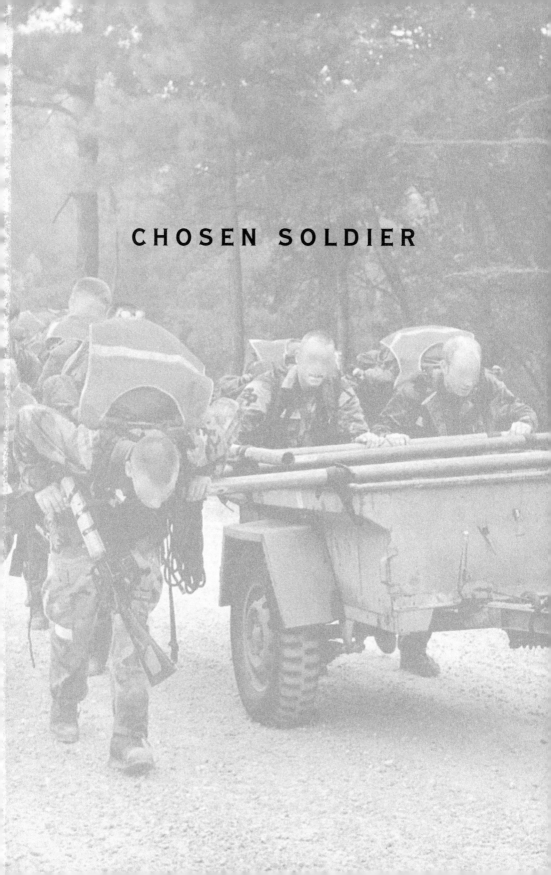

CHOSEN SOLDIER

CHOSEN SOLDIER

THE MAKING OF A SPECIAL FORCES WARRIOR

DICK COUCH

FOREWORD BY ROBERT D. KAPLAN

CROWN PUBLISHERS / NEW YORK

Library of Congress Cataloging-in-Publication Data
Couch, Dick, 1943–
Chosen soldier : the making of a Special Forces warrior / Dick Couch ;
foreword by Robert D. Kaplan.
1. United States. Army. Special Forces.   I. Title.
UA34.S64C68 2006
356'.16—dc22   2006020623

ISBN 978-0-307-33938-6

Printed in the United States of America

Design by Leonard W. Henderson

10 9 8 7 6 5 4 3 2 1

First Edition

This book is dedicated to the volunteers—the young men who join up to become special operations warriors. They are talented, capable, motivated, and intelligent, and all that America has to offer lies before them. Yet these patriots choose to enlist. They turn away from civilian opportunity and fortune for a life of sacrifice, struggle, danger, and service. And because they choose to serve, the rest of us are free to enjoy the bounty of this great nation. God bless and protect these gallant volunteers.

ACKNOWLEDGMENTS

I'd like to thank those in the Army and Army special operations chain of command who allowed me such full and complete access to Special Forces training. A special thanks is due to two commanding generals of the JFK Special Warfare Center and School—Major General Geoffrey Lambert (ret.), who approved the project, and Major General James Parker, who supported my work while he was in command. And start to finish, Colonel Manny Diemer, Commander, 1st Special Warfare Training Group, was always there to help. I especially want to acknowledge and thank the many cadre team sergeants and officers who made time for me while they went about the deadly serious business of training tomorrow's Special Forces chosen soldiers.

"Whom shall I send, and who will go for us?"
Then I said, "Here am I. Send me."
—ISAIAH 6:8

CONTENTS

FOREWORD

ROBERT D. KAPLAN

In the days and weeks after 9/11, the Pentagon scrambled for
options to take down the Taliban regime in Afghanistan. The
most practical and available method turned out to be deploying the
A-Teams of United States Army Special Forces, popularly known as
the Green Berets. It wasn't that these twelve-man detachments were
necessarily the greatest commandos the armed forces could muster:
rather, it was that they were the most adaptable. Whereas Navy
SEALs and Army Rangers—to cite two examples—might kick in
doors faster, the Green Berets could do that very well, too, as well as
deal more effectively with indigenous forces of a very different culture: something that took patience, maturity, and a knack for diplo-
macy. The twelve-man team, which could divide into two six-man
teams because of its duplication of occupational specialties, was also
a perfect bureaucratic instrument that had survived throughout the
decades.

Afghanistan brought Army Special Forces, or SF as it's known within
the special operations community, full circle from the Vietnam days,
involving SF in both training and fighting with indigenous forces for the
first time since the 1960s and early 1970s. Since the Afghanistan campaign, Green Berets have not only fought some of the most difficult battles in Iraq, but haven't let up around the world with their training
missions, which are the bread and butter of SF.

In *Chosen Soldier,* Dick Couch takes us to the heart of the Special
Forces world, focusing on how an Army Special Forces soldier is

created. You can't understand SF unless you delve into the training behind it, which, in turn, reveals the cultural mentality of this branch of the Special Operations community. Thus, this is an essential book.

Never before has SF been so prominent, and, therefore, never before has it faced so many critical decisions, which makes an understanding of Green Beret training doubly important. Think of SF as like the technology company Apple in the early days of the computer revolution, threatened by its own success, vulnerable to being copied and overshadowed by those with bigger budgets. The training missions that SF has thrived on are in the process of being imitated by the Marine Corps and others. The regular Army, for example, is experimenting with new and elite units that partially depend on the SF model. SF simply cannot go on as before. Like a corporation, it has to continually innovate and improve or risk being overtaken by copycats.

In this context, a book about SF training serves two purposes. First, it educates a public that, while closer to its military than are the citizenry of Canada and Europe, is still too distant given the need for healthy civil-military relations. Second, it provides a basis for discussion as military leaders seek to answer thorny questions about how SF must change in the coming years. Ultimately, change and adaptation rest on a knowledge of training.

There isn't one military future confronting the United States, but several contradictory ones. Just as Afghanistan saw a merger of nineteenth-century warfare and twenty-first-century close air support, the next few decades will see a blending of the most basic, rudimentary techniques of counterinsurgency and unconventional warfare (in which language skills could trump technology) with the use of heavy bombers and other conventional assets. Amid this use of varied tactics one thing is clear—business will be booming for SF. And to rise to the challenge, the Green Beret training will have to constantly evolve and be tweaked. Here's a book that can help start the process.

Robert D. Kaplan is a national correspondent for the *Atlantic Monthly* and the author of eleven books, including *Imperial Grunts: The American Military on the Ground*. He is currently the holder of the Class of 1960 National Security Chair at the United States Naval Academy, Annapolis. The views expressed above are his own, and not those of the Academy.

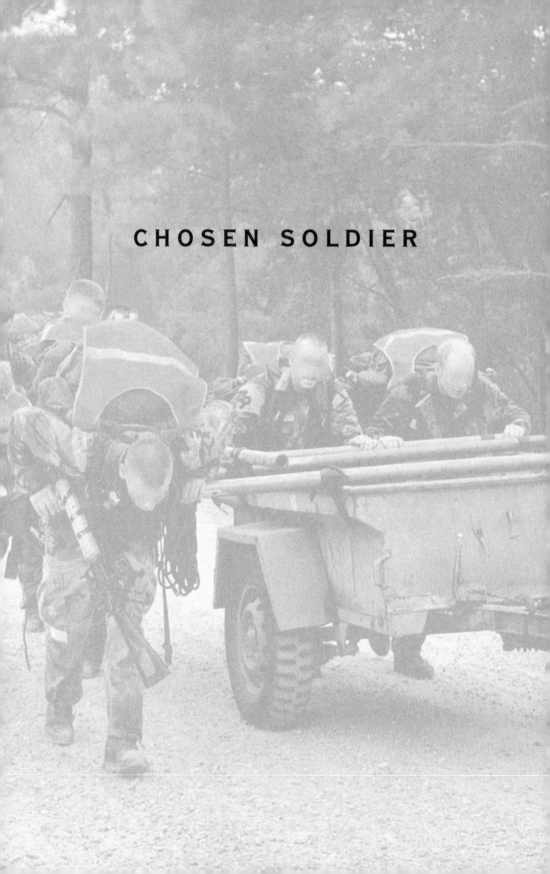

CHOSEN SOLDIER

INTRODUCTION

I am an American Special Forces soldier!

I will do all that my nation requires of me.
I am a volunteer, knowing well the hazards of my profession.

I serve with the memory of those who have gone before me.
I pledge to uphold the honor and integrity of their legacy
in all I am—in all I do.

I am a warrior.
I will teach and fight whenever and wherever my nation requires.
I will strive always to excel in every art and artifice of war.

I know that I will be called upon to perform tasks in isolation,
far from familiar faces and voices.
With the help and guidance of my faith,
I will conquer my fears and succeed.

I will keep my mind and body clean, alert, and strong.
I will maintain my arms and equipment in

COMBAT TEAMWORK. Sergeant Aaron Dunn and Specialist Antonio Costa enter a bunker during a room-clearing tactical drill.

an immaculate state befitting a Special Forces soldier,
for this is my debt to those who depend on me.

I will not fail those with whom I serve.
I will not bring shame upon myself or the Special Forces.

I will never leave a fallen comrade.
I will never surrender though I am the last.
If I am taken, I pray that I have the strength
to defy my enemy.

I am a member of my Nation's Chosen Soldiery.
I serve quietly, not seeking recognition or accolades.
My goal is to succeed in my mission—and live to succeed again.

De Oppresso Liber

This is the creed of the Special Forces soldier—the Green Beret. There's a lot in these few lines that defines this special breed of warrior, but one stands out that defines these chosen soldiers: "I will teach and fight . . ." Special Forces are teachers. Like all good teachers, they have to know their trade, and their trade is the art of war. And like all good teachers, to be effective they have to gain the respect and trust of those they teach. This is not an easy task, since those they teach come from diverse ethnic and religious backgrounds. Quite often they don't speak English. Many can neither read nor write. Yet gaining respect and trust of foreign fighters, on their home ground and within the constraints of their culture, is the stock in trade of the Special Forces soldier. These Green Berets can also fight. They've been engaged in every conflict of military action, declared or otherwise, since their formal inception in 1952. Along the way, twenty Special Forces soldiers have received the Medal of Honor.

After 9/11, Army Special Forces were quickly deployed to Afghanistan. There they executed a classic unconventional-warfare campaign, an astonishing feat of arms in which the Green Berets taught and fought with distinction. The Northern Alliance, with their Army Special Forces mentors and backed by American precision airpower, swept through that feudal nation in only a few months—something the Soviet army couldn't do in more than a decade of fighting. The invasion of Iraq was a classic exercise in conventional maneuver warfare. The 3rd Infantry Division and the 1st Marine Expeditionary Force, under the superb direction of General Tommy Franks, made short work of Saddam's army. In both these campaigns, our conventional military and special operations forces were magnificent. Technically and professionally, our forces were overwhelming. In both cases, and unlike previous wars, we took the ground and were able to leave the infrastructure largely intact. But while we won the physical terrain, we didn't entirely win the human terrain. That's still being contested. In Afghanistan and Iraq, our enemies learned a great deal about how to fight us. It's unlikely that they will ever again expose themselves to our conventional military might or our airpower. They've gone to ground—deep in the mountains and deep into the local populations.

The enemy has taken up the tools of the insurgent. In doing so, they've largely denied us the use of our technology and our conventional military superiority. And now, we must go into the mountains and the cities—among the tribes, the clans, and the urban populations—and find this elusive and deadly foe. To do this, we need the help of the locals. Simply stated, if we lose or fail to gain the popular support of the people, we lose it all. Our initial victories in Afghanistan and Iraq will have been for nothing.

We are currently locked in an insurgent war, one that's likely to go on for a very long while. Our enemies—al-Qaeda, the Baathists, the Islamists, the Taliban, the Wahhabis, or whatever they may be calling themselves or however they are allied—have perfected the art of insurgency warfare. Their battlefield tactics now include suicide bombers, roadside bombs (called improvised explosive devises, or IEDs), kidnapping, random murder, ritual beheadings, chaos, and terror—all in the name of religious ideology. The insurgency is alive and festering in Baghdad, Kabul, and in the mountains of the Hindu Kush. The enemy of this insurgency is not America, although we are a useful and visible target for these insurgents. Their enemy is democracy, the electoral victory of Hamas by the Palestinians notwithstanding. If the people choose—if there is government by consent of the governed—then the insurgents lose. The fact that Hamas rules by virtue of an *election* is against Islamic law. Should elections in Beirut or Damascus bring about a secular government, an insurgency will surely follow. Sharia, a strict and fundamentalist interpretation of Islamic law, simply cannot allow political freedom. Neither can it allow economic freedom. One reason Islamic nations are so poor is that economic freedom generates wealth, and wealth will lead to political freedom—something these insurgents cannot allow to happen.

Since our enemies have taken up the tools of the insurgent, how do we react? How do we defeat this insurgency? Unfortunately, we're a lot better at fighting battles against national, conventional armies than insurgent armies. And unless we want the Middle East and Southwest Asia to go the way of Vietnam, we had best perfect the tools of counterinsurgency warfare. There's a lot at stake here. Our efforts in Afghanistan and Iraq will affect the political landscape of the entire region. How long can the House of Saud last if the Islamists (a term I apply to the radical Muslim extremists) prevail in Iraq? How long can Israel last if the followers of bin Laden and Ayman al-Zawahiri control the vast oil wealth of the Middle East? Do we want to leave our grandchildren a world where these radicals control 70 percent of the world's oil—wealth that will most certainly put nuclear weapons in their hands and finance a host of young zealots schooled in hate? This insurgent war must be won in Iraq and Afghanistan. Right now, our single most effective tool in this war is American Special Forces. I know my SEAL brothers may be surprised at this assertion, but Special Forces are the most valuable asset on this battlefield. The Special Forces soldier is the most important man in uniform—our most essential warrior.

Chosen Soldier is not a book about counterinsurgency warfare per se, but I want to be clear on what is at stake in this fight, and what our nation and the world stand to lose if we flinch. If the Islamists win in Iraq and Afghanistan, they're sure to win in many other places as well. If they can force us out of Iraq and Afghanistan and unhinge the modest democratic reforms our troops are so desperately fighting to safeguard, then I fear the dark cloud of fanaticism will claim most of the world's billion (and growing) Muslims, and we'll recall with some nostalgia the comparative civility of the Cold War.

Chosen Soldier is a book about the training of Special Forces soldiers. It defines who they are, discusses where they come from, and explains what must take place before they ever don a Green Beret. The Army Special Forces soldier is a unique warrior, and the requirements of this special individual are like no other military professional. He must be tough and he must know how to fight, but there's more than professional military skill and physical toughness involved. The Special Forces warrior requires a unique mind-set. We cannot win this insurgent war without the help of the villagers, tribes, and townspeople who represent potential sanctuary for insurgents. Warriors who understand other cultures, and who can live among them and gain their trust, have value beyond measure. These men are hard to find and, once found, must be rigorously trained and tested. Special Forces training is all about finding talented men who have adaptive, creative minds, and developing those abilities to create warriors who can succeed in hostile, ambiguous, unconventional environments. Physical toughness is a requisite; mental agility is essential. As Lieutenant Colonel Richard Carswell, a former company commander in charge of the Special Forces officer-training phase, put it, "We must find and train men who can enter an inhospitable, politically unstable situation and successfully navigate in a foreign culture. They must use all their intellect and cunning to accomplish the mission without compromising

the ethical or moral standards of an American warrior." First Sergeant
Billy Sarno, who helps select and assess Special Forces trainees, said it
this way: "We gotta find guys who are smart, physically fit, and who
play well with others. Then we gotta train the hell out of them."

Not every soldier has the intelligence to learn the interpersonal and
technical skills to live and work with another culture. Not every officer
has the vision, maturity, and unconventional-warfare training to lead
an elite force of professionals with this skill set. It's not easy to assemble the kind of talent and experience found in a twelve-man Special
Forces ODA (Operational Detachment Alpha) team. It takes time—
years, actually. The average age of a Special Forces ODA team is close
to thirty-two. Compare that to the average age of the entire U.S.
Marine Corps—nineteen!

Chosen Soldier is the story of how these special warriors are
recruited, selected, and trained. *Chosen Soldier* is also the story of the
making of heroes. It's the story of unusual young men who have chosen a path of hardship, danger, sacrifice, and service—who they are
and why they volunteer for this duty. For me personally, it was refresh-
ing to find that a nation with an addiction for reality TV and fast food
can still produce real heroes—patriots who embrace a hard and
demanding life to serve their nation and to fight for the things in which
they believe. Each year, some thirty-one hundred enlisted soldiers volunteer for Special Forces training. Each year, about six hundred of
those soldiers are awarded the Green Beret and sew a Special Forces
tab on their shoulder. Over five hundred Army officers apply for Special Forces training each year, mostly captains with five years' experience. Most are infantry officers with combat experience, but they
come from all branches of the Army. Two hundred are selected for
training. Less than half of them make it through the course and go on
to become Special Forces detachment leaders.

Only one writer has ever been allowed the privilege to attend the
modern version of this training start to finish. I'm honored to be that
writer, albeit I only audited the course. The real thing is for the brave,

the bold, and the young. And the talented. My special operations training took place almost forty years ago. In my day, I was a good special operations trainee and graduated first in my SEAL training class, so I believe that I'd have been up to the physical challenge of Special Forces training. But I have to ask myself, would I have been able to master the skill set of these cross-cultural warriors? I was good behind the gun, but would I have been good enough to work alongside and live with others, and teach them to be good behind the gun?

In early January 2004, I received permission from the U.S. Army to do this book, subject to the approval of the U.S. Special Operations Command and U.S. Army Special Operations Command. These commands had the final say since they are, after all, engaged in fighting a war. I was then directed to the commanding general of the John F. Kennedy Special Warfare Center and School at Fort Bragg, North Carolina, Major General Geoffrey Lambert. During our initial meeting, General Lambert made it clear to me, and to his subordinate component commanders, that he wanted me to tell the story of Special Forces training and that I was to have full access to all training venues, students, and training cadres.

I am no stranger to Fort Bragg; in the past, I've lectured to the officer candidates during their Special Forces training. As a young CIA case officer, I attended the Army Military Free-Fall (HALO) School as well as several heavy and special weapons training courses at Bragg. This time I was taken out to Camp Mackall, west of Fort Bragg and just south of Pinehurst and Southern Pines, where the heavy lifting of Special Forces training is done. There's a world of difference, as I was to learn, between the manicured golf courses in these affluent communities and the wooded sand hills of Camp Mackall. Yet I've never been so warmly received or welcomed at a military facility.

Camp Mackall is a fifty-six-thousand-acre military reservation forty miles west of Fort Bragg and the city of Fayetteville. During the Second World War, Camp Mackall was the home of the airborne, where upwards of seventy thousand troops lived and trained for war. The brave men who parachuted and landed in gliders behind the German lines in Normandy prepared for D-day at Camp Mackall. All that remains from those days are the hundreds of concrete foundations that supported the tar-paper barracks and training facilities, and the Mackall Army Airfield, which is still in use. The 82nd Airborne Division, located at Fort Bragg, and other military units still use Camp Mackall for occasional training, but the only permanent training compound at Mackall is the Colonel Nick Rowe Special Forces Training Facility. This is where the serious business of selecting and training Green Berets takes place.

I arrived at Camp Mackall on 1 August 2004, along with my wife, Julia, and our border collie Jenny. We were allowed the use of one of the few residential structures on Camp Mackall. It was a small log cabin built in 1923 by the Baltimore Barber Steamship Company as a getaway for their senior executives. The cabin passed into the hands of the du Pont family for a time before Camp Mackall expanded during the Second World War to train airborne troopers. Following the war, the structure was abandoned and had fallen into disrepair. Only recently had the cabin been renovated by the Special Forces training cadres. It was to be our home for ten months. The last full-time resident of our cabin was the Camp Mackall's commanding officer during World War II.

Special Forces candidates now train, sweat, and struggle over the same ground as those young men in the 13th, 17th, and 101st Airborne Divisions did some sixty-odd years ago—their grandfathers' and great-grandfathers' generation of warriors. As I followed this current generation of warriors over this hallowed ground, I felt the ghostly presence of those bands of brothers who became part of what we now call the Greatest Generation. And with a full measure of respect for those gallant men who helped save the world from fascism, I couldn't help but wonder if the men whose training I was privileged to document will someday be remembered as saving the world from religious fanaticism. How will history judge them? Well, I hope, for I firmly believe they stand between us and those who have sworn to again bring terror to our land.

Before tackling the business of Special Forces and Special Forces training, we need first to take care of some organizational issues. When we refer to Special Forces, or SF, in this book, we are talking about *Army Special Forces*—the Green Berets. Quite often in the media, and even some military circles, they're mistaken for special *operations* forces. There is a difference. Special operations forces, or SOF, refer collectively to the Army, Navy, Air Force, and, most recently, Marine Corps special operations components. Under the Nunn-Cohen Amendment to the 1986 Goldwater-Nichols Defense Reorganization Act, the United States Special Operations Command was created to take ownership of our military special operators. The command's headquarters was located at MacDill Air Force Base in Tampa, Florida. Not only did the new command take control of these SOF components, but it was also given the funding as well as the charter for special operations. Thus, the U.S. Special Operations Command became, in essence, a fifth service. Initially, the Marines elected not to join the new force. General Peter Pace, chairman of the Joint Chiefs, now wants marines in the special operations mix.

Since its inception, the Special Operations Command has grown dramatically in size, funding, and the scope of its responsibilities. Yet it's quite small when compared to the other services. Currently, the command has just over 53,000 personnel and its funding is just over $7 billion. In the context of a $400 billion–plus defense budget, this 2 percent piece of the military-funding pie may seem small for the force that Secretary Donald Rumsfeld has tapped to take the lead in the global war on terror. The U.S. Special Operations Command enjoys an efficient "tooth to tail" ratio of about two to one, which means there are two support personnel for every shooter/flyer/boat driver that goes downrange. For ground combat operations, the command has some

15,000 guns to put into this fight. With the need for ongoing training and some semblance of a family life, we're lucky to keep 5,000 special operators on the ground in Afghanistan, Iraq, and elsewhere around the world. Not that many when compared to upwards of 160,000 military personnel that have been kept on deployment in the active theaters since the fall of Baghdad. Why so few people and so little money? It has to do with politics and the SOF Truths. First, the SOF Truths:

Humans are more important than hardware.
Quality is more important than quantity.
SOF cannot be mass-produced.
Competent SOF cannot be created after the emergency arises.

Basically, it takes time to make these guys. The training is long and expensive, and the attrition is very high. In the case of Special Forces, a soldier may be able to negotiate the training pipeline in a year or eighteen months, but it will be several more years before he becomes a seasoned, competent Special Forces soldier. This is a business where experience and maturity count. The reality is that training is never over; with each deployment, a Special Forces sergeant learns a little more and becomes more proficient at his profession. A senior Special Forces team sergeant brings two decades or more of knowledge to the battlefield; within that team, the Special Forces Operational Detachment Alpha, there may be collectively a century and a half of on-the-job experience.

The politics are important and interesting. The defense establishment is an entrenched bureaucracy, and the defense budget is controlled by Congress. Those many billions of defense dollars flow into congressional districts where the defense plants, shipyards, and military bases are located. Neither the president nor secretary of defense can wave a magic wand and reallocate those dollars without congressional approval. And to be fair about it, there are legitimate competing priorities. Within the defense establishment, there are admirals and generals who feel their ships, planes, and armored divisions are just as important to the defense of our nation as SOF components. I sense there's a general agreement in the Department of Defense and Congress that special operations needs more robust funding, and more money will help—especially in the retention of our experienced SOF operators, whose skills are in high demand in the private sector. Yet it still takes time. Regarding these SOF Truths, the last one may not be so relevant as once thought. This emergency's going to be with us for the foreseeable future.

Just what are the forces that make up the U.S. Special Operations Command? There are four major commands that fall under this command—three of them with their personnel and their roots firmly grounded in the three major service providers. The Air Force component is the Air Force Special Operations Command, located at Eglin Air Force Base in Florida. This command provides special heavy-lift, fixed-wing, and rotary-wing tactical aircraft as well as special-purpose platforms like the deadly AC-130 gunships. Also under the Air Force Special Operations Command are the Air Force Special Tactics Teams, which train and deploy the paramedics, and the Combat Control Teams. Navy-related special operations fall under the Naval Special Warfare Command located in Coronado, California. Their components are the Navy SEAL teams and the Special Boat Teams. The largest of the service SOF providers is the U.S. Army Special Operations Command, which calls Fort Bragg home. While our subject is Special Forces and Special Forces training, it'll be helpful to take a closer look at the various component commands of the Army Special Operations Command.

First, there is the 75th Ranger Regiment. The regimental headquarters and the 1st Ranger Battalion is based at Fort Benning, Georgia. There's a battalion of Rangers at Fort Lewis in Washington State and another at Fort Stewart, Georgia. The Rangers are young, tough, and perhaps the finest airborne light infantry in the world. A Ranger can drop from the sky at night, carry a hundred-pound rucksack for a long distance, and fight like a demon when he gets there. Insurgents around the world try not to gather in large numbers lest they find a company of Rangers in their midst. Next there is the 160th Special Operations Aviation Regiment, nicknamed "the Nightstalkers." They specialize in SOF-configured helicopters, which include the MH-47E Chinook, the MH-60K/L Blackhawk, and the AH/MH-6 "Little Bird." Ask SOF operators on the ground and they'll tell you the Nightstalkers are the finest pilots in the world. Currently, the Army Special Operations Command also oversees the Civil Affairs and Psychological Operations Command. Civil Affairs and Psychological Operations, or "Psyops," serve in that twilight between active conflict and peace, and are very helpful in the conditioning of the human terrain in insurgency environments and war-to-peace transitions. The Army Special Operations Command also operates the training command or schoolhouse—the JFK Special Warfare Center and School. And, finally, there's the Army Special Forces Command, which is the largest single component of both the Army Special Operations Command and the U.S. Special Operations Command. The Special Forces Command is also located at Fort Bragg. In addition to specially trained chemical reconnaissance detachments, the Army Special Forces Command owns the Special Forces groups.

The fourth major component of the U.S. Special Operations Command is the Joint Special Operations Command, also located at Fort Bragg. The composition and missions of this command are closely held information. A significant portion of their portfolio is counterterrorism, which has kept them busy for the last fifteen years and certainly since 9/11. They draw their personnel from Army, Navy, and Air Force veterans of the other special operations components. Collectively, the units within Joint Special Operations Command are known as tier-one forces, and they are some of our very best.

Getting back to the Army Special Forces, the Green Berets. Excluding the 1st Special Warfare Training Group, they are organized into seven operational Special Forces groups. There are five active and two National Guard groups. The organization, location, and regional focus of these groups will be taken up in the next chapter. For now, let's turn to a discussion of SF and SOF missions.

There are four primary missions that the major SOF ground components address in one form or another. The first is direct action, or DA. Direct action is perhaps the most visible of SOF missions, encompassing raids, strike operations, enemy leadership snatches, and the like. These are typically short-duration actions, potentially involving insertion by helo, fire-and-movement activity on the ground, and close-quarter engagement with the enemy. The media loves direct action and direct-action footage. No matter what the in-theater event, the coverage will likely be accompanied by video of some guys leaping out of airplanes, jumping from helos, racing about the battlefield, and doing a lot of shooting. These video clips may or may not be related to the news being reported. And, sadly, the news coverage may be all out of proportion to the relevance of the direct-action mission. It's simply a high-visibility event. This does not imply that direct action is not an important and valuable SOF skill, nor one that does not command a lot of attention in SOF training.

Next there's special reconnaissance, or SR. SR missions have long been a staple of the SOF skill set. In some cases, they may precede or form the basis for a DA mission. Often it's purely an intelligence-gathering operation. A SOF element often may quietly watch a village from afar for several days, observing patterns of movement or waiting for a target individual to show himself. In the current fight, a number of SR missions have been undertaken to secretly observe a target house or compound prior to a precision air strike in an attempt to avoid civilian casualties. These are seldom reported as they may involve clandestine or covert means. A clandestine operation is one that is kept secret from the enemy. A covert operation is one that is secret *and* in which

the hand or presence of the U.S. government is kept quiet or unac-
knowledged. Many military units conduct clandestine operations, but
covert work for uniformed soldiers is usually reserved for SOF. Clandestine and covert operations are most normally linked with SR missions, but both terms can apply to other SOF missions as well.

The third mission is unconventional warfare—UW. This a broad
term, but most usually applies to offensive military operations that are
not conventional, that is, do not involve regular U.S. military forces
such as armored, mechanized, or infantry divisions. These operations
are often clandestine and sometimes covert. In the past, UW has been
closely linked with guerrilla warfare—guerrilla warfare in which the
guerrillas are the good guys and the regimes they oppose or want to
overthrow are the bad guys. A UW campaign is one in which foreign
fighters or a government in exile supplies the troops, and we supply
the arms, the financial backing, and the advisers. A UW operation can
be a long campaign against an entrenched, hostile government, or of a
short duration, as in Afghanistan. In most cases, it's a cheap way to
fight a war and leverages Americans on the ground and the taxpayer's
dollar. When it works, it's a wonderful way to fight a war without
deploying a large conventional presence.

Finally we come to foreign internal defense, or FID. During the Cold
War, foreign internal defense was an active SOF mission. In this effort,
we sent teams of SOF operators to fledgling democracies, and in some
cases friendly dictatorships, to teach them how to protect themselves
from Communist-backed insurgencies. With the passing of the Soviet
Union, much of our FID work centered on helping foreign govern-
ments counter illegal drug production and trafficking. The skill set for
unconventional warfare and foreign internal defense is much the same.
It depends on whether your client is the government in power, which
calls for FID, or those seeking to overthrow a regime in power, which
is a UW mission. Both call for the training of others—to be insurgents
or guerrillas or to conduct counterguerrilla/counterinsurgent opera-

tions. And this brings us to the counterinsurgency struggle we face in Iraq and Afghanistan. Counterinsurgency has its own acronym—COIN. A COIN campaign calls on all four SOF mission disciplines, but it's primarily a derivative of FID.

Regarding these acronyms—DA, SR, UW, FID, COIN, and others in this book—I understand they can be confusing and arresting for you nonmilitary readers. They are freely used in the lexicon of special operators and special operations, almost like a foreign or secret language. However, I'll do my best to use them sparingly in this text.

The four major SOF mission areas are conducted and/or supported by all SOF components. The Air Force and Army aviation components and the Navy Special Boat Teams are usually support elements, but they can act alone for certain mission taskings, such as activity that involves teaching flying or small-craft operations to foreign allied forces. On the ground, this work has fallen to the SEALs, the Rangers, and the Special Forces. The SEALs, in addition to their unique role as the SOF maritime component, have become a superb direct-action and special-reconnaissance force. Since 9/11, they've ranged well inland in Afghanistan and Iraq. But they have limited language and cross-cultural skills, so their capability and utility in counterinsurgency roles has been limited. The Rangers are simply a highly versatile and capable light-infantry force. The bread and butter of the Rangers are small-unit tactics, and while they are capable of teaching this discipline, they're primarily fighters, not teachers. They, too, have their limitations in foreign internal defense and unconventional warfare. The Army Special Forces have neither the maritime capability of the SEALs nor the self-contained, light-infantry capability of their Ranger brothers. But they can do everything else—SR, DA, FID, and UW, especially FID and UW, all of which make them a force of choice in a counterinsurgent environment. Why is it that the Special Forces can do it all? Quite simply, it's because they are teachers. They have to know and practice the full range of SOF disciplines, and they have to have the language and cross-cultural skills to teach them. It's been said that the Special Forces are the Peace Corps with guns. As we will later see from their origins and their deployment history, this is not far from the truth.

To win in an insurgent environment, you have to win the people. That means you have to be close to them and gain their trust. Only the locals know who's an insurgent and who's not. In places like Afghanistan and Iraq, a considerable number of the insurgents are foreign fighters—Saudis, Chechens, Syrians, Egyptians, and the like. They look much the same to us, but not to the locals. They know, and, unless they tell us, we're often unable to distinguish between friend and foe. The key to defeating an insurgency is intelligence—timely, accurate, actionable intelligence. Said another way, kicking the door and dragging out an insurgent leader is the easy part. Knowing which door to kick is far more difficult. Special Forces have the ability to find the right door, and that's what makes them the most important Americans in uniform. Direct-action and military-reconnaissance skills are relatively easy to acquire and can be learned in a short period of time. The language and cross-cultural people skills come much harder. They are not as glamorous or media-genic as the running-and-gunning of direct action or the sneaking-and-peeking of special reconnaissance, but they are essential if we're to defeat the insurgents. The Special Forces also do a lot of other things—coalition building, humanitarian activities, conventional-military support, to name a few—but it's their counterinsurgency skill and expertise that make them our chosen soldiers.

Before we get to the business of Special Forces and their training, I need to speak to the mechanics of how I worked with the SF training cadres and how I was allowed to interface with the SF students and candidates. I was given certain guidelines and latitudes by the training command staffs and the public affairs officers. The bulk of Special Forces training centers on the core skills of small-unit tactics, weapons systems, engineering, first aid and casualty care, communications, mission planning, and the management of unconventional-warfare operations and foreign internal defense. There are a few areas of this training that deal with sensitive or classified information. In any Special Forces training class there are foreign students—a few senior enlisted soldiers, but mostly officers from allied nations. When the allies were asked to leave a training venue or were asked not to attend a presentation, I was usually absent as well. The senior trainers, however, were good enough to give me an unclassified overview of the training that I couldn't attend.

Regarding security classifications, I've held final top secret clearances with the Navy and at the CIA, and have been further cleared for higher levels of sensitive information. That's all history. Now I'm just a guy with a notebook, a camera, and a word processor, and that's how it should be; I have no need to be privy to anything sensitive. I'm often asked how I can write about this if I'm denied access to the classified material—what many would call "the good stuff." This is not a book about classified material or closely held information or secret missions. This is a book about what must take place to make a Special Forces warrior. It's about the men in the arena, and believe me, this is the good stuff—the *really* good stuff.

Another issue in producing this text was the identification and the use of real names of Special Forces training cadre and Special Forces candidates. I handle this issue differently than most writers. In *The Warrior Elite: The Forging of SEAL Class 228*, I used real names, both of the SEAL trainers and the SEAL trainees. This book was written and published prior to the attacks of 11 September 2001. My follow-on works concerning Navy SEALs—*The Finishing School: Earning the Navy SEAL Trident* and *Down Range: Navy SEALs in the War on Terrorism*—use pseudonyms to protect the identities of these special operators. Other authors do this differently. In his fine book *No Room for Error*, John Carney uses real names in telling the story of the Air Force Special Tactics Teams. So does Robin Moore of *The Green Berets* fame in his recent works, *The Hunt for Bin Laden* and *Hunting Down Saddam*. Perhaps the best book on Special Forces operations is *Masters of Chaos*, by Linda Robinson. Ms. Robinson also uses real names. All of these works identify individual special operations soldiers and airmen, their units, and their domestic home base. Interestingly, this use of actual names and personal data about these special warriors is, or was, in keeping with U.S. Special Operations Command guidelines. Yet I was uncomfortable with this policy. These men are on the front line in the global war on terror, and they'll play a pivotal role in defeating the insurgents. Put another way, these men risk enough on deployment without giving out their names. There's no need to place these brave men, and their families, at further risk by making public their identities. When I took this issue to the public affairs and command staffs, they agreed with me. So the men you will meet in these pages are real from the perspective of their personal background and personal history, their motivations and their sacrifices. Their strengths, struggles, and shortcomings are real as well. But with a very few exceptions, I do not use their real names.

My job is to tell their story—in the classrooms, on the road marches, on the timed runs, in the swamps, on the weapons ranges, and on the tactical field problems. You'll see them excel, and you'll see them fail. From the perspective of the Special Forces students and candidates, there's training that is really great and training that really sucks. From the perspective of the training cadre, there are candidates who have the potential to be superb Special Forces soldiers and candidates who shouldn't be here at all—but are. And there are candidates that fool everyone and make it—they blossom in this crucible called Special Forces training. As I followed this curriculum, I was amazed at the passion and desire that is a part of Special Forces training. The fervor of both the training cadres and the trainees was something that continually surprised me. *Chosen Soldier* is the story of young men who desperately want to join this elite force and who dedicate themselves to this goal—physically, intellectually, emotionally, and spiritually. It's also about the training cadres who test and train the men who want to join their ranks—seasoned veterans who must be counselors, taskmasters, mentors, and gatekeepers.

Chosen Soldier is about the forging of Special Forces warriors. Above all, the foundation of this unconventional warrior is his mind-set. His thinking is not "How many terrorists can *I* kill?" It is "How many terrorists can I get *them* to kill—or to expose or expel from their village?" The Special Forces warrior believes that he'll accomplish his mission *by, with, and through* those he trains to fight. He believes in the T. E. Lawrence dictum "It is their country and their war and your time here is limited." But with respect to that limitation, he's committed to his allied fighters—his foreign warrior brothers. This commitment means he will stay in Iraq, Afghanistan, or wherever and train and fight until he's no longer needed.

How important is the Special Forces warrior? In a word, critical, if we're to win the global war on terror and prevail in the current insurgent environments. The unique ability to move within a culture—to gain the trust of the village chief or the tribal elders—is key to success in these campaigns against the Islamists. How successful have the deployed Special Forces detachments been in these efforts? Remember the infamous deck of cards, each of which detailed the name and/or face of one of Saddam's Baathist loyalists. Thirty-nine of the forty-six rogues in that deck were captured by, or taken into custody as a result of intelligence developed by, Army Special Forces.

Concerning our efforts in Iraq and Afghanistan, a great deal of media attention will continue to focus on daring direct-action missions, our Special Mission Units, and our SOF raider components. As with the capture of Saddam and the killing of al-Zarqawi, the raiders cannot do their work without intelligence. When we do get bin Laden and Mullah Muhammad Omar, it'll likely be from a scrap of intelligence provided by some obscure tribesman along the Pakistani-Afghan border. Odds are this scrap of vital intelligence will result from the trust developed by a Special Forces team sergeant among the tribesmen in that obscure village along the Pakistani-Afghan border. How we find, recruit, and train these essential warriors is the focus of *Chosen Soldier*.

CHAPTER ONE

SPECIAL FORCES 101—HISTORY, TRAINING, AND ORGANIZATION

As with most SOF components, the Army Special Forces have a proud history of service to the nation. Special Forces can trace their roots back to the mid-1700s and the tactics of Major Robert Rogers and his men during the French and Indian War. My own notion of Special Forces goes back a ways, but not quite that far.

In January 1965, I received my copy of *National Geographic* magazine. I was a midshipman at the Naval Academy, and my mother back in Indiana saw to it that my subscription never lapsed while I was in school. On the cover was a soldier in a green beret toting a World War II–era M1 carbine and leading two files of Asian soldiers along a dirt road. The beret had a red and yellow flash, which I later came to know as the mark of the 5th Special Forces Group, the group stood up for duty in Vietnam. The handsome officer with the serious look on his face was Major Edwin Brooks. Brooks commanded the U.S. Special

---

GETTING IT RIGHT.   Special Forces soldiers are teachers as well as warriors. Here Sergeant Daniel Barstow, right, briefs Specialist David Altman during Phase II training.

Forces in an area of South Vietnam known simply as the Highlands, a mountainous area populated by thirty-some hill tribes and contested by the North Vietnamese. I was in my second year at Annapolis, and my focus was trying to keep my grades at a passing level, which I did, and prepare for an upcoming Army-Navy indoor track meet, which didn't go so well. I beat my cadet that year, but Army won. For underclass midshipmen at the time, the war in Southeast Asia was still small and very far away. At Annapolis, it was academics, parades, uniform inspections, and all the military stuff that goes with preparing young officers for duty in the fleet. There were a few of us who had an inkling that we wanted something different and hoped to become frogmen— members of the Navy Underwater Demolition Teams. In my class, the Class of 1967, seven of us ultimately became Navy frogmen. We knew little of SEALs, a secret organization that had been in existence only a few years. The men in *National Geographic* certainly appeared to be serious men at war. But what kind of war was this? It seemed to me that what these guys called Army Special Forces were doing looked a lot different from what we midshipmen at the Naval Academy were being groomed for.

The *National Geographic* article featured an Army captain by the name of Vernon Gillespie. Gillespie and another SF officer, along with ten enlisted soldiers, formed what I learned was Special Forces A-Team— the Operational Detachment Alpha, or ODA. Gillespie and his men were encamped near a village called Buon Brieng along with several thousand refugee tribesmen. These twelve soldiers had trained and equipped a seven-hundred-man force of these tribesmen, who were called Montagnards, and led them into the field against the Vietcong. They also helped manage the daily affairs of the village. This was their village and their tribe, the Rhade tribe. Captain Gillespie and his team were running a municipality, fighting a war, and surrounded by Communist insurgents. Gillespie also had to serve as a diplomat as well. In addition to fighting the Vietcong, he had to manage the tension between the small contingent of the Vietnamese army at Buon Brieng and the Montagnards. The Vietnamese and the hill tribes disliked and distrusted each other. However, both liked and trusted Americans like Captain Vernon Gillespie, so he was able to deal with both sides.

Gillespie was like a shuttlecock, bouncing between his team, the Montagnard battalion commander (a man who, by tribal ritual, was his blood brother), the Vietnamese garrison commander, and Major Brooks, who was stationed at Ban Me Thout. Sometimes Gillespie, dressed in a green field uniform, was out inspecting security positions with his Montagnard battalion commander. At other times, he'd be seated with the council of elders, dressed in traditional Rhade tribal attire and sipping rice beer through a long bamboo straw. When he spoke with Major Brooks, they talked about supply problems, enemy movements, air support, and the ongoing Vietnamese-Montagnard tensions. At the council of tribal leaders, topics ranged from military training to veterinary needs. Often this involved ceremonies in which Gillespie and his mountain people consulted with and/or placated the endless number of spirits that control such things among the Rhade. In the photos associated with this story of the Special Forces at Buon Brieng, Captain Gillespie and his team sergeants looked haunted and tired. Whether they were on patrol, on security duty, training with their tribesmen, or catching an hour's sleep in team hut, they were never more than an arm's length from their rifle. Who were these men? I wondered as I reread the article in my room at Annapolis. And how can a twenty-seven-year-old Army captain from Lawton, Oklahoma, have so much responsibility in such a faraway place?

This is a classic example of the work of modern Special Forces. Captain Gillespie and his team were responsible for the care, feeding, and welfare of over two thousand souls and the combat deployment of a seven-hundred-man irregular force. They were forty minutes by air from any American base or any American support. Each day, they made decisions that ranged from life and death to pedestrian. They built schools, hired retainers, established security positions, constructed an airstrip, handled supplies, observed tribal customs, arbitrated local disputes, put down revolts, managed a medical clinic, reasoned with elders, and fought a war. Most combat units today deploy to a base and discharge their duties within a single, narrow focus—security, supply, combat patrol, air control, or some other specialty. Gillespie and his men did it all—what might be expected of a brigade staff with dozens of support personnel and camp followers. War is never inexpensive, but if there is war on the cheap, this was it. In Gillespie's case, compare the cost of keeping a seven-hundred-man U.S. Army battalion or a battalion of marines in the field to the cost of a twelve-man Special Forces team and supplying their indigenous force, usually with obsolete weapons and dated surplus field equipment. And regarding this indigenous force, since it's their homes and their country, they're often more effective than a deployed American combat battalion. Furthermore, when they are fully trained and on the job, our troops can then go home—or never have to leave home. Special Forces have done this all over the world, just as they are today in Afghanistan and Iraq.

Looking back at my own experience in Vietnam as a Navy SEAL, it was primarily a direct-action war. It was dangerous business and often quite terrifying out there at night on the canals or in the mangrove looking for Vietcong. But we SEALs usually had a safe haven to return to, a place where we could get a hot shower, a hot meal, and, if there were no mortar attacks, some undisturbed rest. When we were not in the field, a base security element watched over us. For the most part we were among other Americans or with American support close by. Life was simple—eat, sleep, and go out and look for bad guys. The Special Forces detachments out there living with the hill tribes enjoyed none of these amenities. And detachment commanders like Captain Gillespie had a lot more on their plate than simply leading combat operations. I stand in awe of them and what they were able to accomplish in that war.

A decade after Rogers's Rangers fought the French and Indians, our nation waged a war of independence against England. A man named

Francis Marion, known as the Swamp Fox for his daring raids against the British in South Carolina and Georgia, built on the special operations legacy of Robert Rogers. In the Civil War, Colonel John Mosby formed a band of volunteers that conducted slashing, behind-the-lines actions against Union supply lines. Mosby became known as the Grey Ghost. He not only led a small, well-trained force, but in true guerrilla fashion, he occasionally shared plundered wealth with those in need. Mosby's sensitivity to the local populations was an important step in the evolution of special operations forces. Prior to Mosby, these small, unconventional units were primarily strike forces that relied on discipline, speed, surprise, and daring—characteristics that perhaps have more in common with our modern Rangers than Special Forces. Mosby operated behind the lines in an effort to weaken the enemy's infrastructure and morale while making some effort to care for the civilian population. This set him apart from the pure raiders that came before him.

The First World War was a trench-war slugfest that ground up major armies, and there was little special operations activity in that conflict on the Allied side in Europe. The Germans, however, sent small teams of engineer/sapper-type elements into the Allied lines to generate havoc and confusion. But there were some fine unconventional-warfare practitioners operating away from the European theater on both sides— T. E. Lawrence in the Middle East and Paul von Lettow-Vorbeck in East Africa. It was not until the Second World War that SOF forces on both sides were to play a significant role.

On the German side, Hitler had a love affair with all that was special —jet aircraft, rockets, and commando raiders. The German army was a highly professional force that conducted many special operations. Two stand out as classic SOF actions. The first was the taking of the Belgian fortress Eben Emael. Hitler's army planned to enter France by way of Belgium, but the Belgian fortifications, an extension of the Maginot Line, were arrayed along the Albert Canal and anchored by the largest fortress of its day, Eben Emael. Eben Emael was a concrete, earth, and steel complex that bristled with artillery. Well before dawn

on 10 May 1940, sixty-nine German paratroopers attacked the fortress, landing on the parapets in gliders. They overwhelmed a Belgian force of close to seven hundred. The attack was so meticulously
planned and executed that it succeeded even though the assault leader
was not present. Lieutenant Rudolf Witzig was to lead the attack, but
because of a glider mishap, he arrived after the fortress was taken. The
raiders took and held Eben Emael until they were relieved by advanc-
ing German infantry. Rudolf Witzig, a story unto himself, led other
storied raids and fought in Crete, North Africa, Russia, Poland, Holland, and France. Though severely wounded, he survived the war.

Perhaps the most famous German commando action took place on
12 September 1943, when Otto Skorzeny, know as Hitler's commando,
rescued Benito Mussolini from the Campo Imperatore Hotel on top of
Gran Sasso mountain. That previous July, due to military disasters in
North Africa and Greece, Mussolini, who had ruled Italy since 1922,
was deposed and exiled in secret. The Italians kept Il Duce at several
locations, but German intelligence finally located him at the Campo
Imperatore in early September. Hitler wanted to rescue Mussolini and
keep Italy in the war on the Axis side. The hotel on Gran Sasso was
remote and all but impervious to a surprise ground action. In a classic
glider-borne assault, much in the mold of Witzig's taking of Eben Emael,
the German force under Skorzeny achieved tactical surprise. In a death-
defying act, Skorzeny ordered his glider pilot to crash-land next to the
hotel. The final assault was one characterized by Skorzeny's bravado
rather than force of arms. Skorzeny had brought along an Italian Cara-
biniere general by the name of Ferdinando Soleti. Soleti's presence put
the Italian guard force in check, while Skorzeny brazenly marched
through the hotel lobby and up to the room where Mussolini was being
held. While the German paratroopers took control of the hotel grounds,
Skorzeny took control of Il Duce, all without firing a shot.

On the Allied side, there was also a great deal of SOF activity. A
number of American units came into the public focus as "special."
There were names such as the Devil's Brigade, Merrill's Marauders,

Darby's Rangers, and the Alamo Scouts. These units were not unlike the German commando units under Witzig and Skorzeny. They were highly trained light infantry schooled in quick-strike operations. Considered one of the forerunners of our current Special Forces was the First Special Service Force, a joint U.S.-Canadian unit. Organized in July 1942 at Fort Harrison in Montana, this was an airborne unit that cross-trained in mountain and amphibious warfare. It saw action in Italy and France before it was inactivated in 1944. Today's Special Forces trace their modern military lineage to the 1st Special Service Force. The 2nd and 5th Rangers were activated in June 1942 and scaled the cliffs at Pointe du Hoc during the invasion at Normandy. They went on to fight throughout western Europe. In the China-Burma-India theater, there was the three-thousand-man 5307th Composite Unit, or Galahad Task Force. Called Merrill's Marauders by the press, this unit fought many engagements with the Japanese in the jungles of Burma. Also operating in the Pacific were the Alamo Scouts and the 6th Rangers, both formed by Lieutenant General Walter Krueger. The most storied action of these units was the rescue of American POWs at the Japanese prison camp at Cabanatuan, in the Philippines.

On 30 January 1945, 128 men from the 6th Ranger Battalion, with a contingent of the Alamo Scouts, rescued 512 American POWs from the Japanese prison camp at Cabanatuan during the closing days of the Second World War. The 6th Battalion was commanded and trained by a tough, no-nonsense lieutenant colonel named Henry Mucci. The attack on the POW compound itself was led by the unflappable Captain Robert Prince, a quiet Stanford graduate. The Alamo Scouts guided the Rangers through Japanese lines and close to camp for a night attack. The force executed a clever diversion and made a coordinated assault. It was over in twenty minutes. The Rangers escorted and carried the freed Americans back through enemy lines to safety. While it was true that the Japanese were reeling under the combined forces of the American advance in the Philippines, the fact remains that there were over 8,000 Japanese troops within a five-mile radius of the

Cabanatuan prison compound, and that the Rangers were outnum-
bered two to one in the camp. Accounts vary, but between 300 and
500 Japanese were killed by Rangers and partisans with the loss of
only 2 Rangers. It was a magnificent raid—a classic that's been studied
by generations of special operators. This was one of the few actions in
the Second World War with joint, combined support. Reconnaissance
and diversion sorties were flown by Army Air Corps P-61s and Filipino resistance forces served in a diversionary role and as a blocking
force. This daring rescue is the subject of the bestseller *Ghost Soldiers*,
by Hampton Sides, and the movie *The Great Raid*.

These are only a few of the Ranger/raider-type special operations of
the Second World War. Perhaps the best text on raids is *SPEC OPS*, by
Bill McRaven. This book details these and other modern special operations raids. Again, raids and other direct-action operations are within
the Army Special Forces charter. But Special Forces are not Rangers,
and this is not what makes the Special Forces special. The Second
World War did, however, provide the first examples of the work currently being done on a regular basis by modern Special Forces.

Spectacular raids and daring rescue operations were not all that
were SOF related in World War II. This global conflict saw campaigns
that were characterized by the same "by, with, and through" conduct
of war that characterizes Special Forces today. This new way of fighting was pioneered by a military-style organization, but it was no mere
offshoot or modification of the conventional military. In 1941, an
imposing and brilliant patriot by the name of William Donovan convinced his friend, President Franklin Roosevelt, that America needed
a paramilitary arm that could operate behind enemy lines to gather
intelligence and manage resistance forces. Donovan, a superb orga-
nizer and tough-minded individual who was awarded the Medal of
Honor in World War I, formed an organization called the Office of
the Coordinator of Information. This maverick organization was
quickly stamped in the mold of its founder. Donovan, recalled to
active service with the rank of colonel, set about to hire the brightest

and the best. He carefully selected men and women from the armed forces as well as from civilian life—investment bankers, accountants, lawyers, actors, stuntmen, makeup artists, and photographers. Donovan trained them in parachuting, sabotage, silent killing, communications, and a host of behind-the-lines disciplines, including the recruitment and training of indigenous resistance forces. In 1942, the organization became known as the Office of Strategic Services, or OSS, and Donovan was elevated to the rank of major general. The OSS set up operating bases in North Africa, England, India, Burma, and China.

In the European theater, three-man teams, assigned to an undertaking called the Jedburgh Project, left England at night and parachuted into occupied France, Norway, Belgium, and Holland. Behind German lines, they conducted the organization and training of resistance fighters, and managed the cross-Channel and cross–North Sea resupply of their partisans. Many Jedburghs who survived the war went on to serve as case officers and in the leadership of the Central Intelligence Agency, the successor to the OSS. There were many of them serving at the CIA well into the mid- and late 1970s, including the director of Central Intelligence, William Colby. During my own time at Langley, one of my division chiefs had been a Jedburgh and told some incredible stories. We "young hands," fresh from combat in Vietnam, loved to encourage the Jedburghs to tell us stories of their operations. You don't hear much about them, but they were among the greatest warriors of the Greatest Generation.

Some of the most spectacular OSS operations took place in Asia, specifically in Burma. There, OSS Detachment 101 organized the Kachin and Karen tribesmen into a force of fifteen thousand irregulars that killed many thousands of Japanese and wrecked their supply lines. American forces were stretched pretty thin in the Pacific and in Asia. One of our objectives was to keep China in the war. A great many Japanese divisions were engaged in the China and Burma theaters, much the same as the bulk of the German army was tied down by the

Russians on the eastern front in Europe. Without the OSS irregulars, China may have been knocked out of the war, freeing those Japanese divisions to oppose our island-hopping campaign in the western Pacific. All this was accomplished with the relatively modest effort in men and material, an effort that was greatly appreciated by men like General Joe Stilwell, who commanded the China-Burma-India Theater.

Not all the irregular activity was undertaken by Donovan and the OSS. There were Army officers who, by inclination or necessity, became irregular-force leaders—men who worked with and fought alongside their partisans. Colonel Russell Volkmann, one of the architects of Army Special Forces, learned his trade on the job. Volkmann evaded capture by the Japanese on Bataan and took to the hills after the surrender of American forces in the Philippines. There he organized Filipino partisan groups in northern Luzon that by 1945 had grown to five divisions. Also in the Philippines, an Army reserve major named Wendell Fertig raised a partisan army that totaled twenty thousand irregular fighters by the end of the war. In keeping with the numbers under his command, Fertig informally promoted *himself* to the rank of general officer.

These behind-the-lines efforts were aided by two advantages that in one form or another still exist today in the SOF disciplines of foreign internal defense and unconventional warfare. During World War II, the Germans and Japanese were occupying forces who by and large brutalized the people they occupied. The Jedburgh teams and men like Volkmann and Fertig arrived on the scene to help the locals fight these occupation forces; they provided the training so the people could fight for their own freedom. This is a great advantage, especially when the occupying force is arrogant, vicious, and given to atrocity. Had the German panzer divisions that swept into Russia and the Ukraine not been followed by the butchery of the SS and the Gestapo, the oppressed Russian people might have rallied in support of the Germans. Stalin was anything but a benevolent ruler. The Japanese kicked the white man out of Asia, and ended the exploitation of Asia by the Western colonial powers. The Greater East Asia Co-Prosperity Sphere, as the Japanese called their brand of imperialism, might have worked, but they, like the Germans, brutalized the people they conquered. To this day, Japan still lives with its ill-treatment of the Koreans and the Chinese. Insurgency is a much easier business when the occupiers are thugs.

The second advantage Americans enjoyed was that most people genuinely *liked* Americans. They liked the GIs who fought to repatriate their conquered lands. For the most part, these Americans respected private property and treated the locals humanely. But the locals really liked Americans cut in the mold of Russell Volkmann—men who'd live the austere and dangerous life of a partisan and fight alongside them.

In the Second World War, our behind-the-lines efforts were successful because we helped the locals throw off the yoke of occupation. Let's fast-forward from World War II, when we were seen as liberators, to today's war, in which we are engaged in a vicious insurgency. To the extent we are seen as occupiers, or are portrayed as occupiers by al-Qaeda, Al Jazeera, and insurgent groups, our job is that much harder. A recent study of suicide bombers revealed that the common thread that ran through their twisted thinking was their conviction that Americans in Iraq and Afghanistan are an occupying force.

Donovan's OSS did not survive the war, but the bright and talented men he recruited into his organization did. They went on to form the nucleus of the CIA. Two veterans, Colonel Russell Volkmann and former OSS Jedburgh colonel Aaron Bank, were to figure prominently in the creation of Special Forces. Volkmann, Bank, and a very capable major general on Eisenhower's wartime staff named Robert McClure were successful in convincing the Army that with nuclear weapons making general war unthinkable, "small wars" were sure to follow. These small wars would need clandestine skills developed in the OSS. Aaron Bank, a veteran Jedburgh who spoke French and German, stood up the 10th Special Forces Group on June 19, 1952, and became the father of Army Special Forces. The 10th focused on Europe, but a few of Aaron Bank's soldiers operated from offshore islands during the

Korean War. There, they helped direct North Korean partisans in the conduct of raids, the harassment of enemy supply lines, and the rescue of downed pilots.

The era between the Korean and Vietnam wars saw the slow but steady growth in the Special Forces. The Army's Psychological Warfare Center became the U.S. Army Special Warfare School in December 1956. In September 1961, the 5th Special Forces Group was formed with Colonel Leo Schweitzer as its first commander. It was the 5th that managed the bulk of the irregular-force operations during the Vietnam War. But prior to Vietnam, the considerations of the Cold War and our conventional-force battle plans still called for the Special Forces to play only a supporting role in a breakout of Soviet-backed, Eastern-bloc forces into Western Europe. They were to go in behind the lines to conduct sabotage, interdict supply lines, and support partisan operations as needed in territories overrun by the Communists.

There are three relatively modern wars or conflicts that have defined the character and role of Army Special Forces: Vietnam, El Salvador, and Afghanistan. We've already talked about Captain Vernon Gillespie and the work of his ODA at Buon Brieng. There were close to 250 of those types of operations during the Vietnam period—village or hamlet outposts from which Special Forces detachments worked and managed irregular-force resistance. I think the operations of Gillespie's detachment fairly characterized Special Forces in Vietnam, but there were others. Special Forces personnel served in other operational and advisory roles, including some of the most secret and dangerous cross-border operations conducted by the secret Military and Assistance Command, Vietnam, Studies and Observation Group. The story of MACV-SOG and the Green Berets who served with that organization are beyond the scope of this book, but they're well chronicled in John Plaster's fine book, *SOG: The Secret Wars of America's Commandos in Vietnam*. These advisory roles sometimes led to vicious battles, as in the case of the embattled Special Forces garrison and their Montagnard allies at Lang Vei. On the eve of the siege at Khe Sanh in early 1968, the North

Vietnamese attacked Lang Vei in force and with armor. This heroic stand is the worthy subject of William Phillips's book, *Night of the Silver Stars*. In size and scope, the Vietnam War, more than any conflict before or since, shaped and defined Special Forces. However, given time, the current global war on terror may change that.

The needs of the war in Vietnam and President Kennedy's demands for a counterinsurgency capability in our military prompted a dramatic growth in Special Forces. By 1969, there were almost thirteen thousand men in seven Special Forces groups. The 5th Special Forces Group alone grew to over thirty-five hundred personnel. Yet by 1974, the force had been reduced to three active-duty groups. In 1980, on the eve of our involvement in El Salvador, there were some three thousand Green Berets in uniform and on active duty.

Few conflicts in the history of SOF are so shrouded in secrecy and controversy as our involvement in El Salvador. Like Vietnam, it was an exercise in foreign internal defense. And like Vietnam, we supported a regime that was anti-Communist and corrupt. And again like Vietnam, it was a decade-long struggle. In the early 1960s through the early 1970s, if you were a Special Forces warrior and you were downrange in harm's way, it was Vietnam. In the decade of the 1980s, it was El Salvador. A case can certainly be made that our Special Forces deployed to El Salvador were successful in saving that nation from a takeover by Communist rebels. There were also allegations of human rights violations and the infamous death squads sanctioned by the Duarte regime. The Special Forces personnel I interviewed say they were in El Salvador to train the El Salvadoran armed forces and that they did not tolerate, nor do they condone, these reported abuses. I believe them; I believe they trained the El Salvadorans and, on occasion, fought alongside them. And I believe Special Forces served with honor in El Salvador. Yet it was a messy affair, and the legacy of abuses in El Salvador on the part of the Duarte government is often invoked whenever we try to help a friendly government counter an insurgency. In early 2005, media stories appeared announcing that Special Forces were preparing to undertake the training of indigenous hunter-killer teams to deal with the insurgency in Iraq. This tactic was immediately dubbed the "Salvador Option."

It is not the purpose of this work to deconstruct the Special Forces activity in that Central American nation, but to point out that it was another decade-long foreign-internal-defense effort. It is worth mentioning that insurgencies, with the notable exception of the one we backed in Afghanistan, are historically long and bloody. A great many Special Forces detachments spent a lot of time in those steaming jungles teaching military and counterinsurgency skills to El Salvadoran army troops. It is noteworthy that this was the last major effort in which Special Forces were involved in fighting a Communist insurgency. In the end, they prevailed. In 1992, the government of El Salvador and the Farabundo Martí National Liberation Front reached an agreement that effectively ended the insurgency. Looking back, it was a great training ground for the current efforts in the global war on terror. By the mid-1980s, Special Forces had grown to just under five thousand in four active Special Forces groups. A fifth group, the 3rd Special Forces Group, was stood up in 1990 to complete the current active-duty posture of Special Forces.

While the Special Forces were serving in El Salvador in the 1980s and early 1990s, there were two developments that would shape the future of Special Forces and, indeed, our entire military. The Soviet Union was beginning to unravel, and its support of Communist insurgencies, such as in El Salvador, was on the wane. The Communist government of Fidel Castro in Cuba was a huge drain on the Soviet economy. In November 1989, the Berlin Wall came down, a symbolic end to the failure of the Communist system. But as the world was shaking itself loose from one form of tyranny, another was well under way. Fundamentalist Muslims—the Islamists—had already begun their jihad, their war with the democracies. Many feel, and I'm one of them, that it began formally with the taking of American hostages at the American embassy in Tehran in 1979. Then there were the attacks on the American embassy in Beirut and the bombing of the Marine barracks, both in 1983. In 1988, there was the downing of Pan Am Flight 103 over Lockerbie, Scotland, that killed 259 passengers and crew, along with 11 people on the ground. By the time of the first attack on the World Trade Center in 1993, we were beginning to sense that we had a new enemy. Indeed, prior to the 9/11 attacks on the World Trade Center and Washington, D.C., there were over seventy-five hundred terrorist attacks worldwide. We were at war prior to 9/11, but most of us just didn't realize it.

Throughout the 1990s and prior to 9/11, Special Forces and other SOF components were deployed worldwide on missions that ranged from counterdrug activities to humanitarian assistance to demining operations, but most usually these deployments related to military training. In the vein of foreign military training, there were security assistance programs designed to "provide training assistance in support of legisled programs which provide U.S. Defense articles, military training, and other defense related services." These foreign military-aid programs deployed Special Forces and other SOF elements to foreign shores and allowed them to live and work in foreign lands. Usually, these deployments came under the Joint/Combined Exchange Training Program. This program allowed Special Forces to sharpen their skills in the training and mentoring of foreign and allied forces. They were beneficial to foreign military units *and* our Special Forces detachments. Who can tell when the global war on terror will move into a nation that because of prior SF military visits is trained to conduct counterinsurgency operations and is receptive to U.S. military assistance in the face of a terrorist threat? This exchange program kept our Special Forces detachments on deployment and trained in foreign-internal-defense and unconventional-warfare disciplines. This brings us to the third and most current event in Special Forces history: the campaign in Afghanistan. While Vietnam and El Salvador called on SF to perform primarily in a foreign-internal-defense role, their activity in the early days of the Afghan campaign was pure unconventional warfare, one that will be studied for generations as a classic unconventional-warfare campaign.

I clearly remember those turbulent days following the 9/11 attacks, when the face of this enemy became Osama bin Laden. Americans suddenly became aware that this was a new and dangerous enemy. My work on basic Navy SEAL training, *The Warrior Elite: The Forging of SEAL Class 228,* had just been released. I knew immediately that those fine young men whose SEAL training I documented would soon be actively engaged in this fight. Very quickly we learned that bin Laden and his al-Qaeda Islamist organization operated under the protection of the Taliban in Afghanistan. But Afghanistan was a very nasty place to do battle. The Soviet Union had poured troops and money into that feudal nation for more than a decade, and the Afghan mujahideen, with our help, sent the Soviet army home in defeat. Many feel that the steady flow of body bags with Russian soldiers hastened the fall of the Soviet Union. But we had two things going for us the Soviets didn't: General Tommy Franks and Army Special Forces.

General Franks, as the theater commander, was asked to come up with a battle plan that would remove the Taliban and allow us to pursue bin Laden and his terrorist organization in Afghanistan. The general laid out his plan and sold it to Secretary Don Rumsfeld and President George Bush. Unlike the Soviets, Franks, who was a conventional artillery officer, opted for the unconventional. In a definitive by, with, and through operation, a handful of Special Forces detachments mobilized the Afghan tribesmen, who were loosely organized under the banner of the Northern Alliance, and executed a classic unconventional-warfare offensive. With the help of the CIA and a generous dose of American precision airpower, the Special Forces—in a word—"took" Afghanistan. What they did and how they did it is chronicled in Linda Robinson's fine book, *Masters of Chaos.* It was a marvelous piece of work on the 5th Special Forces Group, who took the lead in this campaign. The details of this action, I'll leave to Ms. Robinson. This work, *Chosen Soldier,* is an inside look at the selection and training of special warriors who can accomplish such feats. I can only imagine the awe and bewilderment of the Soviet generals who watched this amazing feat. It must've stunned them. It stunned all of us.

I also recall the dire predictions that America would be bogged down in a war of attrition, as were the Soviets in Afghanistan and as we were in Vietnam. There was a lot of conventional wisdom about the tenacity of the Afghan fighters—how we were poking a tar baby that would drag us into prolonged bloodletting. Fortunately, Tommy Franks saw things differently and was able to convince the administration that Afghanistan was a candidate for unconventional warfare. And, to Franks's credit, he never wavered. When the campaign stalled for a few days and Congress tried to press conventional forces into the fray, Franks stayed the course. The U.S. marines were not landed at Camp Rhino, southwest of Kandahar, until the Taliban was pretty well beaten. My image of Iraq will always be of brave young soldiers and marines pushing their armored columns along the Tigris and Euphrates toward Baghdad. In Afghanistan, it's of a Special Forces team sergeant, standing at the head of a group of Northern Alliance irregulars. He's bearded, just like his Afghan fighters, and he's dressed as they are—in tribal scarf and native headgear. He has a radio in one hand and an M4 rifle in the other. His Northern Alliance troop leader is standing by his side as they plan their next move against the Taliban. As we move to counter the insurgencies in Iraq, we might do well to reflect on what the Special Forces were able to accomplish in those early days. Well-led irregular forces, fighting on their home ground, can be a huge force multiplier in an unconventional-warfare campaign. They can also be the deciding factor in the internal struggle against insurgents. History will, in my opinion, record our success or failure in Iraq by how we were able to assist the fledgling Iraqi democracy in dealing with its insurgency.

The history of Special Forces training is a story of growth and maturity. In the beginning, back in 1952 when Colonel Aaron Bank stood up the 10th Special Forces Group, he personally selected the volunteers for his new unit. "Most of us came from the 82nd Airborne," one of the originals from the 10th told me. "The only ones who could speak a foreign language were the 'stateless guys,' the Poles and Czechs who were serving the U.S. Army. Initially, there were about two hundred of us. The training lasted fourteen weeks and was a lot like basic training, only we learned about sabotage and assassination techniques. We were training to go behind the lines if the Communists attacked Western Europe. There was a map and compass navigation course, calisthenics, and daily runs. Colonel Bank himself led us on the runs."

That's how it was then. Over the years, Special Forces training has changed dramatically. For the most part, each year, each new commander—and, indeed, each training class—brings change; what was good enough for making a Special Forces warrior yesterday is not good enough for the one we have to train for tomorrow. It's a dynamic, evolving process. Today, Special Forces training is a formal and highly formatted regimen called the Special Forces Qualification Course, or, simply, the Q-Course. *Chosen Soldier* is about that course, but, more to the point, it is also about the men who train to become these special warriors. You will read about the Special Forces candidates who began their training in the summer and fall of 2004. It's the story of but one iteration of Special Forces training—a single Q-Course. As you read this, the Q-Course I experienced has changed; today, it is more focused, more efficient, more professional, and more tailored to the global war on terror. Before we get to the selection and training of Special Forces soldiers, let's take a look at the organization of Special Forces from the bottom up. And I'll apologize in advance as we wade into a few more acronyms and military jargon. Stay with me.

The basic building block of Special Forces is the twelve-man Operational Detachment Alpha, or ODA. There are two officers—a captain (designated as an 18A or 18 Alpha), who is the detachment commander, and a warrant officer (180A), the assistant detachment commander. These officers are often referred to as the team leader and assistant team leader. The detachment or team has ten enlisted non-commissioned officers, or NCOs, and each of them is trained in a military occupational specialty, or MOS. There are two sergeants, a senior and a junior, for each Special Forces MOS—weapons (18B), engineering (18C), medical (18D), and communications (18E). The "18" designator is that assigned by the Army to Special Forces. In addition to these eight specialists, there is an intelligence sergeant (18F) and an operations sergeant (18Z). These enlisted Special Forces "specialists" are usually referred to by their phonetic titles—Bravos, Charlies, Deltas, and Echos. The intelligence sergeant is called the Fox. The 18Z, or 18 Zulu, is a master sergeant and serves as the detachment enlisted leader. He's usually referred to as the team sergeant. Each member of the team fills a specific and important role, but the team sergeant is the element or personality around which the ODA functions. All these men are cross-trained in the various specialties. The Special Forces Qualification Course has one primary goal: to train officers and soldiers to become effective members of an Operational Detachment Alpha. The term "A-Team" is interchangeable with ODA, but those in Special Forces prefer the use of ODA or detachment. During the Q-Course, the trainees are organized into student ODAs for much of their training.

Six ODAs, along with an Operational Detachment Bravo, or ODB, make up a Special Forces company. Three Special Forces companies, together with a support company and a headquarters element, comprise a Special Forces battalion. Although the force can be mixed and matched to suit the requirements, the battalion is a self-contained force and is the basic Special Forces deployment element. Quite often, the battalion staff and support elements will form the backbone of a deployed forward operating base, or FOB. Said another way, each battalion can field eighteen operational detachments and can provide the command, control, and logistical support to keep these teams in an operational environment. Each line company in a Special Forces battalion will have one or more of their company detachments specially trained in military free-fall parachute operations, underwater (scuba) operations, or urban combat operations. And, finally, three battalions, along with a headquarters company and support personnel, constitute a Special Forces group. A Special Forces group will have an authorized strength of about 1,400 personnel, of which some 650 soldiers make up the operational detachments, the ODAs. That doesn't mean that the ODAs are the only guns in the fight. The company bravo detachments and even members of the SF group staff may be called into action when conducting operations. But it's the twelve-man ODAs that carry the operational load. They're the ones who are out there day in and day out, working with the locals and conducting independent combat operations.

There are five active groups and two Army National Guard groups. First, the five active groups. The 1st Special Forces Group is at Fort Lewis in Washington State with one battalion forward deployed to Okinawa. The 1st has responsibilities in the Pacific theater. The 3rd Special Forces Group is based at Fort Bragg and focuses on sub-Saharan Africa. The 5th Special Forces Group, once tasked with Vietnam, is now the group with primary responsibility in the Middle East. They're based at Fort Campbell, Kentucky. The 7th Special Forces Group is oriented toward South and Central America. They call Fort Bragg home. The 10th Special Forces Group is based at Fort Carson, Colorado, with a battalion forward based in Germany. They have responsibility for the European theater. There are two National Guard groups, the 19th and the 20th. The 19th is based in Draper, Utah, and is made up of units generally located in the western half of the nation. They focus on support of the active groups in the Pacific and the Middle East. The 20th, with eastern-U.S. National Guard units, is based in Birmingham, Alabama, and provides support to the 7th Special Forces Group and Latin America. These two National Guard groups play a significant role in the current Special Forces deployment posture in Afghanistan and Iraq.

The active and National Guard Special Forces groups train for and maintain a regional orientation—tactically, operationally, and with the appropriate language skills. The 5th Special Forces Group again carries a heavy operational burden. The men call their area the sandbox, or, simply, "the box," and they deploy on a routine basis to Afghanistan and Iraq. The other groups split time between their duties in their assigned areas and helping the 5th in the active theater. The Guard groups, like many Army National Guard units, are very busy. The "part-timers" in the 19th and the 20th are spending a great deal of time overseas and a great deal of time in harm's way. More than the other SOF organizations, the Army Special Forces Command relies on and deploys its National Guard groups. The active groups have no problem integrating their guardsmen into their deploying units. In reality, they've no choice. Since 9/11, SF soldiers in the active groups are deployed *270 to 275 days a year.* Any way you slice it, that's above and beyond, for the men and for their families back home. And the National Guard groups? They, too, are gone a great deal of the time. Those volunteering for recall, which many reservists have, can be gone as much or more than their active-duty brothers.

Prior to 9/11, the Special Forces groups were undermanned, perhaps as low as 80 percent of their authorized strength. That has changed. With aggressive recruiting and the training pipeline running at full capacity, the active groups are approaching their authorized strengths. If the recent pay incentives and bonuses now being made available to seasoned SOF personnel achieve the desired result, the groups may plus up in excess of these authorized levels. As of this writing, we have something on the order of forty-five hundred Green Berets to carry this fight to the enemy. We could certainly use more, but as you'll see, it takes time to make a Special Forces soldier, and even more time to season him on deployment.

There's another SF group that resides at Fort Bragg and operates under the commanding general of the John F. Kennedy Special Warfare

Center and School, usually shortened to the acronym SWCS. It's the training group, the 1st Special Warfare Training Group. This is the group that is responsible for training Special Forces soldiers. In addition to the Q-Course, the 1st SWTG also conducts Advanced Special Operations Training, Survival, Evasion, Resistance, and Escape (SERE) School, language training, and training for the Civil Affairs and Psychological Operations units. In the course of writing this book, I was under the close supervision and direction of the 1st SWTG. Before we get to the various phases of training, a word or two about the Special Forces training cadres. Special Forces training, like all SOF training, is part teaching, part testing, and part mentoring. The effect of these trainers on young men who want to become Green Berets is incalculable. They're the role models, and the new men watch them carefully. They want to be just like them. The quality and success of the force is in the hands of these Special Forces trainers. Currently, this training staff has never been better. Prior to 9/11, there were only a small number of Special Forces soldiers with combat experience. And duty at the training command was not all that desirable. Most veteran Special Forces sergeants wanted to stay with their detachments and remain in deployment rotation. We were not at war, yet they didn't want to be away from their operational team if there was a chance for an active deployment.

Today, things are different. Almost all of the training cadre are combat veterans; they've been there and done that. Today, deployment rotations are active and dangerous, and they can keep an operator away from home 75 percent of the time. But even the best of the best need time away from the fight. Now, experienced cadre are coming to SWCS after their third or fourth combat rotation. They bring with them current operational experience and knowledge. More than that, they bring a passion for all those things a Special Forces warrior must master—attention to detail, total focus on the mission, cross-cultural awareness, and a sense of duty to their nation and their teammates. And when they go back to the fight, they will go into combat with the men they have trained. This experience, the commitment to excellence, and the inherent role of Special Forces as teachers have produced a superb faculty of Special Forces trainers. Perhaps never in the history of Special Forces has the critical need for top-quality Special Forces operators been met with a more capable and qualified training cadre. I feel privileged for the opportunity to observe their training and write about it.

Before you can train men for this special work, you have to find men—men who are special before they even get to this training. The selection process is critical. For every five men who enter Special Forces training, only about one of them will ever wear a Green Beret. From the perspective of training resources, the higher the quality of the recruit, the fewer men you have to put in the pipeline to get the quality and quantity of Special Forces warriors the groups need. The aptitude and intelligence tests help, but they can only do so much. The tests don't always predict if a man can readily adapt to foreign cultures and play well with others. And there has yet to be a reliable test for heart and determination. Cast the net too narrowly, and we miss out on some good men. Cast it too widely, and the attrition rates drive up the cost of this already expensive training. I came away from Special Forces training with the sense that quality must never be sacrificed for quantity, though as you will see later in this text, that issue can be hotly debated. So where do these men come from? How does the Army find them? Why do they volunteer for this training? This is the stuff of chapter 2.

Chapter Two

RECRUITING THE UNCONVENTIONAL

A great deal of time, effort, and thought goes into the criteria for deciding who comes to Special Forces training and who does not. The Special Forces, just like the rest of the Army, the other military services, and private industry, are looking for bright young people to fill their ranks. In each case, the more adept they are at recruiting the right kind of people, the easier and more effective the training and the more accomplished the finished product. Special Forces has a unique task. It has to train its recruits to a more rigorous, and yet in some ways a more ambiguous, standard than do other organizations. There is a defined military skill set that includes small-unit tactics, marksmanship, inter-personal skills, mission planning, and the like, but much of the Special Forces' work comes under the heading of "getting the job done." So they're looking for men who can think and improvise—men who can operate independently with little or no help, or direction, from a con-ventional command structure or logistics support train. They're also looking for men who can teach, lead, and operate independently from

---

RUCK INSPECTION.   Special Forces recruits in Pre-SFAS Class 8-04 muster for instruction and inspection prior to a field problem.

any other U.S. military presence. Because they are frequently alone and in remote areas, they often *are* the United States of America. They may be on their own, but they still represent our nation. As such, these men must have a firm moral foundation. A Special Forces soldier must abide by the Rules of Land Warfare, theater-specific rules of engagement and the code of the American fighting man.

The Special Forces are looking for more than someone who is tough and smart and plays well with others. They are looking for adaptability and flexibility, men who can look at a given task and come up with any number of ways to solve it. Someone with good entrepreneurial skills is a good candidate for Special Forces, since the work of the Green Berets often involves calculated risk and creative thinking. If one solution to a problem fails, they have to immediately come up with another way to accomplish the mission. Since the work often involves working as a team or in a cross-cultural environment, the Special Forces are looking for candidates who have good interpersonal skills—men who are open to listening and working with other people and foreign communities. More crudely put, it may come down to whether a man is more comfortable in shooting people or trying to make friends with them. Some soldiers are very proficient in a tactical situation and very comfortable behind the gun, but they don't really want to make the effort to communicate with someone different from themselves. A Special Forces soldier has to be good behind the gun *and* be able to deal effectively with other cultures.

There are two predictors of success in Special Forces training. The first is the Ranger tab. Men who have completed Ranger training have two advantages. One is that they have successfully completed a very difficult school. They've been cold, wet, and hungry, and they understand what it is to go days without sleep. They know pain and discomfort, and they know how to cope with it. Second, Ranger school also teaches small-unit tactics, a key skill in the world of Special Forces and SOF ground operations. Perhaps the most valuable carryover skills from Ranger training are confidence and leadership. Physically, nothing in Special Forces training is more difficult than Ranger training. I've heard Rangers in Special Forces training often say, "This is some nasty shit, but it's not Ranger School." Ranger training simply gives them a confidence that many non-Rangers lack. During Phase II of Special Forces training, which focuses on small-unit tactics in an SF environment, the Rangers usually do very well. Phase II cadre often look on their Ranger candidates as teaching assistants. The second predictor is a foreign language. A second language does not guarantee success, but those who speak more than one language seem to have the interpersonal skills that are essential to the mission of Special Forces, or the ability to acquire them. Having a language usually means that a man will have the ability to navigate in another culture more easily.

Finally, there's the issue of diversity. There's the inherent diversity found in a Special Forces detachment that comes from men with different cultural, economic, and educational backgrounds, all of which make the team stronger than the sum of the individual parts. And there's racial diversity. Too often, the perceived need for diversity has to do with a racial or ethnic balance that mirrors our national demographic. Those charged with hiring practices in the corporate or government arenas pay attention to this because, for want of a more politically correct term, it's the right thing to do. Racial balance in the corporate world may even be an evaluation criterion or a competitive advantage in a contractual situation. But in the military, especially in SOF, and most certainly in Army Special Forces, diversity itself is an *operational* advantage. Deployed Special Forces detachments often have the duties and staff responsibility of a large military force or even a community government. In these situations, diversity becomes a force multiplier. Diverse skills and ethnic backgrounds bring a more multidimensional approach to cross-cultural issues that Special Forces teams have to deal with on a routine basis. The more diverse the members of an SF detachment, the better the thinking that may go into problem solving in cross-cultural environment. Another consideration is the image that a multiethnic team projects. Stephen Ambrose, who has written so eloquently of our troops in

World War II, relates that one of the most comforting sights for the war-weary citizens of France or Belgium was a patrol of American GIs coming into their village. They had chocolate for the kids and were re-strained and respectful in dealing with the local population. But that was an all-white patrol of GIs in a western European village. Afghan-istan and Iraq offer none of the homogeneity found in western Europe during the last world war. In these troubled nations and in much of the Middle East and Southwest Asia, there are competing religious and tribal interests. There are deep-seated animosities in the same nation—in the same community. Imagine the impact in these tribal and ethni-cally charged areas when a Special Forces detachment with blacks, whites, Asians, and Hispanics enters a village. Not only do they have the skills to fight and to provide material assistance, they also speak the language and understand and respect the customs. They demonstrate that people who are different can live and work together. They are the new band of brothers.

There are three types of individuals entering Special Forces training: officer candidates, enlisted soldiers currently serving in units of the Army, and men who have been recruited "off the street"—men who joined the Army to become Special Forces soldiers. All three will come together in the first major phase of the Special Forces training pipeline, the Special Forces Assessment and Selection phase. SFAS is conducted at Camp Mackall, the primary Special Forces training base, and oper-ates under the umbrella of Fort Bragg and the JFK Special Warfare Center and School. The officers and enlisted soldiers who are currently serving in the Army will come to SFAS from their current duty station on temporary-duty orders. If they succeed at SFAS, they will be "selected" to continue Special Forces training. As selectees, they will return to their units and at a future time, usually two to four months, be assigned to Fort Bragg on permanent orders. This is a matter of eco-nomics. It costs money to move a man and his family from one duty station to another. Since two-thirds of those attending the selection phase will *not* qualify, they return to their current assignment at their current post and carry on with their duties. Those selected will leave their current units and return to Fort Bragg (unless they're already stationed there) to begin the next phase of Special Forces training.

Officers entering Special Forces training are special before they arrive at Camp Mackall for the assessment and selection process. They are captains and a few first lieutenants who have made the promotion list for captain. In most cases, they've had four or five years or more in the Army and have distinguished themselves as superior leaders in their branch of the Army. Today, these numbers are up from my time at Fort Bragg; something on the order of five hundred or more of these officers apply for Special Forces training each year. Close to three hundred are now chosen to attend SFAS. Most have been to Ranger School, and many of those are veterans of the 75th Ranger Regiment. Most are infantry officers, although there's always a smattering from other branches of the Army—armor, engineering, artillery, and signal corps officers. It might seem that the Special Forces mission is more suited to infantry officers, but a Special Forces battalion commander likes having a mix of talent he can draw upon. The key components an officer brings to the Special Forces table are troop leadership skills and branch experience. Language ability and cross-cultural skills/experience are also very helpful. And today, more than ever, most of these officers are combat veterans. With regard to other SOF units, including SEALs and Rangers, the officer candidates for Special Forces are older, and have more time in service and more leadership experience.

The enlisted Special Forces candidates are also a breed apart in terms of maturity and qualification. While these soldiers are predominately infantryman, they come from all branches of the Army and from all technical specialties. A great many come from the 82nd Airborne Division, which also calls Fort Bragg home, but there are aviation, administrative, and medical specialists, as well as those from the infantry and armored divisions. As a group, they're more senior, with the junior men having reached the rank of specialist, but most are buck sergeants or higher. It's not uncommon to have a number of staff sergeants and a few sergeants first class in a selection class. They are older than most soldiers in conventional units, they have superior performance ratings, and, like the officer candidates, most are combat veterans. We often hear about the Army failing to make its recruitment goals, but the Special Forces recruiters are finding that there's an increasing number of veteran soldiers who want to become Special Forces soldiers. Applications are up and the SF recruiters are able to select the *most* qualified candidates from a larger pool of qualified applicants.

"These are good times for Special Forces, as far as recruiting goes," a Special Forces recruiter told me. "And I should know. I'm the guy who has to tell a veteran sergeant in the 82nd that we can't take him this time around. I tell him to go back to his unit, try to improve his physical qualifications and test scores, and perhaps we can place him in a future class. Who would've thought that four years into a war, we'd have plenty of high-quality soldiers willing to extend their enlistments to become Special Forces soldiers."

The recruiter's job has been made a lot easier because of 9/11 and the global war on terror. Many good men self-select for Special Forces. These are soldiers who have served with or near Special Forces detachments in Afghanistan or Iraq, and they now know how they want to go *back* to the fight. They've seen what Special Forces do and how they do it, and they want to be a part of that world. By far, the most potent recruiting tool for Special Forces among regular soldiers is a deployed Special Forces detachment.

"I was in Kandahar with a rifle company providing perimeter security for the airport there," a sergeant candidate in SFAS told me. "This C-17 lands and taxis to the end of the runway and lowers the tail ramp, engines still running. I thought it might be some black operation or something like that. Then this Humvee pulls up with four guys in it. They all had beards and shaggy hair, and they were dressed in blue jeans and old field jackets. I knew they were Americans because they all had M4 rifles with scopes and laser sights on them. The C-17 crew chief walks down the tail ramp with a big stack of flat boxes. He hands 'em to one of these guys, reboards the C-17, and the big transport takes off. We're in a revetment about fifty meters away. The Humvee pulls over to our position and one of them gets out. 'You guys look like you could use some chow,' he says, and hands us one of the boxes. It was a pepperoni and sausage pizza—and it was *still warm!* Right then and there I said, 'That's the kind of outfit I want to belong to,' and here I am."

"I want to be in the Army for a career," another candidate told me, "and I want to serve with the best. A lot of people think the Green Berets have it easy because they get special pay and they don't have to observe grooming standards when they are deployed in Afghanistan and places like that. But they work hard. They're out there in the bad areas a lot of the time, and when they're back in, they're often not in a secure area. They're real pros, and the locals respect them—you can tell. They look at them a lot different than they do the rest of us."

"I've wanted to be in Special Forces since I was a plebe at West Point," an officer candidate told me. "That was nine years ago. I enjoyed my tour with the 101st, and I was proud of my service in Bosnia and Iraq, but now I finally have a chance to live my dream and be in Special Forces. This is where I want to serve."

The current climate in Special Forces and Special Forces training can be compared to *The Perfect Storm*—much like the movie and the rare storm-pattern phenomenon on which that film was based. This is due to a number of reasons, but three stand out. First of all, the caliber and content of Special Forces training has never been better. I say this not only from my observations, but from the comments of retired Special Forces master sergeants and sergeant majors—men whose experience stretches back to the late 1960s and early 1970s. They say it is better now than they've ever seen it. Better, again, for a number of reasons, but primarily due to the quality of the training cadre—warriors back from war, training new men for war. Something special goes on when trainers and trainees may soon fight side by side. Those few men who were not combat veterans were experienced SF operators chosen for their teaching and leadership skills. Nearly all of the noncombat vets were approaching the end of their three-year tour as Special Forces instructors. They were like grade-schoolers waiting for recess in their eagerness to return to their groups and get into deployment rotation.

The second reason, as we have talked about, is the quality of the soldiers who show up for assessment and selection. These are, for the most part, men who volunteered for the Army when joining the Army meant going into combat in Afghanistan and Iraq. Except for certain specialties, joining the Army now means going to war. And now these soldiers are volunteering *again,* with the prospect of future combat a certainty. They're not here for college credit or for civilian job skills or because they've no options on the outside. They're here for the fight, to become professional warriors in the service of their nation. Not all of them will make the cut, but that's why they show up at SFAS. And there's the brotherhood thing. Special Forces is a brotherhood like no other. I've been privileged to know the close company of good men and to bond with them in difficult or formative times—my classmates at the Naval Academy, my generation of Navy SEALs, my CIA training class, and my lifelong friends, who will follow me into old age. Yet I sensed something a little deeper and more special at work as I watched the Special Forces cadre mentor the new men into their ranks. They're training their new brothers.

The third component of this perfect storm is the need. Insurgency warfare appears to be the weapon of choice for al-Qaeda and its terrorist allies. The lead SOF component for counterinsurgency warfare is Army Special Forces. We'll succeed or fail in Iraq and Afghanistan on our ability to control the insurgents, period. Any form of democracy that breaks out in Beirut or Damascus will attract Islamic insurgents like bees to honey. The Special Forces detachments will be on the front lines of the war on terror far into the foreseeable future. They'll not only have to fight and train their local counterparts to fight, but they're going to have to teach our other SOF components and conventional units to conduct counterinsurgency warfare as well.

This perfect storm of quality training, quality input, and urgent need does not exist with the other major SOF ground components. Navy SEALs, who have come ashore to become ground SOF players in this fight, are still made the old-fashioned way—the training cadre takes sailors from boot camp and fresh Naval Academy ensigns and makes them into SEALs. There's no Navy boot camp or shipboard experience that compares with Army infantry training, nor is there any fleet deployment that prepares a man for special operations that's comparable with a tour in Iraq with the 82nd Airborne or the 3rd Infantry Division. SEAL training is difficult, perhaps more difficult on the pure pain-o-meter scale than Special Forces training. But the skill set of a Navy SEAL—in addition to his behind-the-gun proficiency, which is comparable to an SF soldier's—requires maritime training. Over one-third of basic SEAL training is in-water training; ongoing maritime/underwater certification and proficiency training also take a great deal of time. And the counterinsurgency skills, while being given more attention, are still not the focus of SEAL training nor a primary mission in their deployment rotations. Even the Rangers don't enjoy this "storm" in the manner of Special Forces. Rangers are younger and don't have to be trained to the same rigorous standard of Special Forces. Good as they are and as tough as they are, it's still light-infantry work, and their duties don't carry the language and cross-cultural requirements of their SF brothers. For all of these reasons, Special Forces have found themselves in a special place and circumstance, one that is unprecedented and one that may never happen again.

A final word about these soldiers who abandon their conventional units to try out for Special Forces. When they leave the 101st Airborne or the 3rd Infantry Division, they are, to some extent, breaking faith with *that* band of brothers. They're saying, "I want to leave you and join them." Put yourself in the shoes of a company first sergeant in the 82nd Airborne. His battalion's just returned from deployment, and like any good first sergeant, he's thinking about the next deployment— the veterans he'll have with him and the new men he has to whip into shape to go back to the fight. Suddenly, three of his best sergeants inform him that they're putting in for Special Forces training. Never mind that two of the three will return to his company after an unsuccessful try at SF selection, perhaps better for their experience. They want to leave. In his heart, the first sergeant knows these soldiers are following their dream and are motivated to better serve their country. Still, he can't help but feel betrayed and a little resentful. For the officers, this resentment is deeper. For officers leaving the conventional fold, it borders on infidelity in marriage. In many cases, the officer who leaves for SFAS may well be the best company commander or the most capable staff officer in his battalion or regiment. The senior commanders who rely on these outstanding junior officers can't help but feel a little betrayed. It's my sense, given the deployed working relationships and intelligence-production value of the Special Forces detachments in Afghanistan and Iraq, the wall between SOF elements and the conventional military may not be as formidable as it once was. Still, the U.S. Army, like most standing armies, has its problems and resentments with elite units, even though Army SOF elements are funded differently and often have a separate chain of command. And these fine young captains and first lieutenants who put in for Special Forces, no matter what their accomplishments, may be moving down a path of no return. Burning their bridges is perhaps putting it too strongly, but this breach of faith with their conventional branch may not be soon forgiven if they are unsuccessful at SFAS and have to return to their old unit. In some ways, the defection on the part of these officers represents a bold move on their part—trading a secure place for the uncertain. And in the final analysis, is this not one of the qualities the Special Forces are looking for in their leaders?

This rivalry and resentment doesn't exist in the Navy and Air Force

SOF components. The Navy SEAL teams and Special Boat Teams don't threaten the blue-water Navy. Most officers come from the Naval Academy or college ROTC, and most of the enlisted men come from boot camp. Those officers and petty officers who apply for SEAL training from the fleet don't do so in the numbers or at the experience levels as their Army counterparts who request to go to Special Forces Assessment and Selection. It is much the same with the Air Force Special Tactics Teams and the 1st Special Operations Wing. Neither of these service-related SOF components threaten their parent service, nor do they drain off talent and experience like Army Special Forces. Not even the Rangers pose this issue with "big Army"; indeed, most senior infantry and armor commanders wear Ranger tabs. There's also the question of job description. Neither the blue-water Navy nor the regular Air Force have an interest in doing the work of SEALs or the Special Tactics Teams. Big Army is often colocated with Special Forces, both here at home and on deployment. Some Army and Marine Corps senior officers believe that with a little training, experience, and funding, they can cover the Special Forces mission. I couldn't disagree more strongly. I personally had no idea of just how difficult the SF mission was, nor the intensive skill set required to do the job. It took me ten months at Fort Bragg and Camp Mackall to appreciate what it takes to be *really* proficient at foreign internal defense and unconventional warfare. Hopefully, the needs of our nation in the global war on terror will bring these inter- and intra-service rivalries into perspective.

In *Chosen Soldier,* you will meet and come to know the officers and enlisted soldiers who want to become Green Berets as we follow them through SFAS in chapter 4. But first, we need to talk about the third input or component to current Special Forces training. I'm talking about those men who have been recruited "off the street" for Special Forces training. These are the ones I often call the civilians and some in the Army refer to as the SF Babies. Neither term is accurate. First of all, when they arrive at Fort Bragg to begin their journey to selection, they're already soldiers—airborne-qualified infantrymen, albeit fresh out of basic training. Many of them will go on to become Special Forces soldiers—outstanding Green Berets. The majority will, for one reason or another, find themselves in the 82nd Airborne or the 4th Infantry Division or the 75th Ranger Regiment, where they will serve out their enlistments. Some of those who don't make it on their first try in SFAS will be back to try again. They will join the legion of combat veterans from conventional Army units who want to serve in Special Forces.

This program, which began in 2002, takes men off the street—from high school, college, or civilian jobs—and brings them into the Army for the sole purpose of turning them into Special Forces soldiers. In many ways, these young men are like their counterparts who enlist in the Navy to become Navy SEALs. Big Army and blue-water Navy love these programs. Those who do not become Green Berets or SEALs make superb soldiers and sailors, and go on to serve with distinction in their assigned service components. The program that turns civilians into Special Forces soldiers is called the 18 X-Ray Program, and these men who join the Army for Special Forces training are universally referred to as the X-Rays. Even when these new soldiers are qualified Green Berets, they're often still called X-Rays. When one of them is killed in combat, someone will invariably say, "He was an X-Ray."

There's precedence for the X-Ray Program. On more than one occasion, Special Forces has looked to younger, less-experienced soldiers to fill its ranks. As recently as the early 1990s, the Special Forces began to accept soldiers directly from basic training and assign them to the Special Forces groups. After they had served in the groups in an administrative or support role for six months, they could be recommended by their group to attended Army airborne training and go on to selection. This was done in an attempt to bring up the manpower strength of the groups. This earlier program was only in place for two years, but it did modestly add to the Special Forces manning levels.

In chapter 3, we'll take a close look at these soldiers and the formal training that prepares these men for the selection process at Camp

Mackall, but for now, let's focus on who they are and what happens before they arrive at Fort Bragg to begin their initial Special Forces training. There's no such thing in my mind as a typical X-Ray, but taken as a composite they look something like this:

Average age: twenty-three years old, with the youngest twenty and the oldest twenty-nine.

Rank: Private first class or specialist. Some in the National Guard are more senior.

Army general test score: 120+, high enough to qualify for officer candidate school.

Average physical training score: 265 out of 300, well above average for the Army.

Other: 15 percent are married, most have some college, just under half have college degrees.

The reasons these men join the Army for Special Forces training range from the patriotic to the adventurous. Not a few are bored by their civilian jobs. Many come from military families. Most were deeply moved by the attacks of 9/11, and that event had some bearing on their desire to serve. A few have had prior service, mostly in the Army, and those few choose the X-Ray Program as a way to get back in uniform. The Special Forces National Guard groups send a few of their non-SF-qualified soldiers to join up with the X-Ray Program; these are men who need some physical training before they go to selection. The reserve groups also send some of their new recruits to the program. All of them have their minds and their focus on a single event that will change their lives: Special Forces Assessment and Selection.

Men who join the Army for the X-Ray Program will sign a five- or six-year enlistment contract. They're inducted into the Army as privates and report for basic training. Army basic training has morphed into One Station Unit Training (OSUT), which includes seven weeks of Basic Combat Training immediately followed by seven weeks of

Advanced Individual Training. The basic training course makes a man a soldier. The successful completion of the latter qualifies a soldier and an infantryman. In basic training, the new X-Rays and every other new recruit in the Army learn about Army regulations, physical training, first aid, close-order drill, marksmanship, obstacle courses (now called confidence courses), hand grenades, and marching under a rucksack. The new recruits put these new military skills to work in a three-day field exercise. On graduation, they are soldiers. Following the Basic Combat Training phase of OSUT, the X-Rays and the other infantry candidates move on to Advanced Individual Training. Here they learn soldiering skills that are useful whether they are assigned to an infantry platoon or a Special Forces detachment. These include weapons operation and maintenance, vehicle operation and maintenance, land reconnaissance, land navigation, minefield safety, communications, static firing positions, and teamwork. On completion, they're now soldiers and infantrymen.

During this fourteen-week OSUT process, some recruits, and those include a few X-Rays, decide that this life is not for them—that they don't want to be soldiers under any circumstances. Army life comes with a decided lack of privacy and loss of freedom. For the X-Ray soldiers, the image of donning that Green Beret meets the growing reality that the road to becoming a Green Beret is very hard and very long. So they volunteer out; they quit. Even for the most capable and motivated, the transition from college student or computer technician or management trainee to soldier isn't an easy one. And along with all this new regimentation, barracks life, and the shouting of drill instructors is the sure knowledge that if Basic Combat Training and Advanced Individual Training is hard, what's it going to be like when they get to Fort Bragg and Special Forces training?

After OSUT, the new X-Rays are off to three weeks of Army Airborne School, more commonly referred to as jump school. At this point, a few of the X-Rays decide that while they want to learn to parachute, the long journey of Special Forces training is not for them.

At this point, they may or may not be allowed into jump school, but they have earned themselves a set of orders to the 3rd or 4th Infantry Division, or some other duty station that serves the needs of the Army. After three weeks of Airborne School and five parachute jumps, the same as when I went to jump school almost forty years ago, they are now airborne-qualified infantry soldiers. Friday afternoon after their jump-school graduation, they blouse their trousers into their jump boots, pin on their silver parachute wings, and board the buses for the trip from Fort Benning, Georgia, to Fort Bragg, North Carolina.

On the twelve-hour trip from Benning to Bragg, the X-Rays have some time to think about their sixteen or seventeen weeks in the United States Army. They have three Army schools behind them. They've struggled and sweated, and they've succeeded. With each school, there was a graduation ceremony of sorts and they were congratulated for their achievement—something the Army does very well. The new soldiers were allowed a day or a weekend to savor their achievement, then it was on to the next school. For the most part, few of them have been seriously challenged, although jumping out of a perfectly good airplane is not for sissies, and something that may have never entered their mind six months ago. Now they're about to begin their Special Forces training. They know something of what is ahead. The rumor mill easily reaches from Fort Bragg to Fort Benning—some fact and a lot of fiction. The Special Forces cadres visit them at Fort Benning and candidly tell them something of what's in store when they do get to Fort Bragg. But all they really know is that it'll be hard—harder than anything they have faced in their short Army careers.

Chapter Three

THE PREPARATION

It is well after midnight by the time the three buses finally crawl off I-95 and turn west. Leaving the interstate, they thread their way through the outskirts of Fayetteville and onto the All American Freeway, a short, four-lane superhighway that leads into the bowels of Fort Bragg. At the gate, a guard steps aboard the lead bus and looks down the aisle of sleepy soldiers. They're awake, but just barely. The buses aren't civilian charter buses, but school-type military buses.

"More Special Forces trainees?" the guard asks the driver as he checks the trip pass.

"I reckon," the driver replies. He's as tired as the soldiers he's driving. The guard's an MP, but the driver is a civilian contract employee.

After the buses are checked through, they continue down All American, turn left on Longstreet Road, and continue for nearly a mile, then right on Gruber Road, and right again onto Pratt Street. The sprawling base is quiet but not quite asleep. Fort Bragg is never fully asleep, just busier during the day. The file of buses stops at a gravel parking area

WATER AEROBICS.   Pre-SFAS students pause midstream on a run for some jumping jacks—not unwelcome in the North Carolina summer heat.

between Pike Athletic Field and a row of two-story World War II–style wooden barracks. It's nearly two o'clock on Monday morning. They were supposed to have left Fort Benning Sunday morning to arrive Sunday evening, but due to a scheduling error, they had not left until two that afternoon. A single figure waits for them, clipboard in hand. He's dressed in utility trousers, black sweatshirt, and black baseball cap. He makes his way down the file of buses, shouting into each one.

"Fall in, on the double! Move, people, move!" The soldiers struggle off the buses with their gear—all their worldly Army possessions in a kit bag and a duffel, perhaps a hundred pounds per man. "Fall in beside your gear. I want four ranks, dress and cover down." The mass of troops scramble into a loose formation. "Too slow, people—everyone drop and start pushing them out." The last of them tumble from the door of the buses, struggling under the weight of their gear. They find a piece of gravel, drop their bags, and begin doing push-ups. Finally, the buses are empty. They pull away in a cloud of blue haze, leaving an eerie quiet in their wake, broken only by the grunting of men doing push-ups. The soldiers melt into an undulating field of dark forms— rising and falling. There's no moon, and the area's sparsely lit by a picket of halogen streetlights along the edge of the athletic field. It's August, and the overnight temperature has dropped to a moist seventy-five degrees.

"Recover!" shouts the man in the ball cap. "Fall in and do it smartly this time." After several minutes, they manage a loose assembly of four ranks. There are about a hundred of them. "All right, men, listen up. When I call out your name, I want you to sound off and fall out into a group off to my right, understood?"

"Yes, Sergeant," comes the weak chorus.

"Not loud enough, ladies. Drop!" After another short round of push-ups, he shouts, "Recover. Is that understood?"

"YES, SERGEANT!"

"Now you're getting the idea. OK, Adams."

"Here, Sergeant!"

"Adkins."

"Here, Sergeant!"

The formation is cut to groups of twelve- to fourteen-man groups and sent off to their barracks. After dismissing the last group, the soldier in the black sweatshirt and ball cap, Sergeant First Class Ross Jennings, flips through his roster and again counts the new arrivals. These soldiers are the X-Rays, men who joined the Army specifically to become Green Berets. They'll begin this journey with 18X Pre-SFAS Training—training to prepare them for Special Forces Assessment and Selection. This class is 18X Pre-SFAS Class 8-04. Jennings had 101 names and could only account for 99 soldiers—2 short. How the hell, he says to himself, could they muster 101 airborne-qualified 18 X-Rays at Benning, put them on the bus, and I get only 99 here to begin training?

Sergeant First Class Jennings is the senior TAC NCO for the Pre-SFAS course. TAC is yet another acronym and stands for teach, advise, and counsel. The X-Ray soldiers saw plenty of these TAC noncommissioned officers in their basic training, but Sergeant Jennings is the first TAC NCO they have met who is a Green Beret. He's thirty-six years old and has been at the JFK Special Warfare Center and School for almost three years. Had the buses arrived as scheduled that afternoon, there would have been eighteen TAC NCOs waiting for them, and the class would have been welcomed to Fort Bragg at that time. Now that reception will have to wait until morning formation. Jennings sent his cadre of TAC sergeants home and remained in the area for the arrival of the new class. He's five-nine with soft, regular features, light-brown wavy hair, and an easy smile that creases the corners of his eyes. Ross Jennings grew up in Tacoma and has a degree in history from the University of Washington. He's one of the few TACs who is single. He came to the school from the 10th Special Forces Group. He speaks German and had two rotations in Bosnia before coming to the training command. Jennings arrived at Fort Bragg just as the X-Ray Program was getting off the ground. Much of the training, testing, and course work for the program has been developed by Sergeant Jennings. Since he is the corporate knowledge for this relatively new block of training, he's just been extended in the billet for an additional six months, which doesn't please him. He wants to get back to his group and back into deployment rotation.

"I've been here too long," he told me. "I should have been back with 10th Group a year ago, but they held me over again. We have a big job here. We've got to sort these soldiers out and get them ready for Special Forces selection. We get a new group in here every month or so. I work my TACs like dogs. Hell, I work like a dog. I need to get back to my group."

Jennings glances at his watch: 0230, or 2:30 a.m. He shrugs, knowing it will take the better part of the day to track down his two missing troopers. He thinks about going back to his office, where he might get a few hours sleep in the cot he keeps by his desk. But the class formation is at 0500, so he decides against it. Instead, he heads for the chow hall. There's always a coffee pot on, and maybe he can talk one of the mess cooks into frying him up some eggs.

Meanwhile, the new Special Forces trainees make their way to the barracks. They're wooden frame structures that were built in 1937—open-bay sleeping area in one end with toilets, showers, and laundry facilities at the other. At one time the structures had been modernized to provide sleeping and locker cubicles for four men. Those partitions were taken out when Special Forces Pre-SFAS Training took over the barracks. Overseas, deployed ODAs often don't have the luxury of privacy. In Special Forces, men train like they fight, even men who have only been in the Army for a few months. In Vietnam, Captain Vernon Gillespie's Special Forces detachment slept in open bays, just like Class 8-04. The new X-Rays shuffle through the dim light of their new home, trying to find an empty rack. In every other two or three bunks there's a sleeping soldier. These are rollbacks—soldiers held over from the previous class. One of the new arrivals finds an empty bunk between two sleeping forms. He unceremoniously drops his load to the linoleum floor. One man grunts and rolls over. The other sits up and offers his hand.

"Hey, man, welcome to Fort Bragg. I'm Hal Eshman, a refugee from Class 7-04."

"Um, I'm Tim Baker. Just checking in from Benning."

Eshman glances at his watch and gives him a knowing smile. "Try to get some rest; you're going to need it."

Private First Class Tim Baker is six-one and a well-set, handsome twenty-two-year-old. He was a sophomore at Texas A&M and an Army ROTC student when he decided to quit collage and put in for the X-Ray program. "I always wanted to be in the Army," he told me. "By leaving school, I just pushed up the timetable a little." While waiting for his induction date, he worked on a horse ranch and at Circuit City. He worked hard to get in shape prior to joining the Army, and neither One Station Unit Training nor Airborne School had seriously taxed him. He's looking forward to the challenge of Special Forces training. But now, he's pretty well done in from the long bus ride. Baker quickly stows his gear, lays out a clean uniform for formation, and is asleep in a matter of minutes.

In a dozen other barracks, the newly arrived X-Ray soldiers are wearily making up their bunks, stowing their gear, and trying for a little sleep. In addition to the new arrivals, there are perhaps half again as many men from the previous class who have been rolled into Class 8-04. The 8-04 designator is given to this group of X-Rays as they will form the eighth Pre-SFAS class conducted in fiscal year 2004. Technically, these men are in Special Forces training, but this course, the Pre-SFAS Training, is designed to prepare them for their formal selection to the Special Forces Qualification Course. The mission of Pre-SFAS Training is to *prepare* X-Ray soldiers for the rigorous selection process. The mission of SFAS, or Phase I of the Q-Course, is to *select* soldiers for Special Forces training. The young men who just arrived from Fort Benning understand this, but their horizons are much shorter. For them, the days will begin early and their evening meal is a long way off. Their focus is on the next formation and the next training evolution.

The members of Class 8-04 aren't the only ones entering this training pipeline. This Pre-SFAS class also marks the beginning of my journey in Special Forces. As mentioned previously, Special Forces training is a changing, dynamic business. Each class is a little different than the one before. There are continuous changes, refinements, and modifications, so no two classes are quite the same. Yet there's a continuing awareness of what works and what doesn't work. If something's changed and it doesn't work, they try something else or revert to the old way of doing things. I talked with a lot of old-timers who came through the Qualification Course in the 1960s and 1970s. They're amazed at the refinements and structure of the current version of the Q-Course, and yet some training evolutions have remained unchanged for decades. For this Navy SEAL, it was all new. Yet, from day one, it had the flavor of SOF training—specially selected men training for a difficult and dangerous job.

"Fall in, three ranks, dress and cover down! Come on people, move! I want first platoon to my left, second platoon in front of me, and third platoon to my right. Too slow, way too slow! Everybody drop! Sergeant Jennings, just what in the hell do we have here? What have you got me into? Are you sure these people are soldiers? Don't tell me they are airborne infantrymen. They look like a bunch of old women! What the hell is going on?"

First Sergeant Will Carter is standing on a three-foot raised platform in front of the assembly area. Before him, the 154 men who were struggling into formation are now down on the rough paved roadway trying to do push-ups. The area is bathed in yellow light from the floods mounted on the nearby barracks. This is a small class; normally, there are between 200 and 250 men in a Pre-SFAS class. There's enough room for them to stand in ranks, but not enough for them to do push-ups. Stepping in and around this low, pulsing mass of camouflaged uniforms are the TAC NCOs. They are dressed the same as their students, but they all wear baseball caps.

"That's not a push-up; that's a head bob. This isn't boot camp; that isn't going to cut it!"

"All the way down, all the way up. No, no, no—your chest, not your belly!"

"You, yeah, you. Number 63. Get off your knees!"

"Tired, soldier? You've only been here two minutes. It's only going to get worse."

First Sergeant Carter picks up a bullhorn and addresses the class. "Recover! Now I want you to pretend you're soldiers and get into formation. Quickly, people, quickly." Carter is a hefty six-footer with a barrel chest and a round, amiable face, yet he's a formidable presence. He's the drover of the SFAS preparation course. Master Sergeant Carter isn't the only master sergeant assigned to Alpha Company, 1st Battalion, 1st Special Warfare Training Group, but he's the master sergeant designated as the first sergeant. He's universally addressed as "First Sergeant" or "Top" by his fellow sergeants. Much of the responsibility for preparing these men for their assessment and selection to Special Forces training falls on his shoulders.

First Sergeant Carter is from East Stone Gap, Virginia, and has spent close to twenty-five years in the Army. He was with the 1st Special Forces Group for sixteen years, and is fluent, if not quite native, in several Indonesian and Malay dialects. He spent two tours with the 1st Group battalion that is stationed in Okinawa and has been forward deployed all over Southeast Asia. "This is it for me," he told me soon after I checked in with Alpha Company. "After I finish with this job, my next duty station is Fort Living Room."

The formation is semiorganized chaos. In ranks, the assigned student squad leaders are trying to get a muster and report their roll call up to the assigned student platoon leaders. While this is taking place, the TACs are roaming up and down the files, inspecting the new men.

"You look like crap, soldier. You are to come to every formation in a clean uniform and blackened boots. You are clearly unsat—you hear me! Now drop!"

"Call that a haircut, roster number 133? You come out here tomorrow with that much hair and you'll wish you hadn't. If you want to become a Special Forces soldier, you damn well better become a soldier first."

The students wear their rank insignia on the collars of their camouflaged uniforms, which are called battle dress utilities, or BDUs. Most of them are privates first class—PFCs—or specialists. They are addressed as "PFC" or "Specialist." There's a strip of white adhesive tape above their nametags and below the two cargo pockets on either side of their trousers. Their roster number is boldly written in black Magic Marker on the tape. Their names are visible, but they are simply numbers to the cadre—for now.

"OK, ladies," booms First Sergeant Carter on the bullhorn, "since a decent formation seems to be beyond you, let's do the caterpillar. Formation, right FACE!" Under Carter's direction and the coaching of the TACs, the students string out in a push-up position, hands on the road with their boots on the shoulders of the man behind them.

"OK, down ONE!" The sea of camouflage drops to the roadbed. "And UP!" The mass of bodies collectively rises. "Down TWO!"

For the next half an hour, the formation coalesces into ranks, then breaks down into scattered platoon and squad-sized groupings for push-ups, sit-ups, jumping jacks, squat thrusts, flutter kicks, and exercises like the caterpillar, which I had never seen before. It's still dark. A moist cloud of perspiration and heavy breathing rises from Class 8-04 into the harsh glare of the floodlights. This is 8-04's welcome to Alpha Company and Special Forces training. Slowly, between the shouting and the calisthenics, a muster of the class works its way up to the podium to Sergeant Jennings.

"Found your lost chicks?" I ask.

"Yep. Seems like two of them just went off to their barracks without getting checked off my list. Or"—he grins—"I just missed them."

"You do this with every class?"

"Pretty much. If they get in on time, we like to shake them up Sunday afternoon or Sunday evening. Then we can get right into training on Monday morning. This little welcome session's to get them focused on the work ahead. It helps mold the class. We want to make it hard enough so they have to help each other. These aren't your average soldiers, and many of them weren't challenged before they got here. At one time or another here, everyone needs some help from his buddy. We like that to happen early. It also lets them know that if they're not prepared to give us 110 percent, then they need to be someplace else."

While we talked, a squad of students was doing flutter kicks in front of us. Jennings called them to their feet. "Too slow, men. Drop!" They all drop but for one man. He remains standing, bathed in sweat and looking miserable. "What's your problem, soldier?"

"I want to quit, sir. I don't belong here."

"Quit? I didn't ask you about quitting. I told you to drop. Now *drop!*" The hapless student melts to the pavement under Jennings's scowl. Jennings bends over him. "Now push 'em out and don't ever call me sir. You address me as sergeant, you got that?"

"Y-yes, sir—I mean, yes, Sergeant."

Jennings steps away from the student. "We don't let students quit until a week from today," he tells me in a quiet voice. "This is a rough day for them. If we can get them through the first week and into the weekend, some of them who'd have quit under the stress of the moment will hang in there—at least that's the theory."

"I notice you call them students. Why is that?"

"Here they're students or trainees. They don't become Special Forces candidates until they get out to Camp Mackall for selection."

With just a hint of dawn and another hot, humid day in the making, First Sergeant Carter puts them in road-march formation and leads them out of the area, past Pike Field and down a gravel road. Once on the gravel, he breaks into a brisk trot and Class 8-04 begins to string out behind him. The TAC NCOs run along the flanks, dispensing equal measures of harassment and encouragement. Following along behind the formation is a single officer—the Alpha Company commander, an Army captain. Carter takes them over a bridge that spans a forty-foot slow-moving stream and up a long quarter-mile incline. As I run alongside, I pick out the man who tried to quit.

"I don't understand," he says to one of his fellow students between gasps. "I told them I wanted to quit. I told them."

"Yeah," the other replies, "but you're still here, aren't you?"

After a short run, they return to the bridge. Only this time, Carter takes them into the stream. Most of the TACs and the company commander go in with the students. I keep to the bridge. The first sergeant halts them midstream and starts them on jumping jacks followed by toe touches. The water's depth is about three and a half feet.

"Are there snakes in there?" I ask one of the TACs.

"Sir, this is August in North Carolina. You got water, you got snakes."

Back at the assembly area, the class is put back in formation and First Sergeant Carter asks for a report. The assigned student squad leaders take roll and report to their student platoon leader. They report to the student class leader. It's still confusion, but ordered confusion.

"First Sergeant, the class is formed. One hundred fifty-four men assigned, one hundred fifty-two men present."

"Where're your other two men?" Carter booms at him. Accountability is a big issue. "We've been at this for barely an hour and already you've lost two of my soldiers. You're fired. You"—Carter points to one of the other rollbacks—"get up here. You're now the class leader. Now get me a good muster."

The student class leader, as well as the student platoon and squad leaders, are rotated often; the cadre wants to see as many students in leadership positions as possible. After another round of calisthenics at the assembly area, the class members straggle back to their barracks to change before heading off for morning chow. The new men are a little more than an hour into their training at Fort Bragg, and some are already questioning their suitability for this work. They're comforted to some degree by the comments of their fellow students from the previous class. "The first day is like this," they tell their new classmates. "It won't get any worse. But then, it won't get a whole lot better either."

Most of the first day is spent in the barracks, in their squad bays. Each two-story building holds two sixteen- to eighteen-man squads—one on the first deck and the other on the second. Each squad will normally have two TAC NCOs assigned, one primary and one alternate. These are veteran Special Forces sergeants, usually with the rank of sergeant first class and usually with at least ten years in Special Forces. The TACs introduce the new men to the barracks, and show them how to stow their gear—what has to be locked in their locker and what must be laid out on or near their bunk. As with all special operations military training, there's a host of protocols and ways of doing things that are very specific and exact. There are two reasons for this. First of all, this is high-stress training, and the buildings are very old. The men have to care for them, care for their gear, care for themselves, and live together. This calls for a great deal of regimentation in the mechanics of life during training and nontraining time. The second is that the Special Forces way of life demands a great deal of precision and attention to detail. It may sound simple, but turning out for every evolution properly attired and with the right equipment takes planning and preparation. Cleanliness and personal hygiene in this environment also take time and attention. Deployed Special Forces teams often live in worse conditions than these, so proper physical habits and a structured communal-living etiquette are important. This training begins on day one.

"These are all good kids, and many of them are great kids," Sergeant First Class Donovan Tess tells me. We're in his squad bay, and all around us students are mopping floors, preparing gear, folding uniforms, and polishing boots. "But they all have to get along and work together. There are three showers, two washers, two dryers. This barracks and each individual's gear and bunk have to be up to standard or the whole squad will be called to task. I may miss one of them sloughing off; the other members of their squad won't. The ones who look out only for themselves or who consistently put their welfare over others won't make it in Special Forces. Neither will someone who doesn't pull his own weight. These kids're smart enough or they wouldn't be here. But many have never been in a situation where they had to look out for the other guy. To make it in Special Forces, they all have to get along, and they have to learn to pull together. The graded evolutions are individual efforts, but here in the barracks, they live as a team."

Tess has been in the Army for eighteen years, but in Special Forces for only eight. Before coming to the training command, he was with 10th Group and deployed to the Republic of Georgia, Slovenia, Germany, and Iraq. He grew up in Phoenix and came into the Army right out of high school.

"These men have to forget about where they came from and what they were doing before they got here. That's all old business. Their total focus should be on getting themselves and their buddies ready for the next evolution. They should always be thinking, 'What can I do better?' and 'Who needs my help?' For the most part, those who belong here make it, and those who don't go away. What breaks your heart is when some kid tries his level best and is always there for his teammates, but he simply doesn't have the physical tools or situational awareness to do the work. The TACs will always go the extra mile for that kind of soldier, but if this isn't his thing, we want him gone; we want to get him to someplace in the Army where he can make a contribution. This kind of soldiering's not for everyone."

Sergeant Tess ambles around the squad bay, helping some with their gear, dropping others for a few push-ups, and kidding with most of them.

"Miller, you call that a properly stowed locker? It's a sewer. Drop." He pulls all the uniforms and gear from the locker and dumps them on the floor. "OK, Miller, recover. And the rest of you, gather around. This is how it's done." Tess begins to pull uniforms from the pile, shake them out, fold them, and stow them in the locker. He takes

Miller's rucksack, dumps it out, and repacks it in an orderly manner. Soon Miller's locker and equipment are a picture of organization and neatness. "Last time, Miller. I'm not your mama. I want all your gear and clothing looking like this, or we'll be going on a little trip to guess where?"

"Uh, the swamp, Sergeant Tess?"

"That's right, the swamp. I'll be back in an hour or so, and I want to see some good-looking lockers and bunks." I follow Tess out to ask about the swamp. We walk around the building to a shallow forty-foot square of standing, brackish water. It was ugly and looked like the surface of a cesspool.

"That's the swamp. We used to put 'em all in it as soon as they got off the bus to let them know they were in for a different kind of training than they experienced at Fort Benning. But that was really over the top, and, quite honestly, sent the wrong message. These men're volunteers, and we need to respect that. We're here to teach these guys, not harass them. Now it's more of a remedial thing. Every class has a personality. If the class begins to break down and has real problems, then we run them through the muck to refocus them on their training here and their duty to their squad mates. It may not look like it, but this class is doing pretty well. It's a matter of effort. We keep a certain amount of pressure on no matter what, but as a class, these guys are doing pretty well. They're trying to do their best and looking out for each other, and that counts for a lot."

I return to the barracks and take the stairs. On the second floor, another group of X-Rays is working in their squad bay and tending to their personal equipment, much as Sergeant Tess's squad. I notice one soldier sitting on his bunk, polishing his boots. His locker has some semblance of order, and his rucksack looks packed and ready. He looks a little older than the others.

"How's it going?" I ask.

"Working our butts off, sir, but we'll get through it. So you're the writer?" I nod. The class was briefed that I would be with them for this training. "I'm Antonio Costa," he says, holding out his hand. "Tell me about this book you're writing."

We talk a while, and I steer the conversation to my favorite question for the X-Ray soldiers. "What were you doing before you decided to go into the Army?"

"I was working for Northwest Airlines," he replies.

"Doing what?"

He grins. "I'm an airline pilot."

The grin becomes a chuckle; the surprised look on my face is one I'm sure he's seen before.

"Furloughed?" I ask.

"No, sir. I'm National Guard, and I'm on leave from the airlines for this training."

"Nineteenth Group?" I ask, guessing at one of the two National Guard groups.

"No, sir, the 20th, out of Jacksonville."

"I guess you know the Guard groups are deploying almost as much as the active groups."

"I do. I expect I'll be going over next fall, that is, if they don't kick me out of here."

I do a quick mental calculation. "Next fall? Wouldn't you be in language school about then?"

"I don't think they'll send me. I'm fluent in Spanish and Italian."

Specialist Antonio Costa is five-nine, solidly built, with dark eyes and hair. He has an open and easy smile, and his manner is serious but with a touch of humor. We talk for a while, and I learn that Costa is thirty-three years old, lived in Europe for most of his childhood, and attended high school in Madrid. He has a bachelor of science in aeronautical science from Emory University. Costa tells me that his biggest challenge in training is keeping himself fit and free of injury during those evolutions designed to wear the students down. When I ask about his family, he whips out a picture of his wife and new baby. He is quick to point out that being a good husband and father is one of his goals. I finally get around to my second-favorite X-Ray question: "Why're you here?"

"I've always wanted to serve my country, but like a lot of guys, I kept putting it off. Then you have a family and family comes first, so it's easy to say you're too busy to serve. Then 9/11 happened. I'm a little old to be looking at military aviation. One of the other pilots at Northwest was in Special Forces in the National Guard, and he got me interested. So here I am. I'm lucky. I can do this and return to my job with the airlines. I'm also lucky to have a terrific wife. She's supported me in this, above and beyond."

"What's the difference in the pay of an airline pilot and a specialist in the Army?"

This brings a genuine smile to Specialist Costa. "Well, it's getting smaller, but it's still significant. We planned for this, but I'll admit, it's caused us to make a few changes. Then again, I'm married to a very understanding woman."

The following day, after a normal physical-training session, a four-mile run, and morning chow, Class 8-04 crowds onto a file of Army stake trucks—bench seating and canvas cover—for the trip across base to the Special Operations Academic Facility. This academic facility is a large, four-story concrete building the Special Forces students and candidates call the Grey Elephant. Since my time at Fort Bragg, the Special Operations Academic Facility has been renamed in honor of the father of Army Special Forces, Colonel Aaron Bank, who passed away in 2004 at the age of 101. It's now the Aaron Bank Hall, and home to other phases of training as well as the language laboratories. The class files into the auditorium and quietly takes their seats. On the screen is a PowerPoint slide with yellow lettering on a green background that proclaims, "Introduction to Special Forces Pre-Selection." A speaker's podium stands in the front of the room, off to one side.

"On your FEET!" barks First Sergeant Carter. "The Alpha Company commander will now give you your indoctrination briefing. It *will* behoove you to give him your undivided attention. The captain has some essential word to put out, and if I catch you sleeping, you'll answer to me."

Carter moves away from the podium, and an officer of medium height and a crisp set of BDUs steps up to it. He has short dark hair, neatly trimmed and combed, and a mild, youthful air about him. He glances at the screen and steps to the center of the room.

"Take your seats, men." His voice is soft, confident, and almost conversational. "If you feel sleepy, get up and stand in the back of the room. If you can't hear me, raise your hand and I'll speak louder. My name is Captain Shields, and my job over the next four weeks is to get you ready for Special Forces selection. I'll do my job. My cadre will do their job, and I expect you to do your job. The purpose of this briefing is to let you know what we expect and what you must do to successfully complete this training and prepare yourself for selection—SFAS. There's no silver bullet to this training, and there are no shortcuts. Pay attention and perform to the best of your ability, and you'll do just fine. This is not meant to be a pep talk or to jack you up in any way, but I'll give you some advice, up front. This is a hard course, as many of you know by now. There are standards you have to meet. If you want to successfully complete this course and move on to selection, then put everything else out of your mind and focus on training. Forget about your car, your cell phone, your girlfriend, your dog, your family, everything. If there's a family emergency, we'll find you and let you know. For now, think about nothing but training and doing your very best. It's the only way to get through this course. It's the only way to show us you're ready to move on."

Captain Jason Shields has been in the Army for ten years, half of that in Special Forces. He has a degree in international studies from the Virginia Military Institute. He was in 5th Group for four years and has made deployments to Kuwait and Uzbekistan. Shields was in Afghanistan with the first wave of Special Forces infiltrations following 9/11, and in Iraq before the 3rd Infantry Division and 1st Marine Expeditionary Force crossed the Kuwaiti border on their way to Baghdad. His father was a case officer at CIA, and he's lived all over the world. Captain Shields has a fair command of Arabic.

Shields punches through a list of administrative and housekeeping matters that include uniforms, ID cards, musters, personal appearance, personnel inspections, barracks cleanliness, barracks inspections, and standards of conduct.

"Regarding conduct. You may be a new Special Forces student, but you're still a soldier in the United States Army. It goes without saying, but I'll say it anyway. A soldier does not lie, cheat, or steal. Do that and you're history. It's not tolerated in the Army, and we certainly don't tolerate it here in Special Forces.

"During the first two weeks of this course you'll complete your in-processing for the Special Warfare Center and School, conduct daily physical training and testing, conduct road marches, attend classes that will prepare you for the selection process, and begin classes in basic and advanced land navigation. The second two weeks you'll continue with physical training and participate in the land-navigation practical exercises." While Shields speaks, the PowerPoint slides follow him through the presentation. He pauses a moment and slowly paces the front of the room. "Regarding land navigation. Seven of these eleven land-navigation exercises are graded. If you don't know how to navigate with a map and compass, you soon will, or you won't complete this course. Land navigation tells us a lot about a man's competence and his character. Pay attention in class and during the land-nav problems. If you don't master land navigation here, when you get to the harder land-nav problems during selection, you're going to be in serious trouble. Again, pay attention and do your best.

"All of you here today will leave this course in one of four ways. One way is to work hard and graduate. That's what you want; that's what we want. The second way is VW—voluntary withdrawal. You can do that at any time after morning formation this coming Monday. Some of you might be thinking about this already. It's your choice. The

82nd and 101st are looking for airborne-qualified infantrymen. But you all came here to be Special Forces soldiers. Think about that as well. The third way is IVW—involuntary withdrawal. IVW means we kick you out of here." Shields begins counting on his fingers. "You can get IVWed for safety violations, multiple spot reports—TAC write-ups for course violations—and, of course, integrity and conduct violations. You're also subject to the Uniform Code of Military Justice. Violation of the UCMJ will also get you removed from training and perhaps disciplinary action as well." His head snaps around and he steps close to the front row. "Excuse me, number 103, but am I boring you, or are you just too sleepy to keep your eyes open?"

The young soldier blanches, jumps to his feet, and heads for the back of the room. One of the TACs heads him off and quietly puts him in the leaning rest. Several more students slip from their seats and go to stand in the back.

"The fourth way is as a medical drop. If you get hurt and can't continue, you'll be recycled to the next class or sent to the regular Army for a tour of duty to heal up. We'll let you miss some training for a minor injury, but you have to complete the major portion of the class. We are not here to hurt you. If you have an injury, go to sick call, get some attention, and get back in training. But if you're going to be in Special Forces, in this training and in the groups, you're going to have to take care of yourself, and sometimes you're going to have drive on when you're hurting. That said, if you have an injury that seriously affects your performance, let's get it fixed."

Captain Shields pauses a moment to survey the class. "It boils down to this, gentlemen. Be at the right place, on time, in the right uniform, and have the right equipment. Stay focused and pay attention to detail. In this training, you have the weekends off; that won't always be the case later on. Use your weekend time to rest and take care of your equipment and uniforms. Do the right thing and do your best. That's all I have. First Sergeant?"

"FEET!"

There's a mild commotion as Class 8-04 scrambles to their feet. Carter makes his way to the back of the room, and one of the TACs takes his place at the podium. Several other TACs begin to hand out forms and the class begins to fill out the inevitable paperwork—personal history forms, medical questionnaires, course survey forms—and, as in every phase of Special Forces training, they will sign a statement saying they understand and will adhere to the honor system. Each phase of Special Forces emphasizes the honor system in a slightly different way, but it comes down to the same thing—a soldier cannot lie, cheat, or steal. This means a half-truth is a lie, and concealing the wrongdoing of another is also a violation of the honor system. The honor system demands that a soldier not only conform to a standard of honesty, but that he must be intolerant of other soldiers who are dishonest.

The next morning there is no class physical training or conditioning run. Instead, the class takes the Army Physical Fitness Test, or APFT. Students are graded in three areas: the number of push-ups they can do in two minutes, the number of sit-ups they can do in two minutes, and their time on a two-mile run. The Army APFT standards have a sliding scale for age, but everyone in Class 8-04 will be graded in the seventeen-to-twenty-one age group. Top score in the APFT is three hundred points. To achieve this, a man has to do at least seventy-one push-ups and at least seventy-eight sit-ups, and run two miles under thirteen minutes. Minimum scores in these three events are forty-two push-ups, fifty-three sit-ups, and just under sixteen minutes for the two miles. Six members of Class 8-04 score three hundred points, and ten of them fail to make a minimum score. Those who fail usually have foot problems or other medical issues. They'll have one more chance to make the minimum score.

After the push-ups and sit-ups, the class runs the two-mile course, which is two and a half times around Pike Field. The best two-mile time of the finishers is 11 minutes flat, which is back-to-back

5:30 miles. Standing at the finish line, I follow one of the better runners, noting that he had scored well in push-ups and sit-ups. He is one
of the six who max the APFT.

"Mind if I walk with you while you cool down?"

"Oh no, sir. Glad for the company." He doesn't seem too winded,
yet he had finished under twelve minutes. He is shorter than myself,
about five-seven, and wears the Army-issue field glasses, which are a
combination of glasses and goggles—a banded rubber frame that
holds the lenses straight across the bridge of the nose. "I'm David Altman," he says, holding out his hand. There is another group being
timed, so we have a moment to talk.

Specialist David Altman is a twenty-seven-year-old Korean-American
who grew up in Sweetwater, Tennessee. Before joining the Army, he
worked as a legislative assistant for a congressman in Washington. Altman has a quick, easy smile, yet I find him very serious about Special
Forces training.

"I know I won't quit," he tells me, "but I hope I can make it
through selection. I'm a little worried about the ruck marches." Then
he adds with a self-conscious shrug, "I'm not the biggest guy in the
world."

Altman has a degree in Bible studies and is a licensed, if not a prac-
ticing, minister. To my why-are-you-here question, he answers, "Like
most of the guys, 9/11 was a big factor in my decision. I read a great
deal about Special Forces and decided that if I could handle the physical part, it would be a good fit for me. I want to be with a military unit
that works closely with other government agencies and the CIA."

"Do you speak a foreign language?"

"I understand Korean, because of my mother, and I speak it a little.
It probably won't take much for me to get up to speed. But I think I'd
like to try for 7th Group and learn Spanish." I ask about his personal
goals as he begins his training. "My personal relationship with Jesus
Christ is very important. My goal is to do well here and become a
qualified Special Forces soldier. I was the honor graduate of my basic

training class at Fort Benning; I'm very proud of that. A lot of my friends thought I was crazy for joining the Army, and even crazier for choosing Special Forces, but I think I can make it."

For the balance of the first week and into the second, the Pre-SFAS course is a steady diet of physical training and classroom work for Class 8-04. Days formally begin at 0600 with a run or a rucksack march, but the students are up much earlier to prepare for the day's training. The runs are led by the TACs in platoon formation, and slow runners are segregated for additional work. The road marches are done with full pack and six quarts of water for a total load of close to sixty-five pounds. These marches range from four to six miles, and students are expected to keep a fifteen-minute-per-mile pace. The class breaks for lunch, usually field rations called meals ready-to-eat, or MREs, and ends their day with a physical training session before evening meal. The time between evening meal—the Pre-SFAS students have their own chow hall in the training area—and lights out at 2200, or 10:00 p.m., is for study and gear preparation.

There are classes—lots of classes. There are classes on Special Forces history, organization, and operations. There are classes on nutrition, which go deeply into hydration, diet, and the use—or, more correctly, nonuse—of illegal substances and stimulants. There are classes on first aid and environmental emergencies. Almost a full day is devoted to classes on foot care and the preparation and maintenance of footgear. Several hours in the barracks are given to the packing and carrying of equipment vests and rucksacks. The vest is a canvas or nylon mesh harness worn over a soldier's battle uniform. They're called load-bearing equipment vests; the soldiers simply call them LBEs. This vest carries have-to-have items like survival gear, a map, a compass, emergency rations, and ammunition. They learn what goes into their rucksacks and how to properly carry their rucks. The physical exercise, the classroom work, the field equipment, and the road marches are all in preparation for training in the key skill of the 18X Pre-SFAS course: land navigation.

"All right, I want your undivided attention for the next two hours, because what you learn here today and how you apply it will determine your success in this course and at selection. As a Special Forces soldier, you must be able to navigate with a map, compass, and protractor under any conditions. I'll say that again: A Special Forces soldier must be able to navigate with a map, compass, and protractor under any conditions. Now, you and I know we all go to war with GPSs and Blue Force Trackers and all kinds of neat technology, but you still have to read a map. When your high-speed Garman Etrek or your Magellan Navigator goes south on you, you'd better be able to use a map and compass. And some of the locals that you'll have to train to fight may not read or write, so you're going to have to teach them how to use a map and compass."

The instructor is Sergeant First Class Randy Loften. Loften is from Waycross, Georgia, and has been in the Army for seventeen years, in Special Forces for ten. All his SF time is with 3rd Group. He has two years of college behind him. He's a French speaker and has seen duty in the Ivory Coast, Guinea, Mali, and Kuwait, as well as two tours in Afghanistan. "I wanted to be a Green Beret ever since I was a little kid," he told me. "Why be average?" His fellow cadre instructors told me he is a solid Special Forces sergeant, but in at least one way he is far from average. Loften is a top-tier competitive shooter and competes in national-level combat- and precision-shooting events.

"I'm a competitive shooter," Captain Shields said, referring to Loften. "A lot of us are, but none of us are in his league. Sergeant Loften is one talented marksman."

Each platoon is crammed into a single floor in one of the old wooden buildings for nav classes. Several air conditioners are running wide open to keep the temperature reasonable, but the air is heavy with the smell of sweat and fatigue. The buildings are old and the post-and-beam construction says they were never intended for use as classrooms, even though they're now equipped for modern instruction. Behind Sergeant Loften is a large, flat-screen TV, and there are a number of monitors suspended from the ceiling, so none of the fifty-odd soldiers in the room is far from a monitor.

Sergeant Loften makes his way through the basics of land navigation—grid and magnetic north, the military grid reference system, variation, deviation, azimuths, back azimuths, and the mechanics of the Army lensatic compass. He talks about pace count and time-distance calculations. Area maps are passed out to each student, the same maps that they will be using in their fieldwork. They talk about map orientation and terrain features. All this is in preparation for the land navigation problems that are the heart of the preselection training.

"There's a lot of value," Loften explained to me, "and, to be honest, a lot of tradition that comes with land-navigation training. Some of these kids grew up hunting and fishing, and they have some knowledge of fieldcraft and reading terrain. Others have grown up in the city, and going into the bush was playing in the vacant lot next door or a family outing in a state park. In Special Forces, we usually work in teams and as a team. That said, a man still has to be able to be out there on his own and get the job done. This part of the training's very much the same as when I began my Special Forces training."

"It's more about what this training teaches a man about himself than a skill he'll take with him into the groups or into combat," Captain Shields added. "It's a confidence builder. If a kid from New York City or LA can take what we teach him and go out on a dark night in these swamps and woodlands and find four separate points on the map that're two to four miles apart, then that tells us something. It tells us that he's smart, that he can solve problems in a stressful and unfamiliar environment, and that he's self-reliant. It also tells us he can perform when he's tired, a little beat up, and he's not getting the sleep he's used to. It's a pretty good indication that he can learn the other skills he's going to need to become a Special Forces warrior."

The navigation classes move outside, where the TAC sergeants and navigation instructors work with the students. They walk with them over various types of terrain, point out the relationship between their two-dimensional contour maps and the actual terrain features. These outdoor classes in the Fort Bragg training areas also allow the students to calibrate their pace and to learn to take a bearing with their compasses. Now they're ready to be out on their own—almost. The first two nav problems are a day compass course followed by a night compass course, and these initial outings are done in buddy pairs. The following day, they're out on their own, first in the daytime, then at night. The waypoints on the course are white five-foot plastic posts sunk in the ground. At night they are lit with a chemical light stick, or Chemlite. When they find the point, the students clip their scorecard with the special hand punch tied to the post, take a new bearing, and set out for the next point. On these first iterations, there are a lot of lost soldiers out in the woods, trying to find their way. It takes practice. After two days in the field, walking in the woods with sixty-five pounds of equipment, some of them are getting it and others aren't. The class is brought back to the barracks area for additional classroom work and advanced navigation techniques. The nav instructors are now starting to focus their attention on those students having problems. Then it's back out to the field for more day and night compass courses.

There are seven graded land-navigation problems—three daytime courses and four nighttime courses. Each course has a starting point and four points that each student has to reach in a prescribed period of time. These points or destinations are given to the students in eight-digit military grid coordinates. Students are given their coordinates at the beginning of the course and allowed a few minutes to plot them on their maps. They take a compass bearing to their first coordinate and set off, noting the distance to their first destination and the pace count that will take them there. The courses range from six to ten miles as the crow flies, but that's seldom how the Pre-SFAS students walk the ground. More often than not, they'll walk 20 to 40 percent farther to navigate around obstacles—and even farther if they get lost. The allotted time on the courses ranges from four and a half hours on the earlier, shorter courses to nine hours on the final night problem. A student scores a point for each point he finds on the course—seven courses for a total of twenty-eight points, with consideration given to those who may struggle at first but do well later on.

"This was all new to me," Private First Class Roberto Pantella told me. "I grew up in Queens, and my rural outings were into the city to Central Park or out for a drive with my family on Long Island." PFC Pantella is a twenty-four-year-old Dominican-American. Prior to joining the Army, he was an aircraft maintenance technician working on 747s. He's five-eight with a stocky, solid build. "At first, I was doing very poorly. But then one of the nav instructors gave me some one-on-one help. They yell at us a lot, and that's their job, but when you need help, they're right there. You see, to do the nav courses, there are three things that'll get you from point A to point B. You can shoot a good azimuth—or series of azimuths, which you have to do at night—to get you to the point. Another thing that will get you to your point is you have to walk a good line. By that I mean you can't drift left or right of your azimuth or bearing, and you have to know your pace—dead on. When your pace count says you've covered a thousand meters, you'd better be at a thousand meters, give or take five or ten. It's not easy. And the third thing you can do is find the point by terrain association. That means as you shoot your azimuth and walk your line, you have to be aware of terrain features: low areas or draws, the crowns or hills, the steepness of the slopes, roads that cross the terrain—that kind of thing. I do them all, but for me the key is the pace count. I know almost exactly when I've covered a thousand meters. And I shoot a lot of back azimuths, checking the line of bearing I just walked. This helps me stay on course."

I asked Pantella why he joined the Army. "I always thought I might want to be a soldier, ever since I was a little kid. Then I got into baseball and I was a pretty good catcher. So I worked nights, and in the daytime I went to school and played baseball. I only got as far as double-A ball, but I had my dream. Finally, I got my associate's degree and was making pretty good money working on airplanes. I visited Ground Zero two days after 9/11, and it made an impression on me. Once I'd paid off my school loans, I quit my job with the airlines and here I am. My family thought I was crazy, and maybe I am. This might sound funny to a lot of guys, but the hardest thing for me is that I miss my family. I've never been away from them this long."

"And the land nav was not a problem for you?"

"After a rocky start, I got twenty-five points out of a total of twenty-eight," he said proudly. "That's better than most guys."

During the navigation exercises, I'm assigned to a student and follow him on his compass course. I have my compass, an old Silva Ranger that I had in the SEAL teams, and I soon learn that for me, 1,116 paces is a thousand meters. Yet my role on the nav course is to trail along a few meters to the rear. Wherever my student soldier goes, that's where I go. One night my student and I are terribly lost. That's when I learn about the draw monster. A draw is a low-lying drainage area or slow-moving stream that can be knee-deep mud, waist-deep water, and thick with undergrowth. They have to be crossed walking on a line of bearing, or "boxed." This is a technique whereby the student goes around the draw or marshy area, boxing it, so he comes out on the other side, on course and with some idea how far he's traveled. My soldier crosses these draws on a compass bearing. On one draw we are up to our waist in the swamp at night for forty-five minutes, fighting tangles, vines, mud, and bugs. Then we come out on the *same* side. "Sorry about that, sir, but I think I got it figured out now," he says, and back into the draw we go. It takes us three hours to get to the first point on the course. My soldier only gets two of his four points, but he never quits trying. We walk a long way that night.

Land navigation is a practiced skill, and the students have to learn by doing. I'm assigned different students to walk with, but after my long night in the draw, I ask if there were someone a bit more accomplished that I might follow. "Put Mister Couch with the Kiwi," Sergeant Loften says.

The next day I'm out with Private First Class David Rule. Each of the X-Rays is a story, and Rule is no exception. He grew up in Auckland, New Zealand, and left college there to come to America. He holds dual U.S.-New Zealand citizenship. Rule is twenty-five and was working as a waiter in Denver when he joined the Army.

"I've always been interested in the military," he tells me, "and I like to travel." His accent's very pronounced. "I'd thought about the New Zealand Special Air Service, but you have to have six years' time in service before you can try out for the SAS. That was a bit much for me, so I saw this as an opportunity to serve with a special force and do some traveling."

Rule is six foot and two hundred pounds. He has a soft appearance and a shy manner, and he gives the impression of not being particularly fit. But as I was soon to learn, he can ruck with the best of them. He swings on his pack, and we start out. I literally run to keep up with him. He has sixty-five pounds, while I carry only water, a camera, and a few PowerBars. PFC Rule marches straight to the first point and to the next three in rapid succession. In a little more than three hours of the five-hour allotted time, we are at the fourth and final point.

"I use my compass to give me a general heading—to get me pointed in the right direction," he says of his technique. "From there I follow the terrain features. I generally know where I am on the map, and I try to choose the best route if not the most direct route. I pick way points along the route that keep me off the roads and out of the draws. When I get close to where I need to be, I find a nearby terrain feature and shoot an azimuth to plot my position on the map so I know exactly where I am. Then I plot a course to the nav-course point and walk there on a line of bearing. It seems to work for me."

"What about at night?" I ask.

"Pretty much the same thing, except that I have to go a little slower."

When the Pre-SFAS students finish a compass course, they make their way to a base camp area, which is usually within a mile of their final point. They check in with the cadre, get their compass cards validated, and get their rucks weighed. The cadre sergeants inspect each

man to see if he has any injuries or foot problems. They also check
their water to ensure that their students are drinking enough. Then
they're given an MRE and sent to a holding area to await the completion of the exercise. There's only one other soldier there ahead of PFC
Rule when we get to the base camp. He's a former ranch hand who'd
grown up in Texas, but had worked all over the Southwest.

"I see we're not the first ones here," I say conversationally.

"So we're not," Rule replies. "Maybe next time."

I later learned that this was the first time that PFC Rule had not
been the first one to finish a nav problem. It must've been the distraction of having an overaged Navy SEAL tagging along that held him
back. Getting in early means some time to relax and have a leisurely
meal. The third man in is a soldier from Seattle. He's a University of
Washington graduate with a master's in education. The fourth's a high
school graduate from Minneapolis who'd been working as a carpenter
when he joined the Army. Of the forty-some men due into this base
camp, only twelve make their allotted four points in the time allowed.

For Class 8-04, a total nineteen points on the seven graded navigation courses were the minimum acceptable, and only about half the
class were able to make nineteen or better. Only four members of the
class went twenty-eight for twenty-eight. PFC David Rule was one of
them.

During these day/night compass courses, the three training platoons
of Class 8-04 live in the base camp areas. Their toiletries, change of
clothes, extra boots, socks, underwear, sleeping bag, rain poncho, and
rain shelter all go into or onto their rucksacks. They must carry their
rucks with them on the compass courses and live out of them in the
base camp areas. Living out of a ruck is a practiced art. There are
issues of comfort, because rest and sleep, brief as they may be, are
important in the performance of a soldier. Hygiene in the field is also
important. Oral hygiene, cleanliness, foot care, hydration, nutrition—
all of these require attention to keep a soldier safe and mission capable. In the base camp area, the students set up sentries and roving

patrols, just as they would in hostile territory. It's part of a soldier's life; you sleep while your buddies stand guard, and they sleep while you watch over them. Since the beginning of the second week of training, all Special Forces students carry weapons—sort of.

Weapons, the use of weapons, and weapons safety will follow these men through all phases of training and into their Special Forces groups. It's a way of life. With very few exceptions, a Special Forces soldier is never more than an arm's length from his rifle. This ongoing link between man and rifle is critical because Special Forces often work in highly exposed, remote areas where they have to provide for their own security. They may, literally, have to go for their guns on a moment's notice. For the X-Rays, it begins in the Pre-SFAS course. The guns are realistic-looking, hard-rubber versions of the M16 or M4 rifles—the standard combat rifles used by the U.S. military. These "rubber ducks" are treated as the real thing, which includes general safety, muzzle control, accountability, and proximity. A man goes to the latrine, he takes his rifle. He goes to the water point to refill his canteens, he takes his rifle. He also takes along a buddy. Throughout Special Forces training, students and candidates will always have their rifles with them, and they will never venture out from the barracks or base camp alone. It's much the same for the Special Forces detachments operating in Afghanistan and Iraq. The one exception is the chow hall. Two men will stand guard over the squad's weapons while the squad eats. Those two will be relieved by two of their squad mates so they can get to chow. In the base camps, the meals are MREs, and the students eat alongside their guns. When they sleep, their rifles are right beside them.

Off to one side of each compass-course base camp is an area bounded by colored surveyor's tape and away from the others. It's the VW area—voluntary-withdrawal area. As the nav courses get longer and the students get more weary, more than a few decide that this kind of life is not for them. They quit. It seemed as though there were always one or two men in the voluntary-withdrawal area at the end of every nav course—sometimes more. The cadre questions each of the VWs, as they are called, to make sure it's not a moment's lapse or a decision made without due consideration. Yet once a student says he's through, his decision is respected and the VW is treated with courtesy. He's also isolated from those who are still in training. The voluntary-withdrawal numbers in the nav-course base camps are higher after a night course than after a daytime course, and higher still when it rains. I've no data to prove this, but I sense that those students who spend the most time in the draws tend to leave Special Forces training at a higher rate. On a few of those nights in the draws, I questioned what I was doing there.

Regarding the voluntary-withdrawal issue, it goes on throughout Pre-SFAS Training, but since no one can VW the first week, there are a number of men who quit on the second Monday of training. I watch fourteen men from Class 8-04 step up to the platform and VW on the second Monday morning formation. In something of a ritual, one that reminded me of "the bell" in SEAL basic training, each man who wishes to withdraw has to ring a gong and announce to the formation why he wants to quit. There are a number of reasons, but most simply state, "It's not for me," or "It's not for me at this time." I suspect this public display of quitting, like ringing the bell in SEAL training, is done to make it difficult to quit. The Special Forces training cadre want these young men to stay with the program. Crossing the Rubicon of having to publicly announce your withdrawal in front of your classmates may keep a few men in training a while longer, and a few of those may just find it within themselves to go on and become Green Berets.

There are those who are asked to withdraw. These are the IVWs, or involuntary withdrawals. These are the men who've committed integrity or safety violations, or repeatedly failed to follow specific instructions. The most common of these that relate to the land-nav problems are students walking on the roads or found sleeping on the nav course. The first relates to cheating, and a second offense will lead to involuntary withdrawal. These are called, appropriately enough, roadkills. The second's a safety issue. A man found sleeping on the course or on the roads while waiting for pickup after expiration of the course time limit will be asked to leave. The sleeping issue may seem harsh, as these men are very tired. Sometimes, just to sit down is to doze off. But the 18X Pre-SFAS cadre take safety issues very seriously. Putting this many students out in the woods at night, in rough terrain by themselves, requires strict accountability. None of the cadre, especially Captain Shields and First Sergeant Carter, rest easy until all men are accounted for. If someone has fallen asleep out there and goes missing, training stops and an all-out effort is made to find and recover the missing student.

"One of the best students in my squad sat down on the road to await recovery and fell asleep," Sergeant Loften told me. "He was a super kid; his dad is a Green Beret. I went to the first sergeant and the captain to try to do something for him, but he's gone. He'll have to go to another Army unit for a while and try us again later. But rules are rules. The poor guy was in tears. Hell, I was almost in tears. We told him to do his time in the 82nd Airborne and come back. I hope he does. He's just the kind of kid we want in Special Forces."

While the business of land navigation continues, there are other evolutions and training taking place. If the students are not in the field on a nav problem, there are ruck marches under full pack, squad runs, and the obstacle course. All students are timed on a five-mile run for which the cutoff time is forty minutes. The fastest member of Class 8-04 came across the line right at thirty-two minutes. On the second to the last day, the class is again graded on the Army Physical Fitness Test. A few of the students are able to improve their scores, but not many. The three and a half weeks of training have worn them down, and most score lower than they did on the first test. With the final APFT, time is running out for Class 8-04. Collectively, there are two basic avenues open to the remaining class members—those who have not left training by the voluntary- or involuntary-withdrawal route. They can be sent forward to the Special Forces Assessment and Selection phase, or they can be recycled.

The burden of deciding who will and who will not be advanced to SFAS and Phase I of the Q-Course falls to Captain Shields and First Sergeant Carter, and to the recycle board. Before we talk about the function of the recycle board, there is another evaluation criterion that comes into play. It's called the peer review, or, simply, peers. Midway through the phase and during the last week, the students in each training squad evaluate and rank their peers. Each man rates the members of his squad from top to bottom—one through sixteen or eighteen or however many are in his squad. He puts in a chit on the top man, a blue half-sheet of paper, saying why he's number one or best suited for Special Forces. He also puts in one on the bottom man, and says why he feels this man is last or least suited. These are pink-colored slips. The peer ratings, by average rank and any first or last chits, become part of each man's package.

"Each class is a little different," First Sergeant Carter told me, "but after the last APFT, we complete each man's package and we take a look at them. We have no quotas or numbers, but we do have a clear definition of our role. In the Pre-SFAS course, we prepare; we do not select. If this class is like previous classes, of those still in training, about half of those who came to us four weeks ago will have earned their ticket to selection outright. Of those on their second time through the 18X Pre-SFAS course, about half of *them* will have met the standard, and while it took them two tries, they have made the grade and, in our opinion, have earned a shot at Special Forces selection. The other half of the recycled students who didn't quit, but still didn't make the grade, well, we send them forward anyway. We don't like to advertise the fact that a man goes to selection phase after two rounds of Pre-SFAS Training, even if he hasn't met the standard, but that's about the size of it. Again, our job is preparation, and our job ends when we've put a man through two rounds of this training. Anyway you slice it, the easy calls are the guys who perform to standard and the guys who quit or are dropped from the course."

I watch as Sergeant Jennings goes to each of the three training platoons and calls out the roster numbers of those successful students and quietly takes them aside. "OK, men, congratulations. You've worked hard, and you've met the standards of this course. Next Monday, you start selection." There's a collective cheer from the students. Jennings quiets them down and continues. "Now, you've got the next few days to enjoy your success, rest up, and get your gear ready for Phase I and Special Forces selection. Don't let up; maintain your focus. Remember what you've learned here. Selection is hard—a lot harder than this course. The ruck marches are longer, the nav courses are longer, there's less sleep, and there are team events that will test your stamina and your ability to work together. Above all, don't do something stupid this weekend like get in a fight or drink and drive. Be smart. Look after each other just like you did during this training. And while congratulations are in order, remember: You've just completed one small step on the road to the Green Beret. You're now ready to begin the Q-Course."

Jennings is equally as judicious when he musters those who had quit or were involuntarily withdrawn from training. They are housed in a separate barracks area nearby.

"Men, I want to thank you for being part of this course. This is not easy training and Special Forces is not for everybody. Some of you may, after a tour with the 101st or some other unit, come back to give Special Forces another try. For now, we hope that what you've learned here will make you a better soldier and serve you well in your next unit. Thanks again for your effort, and good luck to each of you."

Close to half of Class 8-04, or some seventy soldiers, will move on immediately to SFAS. Another forty, those who for the most part fall into the VW/IVW category, will soon have orders to somewhere else in the Army. That leaves close to forty men who have to come before the recycle board, where their fate will be determined and/or explained to

them. The board is chaired by Captain Shields, with First Sergeant
Carter sitting at his right elbow and Sergeant First Class Jennings close
by. During my sessions with the recycle board, another first sergeant
from one of the other phases is also present. Normally, the soldier's
TAC NCO briefs the board on the soldier who is about to appear before them. The TACs know the men best, and they're not reluctant to
give their opinion to the board.

"This is a really good kid. I know he tries hard. He's had a lot of
problems with land navigation, but as you can see, his scores continually improved. Both his APFT scores were just below the minimum,
but I watched him closely the second time, and I know he gave it his
best shot."

Another TAC, another student. "This guy is a total misfit. He falls out
of the runs and the ruck marches, and he could only manage twelve
points on nav courses—just one on the final problem. And look at his
peers. His squad thinks he's a shit bag, and most of them have rated him
dead last." The board hears the TAC out and then calls the soldier in.

"Private First Class Jones reporting to the board as ordered, sir."
He's in a clean uniform, and apprehension's written all over him.

Captain Shields, who is seated behind the table with the others,
returns his salute. "Stand at parade rest, Private. You're here before
the board because your performance has not met the course standards,
and it's the duty of this board to determine what will be the next step
for you. Before we do that, what do you have to say for yourself?"

The replies range from "No excuse, sir; I did my best" to a litany of
excuses and/or requests for another chance and promises to do better
next time. The work of the board is serious and emotionally charged.
The future and dreams of some fine young men are being determined.
Even at this first step on the long path to the Green Beret, the composition and quality of the Special Forces is being determined. I didn't
envy the responsibility of the board, and my heart went out to the men
standing before them. Tough business all around. The ones who were
just under the performance standard hear things like this:

"Soldier, you need to pay more attention to terrain association."

"Your physical-fitness test scores are low, and you're going to have to find a way to do better."

"You seem to have trouble meeting the times on the ruck marches. What're you going to do at selection when you have to keep pace on a much longer march?"

"You do OK on the navigation courses at night, but you're having trouble in the daytime. Why is that?"

"There are spot reports in your file that say you come to formations and evolutions unprepared or missing equipment. You want to tell us about that?"

Peer rankings are factored into the performance rankings. If a man has low performance and low peer rankings, then he's probably ill-suited for Special Forces. "The peers often tell us something that we miss," one of the TACs told me, "because we're cadre—we're not privy to everything that goes on in the barracks and the interpersonal relationships within the squad. Sometimes we find that a guy who is a marginal performer is selfless when it comes to helping his team-mates. That's important in Special Forces. Sometimes we learn something negative. A few classes back, there was a kid who was a superstar. He was good on the fitness test, the ruck marches, and only missed one nav point. But he cheated on the land-nav courses. He ran along the roads and bragged to his squad mates about cheating. We never caught him cheating, but his squad mates peered him dead last and said why. When we confronted him, he admitted to cheating. He was recycled, and we watched him closely. He did just fine; he never had to cheat in the first place. So we think the peers are very important." When a man with a stack of pink, low-peer chits came before the board, I hear:

"You seem to have a problem working with others. Your fellow soldiers don't seem to want to serve with you."

"Both the cadre and your peers say you need to watch your mouth. You want to tell us about that?"

"You seem to have a bad attitude about the Army and this training. Why is that?"

After questioning by the board, the soldier is asked to step outside while the board considers its decision. Sometimes it's a brief conference among the board members and the man's TAC sergeant, and sometimes they discuss the case at length. I've watched as they sent for another TAC for his opinion. On occasion, a student is recalled by the board for further questioning. If it's a man's first time through Pre-SFAS, the board usually recycles him.

"Private Jones," Captain Shields tells him, "it's the decision of the board that you are to be recycled to better prepare yourself for selection." This is usually followed, as appropriate, by a comment from First Sergeant Carter. "Son, you need more time here. We want you to succeed in Special Forces, so take this as an opportunity to get stronger and improve your performance. It'll give you a better shot at being selected."

If they send a marginal student on to SFAS, it goes like this:

"Private Jones, the board is considering sending you on to selection. If we do this, do you think you can step up your performance and be successful?"

"Yes, sir. I'll try my best, sir."

"Very well, but you do understand that there are no second chances during Phase I. If you don't cut it there, you'll quickly become an infantryman in a line Army division."

"Yes, sir, I understand. I think I can make it."

"So do we, soldier. Stay focused, work hard, and make us proud. You're dismissed, and good luck at selection."

The really hard ones for the board are the men who are coming before it after their second time through Pre-SFAS Training. Most of those who aren't cut out for Special Forces have quit or been involuntarily withdrawn, but not all. Some don't have the physical tools, others lack the awareness or focus to do land navigation, and some just can't find it within themselves to put forth the effort. But they didn't quit. These are the men who are now before the board, and these are the men who, with a very few exceptions, the board *has* to send to selection. So the purpose of the board is to do what they can to get these men ready for the tough sledding that awaits them at Camp Mackall during SFAS. This usually involves a good talking to by First Sergeant Will Carter.

"Soldier, your performance in this course has been totally unsatisfactory. You need a hell of a lot more preparation, but we just don't have the time for that, and there's no room for you in the next class. We've no choice but to send you to selection. I personally don't think you can do it. So why don't you go out to Camp Mackall and prove me wrong. I don't think you can cut it, but let's see if you can make a liar out of me."

With the findings and disposition of the recycle board, the 18X Pre-SFAS Training course for Class 8-04 is over. The recycle board sends half of the forty boarded men on to Phase I and designates the other twenty to be recycled in the next 18X Pre-SFAS class—Class 1-05. Those X-Rays headed for Phase I and SFAS will be joined in the selection phase by a dozen X-Rays held over from previous Pre-SFAS classes for medical or personal reasons. Next stop, Camp Mackall and Special Forces selection.

> *Author's Note:* Since I observed the training during 18X Pre-SFAS Class 8-04, there have been changes. Among them, the X-Ray soldiers who now arrive from Fort Benning are not hazed on arrival or at their initial formation. The shakedown I described in this chapter is no longer a part of this training. The current thinking is that these are mature, patriotic volunteers, and should be treated as such. Pre–Phase I/pre–Qualification Course training is now built around the goal of doing everything possible to help each soldier succeed at Special Forces selection. The physical, professional, and performance criteria of Pre-SFAS Training is no less strenuous, but the focus is now on giving these new soldiers the tools to succeed in Special Forces.

CHAPTER FOUR

THE SELECTION

Sergeant First Class Byron Hacker is the assigned Special Forces Assessment and Selection duty NCO, which means he'll be at Camp Mackall until he's relieved at 0800 the following morning—Wednesday morning. Most of the phase cadre have the day off. When there's a class in session, they work 24/7. When there's no class in session, the cadre are permitted time off. Sergeant Hacker sits by the door of the cadre hooch that opens out onto the crushed-rock assembly area and waits. It's almost 1600—four o'clock—and only about a third of the class has checked into Phase I and the Rowe Training Facility. It's September, and this is Class 8-04—the eighth and final Special Forces Assessment and Selection class this fiscal year. Sergeant Hacker's duty post and SFAS are at the Rowe Training Facility, a secure compound on Camp Mackall.

The Colonel James "Nick" Rowe Training Facility is named in honor of a legendary Green Beret. Nick Rowe was taken prisoner by the Vietcong and held for five years. The night before they were to

---

THE NASTY NICK.   Swing through the air, crawl through the mud. The obstacle course at Camp Mackall tests the candidates during SFAS and Phase I.

execute him, he made a daring escape and eluded his captors to eventually return to friendly forces. Following the Vietnam War, Rowe was released from the Army, but he returned to active service in 1980 to train a generation of Special Forces at the facility that now bears his name. In 1989, Maoist guerrillas managed what the Vietcong could not. They assassinated Nick Rowe while he was serving in the Philippines. Today, the Rowe Training Facility is a secure compound on Camp Mackall that is home to Special Forces Phase I, Phase II, Phase IV, and Special Forces SERE training. Within the compound there are barracks, classrooms, a chow hall, support facilities, and the headquarters of the 1st Battalion, 1st Special Warfare Training Group. First Battalion is responsible for all training at the Rowe Training Facility. The compound itself is a study in the old and new. Most of the buildings have numbers that begin with "T," which stands for temporary. They date back to World War II. Gradually, these are giving way to new construction, including a modern shower-and-head facility, and an extensive new do-it-yourself laundry. There will soon be a new chow hall. But the sleeping quarters are old and cramped. The soldiers who train there still live in the old-style barracks, very much the same as did the airborne troopers who lived and trained at Camp Mackall before they parachuted into France on D-day, sixty-plus years before.

The buses from Fort Bragg arrive in threes and fours and disgorge soldiers, each one with a duffel bag, a parachute or gear bag, and a rubber M4 rifle. As they do, Hacker goes out to meet them, checks their names from his list, and sends them to their assigned barracks. So far they've all been the regulars, soldiers from conventional units here to try out for Special Forces. They come from all over the nation—all over the world, actually. Many are from the airborne divisions, the 82nd at Fort Bragg and the 101st at Fort Campbell, but some are from units in Germany, Hawaii, Alaska, and remote bases around the globe. The rain has stopped for the moment, but a low overcast hangs over Camp Mackall with the likely prospect of more showers. The bus ride from Fort Bragg to Camp Mackall takes about forty-five minutes. At

1630, three buses arrive with the men from Pre-SFAS Class 8-04. Hacker doesn't have to ask if they're the X-Ray soldiers; he could tell by looking at them.

"Where's the class leader?"

"Right here, Sergeant."

"OK, get them in the five ranks with their gear and be quick about it."

"Yes, Sergeant."

Hacker watches with a quiet detachment as the soldiers form a human conveyor belt, passing their bags from the back of the bus up to the door. Byron Hacker grew up in New York and joined the Army right out of high school. After four years in the 82nd Airborne Division, he put in for Special Forces, and like the men arriving here today, came out to Camp Mackall for selection. That was twelve years ago. He spent all his time in the 3rd Special Forces Group and has made a half dozen deployments to Africa and one to Afghanistan. As soon as the new arrivals achieve some semblance of a formation, he walks over to the class leader.

"The detail is formed, Sergeant. One hundred and four men assigned, one hundred and four men present."

Hacker returns his salute. "OK, listen up, everyone. I'm going to call out your name, followed by your roster number and your barracks number. Sound off when you hear your name. Then take your gear to the barracks and find an empty bunk. Dump your gear on your bunk and fall in back out here in a separate formation. Everyone understand that?"

"YES, SERGEANT!"

"Class leader, when you've got everyone mustered back out here, I want you to go over to the phase headquarters building and get First Sergeant Sarno. He wants to have a word with you, clear?"

"Clear, Sergeant."

Hacker begins taking roll. He speaks loudly, but there's nothing particularly harsh in his tone. Soldiers answer up, then shoulder their gear and stagger off for their barracks. Soon they are forming back up, and the class leader is checking them off as they re-form. They now carry only their rifles—still the rubber rifles for SFAS. The class leader is a specialist who's been in the Army for three years. He was in the medical corps and was trained as a respirational therapist. Since he lacked current field experience, he asked to come to Special Forces through the X-Ray Program. Once he has a good muster, he jogs across the road to the headquarters building, which is a corrugated metal, half-round World War II Quonset hut. Painted on one end is a Special Forces logo and, in block lettering a motto: SFAS: WHERE THE BROTHERHOOD BEGINS. The class leader raps on the screen door and steps inside.

"What can I do for you, soldier?"

"Specialist McAlister, First Sergeant. I was told to report to you when the X-Ray candidates were formed up."

"Where're you from, McAlister?"

"Texas, First Sergeant."

The phase first sergeant, a master sergeant in grade, walks from behind the desk and holds out his hand. "I'm First Sergeant Billy Sarno, soldier. Welcome to Camp Mackall."

"Uh, thank you, First Sergeant. Glad to be here."

"You want to be a Green Beret, McAlister?"

"Yes, First Sergeant."

"Well, that's terrific, 'cause that's what I want, too. You go on back to your men and stand by. I'll be with you in a few minutes."

"Roger that, First Sergeant." Specialist McAlister leaves, more than a little puzzled about the smiling, affable SFAS first sergeant.

First Sergeant Billy Sarno joined the Army right after he graduated from John Marshall High School in Cleveland. That was in 1980. He became a Green Beret in 1987. Sarno is Italian by heritage, but since most of his time has been with the 7th Group, he speaks Spanish much better than he does Italian. Sarno has been to almost every country in Central and South America, and has seen action in Panama, Haiti, the First Gulf War, and Afghanistan. He's been the first sergeant at Bravo

Company, 1st Special Warfare Training Group, for two years, which means he has had a hand in the selection of most new Special Forces soldiers since 9/11. Yet he's still itching to get back to 7th Group—or any group, for that matter. Billy Sarno is a people person; he's not happy unless he's meeting, greeting, listening, or talking. I've watched him stop a car just to meet and talk to a total stranger.

When Sarno steps in front of the former Phase I students, he is the picture of a Special Forces soldier. He's a well-favored man, just under six feet with dark hair, good shoulders, and a confident manner. His dark eyes have a mischievous twinkle in them. There are master sergeant chevrons, ones that designate him as first sergeant, on his collar points, and his Green Beret is set at a rakish angle. His BDUs are freshly starched with sharp creases in the trousers. Specialist McAlister calls the formation to attention.

"Stand at ease men, and bring it around, in close. I want to talk to you guys for a minute." The formation breaks and bends in around the first sergeant. "Welcome to Camp Mackall and SFAS. This is where we select soldiers for Special Forces training. How many of you started basic training together at Fort Benning—two, three hundred? Well, that doesn't really matter now; you're here, and here we play for keeps. You have to make it in this phase or you'll be soldiering with another outfit. But hear me on this, we need you in Special Forces. We need all of you. Assessment for soldiers coming from the regular Army can run between 30 and 40 percent. Because you've just come from basic training, jump school, and Pre-SFAS, we expect better than that from you. But you still have to show us you belong here. You really have to want this and show us some heart. Doing your absolute best here at selection has to be on your front-sight post. This is a tough course. It'll hurt; it's supposed to hurt. Getting through this phase and moving on to Phase II should be your goal. How well you perform should be another goal. Remember, this is a small fraternity and reputation's everything. Your reputation starts right here, today. Are you going to be somebody who does just enough to get by or someone who goes all out? I've been at this a while, and I'll know if you're not doing your best.

"I want you to forget everything but this training. Don't worry about your family; we'll let you know if there's a problem at home. Special Forces is a brotherhood, but your family is everything; your family is forever. In Special Forces, we look after our brothers and their families. God forbid, but if there's a serious problem, we'll get you home to take care of business and get you back in a future class. Are we clear on that?"

"YES, FIRST SERGEANT."

"OK, so what're we looking for here? We're looking for people who are smart, who are physically tough, and who play well with others. And we'll watch how you get on with your buddies. If you can't get along with your fellow candidates, how're you going to get along with the locals in Colombia or Afghanistan? I'm here to evaluate you, and I'm here to help get you through this. But in the end, it's up to you; you have to meet the standard or you're done. You have to perform during ruck marches, the runs, on the land-nav exercises, and in the team events. If you don't understand something, ask questions. Pack your own weight—be a leader on your team. Don't lose your rifle or your equipment—give 110 percent all the time. We will watch your every move, as cadre, as evaluators, and as your future teammates. We'll be looking for a balance of the physical, the mental, and the emotional. We look for how you perform when you are out there at night on your own during the nav courses. We look for maturity. If and when you leave here as a selectee, it's just the beginning. So don't get ahead of yourself. Focus on this phase; take it a day at a time—an evolution at a time.

"A couple of things that I'll insist on while you're here. You will treat my cadre with respect. Disrespect my cadre, and you'll think you were hit by lightning." Sarno folds his arms and kicks at the gravel a moment. "One more thing. Should you decide this is not for you, come see me. You can quit or VW with honor and walk away, anytime, but

I'll want to know why. But don't try to make that call for your fellow candidates; every man has to decide for himself if he wants to be here—if this life's for him. I love you guys, and I want you all to make it through selection and come back out here for Phase II, but it's up to you to show us *you* want it and measure up to our standards. And remember the four Ls: Don't be late; don't be light; don't be lost; and don't be last. We're glad to have you here; make us proud of you. Good luck to each of you."

Phase I training begins in earnest on Wednesday morning, but that doesn't mean that the new Special Forces candidates had not put in two very long days at Fort Bragg. Prior to coming to Camp Mackall and the Rowe Training Facility, the class had completed two days of in-processing and testing at Fort Bragg. Each man had his medical record reviewed, and he had been weighed in and "taped" for an estimate of his body fat. There were briefings and paperwork associated with those regular soldiers coming to Fort Bragg on temporary-duty orders. And there were the tests—lots of tests. The Army and the Special Forces put a great deal of emphasis on psychological, aptitude, and suitability testing. Before the candidates leave Fort Bragg, they undergo seven hours of testing. While at Camp Mackall, they'll be counseled and evaluated on the results of those tests. There's also a basic swim test, which all are expected to pass. Later on, the Special Forces groups that are good in the water and have an aptitude can put in for scuba school and duty on a Special Forces scuba team.

Day one of formal training at Camp Mackall begins at 0400. After personal hygiene and barracks inspection, the entire class takes the Army Physical Fitness Test at 0500. Scores are noted, and any discrepancies are made a part of a candidate's training folder. After morning meal in the chow hall, the class assembles for command briefings next to the battalion headquarters, another World War II–era building. First on the schedule is the 1st Special Warfare Training Group commander, Colonel Manny Diemer. Diemer is a slightly built man with a quiet, measured intensity. He drove out from Fort Bragg to address the

Special Forces candidates. It's a small class as selection classes go, with just over 250 SF candidates. The class leader, inasmuch as there is a class leader in a selection class, is the senior enlisted man, a sergeant first class from the 82nd Airborne. He calls the class to attention on the colonel's arrival.

"Sir, SFAS Class 8-04 is formed."

"Very well, Sergeant," Diemer replies, returning his salute. "Fall in with your men." Diemer pauses to survey the class, then, in a clear, restrained voice that carries to the rear ranks, says, "Good morning, men."

"GOOD MORNING, SIR!"

"Stand easy, men. First of all, I want to thank each and every one of you for being here. The groups need Special Forces soldiers. The nation needs Special Forces soldiers. Each of you has the ability to make it through this selection process. It won't be easy, and we don't want it to be easy. But you can do it—all of you can do it. While we have a pressing need for people, I have no mandate to get a certain number of candidates through selection or any other phase of Special Forces training. There are no quotas. Meet the standard and you can be one of us. If you fail to meet the standard, you will make your next deployment with your current unit. If you young men in the X-Ray Program fail to perform, you're going to find yourself soldiering with an Army unit other than Special Forces. We may be at war, but we'll not lower our standards.

"You are here to be evaluated on your suitability for Special Forces. We cannot select you into Special Forces if you quit, so don't quit. No matter what happens, do your best. We want to assess you on your best effort. If you do poorly on an evolution, put it behind you and focus on the next evolution. All of us have strengths and weaknesses. That's why we assess men into Special Forces on the whole-man concept. We will identify your weaknesses and help you with them. But you'll have to work hard. For some of you, this will be the hardest thing you've done in your life. So hold nothing back. Show us intelligence and show us some heart. Your goal in coming here is to enter Special Forces training and serve in Special Forces. In the days and weeks ahead, when the going gets tough, don't lose sight of that goal. Good luck, men, and carry on."

As Colonel Diemer takes his leave, the class leader shouts from the rear rank, "Class, a-ten-HUT!" The class stands at attention while the colonel leaves the area. After he is gone, Lieutenant Colonel Jim Jackson makes his way from the rear to the front of the formation. Jackson is the commander of the 1st Battalion, 1st Special Warfare Training Group. In addition to the Special Forces phase and SERE training, he's responsible for the daily operation of the Rowe Training Facility. He has a few words for the class, but he is more direct than his superior, and there is an edge to his voice.

"Gentlemen, let me add my welcome to that of the group commander. Ahead of you are twenty-three days of selection—SFAS, or Phase I. During that time, you're going to have to show us you have what it takes to be a Special Forces soldier. This is a warrior's vocation. It's also a technical vocation. We use our training and our smarts to leverage our force in the field. So you have to be smart as well as tough. When the suck factor goes up, each of you'll have to decide if you want to be in this fight as a Special Forces soldier or if you'd rather be someplace else. Our job here is to assess you based on your performance and on your potential to perform in an unconventional environment. That's all I have, except to wish you good luck. Do you have anything, Command Sergeant Major?"

The battalion commander's right-hand man is his command sergeant major, his senior enlisted soldier. At the company level, it's usually the senior master sergeant in the role of first sergeant who holds sway, but at battalion, it's the senior sergeant major—the command sergeant major. At 1st Battalion, he's Command Sergeant Major Frank Zorn. He's standing at the side of the formation and speaks from there.

"Not really, sir. Other than to remind you men that here we play for keeps. You quit or break the rules or do something stupid, and you no longer have a chance to be in Special Forces. I'll give you one piece of advice, though. And that is, smile. This training is serious business, and it will demand your best effort to be successful, but every day, try to smile at least once. A little humor will help you to get through this, and it might even help some when it starts to hurt."

I wasn't surprised to see the group commander and the battalion commander take the time to address the men who are beginning Special Forces Assessment and Selection. All phases of Special Forces training are important, but SFAS is considered a key course on the road to the Green Beret. It's the admission slip to SF training. During my in-brief on my arrival at Fort Bragg, the commanding general of the JFK Special Warfare Center and School, Major General James W. Parker, put it this way.

"Dick, I want you to pay special attention to what goes on during SFAS. The other phases of training are demanding and technical, and we're always tweaking them to produce a more proficient soldier or a soldier that is better equipped to function in the current operational environment. But the selection phase is where we decide who will and who will not enter Special Forces training. This is very important. If we get the right men into the pipeline, then the force will thrive, but we must have the right men. In selection, we are looking for the men who are physically tough, but more importantly, men who have the intelligence, character, and interpersonal skills to be impact players on a Special Forces detachment. Special Forces is one of the only military training programs that seeks out men who can get along with others— who can function in a cross-cultural environment. And it all begins at selection."

I promised General Parker that I'd do my best. And during my time with this SFAS class, I saw the general on several occasions, observing training to one side and speaking quietly with First Sergeant Billy Sarno.

After the battalion commander and his command sergeant major take their leave from Class 8-04, Sergeant Hacker puts the formation at ease and gives them their Camp Mackall orientation briefing: no cell phones, no phone calls out, no post exchange (the compound has a small one-room PX), no Coke or vending machines. He covers uniforms, formation times, gear lists, chow hall protocol, bulletin board notices, barracks security, and a host of other issues that govern the lives of Phase I candidates. Everyone has white adhesive tape on their uniform blouses and trousers with black Magic Marker numbers, but in SFAS they wear the blouse tape strip over their nametags and they wear no rank insignia. For now, the selection candidates are pure numbers. When Hacker gets to the medical issues, he slows.

"If you're hurting, drive on. If you have a medical problem or are injured, get to morning sick call and get it fixed. If you get poison ivy or poison oak, let us know, and we'll get some ointment for you. It's starting to cool off, but the heat's still our number one problem. Hydrate, and hydrate often. You will be issued hydration salts; take them every day. Next to the heat, it's the feet. Take care of your feet. Treat hot spots and blisters early. Moleskin, new skin, second skin, and bacitracin ointment are all helpful. By now you should all know what does and doesn't work for you. Deal with it. Prescription meds are the only meds allowed, so if you're on a prescription, we need to know about it. Out here, Motrin is to be used only as prescribed by the medics." He pauses to consult his notes. "Hygiene. Hygiene is very important. Take care of yourself; shower when you can, and take a whore bath when you can't. Check each other for ticks; we have a lot of ticks. Also be on the lookout for black widows and brown recluse spiders—we've got them, too. There's a lot of snakes out here, so let us know if one bites you. Usually, it will be a copperhead, and most of their bites are defensive and venomless, but we treat them all for real. Cottonmouths are different. They're rare on Camp Mackall, but we see them from time to time. If you get a cottonmouth bite, let us know in a hurry." He again checks his notes. "I guess that's it. Class leader, take charge. I believe the next evolution is equipment issue and gear shakedown. Let's get to it, men."

The following day, the candidates are up at 0500 and out for a four-mile run at 0600. This is a conditioning run, but the pace is brisk. The SFAS cadre run along with the class, cutting them into groups of thirty to forty. There's no shouting or harassment, but the cadre note if any in the class are having problems running. The run also serves in the continuing acclimation to Camp Mackall. The X-Ray candidates have no problems, having trained in North Carolina and Georgia during July and August. Some of the other soldiers have come from colder, more arid conditions. If one of the candidates lags behind, a cadre sergeant will drop back to check on him and offer encouragement. I asked Specialist David Altman about the attitude of the selection cadre compared to his prior training.

"This is something new for us. We've just been through boot camp, jump school, and Pre-SFAS. It seems like for the last six months someone has been yelling at us or ordering us about or dressing us down. It's different here. There are expectations, but the assessment cadre never seem to raise their voices. When something needs to be done, they ask us to do it. And we do it. This is serious business; it's all on us now."

The balance of the day is taken up with a crash course in land navigation. Many of the soldiers coming in from other units have not used a map and compass for a while. Many are competent in using a handheld GPS, but they need to brush up on shooting azimuths and establishing their pace count. This is almost second nature for the infantrymen, but some of the soldiers are coming from maintenance units or technical specialties in which they have had limited time in the field. The information's not new to the regular soldiers, but few have had the recent training of the X-Ray soldiers. That evening, they're back in the classroom. They're given an hour and a half to write out their personal history. This personal history becomes part of their training folder and a component of their psychological assessment.

"We keep these training folders in our file room," First Sergeant Sarno tells me. "They're available for official use or review as needed. The training folders also contain their scores on the physical evolutions, the psychological testing, and their peer reviews. On occasion, when one of my cadre sergeants starts grousing about the deficiencies of these new men, I pull his SFAS training folder." He gives a gentle chuckle. "It seems some of my cadre weren't among the leading performers of their selection class. And to be honest about it, I was no big-time stud when I came through here as a young sergeant. It took everything I had and then some to make it through selection. And that's what it will take for these young soldiers here today. Y'know, sir, what goes around, comes around, even in our little world here at Camp Mackall."

A part of this selection process is that soldiers not only have to perform to standard, but they have to perform to standard when they've been on the go and haven't had all that much sleep. They're kept on the move all of their waking hours with the exception of time in the classroom. During the first week of training, days begin at 0400 or 0500. The days are full, and every evening is scheduled for a classroom evolution that will engage the selection candidates until 2030 or 2100—8:30 or 9:00 p.m. They are often up much later than that, preparing their gear and uniforms for the next day's training. These sixteen-plus-hour days are designed to teach and to tire. In addition to navigation classes and navigation practical work around Camp Mackall, there are physical evolutions. Each morning there is a run or a rucksack march. By the end of the week, the candidates are on the stopwatch. They are timed on four- and six-mile runs and four- and six-mile rucksack marches, the latter under sixty-five pounds of gear. There are teamwork drills with logs—telephone poles, actually—and calisthenic drills with rifles. And there's Nasty Nick. Nasty Nick, named in honor of Colonel Rowe, is the obstacle course at Camp Mackall, and I can honestly say I've never seen a more robust and challenging course. The candidates crawl through water, under barbed wire, walk on elevated logs, climb ropes, hand swing from horizontal ladders, and negotiate cargo nets. Much of the course is high enough above ground that a fall would likely cause injury. At each obstacle, there's a cadre sergeant noting the roster number of those students who fail to properly handle an obstacle. "You failed to properly negotiate that obstacle, soldier," I heard many times. "You can try it again, or you can move on to the next obstacle." Sometimes a candidate would trot back for another try; other times, he would simply move on to the next obstacle. Only those with superior athletic skills or previous climbing experience were able to successfully manage all the obstacles.

At Camp Mackall and Phase I SFAS, there's the ongoing question of standards—what is and what is not *the* standard. From my observation of other SOF training, standards are usually in the form of run times, obstacle course times, swim times, marksmanship, and scores on written tests. Standards also take the form of an acceptable level of performance in leadership roles during field training exercises. Sometimes a standard is subjective and at the discretion of the grading cadre. In most cases, these standards are, in one form or another, sacrosanct; you either meet the standard or you are gone. In Special Forces training, there are minimum standards, but as I was to learn in the weeks and months ahead, exceptions could be and were made to these standards. And these exceptions were not a lowering of the bar. This "moving standard," for want of a better term, has to do with evaluating the whole man. The criteria has to do with what each individual brings to the table in contributing to the Special Forces mission. Some standards, such as those that relate to character and weapons safety, are very sharply drawn. Others, not so. If a candidate's run or ruck march times are not quite up to the minimums but his leadership and language abilities are exceptional, these are taken into consideration. His attitude and adaptability are also considered. And above all, there is the question of whether he gets on well with others—is he a people person? The question of standards is always a difficult one, both in the evaluation and the application. What if a young soldier has great potential, but lacks maturity? What if a promising candidate works diligently on a single weakness, shows dramatic improvement, but still doesn't meet the minimum posted standard. The phase cadres wrestle with these questions throughout the Q-Course. None deal with the issue of standards more openly and contentiously than the SFAS cadre. They are evaluators, but they are also the gatekeepers.

On the Friday of their first week, the candidates are out on short land-navigation exercises around Camp Mackall. They take their classroom work out into the field and conduct day and night compass courses in mild terrain. After these three-hour day and night navigation exercises, they're back in the classrooms to talk about land-navigation technique—reading elevation and relief on their contour maps, compass intersections and resections, and route planning. The methodology is that after some instruction, they're put in the field for short periods to test their skills. Then they come back in the classroom to talk about what worked and what didn't. By and large, the X-Ray candidates are proficient at the basics of land navigation. The veteran soldiers struggle to some degree, depending on their experience and aptitude.

One of the training aids right next to the Rowe Training Facility is the mini stakes compass course. It is a four-point course, with each leg of the course only about 200 to 250 meters. The terrain is relatively flat with sparse vegetation. This evolution is under the supervision of Sergeant First Class Reynard Cara. Cara is from Garland, Texas, and is fluent in Spanish. He has been in the Army for nineteen years—sixteen in Special Forces and two with the 75th Ranger Regiment. While a Spanish speaker, most of his time has been with the 1st Special Forces Group. Cara is competitive in civilian orienteering competitions. He assigns one of the candidates to explain the mini stakes course and walk me through it.

"It works like this," Specialist Tom Kendall says. "We shoot an azimuth and walk a line of bearing, keeping an eye on our compass and noting our pace count. When we get to where the point should be, we stop and see how far off we are."

Kendall shoulders his pack and slings his weapon. He takes a bearing, so do I, and off we go. Both of us pace the first point a little short, but his line of bearing is better than mine. We both take a new bearing and set off for the second point, trying to walk a better line, given the error on the first point. At the end of four points, Specialist Kendall takes his pace and azimuth errors to Sergeant Cara. He has a conversion chart that takes Kendall's errors and tells him how far off he would be on a thousand-meter distance.

"Your pace is pretty good, soldier," Sergeant Cara tells him, "but you seem to drift left when you walk. You're going to have to be mindful of that on the longer course legs." This is not a graded evolution, and sections of the class rotate through the course to sharpen their land-nav skills and to try to eliminate their errors. "If you're having trouble," Cara tells the candidates, "see me and we'll give you another set of points. This is for your benefit. Myself and the other cadre sergeants will be out here as long as you need us; we're here for you." To me he says, "This is an important skill, one that they will use as well as teach. On deployment, they'll have a GPS to get around with, but if you're walking, you still have to plan for how much ground you can cover over various types of terrain and how much ground you can cover under various weight conditions—how much gear they have on. If it's a quick tactical mission with bullets and radios, that's one thing. But you have to know what you can do with one hundred and ten pounds of gear strapped on your back. A line of bearing is important, but pace count is everything."

"Think you have this down?" I ask Specialist Kendall.

"I think so. All of us X-Rays got a lot of this in Pre-SFAS, but it's good to go over it again. We all know it'll be more difficult here than back at Fort Bragg, and a lot more important."

"What were you doing before you joined the Army?"

Tom Kendall is a measured, solid-looking twenty-four-year-old with a serious, direct manner. "I was going to college—graduate school, actually—and working as a firefighter and emergency medical technician. I'm also a professional martial artist."

"A what?"

"I get that a lot from people," he says quietly. "I taught kickboxing and jujitsu, and I competed professionally in martial-arts competitions and ultimate-fighting events."

"Then the physical side of this training must be a breeze for you, right?"

"Yes and no. Even for a kickboxer, this training's very hard on your feet, and I'm not the best distance runner. It's a different type of physical conditioning. Still, I'm either at or very close to three hundred on the Army fitness test. But in general, this training has been impressive, and far more comprehensive and professional than I ever imagined. I'm learning a lot."

"You have more choices in life than most," I venture, "so why are you here?"

He shakes his head with a smile. "I've asked myself that on a few of the night compass courses back at Fort Bragg. This may sound corny, but it has to do with issues of genocide and injustice. Given the suffering in the world, I feel I have to do something. It was Special Forces or the Peace Corps. With my background and what I have to offer, this seemed to be the best way to make a contribution."

"So what does your family think about your decision?" I ask.

"My family?" He pauses a moment before continuing. "Well, without my family, I couldn't be here. I'm from California and my parents are liberal—very liberal. We talked at length about what I wanted to do and what I was getting into. They have some serious issues with the current administration and our nation's foreign policy. But they've been there for me. You see, I'm a single parent with a two-year-old daughter. She's with them while I complete this training. I can do this because my daughter has a structured and stable home life. I miss her terribly. Right now, I'm living for the times I can get back and see her. When I think about it, I'm forced to admit that any sacrifice on my part is small compared to that of my parents. I'm blessed with wonderful parents, and my daughter's blessed to have such loving grandparents."

The attrition of SFAS Phase I Class 8-04 has already begun. A few of the candidates, mostly soldiers coming to Camp Mackall from other Army units, have voluntarily withdrawn. Their reasons for choosing to leave range from the medical to the physical. Some men have foot problems and the pace of training simply does not allow them time to heal. Men take to pain differently. Some candidates can soldier through it and others can't, or won't. Some of them understand that they are unready for this kind of extended physical ordeal, and plan to return when they're better prepared. Each day, a few more leave their barracks and take up residence in the voluntary-withdrawal quarters, where they will await the paperwork that will return them to their units. That may take a week or more. While they wait, they'll become a part of a labor pool for the upkeep of the Rowe Training Facility. While their former classmates continue with SF selection, these men will cut grass, repair obstacles on Nasty Nick, and work on maintaining the dated facilities in the compound. There are only a few men in the barracks now, but there's room for a great many more. I spoke with several of these men who decided early on to leave selection. Most said they'd be back for another try.

"I didn't understand how physical it would be. I'll be better prepared next time."

"My feet are shot," another told me. "I need to heal up and get my feet toughened up before I come back."

And a few expressed regret. "I quit on the six-mile ruck march. I shouldn't have, but I did. It was a spur-of-the-moment thing, but I'll have to live with it. The straps were cutting into my shoulders and I got to feeling queasy. I knew I wouldn't make the time. Still, I shouldn't have quit. I'm going to give up cigarettes, get healthy, and come back for another try."

Beginning on day nine, after a before-dawn rucksack march, the class begins the first of their land-navigation practical exercises. These are very much in scope and duration of the initial practical exercises the X-Ray soldiers negotiated during Pre-SFAS at Fort Bragg. Each one has four points, with each leg of the course between two and four miles. Each student has a different lane, meaning that his four points and his route to them are unique. The navigation courses are laid out on Camp Mackall and stretch into the state game lands that border the camp. The terrain is similar to that at Fort Bragg, but here there are more streams to ford and more marshlands to deal with. "There's some bogs out there that will swallow you up," First Sergeant Sarno told me. "The meat missiles, the guys who walk a straight line of bearing no matter what, are going to have some long and frustrating hours out there."

For the X-Rays, the most striking change on these nav exercises are the point sitters. During their nav problems at Fort Bragg, they were given four sets of eight-digit coordinates. They plotted their four points—one, two, three, four—and set out to find them. At each nav-course point, there was a punch tool to document that they successfully reached the point. In SFAS, the points are real people. The SFAS candidates are taken to a starting point and given a single set of coordinates. At the start time, they set off to find their first point. When they reach it, they find a man sitting there, often by a fire with a tent or a makeshift shelter. These point sitters are usually retired Green Berets who live in the area and come out to help with training evolutions like the navigation practical exercises. When a candidate reports in to a point sitter, he hands him his score sheet. The point sitter checks to ensure that the candidate should be there and that he's reached the point in proper sequence. He then gives the candidate a set of coordinates for the next point.

For Class 8-04, there are four land-navigation practical exercises on Camp Mackall—two in the daytime and two at night. The time limit of these exercises is five hours, and they range in total distance between ten and twelve miles. Each candidate, with his load-bearing equipment, ruck, and six quarts of water, carries between sixty-five and seventy pounds. In order to get all four points in the allotted time, a candidate has to walk fast and find the point fairly quickly. I walk one day and one night with assigned students—both 18 X-Rays. For the other two exercises, I sit with a point sitter and watch the students as they passed through.

During my daytime trek, I follow a young soldier from Hacketts-town, New Jersey. He'd been accepted into the X-Ray program right out of high school. While he could have gone to college on a soccer scholarship, he elected to join the Army because of 9/11. His father is an FBI agent and encouraged him to join the Army when he decided not to go to college. We do well on the first two points, but the third one proves elusive. Just before the allotted time, he finds the third one to go three-for-four on the nav exercise. The following evening, I go out with another X-Ray for a night course.

"What's your technique?" I ask my candidate as he plots his first course.

"I use mostly terrain association, sir, and I think we got lucky. In the barracks, we talk about these nav problems, and they usually have a long leg, two medium legs, and a short one. Our first leg is just over four miles, so we got the long one first. That's a break. If we hustle, we can get most of it done while it's still light."

The night courses begin at 2030, or 8:30 p.m., so the candidates have close to an hour of daylight and dusk on the course. My candidate that evening is a nineteen-year-old PFC from Texas. He is a year out of high school and managed a Dairy Queen before he decided to join the Army. He didn't know what he wanted to do after high school, and college didn't seem to be for him. His father served a tour in the Army and his brother was in ROTC in college; both encouraged him to take a hard look at the X-Ray Program. He is a small man, slender and just under five-nine. The hardest thing for him, he tells me, were the ruck runs.

"You mean the ruck marches?"

"No, sir. For me, they're ruck runs. I have to run to keep up with the bigger guys, but I can do it. I usually finish in the middle of the pack, maybe a little better than the middle." I'd been out with the class on most of the ruck marches. In order to make the cutoff time, the candidates have to run at least part of the way. The technique favored by most is to walk up the hills and run down them. The faster candidates on the ruck marches run the flats as well.

My candidate and I set off on the night nav exercise, and I have to struggle to keep up. I didn't know a guy that small could move through the woods that fast carrying almost half his body weight. I have only a Camelback canteen, a few PowerBars, and a notebook—about ten pounds. We make our first point just after dark, and he moves well on to the others. I appreciate that he keeps me out of the swamp, and we only get wet fording streams. What amazes me most is his eyesight. When he stops to orient and consult his map, he can read terrain features and contour lines that for me, even with my reading glasses, are a blur. Walking, he sees the ground well. I find every snag, hole, and stump.

"I tested out close to 20/10, and I see well at night. I didn't do all that well in land nav during Pre-SFAS, but it all seems to be coming together for me now. I think I can make it through this course." He had me at the last point in just under four hours—four-for-four.

My point-sitting time is equally rewarding, if less taxing. And it is educational. When you sit out in the woods for five or six hours with a retired Special Forces sergeant, you hear some pretty good stories. One of my point sitters was a Son Tay raider—one of the eighty-some Green Berets who crashed into the POW camp in North Vietnam in 1970, only to find that the Americans held there had just been moved. One of my friends in Idaho was the senior POW at Son Tay and missed freedom by only a few days. The Americans held by the North Vietnamese soon learned about the attempted rescue, and it did wonders for their morale. It told them that their nation had not forgotten them. When a candidate comes into our point, he makes his way over to a point sitter and drops to one knee. Usually, he is soaked from sweat and wading the streams and draws.

"Number 141 reporting in, sir." SFAS candidates treat these retired Green Berets with near reverence.

"What point do you think you're at, son?"

"Point number three, sir."

"I agree; good job. Do you have all your gear?"

The candidate checks himself quickly. "Yes, sir."

"OK, while I get you logged in on my sheet, go over there, dump your gear, and take a break. There's a jerry can with water if you need to top off your canteens."

"Roger that, sir. Thank you, sir."

After a few moments, he calls the candidate back over. "Here are your new coordinates." He reads them aloud and the candidate reads them back to him. "That's a good copy. Take whatever time you need to plot your point and plan your route. When you're ready, saddle up and drive on. What time do you have?"

"Twenty-three forty, sir."

"Close enough. That gives you a little more than an hour to make your last point. Good luck."

"Understood. Thank you, sir."

A great deal of what goes on during Phase I to date is to prepare the class for the Star. The Star is a navigation course that serves as a final exam for the land-nav requirement for Special Forces selection. The Star is nothing that the candidates haven't seen or trained for. This nav course is simply longer and more difficult. This evolution is conducted at the Hoffman training area, a state game lands tract about fifteen miles from Camp Mackall. It is a large wooded area that the candidates have not seen before, and the ground is a little higher. There are streams and draws, but the terrain is less marshy than Camp Mackall. The entire class moves from Camp Mackall to a base camp at Hoffman and prepares for the Star course. Base camp is perhaps a poor term for the bivouac area. It consists of a large, six-by-six cadre truck that serves as a mobile command center. The truck is served by a generator and a portable, telescoping antenna. This command center keeps track of the students on large status boards and is in radio contact with the point sitters and the cadre who roam the Hoffman area in pickup trucks. For the roving cadre, it's an issue of compliance and safety. Candidates caught on the roads become roadkill, and are taken off the course and removed from training. If a candidate gets into trouble or is injured, he can come out to a road and await help.

At Hoffman, the candidates live out of their rucks for five days and five nights. The only concession for their comfort is a line of Porta-Pottis and a water buffalo to refill their canteens. They live in designated patches of woods and assemble near the command truck for orientations and briefings. Meals are MREs. On the first afternoon at Hoffman, the candidates are briefed on the area—what areas are inbounds and what areas are out of bounds. The inbounds area consists of several thousands acres that the students will crisscross in search of their navigation points. Often their route will angle back and across the area in a star pattern, which gives the final nav problem its name.

Following their initial briefing, the candidates are given an area familiarization to acquaint them with the terrain they will have to negotiate on the Star. This orientation is the Hoffman stakes course, a four-point land-nav course with points just one to two thousand meters apart. It allows the candidates to once again calibrate their compass bearings and pace count. This is an ungraded evolution—simply a practice exercise for the benefit of the candidates. They walk the stakes course in the daylight and once again at night. It's a good final validation of their navigation skills, and, for many of the candidates, a confidence builder—a last opportunity to refine their navigation technique. But it's also time on their feet. These men are getting tired and worn down, and this fatigue is a cumulative condition. This is by design. The Hoffman stakes course will walk them, with their rifle and seventy pounds of gear, for another four to six miles, also by design.

"How're you holding up?" I ask my candidate on the stakes course.

"Pretty well, sir. I've got some blisters I'm concerned about, but otherwise I'm good to go."

It's raining lightly, so we both get soaked as I follow him around the course. My candidate this time is the senior soldier that came to selection with this group of X-Rays. He's a staff sergeant and a former Ranger. He served a tour in the Army and left to join his family's retail business. After three years out of uniform, he's back. He chose the X-Ray program as a way back into the Army and into Special Forces.

"Two things brought me back. The first was 9/11. The second was my life on the outside. I'm just not cut out to be a nine-to-fiver. My family couldn't have been better about it, and my brothers are doing a great job at home helping mom and dad with the business. My family doesn't need me, but my country does."

We arrive back at the base camp area soaking wet. I go to the fire to dry out and get warm. It's a mild afternoon, but I'm teeth-chattering wet. My candidate strings up a poncho, Ranger style, to get himself and his gear out of the rain. He changes into a dry uniform and then sets about retaping his feet. A few hours later, we're back out on the stakes course—same course, still raining, only it's dark. We finish the course just before midnight. The next day, the candidates are allowed to sleep in. Reveille is a leisurely 0700, breakfast is MREs. The morning and early afternoon are given to gear preparation, drying out, a land-nav review, and Star briefings. Each candidate is given two MREs, and at 1430 that afternoon, they board trucks that take them to their Star starting points. At the starting points, they're on their own time to sleep and ready themselves for the Star. At 0130, the candidates are given their first set of coordinates. At my initial Star point, I watch as they plot their first point on their terrain maps and, one by one, disappear into the woods. I do not walk the Star. This is a final exam, and no candidate needs the distraction of a writer/straphanger on this important evolution.

The Star navigation course is run three times on three consecutive days. Each time window is the same—they begin at 0130, and end at 1200, or noon. Given the number of points, there are endless variations on how a candidate might be asked to get through his four points. The individual courses or lanes are computer generated, and each lane is between ten and eleven miles. The good land navigators will walk perhaps 15 percent more than that to find their points, most will add 25 percent to the straight-line total, and those having trouble can walk as much as 40 percent farther. A Star course will take a candidate and his seventy-odd pounds of gear over some thirteen to sixteen miles of terrain. If he's moving through the course well, most of it will be at night.

It's a long night for the cadre as well. They rove the area in pickup trucks as safety observers and to ensure the candidates remain off the roads. On the first Star, I ride with one of the cadre. It is a long night as we bore holes in the woodlands of North Carolina over dirt roads. Sometimes the cadre sergeant coasts slowly using only his parking lights, thus preserving his night vision; other times, he parks on a shallow rise affording a vantage to see the road. Candidates are allowed to cross the roads, but they must move quickly from one side to the other, and at no time can they walk along the road. That's cheating and an honor violation. Men caught moving on the roads or going out of bounds on the Star course become involuntary withdrawals. We see several candidates crossing properly, but none who are walking on the roads. Other cadre do. Five candidates are taken off the course for walking along the roads or being out of bounds. My cadre sergeant does, however, give two candidates a ride back. Just after sunup, we come upon two of them sitting by the side of the road.

"What's the problem, guys?"

"We've had enough, Sergeant. We want to VW."

"OK, fellows, put your gear in the back and climb aboard."

"Roger that, Sergeant."

We take them back to the base camp area and continue our patrol in the daylight.

The first iteration of the Star course begins a curious division within Class 8-04. About 80 percent of those who entered the phase two weeks ago are still in training and began the first Star navigation problem. It takes until midafternoon to get all the candidates off the course, accounted for, and back into the base camp area. Of these candidates, 40 percent go four-for-four while some 50 percent, roughly half, reach three or less. About 10 percent decide they've had enough and VW. The remaining candidates are cut into two groups—winners and losers. The larger group of unsuccessful candidates bivouacs in an area near the command center truck, draws more MREs, and begins to rest and prepare for the next Star evolution. Sergeant Cara and some of the other cadre navigation instructors roam among these candidates.

"If you didn't get your four points, let us know why. If there is a problem, let's try to get it fixed before you go back out there tomorrow morning. What can we do to help?" Several candidates seek out these cadre sergeants to go over their routes to review their mistakes.

I find my X-Ray Ranger candidate in this group, and am surprised to see him there. "I screwed up," he quickly admits. "I plotted my second set of coordinates wrong, and by the time I figured it out, it was daylight. I ran the rest of the course, but got to the last point five minutes late. Jeez, was I pissed. I'll get 'em all next time—guaranteed."

"How are your feet?" I ask.

"Not good, but I'll still be back out there tonight."

There's a second, much smaller grouping of the unsuccessful Star candidates off to one side in an area marked by pink surveyor's tape. This was the VW/IVW holding area, much like the one I had seen on the nav courses at Fort Bragg during the 18X Pre-SFAS Course. This is a sad lot of soldiers, and I hesitate to intrude. I catch the eye of one of the X-Ray candidates I'd spoken with at Fort Bragg, so I approach him.

"I'm sorry to see you here," I venture.

"It's OK, sir. I've done my best, but this is just not working out for me. I hurt all over and my feet are killing me. I don't know if I'll come back, but if I do, I'll know what to expect and be prepared for it. Right now, I don't belong here. It's time for me to go."

I wish him well and make my way across an open meadow to a separate, wooded bivouac area, well away from the base camp. It's a wonderful place called Andersonville.

Andersonville was a prison in Georgia where Northern POWs were interned during the Civil War. It was a dreadful place, rife with disease and dying soldiers, and, at the time, one of the largest cities in the Confederacy. Old tintypes of Andersonville show it as a shantytown with bearded soldiers idling under canvas tarps. The Andersonville at the Hoffman training area near Camp Mackall resembles its namesake only in the scattering of poncho shelters strung up in the wooded bivouac area. This is the winner's circle where the candidates who went four-for-four on the initial Star course are bivouacked. These soldiers will not have to go back out; they've passed the navigation portion of SFAS. It's a very happy place. The eighty-some successful candidates sleep, lounge, sit by a fire, or simply bask in the warm glow of accomplishment.

It's hard to put into words, but I know this feeling from my SEAL training, way back when. It's an emotion, or sense of being, that is given to few in the military and, from my experience, far fewer in civilian life. It's a feeling one gets after a hard-won rite of passage. In the case of the Star, it's an evolution that demands a certain amount of intellectual skill and a maximum physical effort. It's a personal victory over what you previously thought of as your own limitations. It's also a powerful engine for future growth. Those who train to become SEALs, Rangers, Air Force Special Tactics Team members, and Special Forces all know this feeling. It's a delicious sense of fulfillment and accomplishment. It's also fleeting. For that's the nature of all special operations training—attaining one difficult, seemingly impossible goal and moving on to the next. This aura of accomplishment in Andersonville was so thick you almost had to swim through it.

The second night I journey around to visit with a few of the point sitters and to watch candidates pass through, get their point recorded, and plot their next set of coordinates. Midmorning, I stay with a point sitter to watch the final hours of the second Star. Twelve candidates are slated to be at that location as their fourth and final point. Four make it in time to go four-for-four, while one other comes through to make his third point with a good chance to get to his fourth. Two others come for only their second point; one has time for a chance at his third. The first man to arrive at my location to get his fourth point has over three hours to spare. He carries his load easily, tired but not as exhausted as I'd seen other candidates on the course.

"Congratulations," I say, offering him my hand. "Good job, and you had a good time."

"Thank you, sir," he replies as he shucks his pack and takes out a canteen. "I'm very glad to have this behind me."

"You seem pretty fresh," I tell him. "What happened to you on the first Star?"

"Well, that's a little embarrassing." He smiles and shakes his head. "Took a wrong bearing and missed my second point—walked way past it. By the time I got sorted out and found the point, it was too late. Never missed a single point on the land-nav practicals at Camp Mackall, and then I get lost on the first Star. Go figure."

"Where are you coming from?" I ask.

"I was just detached from the 101st Airborne."

"Why Special Forces?"

"It's something I've wanted to do ever since I was a plebe at West Point."

There is no way to tell he is an officer; he wears no rank and has only a number over his nametag. He is First Lieutenant Matt Betters. Betters had grown up in Annapolis, Maryland. He turned down an appointment to the Naval Academy because he didn't want to go to college in the same town in which he was raised. He is Ranger qualified and has seen action in Afghanistan and Iraq.

"So what's next?"

"Next month I report to Fort Benning. There's a six-month course there for new Army captains. Then, after Benning, assuming I'm selected, I'll be back here to continue with Phase II sometime in the spring or summer."

"Are you in for a career?"

"Yes, sir. Hopefully a career in Special Forces."

Later that day, another increment of men, including First Lieutenant Betters and my Ranger X-Ray candidate, achieve the magic four-for-four and made their way into Andersonville.

There are two ways to pass the Star course and the land-navigation requirement at Special Forces selection. A candidate can pass any one of the three Star evolutions by making all four points in the allotted time. Or he can make it to at least eight of the points during all three Stars, thus going eight-for-twelve (or better). Some of the grittiest men I observed during Phase I were those tired souls who shouldered their rucks and set off for their third Star evolution.

While the men in Andersonville don't have the heavy burden of the men still on the Star course, they are not given a day off. "We take the winners out for an eight- to ten-mile ruck march in the afternoon," one of the cadre sergeants told me. "They've passed the navigation portion of this phase, but they still have the team events. We want them all tired and a little foot-weary going into the team events."

Yet as I walk around the cluttered, poncho-strung ghetto, I meet nothing but smiles. Each man is told to bring one book with him to Phase I and keep it with him in his ruck. When they aren't sleeping, eating, talking, or tending their blistered feet, I find many of the Andersonville residents reading. The most popular book is the Bible, followed by books written by Tom Clancy. I note more than one copy of *Shadow Warriors* and *The Teeth of the Tiger.* I also see *To Kill a Mockingbird, Red Badge of Courage, Gates of Fire,* and *Black Hawk Down.* I even find a candidate with a novel by Dick Couch. There is one candidate sitting by the fire, reading a book with Cyrillic writing on the spine. He'd gone four-for-four on the first Star. When I approach, he scrambles to his feet.

"Good afternoon, sir. You must be the writer."

"I am. Glad to be here?"

"Yes, sir. A little bit of time to heal up and get ready for the team events." He holds out his hand. "I'm Alex Lawson, by the way."

He has a firm grip, and I don't recognize him as one of the X-Rays. "What were you doing before you came to selection?"

"Well"—he grins self-consciously—"that's a bit of a story."

"Hey, that's what I do. Have a seat." We both sit by the fire. It is now late September and damp, and most of the poncho groupings have at least one fire.

Alex Lawson is a slender, dark-haired soldier with a shy but confident manner. I learn he was a National Guard officer assigned to the 20th Group with a National Guard unit out of Charleston. Within months of his high school graduation, he had married and joined the Marine Corps. Four years later, he was single and an ex-Marine infantryman. Armed with his GI benefits, he plunged into college. He worked part-time and joined the Army National Guard for the extra money. In another four years, he had a degree in Russian studies from George Washington University and gained admission to Georgetown University's law school. Along the way, he completed Officer Candidate School. With his law degree, he became a full-time staffer on the Senate Foreign Relations Committee and remained a part-time soldier. He had recently moved to Charleston and established a practice that represented contract security firms. He was only recently promoted to captain.

"I guess you know you're not going to have all that much time to practice law."

"That's true," Lawson replies. "My unit is scheduled for deployment early in 2006. If everything goes as planned, I'll be able to get back here to complete the Q-Course in time for that deployment."

I make a quick mental calculation. "So that means you can validate your language requirement?"

"That's my plan. I'd like to do it in Russian, but my Russian is only fair." He taps the book. "I read it a lot better than I speak it, but I'm fluent in French."

"Obviously, you have options, in or out of uniform. Why Special Forces?"

He tilts his head and is silent for a moment, as if he is reviewing a well-worn line of thinking. "I think on balance, it's the challenge. Special Forces offers the chance to lead men in a very difficult and challenging environment, and to operate independently without the close supervision of the regular Army chain of command. The senior SF sergeants in my National Guard unit are sharp guys, very intelligent and very experienced. I admire them. My goal is to deploy as a detachment leader with these men. It's a leadership challenge and a cultural challenge. I guess that's why I'm here."

"Career soldier or a career lawyer?" I ask.

"We'll see," Captain Lawson replies. "Perhaps neither. My real passion is Russian literature. It could be that I'll want to get an advanced degree in that area and teach. Right now I have to focus on getting through selection, then get back here to finish the Q-Course."

On the afternoon of the third Star, another increment of successful land-nav candidates joins their classmates at Andersonville. Though they will only be there a short while, they're overjoyed. At a holding area near the command truck, there's a group of close to thirty candidates. Those soldiers who have quit or been involuntarily withdrawn from selection have all been taken back to Camp Mackall. These remaining candidates are the men who, for one reason or another, didn't find four points on any of the three Stars and found less than eight points on all three evolutions. They are quietly attending to their gear or sitting dejectedly on their rucks. A few have taken a seat without taking off their rucks. They're levered back on their packs, passed out from sheer exhaustion. Some are talking quietly among themselves, but most are silent. In the background is the drone of the generator that serves the command-center truck. A lone figure makes his way over to the unsuccessful candidates.

"OK, guys, bring it over here and bring it in close. Yeah, wake that guy up and get him over here." First Sergeant Billy Sarno ducks under the pink marking tape so he can be with them in the penalty area. A candidate nearby is struggling to rise and Sarno offers him a hand, pulling him to his feet. He is in a fresh set of utilities, and the bill of his starched fatigue cap rides characteristically low, close to his nose. Sarno surveys the sad group a long moment with his arms folded across his chest. Then he removes his cap. "Men, I gotta take my hat off to you. None of you quit; you gave it your best shot. You didn't make it through the Star, and that means your training here is over. Right now, it's just not for you, but I want you to know that I'm proud of you, and I want to thank you for trying. If it works out, come back next year or after your next deployment and try again. Very few people in this man's Army can do what you've just done. As you go back to your units or to a new assignment, you can walk with your head up. You're not quitters, and I'd be proud to soldier with you anytime, anywhere. I love you guys. Thanks for being here." Sarno replaces his cover, comes to attention, and salutes them. One or two manage to return his salute. "Good luck to each of you. The trucks'll be here in a few minutes to take you back to Camp Mackall."

The successful candidates break down Andersonville and clean up the area. When they leave, it's like they hadn't been there. Then they help police the base-camp area, and they, too, board the trucks for Camp Mackall. That evening they have their first hot meal and shower in five days.

Two-thirds of the assessment and selection phase of Special Forces training is over. The physical grind, the timed runs and ruck marches, and the long navigation courses have cut Class 8-04 in half. While the candidates overhaul their gear, the cadre sergeants begin to organize the survivors into twelve- to fourteen-man teams. Over in the headquarters hut, the senior members of the Phase I cadre work out the final details of the remaining training. Ahead are the Long Range Team Movements, or team events, and the SAREs—Situational Awareness Reaction Exercises. The SARE has since been renamed the Human Terrain

Adaptability Exercise, but for this work I'll stick with the term "SARE." Also still ahead are the psych evaluations and, for some, the commander's review board. The senior cadre work late into the night, and the last two to leave are First Sergeant Billy Sarno and Captain Walt Carson. Billy Sarno provides the energy and combustion to the selection phase; Walt Carson provides the passion and intensity.

Walt Carson grew up in Charleston, South Carolina, and had wanted to be a Green Beret ever since he was a little boy. He attended the nearby Citadel, where he earned a bachelor of arts in history. Captain Carson has been in the army for ten years and a Green Beret for six. On his desk in the phase headquarters building is a .44 revolver carried by a Confederate ancestor in the Civil War. Like his first sergeant, he's from 7th Group and a Spanish speaker. He has deployed to Haiti, Costa Rica, and Afghanistan. For the last two years, he has command Bravo Company, 1st Battalion, 1st Special Warfare Training Group. He and Billy Sarno, more than any other two individuals during that period, have been responsible for the evaluation and selection of new men for Special Forces and Special Forces Training.

"We have a difficult and important job here," he told me one evening, after the rest of the cadre had left. "We have to assess and select men who have the traits and characteristics that have proven successful in the force. This is a great responsibility. Special Forces is an officer-led, enlisted-run organization. Some officers find it difficult to lead in this kind of environment, and I was one of them. I tended to be a micromanager as a Special Forces detachment leader. You can't do that when you lead smart, professional, type A SF soldiers. That's something I've had to work on. Fortunately, the battalion commander who hired me into this job recognized this and teamed me with Billy Sarno. I spin around and want to fix everything myself. Billy doesn't let that happen. He and the other senior cadre force me to forget about the details, which they take care of, and focus on the big picture. It's made me be a better officer and a better leader. I have another issue; I'm a very devout Christian. I feel I have a duty to preach the word of

Christ and to share his teachings with others. One of my former company commander finally took me aside and asked if I wanted to be a chaplain or a Special Forces officer. I still have a duty to the Lord, but I'm a Special Forces officer. It's the path I've chosen, and I will give it my full attention and best effort."

This gregarious, sometimes ribald first sergeant and his thoughtful and devout captain make an odd but effective pair of leaders. They differ in temperament and personality, but I watched both work long days in harness together to select the right men for Special Forces. On more than one occasion, when I was with alone with one of them, he would take a moment to tell me how much he admired and respected the other. The first sergeant and cadre sergeants ran the training for the most part, and I saw very little of Captain Carson as I observed the first two weeks of training. That was to change, especially during the SAREs and during the commander's review board.

Along with the physical and professional assessment evolutions, there's the mental and psychological screening. The approach of Special Forces in their efforts to get a read on a candidate is like nothing I have ever seen. As I was to learn, a man could be a physical stud and professionally competent, but still be unsuitable for Special Forces. All candidates for Special Forces training undergo a battery of psychological and aptitude testing. There are three basic instruments that are used in the selection process. One of these is the Wonderlic Personnel Test, a short exam used to predict an individual's ability to learn, adapt, solve problems, and understand instructions. Another is the TABE—the Test for Adult Basic Education. The TABE assesses reading and basic math ability and a candidate's aptitude for language. The scores from the TABE reflect reading and math ability in grade levels. It may suggest that a candidate reads at the tenth-grade level and has twelfth-grade math skills. The third test is a version of the Minnesota Multiphasic Personality Inventory, or MMPI. The MMPI is one of oldest psychological assessment tests, and can be used to evaluate thoughts, emotions, attitudes, and behavioral traits that relate to an individual's personality. It can also be used to diagnose mental disorders. These tests are administered and evaluated by an experienced team of trained psychologists and psychiatrists. Results are held in confidence, and their combined results are made available to the senior training cadres for candidate-evaluation purposes and at the commander's review board.

"We get a lot of men through here, and we look at the psychological health of all of them," Lieutenant Colonel Scott Middleton told me. Middleton is the senior psychologist who oversees the testing and the team of psychologists who work with the Special Forces candidates. "Most are well-adjusted soldiers. A few may have problems that would not be an issue in a conventional military organization, but considering the stress and the nature of the Special Forces mission, we may want to take a closer look at these soldiers.

"Initially, we look for flags that may suggest possible pathologies. So yes, we're looking for potential problems and for those who may be unsuitable—guys with serious problems. Occasionally, we find a man who is very smart, but lacks ethical balance. Too much intellect without a firm moral grounding is like a big engine without a transmission. But we have to be careful in the application of our testing and evaluation. The men who come here and go on to be successful special operators are a breed apart. They are not 'normal' compared to a group of civilian men their age or even a group of regular soldiers. They're aggressive, adventurous, extroverted, intelligent, type A individuals. Many of them are thrill seekers. That's OK, but these traits have to be balanced with maturity and framed with a sense of responsibility."

During the selection process, about 15 percent of the enlisted candidates are brought in for psychological counseling. Army psychologists meet one-on-one with these candidates to further explore issues raised in their testing—issues that need clarification or explanation. All officers meet with a psychologist for a session to review their test results.

"Initially, we're looking for the problem soldiers—pure suitability issues. Past that, these tests and our work with the candidates become positive. Where are they weak and what do they need to work on? What are their strong points and how can they use their strengths to offset their weaknesses? Of course, some of the candidates see us simply as shrinks—that these exams and evaluations are mumbo jumbo that might adversely affect their chance at selection. But you'd be surprised how many agree with our assessments and use the information we give them in a constructive way. The bottom line is that these men will often have to be on their own doing a difficult and dangerous job, well away from traditional military structure. They have to be professionally, ethically, and morally self-sufficient.

"Our input to the training cadre comes in three general areas," Lieutenant Colonel Middleton said. "The first is the intellect of the candidate. Is this soldier smart enough to handle the technical part of Special Forces training? In many cases, it identifies men who need more education in a specific area to perform in an SF role. For our work here, we try to measure intellectual capacity, academic training, and potential creativity as they relate to the Special Forces mission. The second is vocational. Which Special Forces military occupational specialty may be appropriate for the man, and what might be his limitations if he is assigned to one MOS or another. We've an immense body of evidence that supports our input to the process. For example, we can predict that a man with a given set of scores will have 40 or 70 or 95 percent chance of completing the academic portion of Special Forces training for, say, an 18 Echo—a communications sergeant. And, finally, there's the psychological assessment. These are the social and adaptability indicators—the people skills—which are so important in Special Forces."

"The psych evaluations and psych input to the process are very helpful," Captain Walt Carson told me. "Sometimes it confirms what the cadre sees in a man, and occasionally they raise an issue which we knew nothing about. In some ways, it's like the peer review; it's another perspective. While it is valuable, it's still just an input to the process. The final assessment of a man's fitness and suitability for

Special Forces rest with the cadre sergeants' evaluations and the commander's review board. But we take seriously what the psychs have to say. As an extreme example, you know that Timothy McVeigh came through here?"

"I'd heard that," I replied.

"It was well before my time, but he was here. He was a poor candidate and quit before he even got to the Star course, but he surfaced bigtime on the psych profiles as a highly unsuitable candidate. Special Forces soldiers often have a great deal of responsibility on deployment. We have to make sure they have the mental and moral equipment as well as physical and professional tools to do this job."

For the next two days, the candidates will be fully immersed in the team events. The previous two weeks have reduced Phase I Class 8-04 to a group of individual candidates who've physically endured the phase up to this point and who've shown themselves smart enough to negotiate the land-navigation courses. Now these exhausted men will be evaluated in a team environment. They are segregated into teams, and each team is assigned a phase cadre sergeant. The cadre sergeant gives them a general set of instructions regarding the task before them, and monitors the team as they execute the task. These tasks come in the form of physically challenging, team-centric movements that put a premium on leadership, organization, and teamwork.

My team is given the initial task of moving an old jeep trailer, with only one wheel, from the starting point at the Rowe Training Facility to a distant location on Camp Mackall. To assist them, the teams are given lashing materials, twelve-foot metal pipe sections, and a hundred-foot length of rope. At the start time, the team sets about rigging the crippled trailer using the pipes to set up a counterbalance for the one-wheeled vehicle and crosspieces for pushing bars. They use the rope to fashion a makeshift harness for members of the team. When rigged and balanced on the single wheel, the team begins to move this part wheelbarrow, part unicycle toward a set of coordinates across

Camp Mackall. The cadre sergeant designates one of the enlisted men as the team leader. Throughout this and subsequent evolutions, the team leader is always an enlisted soldier, and each enlisted soldier takes his turn as team leader. The trailer is rigged and moved under the direction of the assigned team leader.

My team leaves the training facility about 0800 and begins to make its way along the sandy roads that border the Camp Mackall Army Airfield. The team I'm following includes a big candidate who played football at Iowa, a former professional snowboarder, a tall redhead whose father is a career navy man, a Pennsylvanian who worked in the family farm implement business, and a Coloradan in his early thirties who owned a shop that sold mountain-climbing equipment.

Nursing this unwieldy vehicle through the soft sandy roads takes teamwork—some men pull, some push, some lift, and some work to balance the trailer. Most of the jobs are very taxing; the others, not so much. It's the job of the team leader to assign and rotate his men, give orders, and make adjustments, always seeking to get the trailer to its destination within the proscribed time. He must use his men carefully—men who are very tired and who'll be on their feet for this and other team events for the next two days. For these enlisted team leaders, it may be the first time they've had to weigh the welfare of their men against the needs of the mission. If they become Green Berets, they'll do this routinely and in harm's way. Halfway to the first destination, the cadre sergeant chooses a new team leader, makes a few suggestions about the movement of the trailer, and off we go. The new team leader assigns duties to his men and shouts encouragement as they bend to the task. The trailer waddles down the road while the cadre sergeant and I follow along behind. While the team pushes and pulls the trailer over sand and gravel roads, there's ample opportunity for cooperation, bitching, team spirit, and leadership. The cadre sergeant watches how each man leads—men who aren't necessarily the team leader—and how they follow. It's leadership and followership.

We reach our destination about 1400 that afternoon. There the team leader checks in with a "Pinelander," while the rest of the team fans out in a security perimeter. Pinelanders are citizens of the mythical nation of Pineland, one of the nations in the unconventional scenario that is to be played out in some detail during Phase IV. Here the Pinelander is a civilian role player who, like the point sitters on the navigation courses, gives them a new set of coordinates. He also takes possession of their one-wheeled jeep trailer and gives them the parameters of their next evolution, the movement of the deadman. The deadman is a five-hundred-pound duffel bag filled with sand. Our cadre sergeant appoints a new team leader and takes the old one aside.

"You made it here within the time limit, but that was only due to the sweat and determination of your men. They busted their butts for you. But if you'd rigged the trailer better and rotated your men on a more consistent basis, you could've made better time and not worked them as hard. You have to get the job done, but you also have to take care of your men, understand what I'm saying?"

"Roger that, Sergeant."

"Fair enough. Get back with your team and let's drive on."

While the cadre sergeant speaks with the outgoing team leader, the new team leader is directing the lashing of the poles to carry the deadman at a shoulder carry. They use one of their soft litters to hold the weighted duffel and lash their four poles in a tic-tac-toe or pound-sign configuration to support the litter. The team leader briefs the Pinelander and the cadre sergeant on his route and rotation schedule. Then the team members ruck up, shoulder their load, and set off. They are able to get eight men under the load at one time. Counting the weight of their rucks, each man has to bear up under a little over 125 pounds when he's under the litter. The initial movement is along an uneven road through a wooded area. They move for four hours, pausing only for water breaks and to rotate fresh men under the load. All the while, the cadre sergeant notes who shoulders their weight and who does not. When the team takes a break and the team leader calls them back to continue their journey, he observes who is first up and who helps his buddy up—who complains and who contributes. When they're all tired and beat, who still manages to be a team player and who does not. Our cadre sergeant is also keeping a close eye on his candidates for injuries. At this stage of selection, they all hurt, but the cadre sergeant doesn't want to lose a man who is performing well to a minor, nagging injury or have a man sustain a permanent injury.

The team events continue for fifty hours. One event has them moving metal cans of sand, each weighing upwards of 120 pounds. In another, they must move a forty-foot telephone pole. Still another has them pushing an old derelict jeep. There are short periods where they can catch an hour of sleep here or a half hour there, but they're on the move most of their waking hours. Meals are MRE rations by the side of the road. As they move from event to event and team leader to team leader, the dynamics of the team unfold. Some men who I watched struggle on the ruck marches and on the Star emerge as quiet, determined team players. Others evolve as peacemakers, taking charge of teammates who start to grumble and quieting them down. A few, while doing their best, are starting to break down physically. On my team, one of the men was limping noticeably under the load.

"Here, I got it," one of his teammates says as he steps beside him and takes the weight of the bar from his shoulders.

"Hey, it's not your turn yet," the limping man replies.

"It's OK. I'm feeling strong. You take a break and jump back in on the next rotation."

We drop back a little, and the cadre sergeant says to me, "These are great kids for the most part. With a few exceptions, I'd have any one of them on my team." His comment rather surprises me, as he shows none of this to the candidates.

At one of the Pinelander's posts, Captain Carson and First Sergeant Sarno are there to observe the changeover. "Now is the time when the good leaders and good followers emerge—leaders who lead by example and followers who quietly lead from the rear," Sarno explains. "It gives the cadre a chance to see if they can play well with others when they're really dragging butt. Sometimes my cadre sergeants get a little caustic about the new men we're training. So every once in a while, we go out and do a Star or we do these team events as a cadre team. It refocuses them on just how hard and taxing this can be. These guys haven't had a real night's sleep in close to three weeks."

"Periodically, we do a team event with the higher-ups," Walt Carson tells me. "Soon after I took over the company, we had a headquarters element from the 1st Special Warfare Training Group come out here for team events. I had a bunch of lieutenant colonels and majors on my team. As the junior man, I was the team leader. You couldn't believe the bitching and the power struggles at first. Finally, I had to almost shout, 'Gentlemen, can we just please soldier on and get through this.' They all laughed, sucked it up, and we made it happen. It's good for us to get regrounded on what we ask the new men to do."

The final team event has them back at the Rowe Training Facility late morning on the third day, exhausted beyond measure. It's the last physical evolution of Phase I—almost. After securing the materials from their last team event, each team is sent to the classroom, where they conduct a peer review of their team. With the peers' input, each man will have in his training record an evaluation of how the cadre rated his performance in the team events and how his teammates rated him in the team events. There's also a cadre debriefing. A cadre sergeant sits for ten or fifteen minutes with each man, one-on-one, and talks about his performance. He tells the candidate where he did well, where in the cadre sergeant's estimation he came up short, and what he might do to improve. And finally, after a hot meal and a hot shower, they're allowed some rest. Those who performed well will eventually be selected for continuation in Special Forces training. Those who did not perform or test well will have their training record examined by the commander's review board.

Early the next morning, they are up at 0300 for their last physical evolution—a twenty-mile ruck march. There is no time limit, but they're expected to complete the march in twelve hours. All but two finish, but many in SFAS Class 8-04 are nearly sleepwalking by the time they return to their barracks at the Rowe Training Facility.

The officers in Class 8-04 are asked only to follow during the team events, though they're ranked along with their teammates in the peer review. The cadre sergeants know who the officers are and watch carefully to see how they follow and support the assigned team leaders from the ranks. This input is noted in each officer's training folder. One of the more important inputs for the officer candidates is their performance in the SAREs. All of these Green Beret hopefuls are looked at carefully, but none more so than the officer candidates. In fact, few men in or out of uniform are as closely scrutinized as these prospective Special Forces detachment leaders. Here in Phase I and in subsequent phases, their physical, mental, moral, and decision-making abilities will be continually challenged and evaluated. Their screening is on the order of a full-on, in-depth psychological examination and a Senate confirmation hearing—combined. The first of these challenges is the SAREs.

Following their completion of the Stars and continuing through the team events, each officer is called away and sent on a series of two to three orchestrated situations that will challenge and evaluate his judgment, his decision making, and his interpersonal skills. These role-playing situations with professional role players following a loosely choreographed script. Often, there are hard left and right boundaries— what is clearly right and wrong or what is acceptable and what is unacceptable—but there's also ambiguity. The officer candidates have been leaders in the Army long enough to know the black and white of most issues. Now they will have to use their experience and interpersonal skills to negotiate the gray areas—the difficult moral terrain often found in the conduct of Special Forces operations. Most of the scenarios in the SAREs come from actual events that have confronted deployed detachment leaders. These real-time dilemmas range from how to stop a war crime when you have little power or influence to how to deal with a village elder who has honored you with the gift of his ten-year-old daughter. Few captains in line infantry units deal with these problems. Those that do usually have the luxury of a senior officer nearby for consultation. The substance and particulars of these SAREs are closely held, if not confidential. I'll describe one of the SAREs that I observed and am permitted to describe.

A captain candidate is summoned from Andersonville. Under his rucksack, with his weapon at port arms, he jogs down a dirt road to where Captain Walt Carson waits for him, just outside the base camp at the Hoffman training area. It's almost dark, and Carson holds a small flashlight to see his briefing sheet.

"All right, Captain Smith, this is how it works. I'm going to brief you on a scenario that'll move you into your first SARE. Here's the situation."

The dilemma that Captain Smith must resolve is one that actually happened. Smith, as a Special Forces detachment leader, is to meet with an Afghan subtribal leader. Notionally, his team sergeant is nearby, but he's alone for this meeting and well away from any other American assistance—he's on his own. His mission is to find out how many Afghan fighters are in this tribe or clan, and how well they're armed. Smith's battalion commander is considering moving an operational detachment into the area, and he needs this information. The battalion commander also wants Smith's impression of this subtribal leader. Is he easy to work with? Will he be amenable to taking direction and assistance from an SF detachment? What's his attitude toward having Americans in his area? With the situation and requirements in mind, Captain Smith continues down the road toward his first SARE. A quarter of a mile on the road, he comes to a small camp—a tent and a campfire. A man in a shabby coat welcomes him to the fire.

"You are American. Good, good. I have been expecting you—come, share my fire. Would you like tea?" A young girl with a head scarf brings them tea. The man takes a drink from a liquor bottle and offers it to Smith; he declines. "So, you Americans will come to help us, and you will bring money, am I right? Do you have money for me now?"

Smith and the tribal leader verbally fence for a while. Smith tries to guide the discussion to get the information he needs while his host at the fire wants only to talk about money. The girl hovers nearby, refilling their mugs with tea. Then she approaches Smith.

"You are American—you must help me—only you can help me." The tribal leader gruffly shoos her away, but after a while, she returns. "Please, I am Indian. I am UN aid worker. They keep me here for prostitution. You must help. Please help me."

Finally, Captain Smith asks the tribal leader if this is true. "So what if it is," the man tells Smith, "she is of no consequence—she is a woman. We need money. We must fight the Taliban. What does this have to do with our affair?"

In the shadows beyond the glow of the fire, Captain Carson, myself, and a psychologist—a medical officer—watch this play out. There are any number of ways Smith can take this, but clearly he has a dilemma. He also has a mission. Smith chooses to ignore the woman's pleas for help and continues to try to engage the tribal leader. Finally, the tribal leader becomes upset because Smith has no money for him, and asks that he leave. Smith shoulders his ruck and starts up the road. There he is intercepted by the psychologist. They huddle by the tailgate of a parked roadside pickup.

"OK, Captain, you chose to engage the tribesman and ignore the girl. Tell me, what was your thinking?"

"I had a mission to get information," Captain Smith began, "and I did what I could to carry it out. As for the girl, I felt there was nothing I could do for her right then. She's about five-two, in her late twenties, and there's a small mole on her left temple. When I get to a radio or back to a rear area, I'll report it."

"OK," the psychologist replies as he takes notes. "And in retrospect, what do you think you could've done differently or done better?"

Smith considers this. "When she refilled my tea, I might've asked for her name—maybe introduced myself and see if she would tell me. Then I'd have a name to report."

"OK, that's reasonable," the psych replies neutrally. "Let me brief you on your next problem."

Candidate-Captain Smith heads off for his next dilemma, and the psychologist returns to the shadows near the fire to wait for the next officer. Later on, each officer will be debriefed by the team of psychs working this series of SAREs. At that time, they'll have a full discussion of the possible range of responses and the merits of the one chosen by each officer candidate. Those who elect a clearly inappropriate course of action may be asked to address that position at the commander's review board.

During the last few days of Phase I, the lives of the members of Class 8-04 are driven with continuing interviews, equipment maintenance and overhaul, and barracks cleanup. The remaining candidates are notified by their cadre sergeants that they fall in one of two categories: successful candidates who will move on to Phase II of Special Forces training, and those who will appear before the commander's review board to have their fate determined—relief for the former, angst and apprehension for the latter. First Sergeant Sarno musters the successful candidate at the assembly area outside the barracks.

"All right men, congratulations. We didn't vote you off the island. I hope to see all of you back out here in the future for Phase II and again for Phase IV. I can't say welcome to the brotherhood just yet, but each of you've shown that you've got what it takes to become a Green Beret. So now it's your job to stay focused and stay fit between now and when you begin Phase II. Phase II is hard; prepare yourself for it. Again, while you're to be congratulated on your selection for Special Forces training, remember, it's just that—selection. The real training begins when you come back for Phase II and small-unit tactics. Now, as you savor this moment, be mindful of your classmates and teammates whose fates are yet to be decided. Some will be joining you in Phase II, and some will not. Those who will not, let them leave this training with dignity. Good job, all of you."

The commander's review board is an impressive gathering of Special Forces talent. The board is chaired by the battalion commander, Lieutenant Colonel Jim Jackson. Joining him are Captain Walt Carson, Command Sergeant Major Frank Zorn, and First Sergeant Billy Sarno. There are three other men on the board for SFAS Class 8-04: Captain John Block and First Sergeant Stewart Donnally from Phase II, and Sergeant Major Del Mallick from Phase IV. These men will decide the fate of some thirty enlisted soldiers and six officers who'll appear before them. Unlike the 18X Pre-SFAS board, this review board has a clear mandate to assess and select men for Special Forces. It is very serious business.

The board begins with a single stack of training records. They review each of them in light of a number of criteria—among them, demonstrated performance, future potential, intelligence, maturity, personality, adaptability, creativity, and a mix of this stew that is often referred to as the whole-man concept. The mix is critical in the makeup of a Special Forces soldier, and subject to board deliberation. Can talent and intelligence overcome immaturity and inattention to detail? If a candidate's performance is below standard, but he's shown rapid improvement, do they send him on to Phase II or back to a conventional unit for more seasoning—and risk losing this promising candidate? What if he's scored low on intelligence, but is all heart? These are the men and the issues before this board.

The first task before the board is to cut the men and their training record into three piles. First, there are those whose performance and evaluations are too weak on too many levels for them to be selected. Then there are those whose performance is marginal, but could be considered for selection after meeting with the board. And still others are pretty much good to go, but the board wants to take a final look at them. Often, this is to address an attitude issue of a capable candidate. That said, I've seen men in the first category selected because of their comportment at the board or a spirited endorsement by a cadre sergeant, and I saw one candidate whose arrogance before the board cost him selection. All of these men have passed land navigation and none of them have quit. Anything is possible. The board is guided by two criteria; first, what's good for the force; second, what's good for the man.

Procedurally, all of the men slated for consideration by the board will appear personally before the board. Prior to a candidate's appearance, his training record is brought under review. One or more cadre sergeants addresses the board on his personal observations of the man's performance in a team environment and in a team leadership role. One or more of the psychologists is on hand to speak to the candidate's profile with respect to his intellect, personality, and social behavior. If the psych evaluation suggests a man may be a training risk in one or more of these areas, the board will then have to decide if the candidate's positive qualities justify the risk of sending him to Phase II. After a general discussion of the individual's potential and deficiencies, the candidate is called into the room. He salutes, stands at attention, and reports to the board.

As the board wades through these candidates, the atmosphere in the room, which is the front portion of one of the two large classrooms at the Rowe Training Facility, is tense. Lieutenant Colonel Jackson directs the deliberations, and he's careful to canvass the opinion of each member. He especially wants to hear from Captain Carson and First Sergeant Sarno, and allows the cadre sergeants who observed the candidate to fully speak their minds. When the candidates are before the board, they're asked to speak to their performance, or lack of performance. Some of the questions they hear from the board:

"Your performance is marginal in several areas; why should we select you?"

"We're an interdependent community, and your teammates have rated you very low in the peer review. If you can't work with your peers, how're you going to work with people from another culture?"

"You led poorly in the team events. In Phase II, you'll have to show that you can lead in a tactical situation and under stress. Tell us why you think you can do this."

"Your psych exam says you're something of a loner. Your cadre sergeant saw that as well. We're a family in Special Forces—a brotherhood; we share each other's problems. You earn your beret every day by helping others. Is it in you to be a good teammate?"

"If you were to go forward in training and someday join an ODA, what would you bring to that detachment?"

Most often, the candidates are questioned by the board, then sent from the room while their case is discussed. These discussions invariably invite input from a cadre sergeant who observed the candidate firsthand. The individual who directs much of the questioning and often speaks for this board is the senior enlisted man present, Battalion Command Sergeant Major Frank Zorn. This was my first close encounter with a command sergeant major. Special Forces first sergeants are in a league of their own, but command sergeant majors are on a planet of their own. They're a product of an evolutionary process that produces some of the most shrewd, savvy, intelligent, committed, capable, and colorful leaders in the U.S. Army—in the U.S. military. Lieutenant Colonel Jackson controlled the proceedings, but it was usually his command sergeant major who laid it out for the boarded candidate. These are some of the board findings as articulated by Command Sergeant Major Zorn.

For a clearly unsuitable candidate: "We've observed your performance and you're just not what we're looking for. The input from your peers and the cadre suggests that you're selfish and that you think only of yourself. There's no place here for someone who doesn't look out for his teammates. This business is all about sacrifice for others and working in a team environment. Furthermore, we recommended that you not return for a future assessment. There's too much you have to change to succeed here; however, you can ask for a waiver, and it may be considered. That's all I have." The colonel then formally dismisses the candidate.

To a candidate who has tried, but hasn't shown an unacceptable level of performance: "The board has considered your case, and you'll not be going forward. We work in human terrain here in Special Forces. You've not displayed the situational awareness to succeed in this business. Right now, son, this is not where you can make a contribution. If you really want to be in Special Forces, you'll have to make some changes and come back when you're better prepared. This is our assessment of your suitability for this work; this is not an assessment of your character."

To a similar candidate: "Go get some operational experience and a little more maturity and come back. It's just not for you right now. You've got too many holes in your game. Go to the 82nd or the 101st, get a deployment or two under your belt, and then try us again. Show us you can succeed there, and then you'll have a better chance of succeeding here." More than once I heard the command sergeant major say to younger candidates, "You've shown us something, but not enough and not right now. Put in for the Ranger regiment and get yourself to Ranger School. They'll grow you up right."

I later asked him about sending unsuccessful candidates to other units for, lacking a better term, rehabilitation. "This has nothing to do with the quality or capability of the airborne divisions or the Rangers or any other unit for that matter," Zorn told me. "They have a job to do, and they're damn good at it. But these conventional units and the Rangers work in a far more structured environment than we do. That structure's tailor-made for developing maturity and professional soldiering skills, including leadership. We need those qualities, among other things, to be at a certain level before we can send a man on for Special Forces training."

And I recalled his advice for a very strong candidate whose attitude and demeanor were not to the cadre's liking. "Son, we're going to send you forward, but before you come back here for Phase II, you better sit down and have a good talk with yourself. Your performance here was very good, but you've given the cadre the impression that you think you're better than everyone else. Your teammates peered you low for that very reason. Are you really that good?"

"No, Sergeant Major."

"I recommend you find yourself a good ration of humility before you come back. Start thinking about others and stop thinking about yourself. You hear what I'm saying?"

"Roger that, Sergeant Major."

"Say that again, a little louder."

"Roger that, Sergeant Major."

"One more time."

"Roger that, Sergeant Major!"

"Good. That kind of response'll take you a long way in this training."

Most of the enlisted candidates who come before the Class 8-04 review board aren't selected for Special Forces training, but many are. It seems to me the board is always looking for some way to keep a man in training—some positive input or rationale that will allow them to keep a marginal performer.

That input often comes from a cadre sergeant. "This is a kid who tries hard and who was an asset to his team; he peered very well. Physically, he needs work, but there's no quit in him. If we're going to bend a little, let's bend for him."

Usually, it is a board consensus that keeps a boarded candidate in training. "Congratulations," Zorn tells one candidate, "we're going to select you for Special Forces training."

"Roger, Sergeant Major. Thank you, Sergeant Major."

"Don't thank me yet, soldier. You've some work to do before you're ready for the next phase of training. You need to work every day on your upper-body strength and your overall conditioning. We all have weaknesses; we've talked about yours—it's up to you to fix them before you come back here for Phase II. Can you do that?"

"Yes, Sergeant Major."

"The board's accepting some risk in sending you forward. Don't let us down, you hear me?"

"Roger that, Sergeant Major."

One soldier the board sends through to Phase II is an excellent performer but has an incident with spousal abuse in his record. He has also spent two years on deployment, a year in Afghanistan and a year in Iraq. The man is apologetic and forthcoming when he speaks about the incident, and talks about the counseling he and his wife received. Yet there is a special passion in the command sergeant major's voice when he spoke to this candidate.

"There is something you better understand before you leave here. There's no place for abuse or dysfunction at home—here or anywhere else in this man's Army. I mean, absolutely none, understand? We take care of our teammates, and we take care of our families. This comes up again while you're here at the training command and you are history. You hear me, soldier?"

"Yes, Sergeant Major."

"I've got your name on my blotter, and I'm going to be looking for you," First Sergeant Stew Donnally from Phase II tells him. "Your team sergeant and I are going to be closely monitoring your performance, and we're going to be asking you how things are at home. You're definitely on my radar, understood?"

"Understood, First Sergeant."

As this candidate takes his leave from the board, First Sergeant Billy Sarno follows him out, wanting a further word with him before he left his phase.

The board addresses the officers in their final session. It's my sense that they are far more critical and exacting with officer candidates than enlisted candidates. Most of the issues concerning the officers appearing before the board have to do with leadership and their performance on the SAREs, but not all. One officer is a very strong leader but has a two-year-old notation in his record for getting into a barroom brawl. He is also a bit cocky.

"You'd better get straight on something, Captain," Lieutenant Colonel Jackson tells him. "We don't need guys who can fight in bars. In fact, we need guys who can walk away from a bar fight. You're paid to use your smarts and your judgment to lead your detachment. We're at war, and you need to channel any aggression you may have into leading your men and setting a good example, understand?"

"Yes, sir."

"You'd better, or you are going to find yourself in another line of work. We hold our officers to a high standard. Understand this and take it to heart. Captain, you have all the tools to be a good detachment leader, but you have to be in control of yourself at all times. Are we clear on this?"

"Yes, sir, very clear."

Of the six officers boarded in Class 8-04, four are selected to continue in Phase II. One is nonselected for his poor performance on the SAREs and another for his leadership deficiencies. Officer attrition can often be more dramatic. In a more recent class, twenty-nine officers began the selection process in a Phase I class. Twenty-four made it through to the end of the team events. Only sixteen were selected for Phase II.

After twenty-five days at Camp Mackall and the Rowe Training Facility, the books are closed on SFAS Class 8-04. Their numbers are close to the historical averages. One in three was selected and will move on to Phase II to continue along the road to the Green Beret. The success rate for the X-Rays is higher than for the regular soldiers. This, too, is about average. The continuous training cycle of basic training, then airborne training, then Pre-SFAS seems to bring these soldiers to the selection phase in better physical condition than their counterparts coming from the regular Army units. Another factor that seems to favor the X-Rays is their recent land-navigation training and the ruck marches during the 18X Pre-SFAS course.

The regular Army soldiers who were selected for continuation in Special Forces training will return to their units and await orders to return to Fort Bragg and Phase II. The X-Rays will stay in "the pipeline," as they receive additional leadership and small-unit tactics training to prepare them for Phase II.

CHAPTER FIVE

SPECIAL FORCES TACTICS

The Special Forces Qualification Course, up to this point in time, has been focused on preparing and selecting men for Special Forces training—a process designed to screen for the right men. Phase II marks the beginning of the serious training that will train and equip those men to do the work of a Green Beret overseas. Phase II is all about small-unit tactics and leading in a small-unit tactical environment. To put a fine point on it, the phase focuses on small-unit tactics as applied to the unique environment of special operations. The regular soldiers who've earned the right to begin Phase II with SFAS Phase I Class 8-04 now return to their current duty stations. They'll come back to Fort Bragg in two to six months and be assigned to a future Phase II course. Now that they've been selected for Special Forces, the Army will move them, along with their families, to Fort Bragg on a permanent change-of-duty assignment. Oddly enough, one in ten of those soldiers will elect *not* to continue with Special Forces training. I

STUDENT ODA 811.   Operational Detachment Alpha 811 musters outside its team room, ready for a four-day tactical field exercise during Phase II.

asked about this. Why would a man undergo the rigors of selection and not choose to return for Phase II? There are several reasons.

Many of the soldiers who put in for Special Forces from regular Army units come to selection to see if this is for them—if this is how they want to spend their career in the Army. In the pressure cooker of the assessment and selection process at Camp Mackall and the Rowe Training Facility, they get those questions answered. A few of those take a hard look at the months of training ahead, the lifestyle, and the rigorous deployment schedule, and they decide that this is not for them or not for their family situation. Most experienced soldiers who come for selection are proven soldiers and leaders. They've enjoyed some measure of success in their conventional units. When they return to those units after selection for Special Forces, some are approached by their first sergeants, command sergeant majors, and company officers and asked to stay on at their current unit. Sometimes they're offered positions of increased leadership and responsibility within their unit. These are good men, and their current commands want that talent to remain in place for their next deployment rotation. So one in ten decline orders to Phase II and Special Forces training. Special Forces lose a potential Green Beret, and the regular Army retains a good man, perhaps a better soldier for his experience at SFAS. In any case, I'll lose track of those nine in ten from SFAS Class 8-04 who will return for Phase II at a future date. I'm scheduled for the next Phase II class, as are the X-Ray soldiers who are to begin Phase II about five weeks from the completion of their selection. For the X-Rays, there are two interim courses they must complete before they begin Phase II: the X-Ray Special Forces Preparation Course, and the combined Primary Leadership Development Course/Basic Non-Commissioned Officers Course—SFPC and PLDC/BNCOC, respectively. Since these acronyms are a mouthful, I'll refer to the former as the preparation course and the latter as the leadership course. The prep course is designed to give these new soldiers some background in small-unit tactics to better equip them for the intensive tactical training in Phase II. The leadership course is the requirement for leadership training before a man becomes a sergeant in the United States Army. All men who graduate from the Q-course and don a Green Beret and haven't made sergeant, which includes most of the X-Rays, are then advanced to sergeant. Before they are allowed to sew on the coveted three chevrons of a buck sergeant, they must have completed this leadership requirement.

The X-Ray Special Forces selectees return to Fort Bragg for their Special Forces Preparation Course. They are once again in barracks that appear identical to those where they suffered through their Pre-SFAS Training. The prep-course barracks are located next to the Pre-SFAS Training buildings, but inside they're arranged very differently. They are set up in "ODA configuration," a living/working arrangement that'll characterize much of their training in the Q-Course and much of their operational life as a Green Beret. Each floor of the dated, two-story structures houses a student Operational Detachment Alpha, or student ODA—a team of twelve to fourteen students. For much of the Special Forces Qualification Course, the trainees or students (they are no longer candidates) will train and learn in these ODA-sized student groupings. Most of these men will go to war as young sergeants in a Special Forces Operational Detachment Alpha. One end of the barracks houses a small head/laundry/shower facility, much the same as the Pre-SFAS barracks. Next is a bay that takes perhaps half the assigned floor space. This is the team area, or team room, where the daily planning, preparation, and instructional life of the team takes place. Along the walls are racks for weapons, and lockers and shelving for ammunition and operational equipment. The interior of the team room is taken with a ring or U-shaped arrangement of tables surrounded by chairs—one for each member of the team. The tables encircle two sand tables—four-foot-square, shallow sandboxes where the student ODAs can build terrain models for operational planning. In and around this team bay are whiteboards, butcher-block paper pads, and easels for planning and briefing. These mission-planning/mission-briefing areas are where the

new X-Ray selectees will spend most of their waking hours. At one end
of the room is a stack of boxed MREs. When the student ODAs aren't
in the field, they'll live and eat most of their meals in the team room.
The third section of each team's space is a small sleeping bay crammed
with double bunks and just enough room for a man to slip between
them and crawl into his rack. Special Forces detachments live in similar
eat-sleep-work environments all around the world.

The prep course is a sixteen-day course of instruction that teaches
individual movement, patrol movement formations, types of patrols
(including reconnaissance, ambush, and raid patrols), mission planning, and troop-leading procedures. Unlike Pre-SFAS Training, the
prep course is continuous, 24/7—no weekends off. The information is
presented in the classrooms, and then the student teams move into the
training areas on Fort Bragg to practice in the field what they learned
in the classroom—a day in class, then a day out in the woods. These
days begin with physical training (PT) at 0600 and often end with a
patrolling practical at 2130 (9:30 p.m.). Each team has an assigned
cadre sergeant who is a sergeant first class. This veteran Green Beret is
assigned to each student team or student ODA in the prep course. My
student ODA cadre sergeant is Sergeant First Class Owen Tell.

"We have a little over two weeks to get these soldiers through the
basics of small-unit tactics. In that short amount of time, they're literally drinking from a fire hose. Most of what we teach here they'll see
again in Phase II, but having seen it here, they'll have a better chance of
bringing their skills up to an acceptable level when it really counts.
These men've had infantry training as a part of their basic training or
OSUT. That training gave them the basics of soldiering in a platoon or
company-level unit. But this only taught them to function as a rifleman
in a rifle platoon, and to follow orders on the battlefield. Now we have
to get them used to working, planning, and leading in a small-unit
environment."

"How are they doing?" I ask.

"They're doing pretty well considering where they've come from and the limited time we have with them."

Sergeant Tell is a short man with an efficient compact build, dark hair, and dark eyes that give him something of a Native American look. He joined the Army sixteen years ago after graduating from high school in Tucson. Before reporting to the Special Warfare Center and School, he had spent twelve years, his entire Special Forces career, with 3rd Group. Sergeant Tell can make himself understood in both French and Arabic, but is fluent in neither. He's made deployments to half a dozen sub-Saharan African nations and one to Afghanistan. He struck me as a very measured and precise individual, yet there's no misreading his passion for teaching and mentoring these young soldiers.

"They arrive the same day they graduate from Phase I and are selected for SF training," Sergeant Tell says. "Naturally, they're a little cocky, and they literally swagger as they get off the bus. The first sergeant has a quick talk with them and settles them in. 'Congratulations,' he tells them, 'but now it's time to get ready for the real Special Forces training.' That first afternoon we have them lay out all of their gear, what they have and what we issue them. It's a full-on personnel and equipment inspection, and we give them a little of the drill-instructor treatment. It refocuses them and gets their minds set for the serious business of learning small-unit tactics.

"Myself and the other cadre sergeants also talk to them every day about staying focused and keeping their goals and priorities in order— preparing for Phase II and working to earn their beret, nothing else. We spend a lot of our evenings here with them, talking about life in the groups and on deployment. We tell them not to get married, get engaged, buy a car, or get a tattoo. We also talk to them about drinking, not that these guys have much time for that, but one DUI or an incident in a bar and they're gone."

The preparation course trainees draw weapons for this training— real weapons equipped with blank firing adapters. These are metal appendages attached to the muzzles of their weapon that allow them to fire blank ammunition, either in single rounds or on automatic fire. As with their two previous phases, they take their weapons with them everywhere and are never to be more than an arm's length from their weapon. These are real guns, and they come with real weapons safety violations. Except for the first day's inspection, the Special Forces Preparation Course is a pure teaching environment. Very few students VW from this training, and there are few IVWs. The involuntary withdrawals that do occur are for safety violations; these are always taken seriously, even with blank-loaded weapons. Safety violations include sweeping someone with the muzzle of your weapon, inappropriate handling of the weapon, and an accidental discharge. Failing to have a round in the chamber and the weapon locked (on safe) is also a safety violation, as it will be for the rest of their Special Forces training. In addition to M4 rifles, each student ODA is assigned two M249 squad assault weapons (SAWs) and a single M240 medium machine gun.

On day thirteen, they sit for a two-hour exam at their tables in the team bay. Following the test, Sergeant Tell gives them their operations order for their final field training exercise. The honor of leading Tell's student ODA team on this final exercise is given to Specialist Tom Kendall.

"He's one of the better soldiers in this group, and he's already breaking out as a leader. He's also a quick study in picking up the mechanics of small-unit tactics." Sergeant Tell knows about Kendall's martial-arts background, just as he knows the first name and background of everyone in his student ODA.

That afternoon Kendall puts out a formatted warning order, a short briefing that alerts his team of the mission, itemizes what equipment they need to prepare, and makes team assignments for the mission. The team plans for the mission most of the afternoon and evening and, at 2200, Kendall gives his team their operations order, a premission briefing that walks the men through the mission, start to finish. Various team members step before the group to give their portion of the briefing—weather, communications, routes to and from the objective, enemy forces in the area, and so on. All of them are in battle dress and their faces are camouflaged. Kendall gives the all-important actions-on-target portion of the briefing, using the sand tables on which scale models of the target area have been created. Sandbox 101 is a required course in Special Forces training. There are toy trucks, toy soldiers, and vegetation scrounged from the nearby woods. The mission is an ambush of a squad of enemy soldiers. Kendall covers setting the ambush, executing the ambush, searching the bodies, and the exfiltration plan. He also covers a dizzying array of details, contingencies, and procedural issues. The briefing concludes just before midnight. After a quick critique from Sergeant Tell, the squad saddles up for inspection and a brief rehearsal at nearby Pike Field. The team then boards a truck waiting for them outside the barracks. Other trucks are waiting or loading student ODA teams for other missions.

It is a half-hour ride to the infiltration point. The team piles from the bed of the big four-by-four Army truck called an LMTV—light medium tactical vehicle. These are the beefy trucks like the ones on convoy duty in Iraq. The team expands into a security perimeter, just as they would if they were being inserted by helo. Then Kendall signals them to move out, and the team files into the bush. It's 0300. For most of the night and through dawn, the team moves through ravines and wooded areas in a section of Fort Bragg known simply as Area K—one of the many training areas on the huge Army post. Shortly after dawn, Kendall has his team 250 meters from its ambush site. Specialist Kendall and his subordinate team leaders move cautiously to the roadside ambush site and position each man and weapon. Primary considerations are security, firepower, and command and control. Then they wait.

Walking along the road, I can see nothing of the men in hiding. "Not bad, but they were pretty sloppy patrolling in, and it took too long for them to get set up. But each time out, they do it a little better." My companion is a staff sergeant named Carlos.

Carlos had been selected for Special Forces training well over a year ago, but was requested by his company in the 82nd Airborne to make a

deployment with them. After close to a year in Iraq, he is back and waiting for the next Phase II class to begin. He's also spent time in the 75th
Ranger Regiment. Detached from the 82nd and waiting for Phase II, he's
assigned as an assistant SFPC instructor. Carlos usually shadows the student ODA when it's in the field. I've watched him work with the X-Rays
over the past two weeks, and he's been a wealth of knowledge in fieldcraft. Carlos has been in the Army for seven years and has two combat
deployments behind him.

"You think they're ready for Phase II?"

Carlos gives me shrug and a grin. "They're smart and they learn
quickly, but we won't know until we get to Phase II. I won't know myself
until I get to Phase II. These soldiers will be my classmates there. We'll all
find out together."

Shortly before 0930, four men file up the road toward the ambush
site. They carry AK-47 rifles and their heads are swathed in Arab headgear. When they are in the kill zone, Kendall keys the initiator of the
claymore mine, which produces the bang from a large M-80-type fire-
cracker. The automatic weapons hidden along the ambush line begin
to chatter. Loudest of all is the POP-POP-POP of the M240 machine
gun. The enemy tries to return fire but is overwhelmed by the concen-
trated firepower of the student ODA. Kendall shouts above the din,
calling for a cease-fire. He then directs the team's actions as they sweep
through the target, checking the downed enemy soldiers and disarming
them. Moments later, Sergeant Tell calls the proceedings to a halt and
conducts a field critique. He tells his students what he saw and asks for
comments from Carlos and the Arab role players who have risen from
the dead. The student ODA is back in the team bay by midafternoon
for a final critique and course review. A few days later, the new Special
Forces Preparation Course graduates are on their way back out to
Camp Mackall. They have one more stop before Phase II.

The leadership course conducted at Camp Mackall fulfills the Army's
noncommissioned-officer leadership requirement with a Special Forces

bias. The X-Ray soldiers, now selected and prepared for Special Forces training, are housed in clean, new, but still temporary billeting modules at the rear of the Rowe Training Facility. Again, the students are cut into ODA-sized squads for billeting and training. The interior living arrangements are not unlike those they just left at the preparation course at Fort Bragg. The barracks area is a little more generous with wall lockers beside each double rack, and the operations-planning bay is arranged in a classroom setting with the familiar U-shaped student-table arrangement. Since their arrival from Fort Benning, this is the first time the 18 X-Ray soldiers have been in some semblance of an academic environment, albeit a Special Forces academic environment.

Each day begins at 0600 with an hour and a half of physical training—stretching, group calisthenics, and then a run. These are led initially by the cadre sergeants, but those leadership duties are quickly turned over to the students and rotated among the student teams. On the first day after formation and inspection, they are briefed by the course first sergeant, a laconic Georgian and a twenty-four-year Special Forces veteran. The men stand in ranks by team, at parade rest: left hands resting at the small of their backs, right hands holding the barrels of their rifles—rubber M4s for this training. The first sergeant quickly goes over the rules and restrictions. They are to be on time, in the right place and in the right uniform. There's to be no talking with those in other phases of training, no cell phones, no use of the PX, and so on, and so on. Then he cuts to the heart of the training.

"This course is a standing requirement to become a sergeant in this man's Army. It will also equip you for the leadership challenges you will face in Special Forces training and Special Forces duty. In every Phase II, we lose a few of you guys because you lack the ability to lead in a tactical situation. There's information in this course you're going to need to get you through Phase II and the other phases of the Q-Course. Now, this course is not as intense as what you've been through in previous courses. It's not intended to be. Nor is it as intense as what awaits you in Phase II. Nonetheless, it's important. It's a time to listen, learn, and practice the techniques and disciplines you are going to need if you want to earn that Green Beret and deploy as a member of a Special Forces detachment. It's a time to regroup and prepare yourself mentally and physically for the challenges ahead. Use this time well. Ask questions. Get to know your classmates and your cadre sergeants. Leadership's a key skill of a Special Forces soldier. Leadership extends to all aspects of military life. Now, some of you might think the accountability and the uniform inspections and the close-order drill we do here is chicken-shit. But let me ask you this. How are you going to ask a subordinate, a fellow American or an allied soldier, to fight and die for you if you can't get them to wear a proper uniform or properly maintain their equipment? Special Forces soldiers are leaders; don't you ever forget that.

"This course is designed to be an academic experience in a learning environment. Now, that means you have to be ready and willing to learn—to give it 100 percent. We hope you will. But if you don't, my cadre sergeants have my blessing to take you out to one of those swampy draws here at beautiful Camp Mackall and conduct a little attitude-adjustment training. I hope that won't be necessary, but we want your full attention while you're here. Y'all clear on that?"

"YES, FIRST SERGEANT!"

"Good, good. That's what I like to hear. We don't want any failures of communication while you're here. Good luck to y'all. Class First Sergeant?"

"Right here, First Sergeant." The class chain of command has a student first sergeant in charge of the class and student team sergeants in charge of each student ODA. These leadership positions are changed and rotated often during the course.

"Take charge of the formation and carry on."

"Yes, First Sergeant." The assigned class first sergeant salutes and does a crisp about-face. "Team sergeants, take charge of your squads and fall into your classrooms."

When they hit the classroom at 1000 on the first day, there's an impressive stack of reading and reference material at each student's place in the classroom. I counted twelve manuals, plus that many or more pamphlets and handouts. The sheer volume seemed more suited to a semester of law school than a sixteen-day leadership course. They ranged from *The Army Noncommissioned Officer Guide,* on the leadership side, to the *Ranger Handbook,* on the tactical side, but the course is all about leadership. These reference materials will leave with the students on the completion of the training. Each day the students are assigned mandatory reading to prepare them for the next day's classes. In addition to a host of leadership topics, the subject matter includes the Army writing style, subordinate supervision, close-order drill, tactical supply procedures, environmental awareness, NBC (nuclear, chemical, biological) precautions, joint operations, and how to give a military briefing. The evenings are taken with study and cadre presentations on the Special Forces history and Special Forces current operations. I was pressed into service for my SOF presentation on warriorship and moral conduct on the battlefield.

"These are skills and information they will need," Sergeant First Class Don Langston tells me, "in SF training and later when they're assigned to an operational ODA. Our job is to see that they get this information and that they have a personal library of leadership and tactical material to refer to in the future. We also try to put them in as many leadership and supervisory roles as we can, consistent with the teaching that has to take place to get through this material."

Langston's a handsome, blond six-footer from upstate New York. He has his associate's degree and is currently studying for a BA in history; he wants to teach high school history when he retires from the Army. Langston has been in the Army fourteen years and in Special Forces for eight. He is from 3rd Group and has made deployments to Uganda, Mali, Zimbabwe, Bosnia, Afghanistan, and Iraq. Langston gathered two Bronze Stars and a single Purple Heart for his combat tours. His goals in the military are to become a master sergeant and a detachment team sergeant. He has fourteen men in his training squad; I'm assigned to Langston's group.

"The course work here is driven by a set curriculum, but we've a lot of latitude to spend more time on one topic at the expense of another, or to probe more deeply into a subject after hours. We spend a lot of time with these soldiers in the evenings." We walk to the whiteboard at the front of his group's classroom bay. "For example, these are their goals as we developed them in general group discussion." He points to a list on the whiteboard.

1. Have the highest team average on the Army Physical Fitness Test.
2. Win all course team events.
3. Get to know everyone in your team.
4. Don't lose anyone in the team from training.
5. Exceed all standards.

"These are our team goals, and every few days we go over them to see how we're doing. Chances are we may not achieve them all, but they're realistic goals and each man in the team is committed to them."

I notice that the members of the team all call each other by their first names. They address him as Sergeant Langston, and he calls them by their first names. Several afternoons are taken up with class presentations. Each man must submit an outline of a military presentation, and after it is approved by Langston, the student has to give an eight- to ten-minute talk on the subject, complete with visual aids. Probably one of the best and clearest presentations I've ever attended on sighting in an M4 rifle was given by one of Sergeant Langston's soldiers.

In addition to the classroom work, there is close-order drill, usually a single student marching four or five of his classmates about the compound—column left, column right, to the rear, harch! There are also uniform inspections with sections of students turned out in dress greens, complete with red berets, bloused trousers, and spit-shined jump boots. The only concession to SF protocol is that the inspectees fall in with their rifles. Both the drill and the uniform inspections are unusual activity for the Rowe Training Facility, where most soldiers are dressed and outfitted for combat-related training, often with their face and hands camouflaged. The most welcome nonclassroom activities are the team competitions. Again, a squad leader or student team sergeant is chosen to lead each evolution. He has to organize his team, make assignments, and direct his men in the competition. These contests range from a barnyard version of soccer in a nearby meadow to a four-mile run, during which one or more members of the squad have to be carried by the others. The one I liked was the Nasty Nick relay. Each team is scattered around the obstacle course. The first man takes two or three obstacles, then hands off his helmet—the baton in this race—to the next man, and he negotiates the next few obstacles. As the event progresses, the squad members who have completed their leg of the race run alongside to cheer on their teammates as they take on their obstacles. At the last obstacle, there is a single, helmeted competitor and a dozen or more cheerleaders. They have to finish together, as a team. These are spirited contests on the Nasty Nick course, and the race is run more than once. Winning squad leaders take their men for a break, losing squad leaders lead their men in push-ups.

"This is a relatively easy two weeks for them," Sergeant Langston tells me, "and it's supposed to be. We have to give them the leadership training in keeping with Army requirements, but since we have them 24/7 for fifteen days, we can also expose them to Special Forces team-centric leadership training. They've been worked hard for the last six months or so. We want them to rest up and, in some cases, heal up for Phase II, but we also want them to stay mentally focused. We also want them to understand the key role leadership plays in Special Forces."

Most are 18 X-Ray soldiers, but not all. A few are soldiers who have been selected for Special Forces training from conventional units. They are there for the Army NCO leadership requirement. In one of these courses, I met a former Navy SEAL. He had been released from the SEAL teams before 9/11 and had decided get back in the fight—this time as a Green Beret. Though he had been a second class petty officer in the Navy, he still needed this course to become a sergeant in the Army.

"This has been a good few weeks for us," Specialist Justin Keller, one of the X-Rays, tells me. "It's been challenging but not too challenging, and you can feel the guys' confidence growing as we get ready for Phase II." Justin Keller is a big man, some 250 pounds, down from the 270 he was carrying when he reported to boot camp. He's the largest man in Sergeant Langston's squad. He grew up in Denver and attended a small college in Iowa, where he was a heavyweight wrestler. He has a degree in physical education and secondary education. Keller has a brother serving in the Army, and his father and uncle are both retired from the Army National Guard. He has soft, rounded features, and while his hair is closely cropped, it's clear that he is balding. He's twenty-six. Prior to enlisting in the Army for the X-Ray Program, he was working as a bouncer and as a laborer in the warehouse of a flooring company. Keller has a soft intensity offset by an easy smile and intelligent eyes.

"So you're ready for Phase II?"

"I suppose so, at least as ready as I'll ever be." There's a flash of an easy smile. "I guess I'm like Grasshopper in the *Kung Fu* TV series. It's time for me to go."

On an overcast Monday morning in early November, 341 souls in starched BDUs file into the large auditorium at the JFK Special Warfare Center and School building at Fort Bragg. The only color on their uniforms are the small American-flag shoulder patches. Collectively, they're a sober group, each man pulling off his cap as he enters to reveal a military haircut—high and tight. These soldiers—veteran officers and enlisted men, along with a hundred-plus X-Ray candidates—are at the auditorium to begin Phase II. Collectively, they make up

Phase II Class 1-05. It's still calendar year 2004, but fiscal 2005 began on 1 October. They speak quietly among themselves, but it is hushed, careful murmuring. All talking stops when the company first sergeant steps to the front of the room.

"Good morning, men, and welcome to Phase II of Special Forces training. For the next thirty-five days you belong to me and my cadre—every waking hour, and those waking hours will take up most of the day." First Sergeant Stewart Donnally is a measured, even-tempered master sergeant from 3rd Group. He doesn't raise his voice, but it easily carries across the quiet auditorium to the back rows of soldiers. "Most of you know what to expect here; Phase II is all about patrolling and small-unit tactics. The phase has standards, and you must meet them. Within the boundaries of those standards, we will keep the guys we want to keep. We make subjective evaluations all the time. The cadre's here to evaluate you and to help you learn, or to help you out. It's your choice." He pauses a long moment before continuing. "Be clear on one thing, people. We are here to train warriors, and we are deadly serious about this. The reputation you established during selection will continue after you leave here. We are still a small force, and reputation is everything."

First Sergeant Donnally goes through a litany of rules and restrictions that will govern training and their life at Camp Mackall and the Rowe Training Facility during his phase. Then he yields to his company commander, a square-shouldered, solidly built captain with a shock of dark hair across his forehead.

"Good morning, men."

"GOOD MORNING, SIR!"

"I'm Captain John Block, Charlie Company commander, 1st Battalion, 1st Special Warfare Training Group. Let me echo the first sergeant's welcome. Let me also emphasize what he said about training warriors. If you don't want to be a warrior, this is the wrong place for you and you're wasting our time. If you want to be a warrior, then show us you want to be a warrior—a Special Forces warrior. Like the first sergeant, I've been at this a while. I earned my tab back in 1988 as a young staff sergeant. Back then and through most of the nineties, we worked mostly in a foreign-internal-defense environment. Our country is now at war, and you will be asked to do it all—foreign internal defense, direct action, special reconnaissance, and unconventional warfare. Phase II is about patrolling and tactics, the foundation of your warrior skill set. You'll use and teach these skills for the rest of your Special Forces career. This is not a mini Ranger course; this is small-unit tactics adapted for the Special Forces mission. We expect you to do your best, show us some heart, and take care of your teammates. Fail to show us you can lead, follow, and perform in a small-unit tactical environment and you'll be soldiering in another outfit."

Block, like all enlisted Green Berets who become officers, has been through the Q-Course twice. When an enlisted Special Forces soldier elects to become an officer and qualifies for officer training, he does not have to reselect, but he must, as a newly commissioned officer, again complete Phases II, III, and IV.

"The groups need every one of you," Captain Block continues, "but we'll not cut corners and we'll not relax our standards. You have to perform, and you have to demonstrate character. Show us you want to be a Special Forces warrior, and forget about everything else. For the next five weeks, consider yourself on deployment. And good luck to each of you."

The following day, the class draws weapons at Fort Bragg and moves en masse to Camp Mackall and the Rowe Training Facility. The Phase II area is a scattering of temporary metal buildings dating back to the 1950s. The twenty-five-by-fifty-foot metal-sided structures each house a student detachment of twelve to fourteen students—a student Operational Detachment Alpha. Most of the student ODAs are assigned their own building, but given the needs of the Special Forces groups and the nation for more Green Berets, some of the Phase II ODAs are billeted in recently erected tents near the main compound. These are semipermanent structures served by generators and portable toilets. The tents are erected on existing concrete slabs—pads that date back to World War II, when they served as foundations for the temporary barracks hastily built for soldiers preparing for the invasion of occupied France. Both the tents and the buildings are partitioned in the now-familiar barracks-area/operational-bay configuration. The shower, mess, and laundry facilities are in the central area of the Rowe Training Facility and serve Phase II students as well as other training venues at the facility.

Life in the team huts and tents is conducted as if the student ODAs were on operational deployment, which means they move about the Rowe Training Facility as a team or in pairs, and when they sleep in the barracks, two men will always be awake and on guard duty. They have to be prepared to move, fight, or fend off an attack at all times.

Class 1-05 is organized as student ODAs, and all training evolutions are conducted within the individual ODA or a pair of ODAs. Each ODA or team is assigned a cadre team sergeant who is a veteran sergeant first class. Most student ODAs also have an assigned teaching/training assistant. He is a civilian employee of the Northrop Grumman Corporation and, almost without exception, a retired Green Beret. These civilian trainers are called different things in different phases, but in Phase II, they are referred to as training assistants and considered cadre. Like the soldiers in Class 1-05, I'm also assigned to a student ODA. My team is ODA 811, usually referred to simply as "eight-one-one." My cadre sergeant is Sergeant First Class Paul Janss.

A word about student ODAs and cadre sergeants. Much of Special Forces training is conducted in groupings or teams that reflect the basic deployment unit of Special Forces, the Operational Detachment Alpha (ODA). The student ODA will often mirror the deployed ODA in size and composition. Operationally, it's usually twelve Green Berets per ODA, but in training that number can range from ten to sixteen soldiers per student ODA. It's the same for assignments within the student ODA—detachment commander or team leader, team sergeant, intel sergeant, weapons sergeant, and so on. The numbering—say,

811, as in the case of my student ODA for Phase II—would also reflect a functioning ODA's group, battalion, and company affiliation. For training in the Q-Course, they're somewhat artificial. An instructor in the form of a cadre sergeant or assigned cadre officer will often accompany these student ODAs throughout a phase or for certain portions of phase training.

Paul Janss was born in Norway and went to high school in Alexandria, Virginia. He speaks Norwegian and Russian, and is a veteran of the 3rd and 5th Special Forces Groups, but now calls 5th Group home. Jan, as he's called, enlisted in the Army in 1980 and served in the 75th Ranger Regiment from '83 through '85. He has deployed extensively in Africa and the Middle East. Sergeant Janss is five-nine, lean, and as hard as dried leather. Though he's one of the older cadre sergeants, he can run—effortlessly, mile after mile. Few of his cadre sergeants want to run with him; few can. He is quiet, personable, and approachable. While he yearns to return to group and operational-deployment rotation, he's totally committed to teaching small-unit tactics to the next generation of Green Berets. Jan is qualified as an 18 Charlie SF engineering sergeant and as an 18 Delta SF combat medic.

Jan's training ODA for Class 1-05 has thirteen men: two captains and five enlisted soldiers who have returned to Fort Bragg for Phase II, and six X-Rays—a much higher percentage than with most student ODAs. Once they're settled into their billets, Sergeant Janss takes them on a tour of the Phase II area and the Rowe Training Facility. For all, this is a reacquaintance of the area, except for the weapons-cleaning shed and the Phase II team huts. This is the first time any of them have carried real weapons, with blank adapters, at Camp Mackall. Before we look at the training, let's take a look at the men in 811—my student ODA. First, the X-Rays.

They are Specialists Antonio Costa, David Altman, and Tom Kendall and PFCs Roberto Pantella, Tim Baker, and Jamie Wagner. All of them, with the exception of Wagner, went to selection right after their first iteration of the Pre-SFAS course. Wagner is a twenty-eight-year-old from Baton Rouge. He arrived at Fort Bragg from basic and airborne training insufficiently prepared physically for the rigors of Special Forces training. After his second round of Pre-SFAS, he was selected for Special Forces along with Baker, Costa, Altman, Pantella, and Kendall.

"Back home, I was a computer tech when I decided to join the Army," he tells me. "Basic training and jump school got me in shape, but not enough for SF training. I needed the extra work, and they were right to hold me back for a second Pre-SFAS. Now that I've been selected, I'm ready to move ahead."

The five experienced soldiers assigned to student ODA 811 all come from the conventional Army, and as in all small units, these veterans will form the backbone of the student ODA. They're led by Sergeant First Class Stan Hall. Hall's father was a career infantry officer, and he grew up in the Army and on the move; he went to four different high schools. He's an experienced soldier with four years in the 25th Infantry Division, four years in the 82nd Airborne, and a year and a half as a drill sergeant. He's also Ranger qualified. When I met him, Hall struck me as a mature, efficient leader, and probably one of the reasons the Phase II cadre assigned so many X-Rays to his training ODA.

"I went through selection almost two years ago," he tells me, "and then I got orders to Fort Benning as a drill instructor. I thought I'd never have the chance to go SF. But I managed to get an early release to come to Phase II. I'm twenty-seven, and I need to get on with this before I get too much older."

There are three sergeants or buck sergeants assigned to 811: Daniel Barstow, Byron O'Kane, and Aaron Dunn. Dan Barstow is from Canton, Ohio, and joined the Army right out of high school. He's been in the Army for four years and came from a military police unit assigned to Schofield Barracks and the 25th Infantry Division in Hawaii. He met his wife, also an MP, in Hawaii. While he attends Phase II, she's serving in a security role in Kabul, Afghanistan. Byron O'Kane is a seven-year Army veteran from Wichita, Kansas. He's an infantryman and saw action in Iraq with the 1st Infantry Division. He married just before he joined the Army and the couple now has a new baby girl, their first. Before enlisting, he was training as an emergency medical technician and hopes to become an 18 Delta Special Forces medic. O'Kane and his young family just arrived at Fort Bragg from a tour in Germany. Aaron Dunn is from Dallas and has been in the Army five years. He is a tall, thin, quiet Korean–African American with a striking resemblance to Tiger Woods. He's married with a three-year-old son. Dunn came from a technical billet in the Army; he's a radar technician. For most of his Army career, he has been repairing radars and aviation electronics. When we spoke, he was concerned about Phase II and small-unit tactics since he's been with an aviation battalion for the last three years and has spent very little time in the field.

Specialist Frank Dolemont is the most junior of the "regulars" and, in terms of combat, the most experienced. Dolemont dropped out of high school in his junior year to work the family farm in Oklahoma. After a series of odd jobs, he joined the Army at twenty-five. Following basic and advanced training, he went straight to the 75th Ranger Regiment. He has two combat tours as a Ranger.

"My last tour, I was a squad leader," he tells me, "and it was on that second tour that it all came together for me. I knew that this is what I was born to do—to lead in combat and to teach others how to perform in combat. I'm finally where I belong."

The two officers are very experienced and very different. Captain Matt Anderson grew up in Meridian, Mississippi, and enlisted in the Army after his high school graduation in 1991. He has served in the 82nd Airborne and the 75th Ranger Regiment. He's also worked in Army intelligence and counterintelligence. He attended college at night to earn a degree in psychology while at Fort Bragg, which allowed him to qualify for Officer Candidate School. Like many SF officer candidates, he's an infantry officer. Anderson is handsome, easygoing, and outgoing; it seems as if he knows everyone and they seem to know him. He is unmarried, but has two daughters from a previous marriage. Anderson is six foot and a solid two hundred pounds. I have to finally ask him about his ethnic background—he looks as if he could be Arab or Lebanese. "No, sir," he chuckles, "I'm just a black guy."

Captain Miguel Santos grew up in a small town in Georgia. His parents are both Cuban immigrants. He's been in the Army nine years: four at West Point and five as an armor officer—a tanker. Like Anderson, Hall, and Dolemont, he has earned his Ranger tab. He spent close to a year in Iraq, where he saw action as an armored scout platoon leader. He came to selection from a tour in Germany, where he met his wife. They're expecting their first child while Santos is in the Q-Course— during Phase IV, if the captain and the baby both stay on schedule. Miguel Santos is short, perhaps five-six, and in superb physical condition. He is quiet, observant, and very intelligent.

"There are two things that made me want a career in Special Forces," he says to me. "The first is 9/11 and the role SF will play in the war on terrorism. The second is the quality of the NCOs in Special Forces; they're the best in the Army. These are the kind of men I want to serve with and to lead. That's why I'm here."

"I think we have a pretty good group," Sergeant Janss tells me on the first day of training. "The two officers seem solid and focused, and there's a good range of experience in the veteran soldiers. Sergeant Hall is particularly strong. I've spent some time with the records of the X-Rays, and they are a talented bunch—inexperienced, but there's a lot of potential there. Phase II will be particularly important for them as they will have to display leadership in small-unit tactical situations. And we have four Rangers. For them, some of this will be a review— they've seen it before. My job is to teach, monitor, coach, and evaluate these men. I expect the Rangers to serve as my teaching assistants."

In addition to the Rangers in his ODA, Jan has Gary Courtland, or "Mister" Courtland as the candidates refer to him. Courtland is a recent Army retiree working for Northrop Grumman with seventeen years of his twenty-year Army career in Special Forces. He works part-time with Phase II while pursuing a master's degree in education.

In the late 1980s, he was with 7th Group and in El Salvador. He was a qualified 18 Echo and 18 Foxtrot—communications sergeant and intelligence sergeant—and a qualified sniper. Courtland is a mild, neutral man and looks like what he is studying to become: a high school math teacher.

The day after the candidates move into their team barracks, the cadre sergeants take them out for a four-mile ruck march—a brisk shakedown walk to reacquaint them with moving under their rucks. Under Sergeant Stan Hall's direction, the X-Rays carry the machine guns. Tom Kendall carries the big M240 while Roberto Pantella and Jamie Wagner carry the squad assault weapons, or SAWs. Tim Baker straps on the M240 tripod, which weighs as much as gun itself, to the top of his ruck. That afternoon, they shed their combat load and each man runs the obstacle course twice. The cadre sergeants are watching to see who is having trouble under their rucks and who lacks upper-body strength, which is a prerequisite to performing well on Nasty Nick. The X-Rays are all well conditioned to this, but a few of the veterans are found to have let their conditioning slip between their selection and coming back for Phase II.

The next day, between a 0500 reveille and breakfast, the class gets the first of four sessions in hand-to-hand fighting, or unarmed combat training. After breakfast in the facility chow hall, the rest of the day is taken with round-robin combat tactical training. As a student ODA, they spend an hour at each training station. There are nine of them: loading and firing the M240 and M249 SAW machine guns; arming and positioning of claymore mines; operating the PRC-119 radio; securing and searching an enemy prisoner of war—an EPW; using night-vision goggles (NVGs); using a laser target designator; calling for artillery fire; encrypting and operating the PRC-148 radio; and properly conducting a vehicle search. They work as a team except during the EPW and vehicle searches. At these two training stations, they work in pairs, one man covering while the other executes a phase of the search. For the vehicle searches, they use a Humvee configured as a pickup truck. For the EPWs, they use each other, and this requires some discomfort on the part of the EPW role players. There are too many stories coming back from Iraq about insurgents playing possum with a live grenade, waiting to be searched by Americans. The cadre sees that the training is realistic, and that means it's a little rough on the men who serve as EPW training partners. Interestingly, the term "POW," or "prisoner of war," refers to Americans taken captive, but enemy prisoners are always referred to as EPWs.

The next day, the student ODAs head into the field for five days and four nights of training. Eight-one-one and its sister ODA, 812, bivouac in a wooded area near one of the many lakes in Camp Mackall. Individually, the two ODAs move under their rucks down a dirt road for a mile or more to their training area, a large meadow bordered by a stand of scrub oak and pine. One corner of the meadow serves as a classroom while the large, open area is suitable for walking through formations and battle drills. Once the teams become proficient in their movements in the open, they take the drills into the woods. Jan and Sergeant First Class Sid Warner, 812's cadre sergeant, begin with the basics of individual movement before moving on to squad and fire-team movements.

For several hours, they run individual battle drills in the meadow and woods. Over a hundred-meter stretch of ground, they work in six- and seven-man squads to practice fire-and-maneuver drills. This calls for three or four of them to jump to their feet, sprint for ten or fifteen meters, and dive for cover—up, bound forward, and down. Once down, they lay down a base of fire, while their squad mates make their dash. They start by yelling BANG-BANG, BANG-BANG. Very soon they are firing blanks and quickly changing magazines. They do this with their LBEs, or combat vests, and, occasionally, with full rucks. The temperature is in the mid-fifties, and it's raining lightly. Soon they are drenched from the precipitation and their own sweat. As they run, they're told to look for cover and/or concealment at the end of their sprint. They are also reminded to keep their dashes short so as not to remain a target for too long.

"Think like an enemy gunner," Sergeant Warner tells them. "Always be thinking, 'I'm up, he sees me, I'm down.' And just before you go down, try to locate the next place you'll run to."

On dash after dash, between the chatter of automatic fire, the woods echo with the soldiers yelling, "I'm up, he sees me, I'm down!"

"There's nothing magical about small-unit tactics," Jan says, "but it's a core discipline of just about everything we do on deployment today. These guys will spend a lot of their time teaching this when they get to their groups. They'll teach it to Afghans, Iraqis, and Kuwaitis. They'll teach it in South America, Africa, Southwest Asia—all over the world. But before we get into small-unit tactics, we work on basic individual and squad movement."

After a day of movement drills, the two ODAs move on to squad tactics. There are variations and permutations, but as a small unit—a squad or a platoon—they move in three basic elements: A-team, B-team, and C-team. The A-team is usually the assault element and the C-team is the fire-support element. The B-team, with the squad leader or patrol leader, is the command-and-control element. The essence of small-unit tactics is the management and coordination of these three elements in a tactical environment. Under the watchful eyes of the cadre, the teams practice group movements, danger crossings, security halts, recons, assaults, fire support, and actions on the objective. They use hand, arm, and various recognition signals. Toward the end of the five-day field exercise, they are running ambush drills—again and again—and rotating squad members through leadership positions. For the Rangers and combat veterans like Dolemont, it's practice and review. For soldiers like Aaron Dunn who have come from a technical specialty, it's the first time they've seen this training.

After every tactical evolution, there is a critique. "All right," Sergeant Warner says to 812 while 811 runs a battle drill, "while they train and we watch, we can still learn." When 811 is finished, they are called in for a critique. "Give me three things eight-one-one did wrong," Warner tells 812, and the men do. "Now three things they did right." Again, the men in 812 offer their observations. "Now, eight-one-two, it's your turn. Let's go out there and make some *new* mistakes. Mistakes are OK, but don't make the same mistake twice. Eight-one-one, it's your turn to watch and learn."

While 812 prepares for the next drill, he turns to 811. "OK, think about what you did out there. What's the one thing we can do to overcome mistakes when the bullets start flying?" Sid Warner is a combat veteran from 5th Group and recently back from duty in Afghanistan. "Violence of action, right? So don't let the volume of fire slack off. Keep the pressure on the enemy; don't let him regroup. And talk it up; yell it out along the line. Once the shooting starts, there's no need for stealth—let the bad guys think there's a battalion of you out there. Winning a firefight is often a matter of gaining the initiative and maintaining the initiative."

When they return to their classroom in the meadow, three men have their weapons slung and chant in unison, "My weapon is slung because I almost killed my friend; my weapon is slung because I almost killed my friend." These men were inattentive in just where they pointed their rifles.

"Fratricide is something we all must work to prevent," Jan tells 811 and 812. "Muzzle control has to be a religion. You cannot point that weapon at one of your brothers—or yourself. Know where your barrel is at all times, and know the condition of your weapon—loaded or unloaded, bolt forward or to the rear, round in the chamber or not, safety on or off. Keep your finger off the trigger unless you're going to kill something. This is basic; you have to do the basics right—we won't move to the next block of training until you get this one right."

For five days, the two student ODAs run battle drill after battle drill, patrol after patrol, danger crossing after danger crossing, recon after recon, ambush after ambush—beginning at dawn and continuing until well after dark. Nearly all the training drills deal with security of movement, accountability, and communication. During movement to and from the bivouac area, training continues with cadre ranging out in front of the student patrols to ambush them with automatic-weapons fire and artillery simulators. At the bivouac area, the student ODAs set security, eat, clean and oil their weapons, reload their magazines with blank ammo, and try for a few hours sleep. They set up at a different location each night. It's usually well after midnight before they've settled in, and the bivouac area becomes a scattering of low poncho tents and Gortex-encased human forms that emanate a soft rumble of snoring. While they sleep, two men are always awake and on guard. For most of the nights during this initial field exercise of Phase II, it rains.

"These guys will work hard for the next four weeks, but we'll work even harder," Jan says with no trace of malice. "We get less sleep than the students. After they work a day and into the night, they can go to ground and get a little sleep. We have to spend time documenting the training and grading them. Who's proficient, and who needs work. Which of them are leading well, and which of them need to be put into more leadership roles. The Rangers and the men who are doing well, we try to let them polish their fieldcraft and try different techniques. A typical Phase II student ODA will have a range of abilities, and while we must train those who need it to an acceptable standard, we have to challenge those who are more accomplished."

After five wet days in the field, the student ODAs hump it back to the Rowe Training Facility and are given time to overhaul their gear, refit, and get a hot meal and a hot shower. Then, for the next several days, they train in and around the facility compound. Except for the initial briefing by the phase first sergeant and the phase company commander, there are no speeches or visits by seniors from higher commands—with one exception. On the morning following their return from the field, Class 1-05 crowds into one of the two large classrooms for an address by the 1st Special Warfare Training Group command sergeant major.

Command Sergeant Major Van Atkins, a bull of a man with twenty-eight years in the Army, is the senior enlisted man responsible for making Green Berets. He works directly for the group commander, Colonel Manny Diemer—or, as some of his subordinate battalion sergeant majors see it, Diemer works for him.

"Thanks for being here," Atkins tells the candidates of Class 1-05. "Thanks for wanting to be a Green Beret. How you guys holding up? They treating you all right out here?" There's a soft murmur of grumbling and chuckles. Atkins grins at them. "Training's hard, men; it's supposed to be hard. Not everyone can be a Green Beret, but you can. You all showed that when you were selected. Suck it up; make it happen. The Special Forces groups need you, and your nation needs you. Hell, I need you. Some of you are hurt, and most of you got a little cold and wet out there the last few days. Guys, this is as good as it gets. In the groups and on deployment, you will get less sleep, be colder, carry more, do more—and you know what? You'll have a helluva lot of fun doing it. Being a Green Beret is the greatest thing in the world. All my friends are Green Berets. I don't have any friends who are not Green Berets. I even wonder why I like my mother, because she's not a Green Beret."

"He's got a mother?" one of the candidates within my earshot whispers.

"Get through this, men," the group command sergeant major tells them. "Don't quit. If you quit, six hours later or six days later, you'll hate yourself for it. This is the best organization in the Army—in the world. So when it gets cold and you're hurting, drive on. We have to play with pain in Special Forces. If you're really hurt, get it fixed and get back into training—don't let a little owie become a big owie and get you medically dropped. This is serious stuff. Your nation is at war. All of you are going to war—if not with a Special Forces ODA team, then with some conventional unit. So if you're going to the fight, why not go with the best—where you can make the biggest contribution in fighting your nation's enemies. Think about it when you're hurting or it gets a little cold. I'm not gonna say good luck to you men—that's up to each one of you. Drive on."

Eight-one-one and the other student ODAs plow through classes on warning orders, operational orders, and a whole litany of standard tactical procedures. Often they're out in the field at night—a long patrol, an ambush, and a long walk back to the Rowe Training Facility. The class buses to Fort Bragg for a day of live shooting, a half day with M-9 Beretta pistols and a half day with their M4 rifles. They use the same M4s they've been carrying in the field without the blank firing adapters. On the live ranges, the Phase II students zero in their rifles and get a quick combat-rifle class with each man firing about 350 rounds. The pistol range, also a combat shooting range, allows for just over 300 rounds per man. During both combat shooting courses, those who are shooting well are moved quickly off the range, and the Army shooting instructors focus on those who are having problems. The class shoots for score only on the automated combat-rifle range. It is a very sophisticated range with human-sized targets that pop up at ranges from thirty to three hundred yards and records shooting scores electronically. Following training on the live shooting ranges, Class 1-05 is treated to one of the few breaks during a Phase II—a break for Thanksgiving. After completing a round of peer reviews, 811 and the other student ODAs are bused to Fort Bragg late on Wednesday. They're all back and in training Saturday morning after a two-day hiatus. While Phase II enjoys a break, this time off does not apply to the SFAS class in session at Camp Mackall. They drive on through the holiday. The Rowe Training Facility chow hall does, however, serve up a turkey dinner at the evening meal.

The Monday after Thanksgiving, the Phase II student ODAs are back out conducting more field training, which means more recons and ambushes. The field training falls into something of a pattern—or, from the candidates' perspective, a grind: three or four days in the field and two days back at the Rowe Training Facility for classroom work and to refit for the next field outing. In the field, they lay up for a portion of the day, usually in a draw where the vegetation is the heaviest and they can't be seen. They are damp and uncomfortable, but secure. During the rest of the day and most of the night, they're out training. Camp Mackall is a perfect venue for this, as there are numerous targets for training purposes: airfields, control towers, old locomotives and train cars, bunkers, buildings, bridges, compounds, and lots of old, disused military hardware—tanks, aircraft, and artillery pieces.

One full day of training is devoted to close-quarter battle, or CQB— fighting in enclosed spaces and conducting room-clearing drills. None of the 811's X-Rays have trained in this, nor has Sergeant Dunn, the radar tech. Under the watchful eye of Jan and Gary Courtland, 811 begins training in a sparsely wooded piece of ground not far from their team barracks. In a small clearing, there's an area marked off on the floor of the pine forest with two-by-fours. The wooden planks are laid out to simulate two rooms and two entryways. In twos, threes, and fours, variously constituted combat teams from 811 run room-clearing drill after room-clearing drill in this wall-less training area. Like mini SWAT teams, they approach the "door," M4 at the ready in one hand with the other hand on the shoulder of the man in front of them. They then burst through the door in a file, covering their designated areas of responsibility. Communication is essential in close-quarter combat.

"Clear left!"

"Clear right!"

"I'm moving!"

"Most of us have done this in one form or another," Captain Santos tells me on a break from the drills. "The Army has some pretty sophisticated CQB training facilities—some of them use paint guns and you get immediate feedback from opposing role players as you go from room to room. This is pretty basic, but it's still good training, especially for the guys who have never done it before. Even for guys like Dolemont who have done it for real down range, it's good to go through it again."

Eight-one-one moves from the two-by-four floor plan to a nearby

bunker for full-on room-clearing drills. Once they have shown proficiency in these drills, the whole ODA attacks the bunker as if it were
an enemy installation. The designated squad leader, also the B-team
leader, moves his men into position while his A-team and B-team leaders direct their elements. After a quick evaluation of the problem, the
squad leader sends his C-team to a fire-support position off to one
flank and puts his A-team into an assault line. The action is initiated
when the C-team opens up with the M240 followed by a base of sustained, measured automatic-weapons fire. The A-team assaults the
bunker, half of them bounding forward while the other half provides
supporting fire—just as they have done in so many previous drills. As
the assault team closes on the bunker, the C-team shifts fire off the
bunker, allowing the assaulters to close on the objective. It's organized
chaos with lots of automatic fire and yelling. Once at the bunker, the
squad leader moves up with his B-team and directs two of his men to
clear the bunker.

"OK, cease fire, cease fire!" Jan calls over the din. "Team leaders,
bring it in and let's talk about this." Soon the student ODA is gathered
around its cadre sergeant. "You're getting better, but I'm still not seeing the communication between the B- and C-team leaders. The order
to shift the supporting fire off the objective has to be given and
acknowledged before the assault element can move in on the target. I
know it's noisy, but you have to yell out and make yourself understood. The same goes for the two sections of the assault element—one
section firing while the other moves. It's that steady volume of supporting fire that is the key to effective fire and movement during an
assault. Now, let's do it again—same team assignments, only Altman,
you're now the B-team leader. Wagner, you're the A-team leader;
Sergeant Barstow, you have the C-team. Altman, take whatever time
you need to brief your squad, and let's get set up for another assault. I
want to see a steady volume of fire, and I want to hear lots of shouting.
OK, men, make it happen."

They drill all afternoon, pausing only for critiques, to reload, and to change leadership and team assignments. They break for an MRE and continue the drills well after dark. On one iteration, Gary Courtland fires on the team from a position near the bunker, forcing the squad leader to reform his A-team to deal with this new threat. Another time, Jan returns fire from the bunker, then poses as a wounded EPW during the assault phase. The team has to search and secure him after clearing the bunker.

"Dolemont."

"Here, Sergeant Janss."

"You conduct the critique. What went well, and what do we need to work on during the next drill?"

After the CQB training, the student ODAs prepare for another three days in the field. But before the Phase II ODAs go back out, they take a day for a parachute jump. The candidates are bused to the Luzon Drop Zone in Camp Mackall, where they draw parachutes and prepare for the drop. It's an equipment jump with full rucks and weapons. Military parachuting is time consuming and procedure driven; each "stick," or group of jumpers, has to be briefed and thoroughly checked by a jumpmaster. The C-130s land on the dirt strip, and the candidates waddle aboard. It takes the better part of a full day to get close to three hundred soldiers geared up, dropped, and recovered. For the X-Rays, it's the first time they've parachuted since jump school at Fort Benning. Class 1-05 is now twenty-two days into Phase II.

"How're they doing?" I ask Jan. The previous evening, he had counseled each of them and went over their peer reviews and peer rankings.

"Overall, they're doing fine. It's a strong group. The two officers are solid and Sergeant Hall's a very stable influence on the younger and less-experienced men. We in the cadre can only do so much through drills and exercises. They need to be talking to each other in the barracks and in their bivouacs out in the field—talking about what they did and how to improve when they go back out. They learn from each other as much as from us. Hall keeps them centered and focused. All of them are performing to standard with the exception of three—two of the X-Rays and one of the others."

Each man, Jan explains, has to move properly in a tactical environment and demonstrate individual skills during the drills—patrolling, proper fire discipline, fire and movement, CQB, EPW searches, safety, and the like. They have to show situational awareness in a tactical situation and move quickly and professionally under the direction of the team leaders. But they also have to lead. Each man has to display tactical leadership in the three key roles—squad or B-team leader, A-team leader, and C-team leader. In 811, three men have failed to do that to Sergeant Janss's satisfaction.

"During the next three days of fieldwork," Jan continues, "they'll all get a turn as team leaders, but I'll be focusing on the three who need the work. Last time out it was recons and ambushes. This time out it'll be recons and raids."

The skill set is much the same for a raid or an ambush. In an ambush, the target is moving, and the reconnaissance is primarily done to find a site suitable to attack the moving target. A good ambush site is one where the team leader can establish proper security and position his A- and C-teams to good advantage. The C-team needs a good field of fire to engage the enemy, and the A-team needs a concealed position from which it can conduct an assault once the C-team has the enemy under fire. The team leader and his B-team have to be in a position where they can initiate the action and control the ambush. In a raid, the target is stationary.

"In a raid, the reconnaissance is everything," Jan explains. "We compress the time frames here for training purposes, but to conduct a good raid, you want to observe the target for at least twenty-four hours before you make the hit. You want to study the activity around the target—sentries, guard posts, barbed wire or land-mine defenses, strong and weak points of the security, and so on. Then you want to plan your attack accordingly. There may be intelligence about an enemy reaction force nearby, which will limit your time on target—force you to make a rapid strike and clear off the target quickly. In a real situation, the patrol leader would lead a recon element to the target, then make his way back to a secure position to brief his team. For this training, we do it differently. There's no training value in guys sitting around waiting for the squad leader's return, so we'll send out two or three recon teams and have them work the target for twelve hours or so. Then we'll run three separate raid drills on a single target."

Eight-one-one has three targets on this field outing: an enemy base camp with a derelict helicopter parked nearby, a makeshift control tower near one of the parachute drop zones (DZs), and a cruise missile installation with an old Air Force Regulus cruise missile blocked up on a wooden cradle.

"What I'm looking for is tactical surprise and violence of action," Jan says as we stand off to one side to watch 811 attack the base camp. Dawn has just broken, and four role players with AK-47s sit at a campfire near two tents. The silence is shattered by the bark of the M240, followed by the chatter of the SAWs and the yelling of the assault team. We watch as 811 swarms into the base camp on a skirmish line, sets security, and begins to search the area and the downed EPWs. The radioman calls out the time every thirty seconds while the squad leader directs traffic. The C-team leader is the last man off target. It's his responsibility to get a count of every man in the squad. At that point, Jan calls a halt to the exercise play and the team circles up for an after-action critique. Virtually every training exercise is followed by an in-depth critique or after-action review.

Between targets, 811 rucks up and patrols to the new target location. They move carefully to a location four to five hundred yards from the target and set up a security position in a shallow draw, well hidden from view. The men dump their rucks, break out MREs, reload, and refit for the next raid. Depending on the timeline, they may or may not get a few hours sleep before the recon teams go out.

"So how's it going?" I ask Aaron Dunn as I slide my MRE, a beef stew this time, into its heater pouch. He's preparing a chicken entrée. It's early December, and evening temperatures head for the mid-thirties.

"Better, I think," Sergeant Dunn replies. "There's so much to learn, and when the raid or the ambush is initiated, you have to move and react. At first, I was very intimidated when I was a team leader, but I'm starting to feel better. I'm scheduled to be the A-team leader for this raid. The A-team leader has a lot of responsibility. The success of the assault is with him—with me."

Seated nearby, loading M4 magazines, is Tim Baker. "It's challenging all right, and you have to be thinking all the time, even when patrolling—where to step, what may happen next. You have to scan your area of responsibility, but you also have to know where the other guys are and keep alert for hand signals. During an assault, you have to do it all—move, think, react, and shoot. When we first learned this back in the preparation course and we did everything at a walk, it seemed so easy. Moving at full speed and at night, it takes all your concentration. I never thought I'd be able to do this so fast—especially when we're averaging about four hours' sleep."

"You have the C-team for this target, right?"

"That's right, sir. And I have the experience. I have Captain Santos on one SAW and Sergeant Hall on the other. Dolemont will be on the gun. Imagine me telling those guys what to do." The M240 machine gun is referred to simply as "the gun." The 240 fires a heavier-caliber bullet than the other squad weapons. Eight-one-one is quickly learning that their tactical success often comes down to getting the 240 in the most effective and advantageous position. It's the big dog in a small-unit action, both in the Q-Course and often down range in the real world.

As ODA 811 works its way through the raid and recon portion of the fieldwork, the four Rangers are very seldom put in leadership positions. Sergeant Janss has seen enough of them, in their briefing skills as well as their tactical leadership, that he is satisfied. Now he wants to see the less-experienced men in leadership roles. Often, he will isolate the 811 Rangers so as to force the team leaders to direct other members of the squad who may be as inexperienced as themselves.

On the last evening, I catch Captain Matt Anderson during a quiet moment waiting for darkness to fall. We are down in yet another draw—well concealed, but it is cold and wet.

"How does this training compare with what you did in Ranger School?" I ask.

Anderson considers this. "In some ways, we're learning a lot more here because we go quickly from scenario to scenario. Every day there are multiple opportunities for tactical execution as a team. In Ranger School, we covered much more ground between missions—sometimes it seemed like we walked for days between an operation."

"Is it as hard?"

Again, he pauses before answering. "We're not finished yet, but so far, this is not physically as hard. Ranger School is all about long-range patrols with little or no sleep. In Ranger School, you go until you hit the wall, and then you keep going. But if you weren't in a leadership role, it was just a long slog. On balance, I think you learn more about small-unit tactics here in Phase II, but you learn more about yourself in Ranger School."

"You've been in the Army a while and more than a few Army schools. What do you think of SF training so far?"

"Hey, sir, this is awesome." Anderson gives me his patented, infectious grin. "We lucked out drawing Sergeant Janss as a cadre sergeant. He's a great teacher. The guys are all working hard, and they don't want to disappoint him. Past the basics of small-unit tactics, there are a lot of different ideas and techniques. For those of us who pretty much have the basics down, he allows us to improvise and try new things. We're all learning, especially the newer guys."

The Phase II cadre sergeants all run their student ODAs a little differently. Some are more hands on and more regimented. As I roam about the various training venues, I watch a few of the other cadre sergeants work their teams with more of a heavy hand. If they are unhappy with the conduct of a raid, an ambush, or a patrol, they take remedial action—sometimes almost punitive in nature—as they run basic drills on the spot to correct the deficiency. Sergeant First Class Janss is a pure teacher, but he demands that his candidates perform. When he sees something that's not right, he calls a halt to the training and holds a class. "Let's get this right, gentlemen," I hear him say on more than one occasion, sometimes at night in a cold rain, "because we are going to stay out here until we get it right." Even when he is displeased with the performance of his students, I never hear Jan raise his voice.

The student ODAs return to the Rowe Training Facility after their recon and raid field training during the second week of December, late on day twenty-six of the thirty-five-day course. At this time, each individual in the class is evaluated: Which men have performed to standard, which men have yet to demonstrate that performance, and which men appear unsuitable for future training? Attrition in Class 1-05 to this stage has been modest but ongoing. A few soldiers withdraw because of medical, personal, and, on occasion, family-related issues. Some are involuntarily withdrawn because of safety issues, gross underperformance, and suitability considerations. Though the phase is well past the halfway point, a midcourse review board is convened after the raid and recon fieldwork. This board considers those phase candidates who have been identified by the cadre as clearly failing to meet phase standards. The board disposes of these candidates in three basic ways. A candidate can be relieved or removed from training, and made eligible for reassignment to another Army unit. Such a candidate may leave with a recommendation that he return for a future try at the Q-Course, or not. Second, a candidate can be recycled, which means he'll leave Class 1-05 and return to Phase II with Class 2-05. This is usually done for medical reasons or when a candidate has to miss more than a day or two of training for a family issue or emergency. Third, a candidate can be recommended for reassessment. From my ODA, 811, PFC Jamie Wagner is sent to the midcourse review board because he has failed to show an acceptable level of performance.

"I sent him to the board with a recommendation for reassessment," Jan says. "Perhaps he can show the reassessment cadre something he hasn't shown me. He's a hard worker and I know he's holding nothing back, but right now, he lacks the situational awareness needed for small-unit operations. He's confused out there; at best, he can only do what he's told. He's yet to demonstrate the ability to take charge and direct his teammates in a fast-moving tactical situation."

As the board, which is similar to that of the SFAS selection board, sorts through Class 1-05, there's a growing number of candidates gathering in the holding area outside the classroom where the board conducts its deliberations. When they are finished, eighteen candidates join PFC Wagner in the reassessment group. There's an even mix of X-Rays and veteran soldiers. Only one of them is an officer. For those eighteen, their chances of continuing in Special Forces training are still alive. The board also relieves nineteen candidates from Phase II. They are no longer members of Class 1-05 and are bused back to Fort Bragg. Two candidates with minor medical problems are recommended for recycle in Phase II Class 2-05.

"This is a tough cut," Sergeant Major Frank Zorn tells me after the midcourse board adjourned. "A lot of dreams end at the Phase II midcourse board. For the men in the reevaluation squad, it's their last chance. They're still having problems with small-unit tactics, and it would be wrong to send them forward. But each has shown us something, and all of them have the desire. They've come a long way, and we owe them another look before we make a final decision. For most, it's a proficiency issue. The guys with bad attitudes or who have character issues or who are physically weak have gone away. For the most part, these guys're giving it their best shot, but they're just not cutting it."

I notice one soldier with Wagner and the others who has a large coil of climbing rope draped over his torso. One end is tied to his belt and the other to his rifle. I ask Zorn about this. He chuckles and shakes his head.

"That kid is something of a story."

"Sergeant Major, that's why I'm here—for the stories."

"That's Specialist Scott. We saw him at the board during assessment and selection. He was having problems then, and he's still having them. He's prone to get a little too far from his rifle, and the rope is to remind him to stay close to his gun. He's also having problems in the field. But he has a talent, and we'd like to keep him if at all possible. Scott came to us from Germany; he was a truck driver, and he's fluent in German. At the SFAS board, his personal statement said he spoke Russian. One of the board members was a Russian speaker, and he and Scott carried on a lively conversation in Russian. Scott also claimed he spoke Arabic, and he did—almost without an accent. I ask him how it was he spoke Arabic. 'When I was in Germany,' he told the board, 'I watched a lot of TV.' So I asked, what's that got to do with it? 'Sergeant Major,' he says, 'I watched Al Jazeera.' "

Two senior instructors are assigned to the retraining detachment along with an experienced contractor. The detachment is formed up in a single retraining ODA and given a crash course in basic small-unit tactics. After a few hours in the classroom, the ODA returns to the field for tactical reevaluation.

"This was one of the toughest assignments I've had since I became an instructor," one of the retraining cadre sergeants told me of the assignment. "We had to give each of them a chance to succeed, to prove they had sufficient command of small-unit tactics to remain in the training pipeline. They had to show us they can lead well and they can follow well. When it was over, they were exhausted and I was exhausted."

The other student ODAs—including ODA 811, with its remaining twelve soldiers—start preparing for their final field training exercise. "This training exercise is designed to sharpen their skills and to challenge them in different tactical scenarios," Jan explains. "At this stage of the game, those who remain are pretty much good to go unless they really screw up or are careless about safety. We put a lot of time and effort into this final exercise, and we ask the student ODAs to, within the constraints of the exercise, play it for real—to improvise and use their imagination to get the job done. When a Special Forces ODA is on their game in a tactical environment, they're like jazz musicians. They know the basics, and they know each other. This allows them to change or modify their tactics to better deal with a mission objective. They can do this quickly, often without conversation—with a hand signal or a nod of the head. This is where our small-unit tactics differ from those taught at Ranger School. Up until now, we have expected them to go pretty much by the book. We don't necessarily want them to abandon the basics, but we want them to use their initiative and creativity to get the job done. This exercise is designed to allow for a variety of tactical applications and for them to show us some resourcefulness."

The day before the final exercise is a Sunday. Every day is a training day, in the field or at the Rowe Training Facility, but if the class is training at the compound on a Sunday, an evening chaplain service is held for those who wish to attend. It's a nondenominational service conducted by an Army chaplain from Fort Bragg. This Sunday, thirty-five candidates of Class 1-05 elect to attend the service. Five are from 811. The chaplain, a Presbyterian by ordination, welcomes the soldiers at the door of the classroom. The service begins with hymns as requested by the soldiers attending the service. As it's mid-December, we move on to some Christmas carols. The chaplain is a short, kindly mannered major with a beautiful baritone voice. Following the singing, he asks if anyone would like a special remembrance in prayer for others. There are several—for family members, pregnant wives, sick relatives, lost comrades, and comrades in harm's way. The chaplain then delivers a ten-minute sermon on helping others and being a good friend—it's a vanilla discourse, but there is sincerity and even a touch of passion in his voice. He then offers communion to the group, a generic wafer symbolic of the sacrament of their particular faith. The service ends with a closing hymn. I seldom go to church, but I thoroughly enjoyed this service. It was a first for me, praying in the company of warriors, and I was very moved by it.

I came away with a thin, paper-laminate booklet titled *Soldiers'*

Book of Worship. It contains a short section of Catholic, Protestant, and Jewish prayers, a generous number of hymns, statements of faith, and a section devoted to support of the dying. The statements of faith include the Protestant, Catholic, and Jewish persuasions, along with the Five Pillars of Islam and a statement of Muslim beliefs. In the section for the dying, there's a prayer for a Muslim soldier. It asks whoever reads that prayer to stand facing Mecca, if possible. How strange, I thought. Here I am, reading the prayer for a dead or dying Muslim soldier at a U.S. military Christian/Jewish service on an American Special Forces training base. My cynical self wonders if a prayer for a dying Christian soldier, let alone a dying Jewish soldier, was in any Muslim book of worship at an al-Qaeda training base or some Saudi madrassa training the next generation of suicide bombers.

The service is mostly attended by veteran soldiers, but there are a few X-Rays like Kendall and Altman. When we return to the 811 team hut, I find Dolemont in the squad bay, tipped back in a metal folding chair with his boots parked on a table, reading a Bible.

Eight-one-one has spent most of Sunday overhauling its personal gear, cleaning weapons, and preparing for the final exercise. The men will be in the field for four days and will carry everything they will need for the training. This time they will be working in one of the training areas on the western edge of Fort Bragg proper. Earlier that afternoon, Sergeant Stan Hall was tasked with the first mission. After the chaplain's service, he gives his warning order. It's a very slick and concise, by the *Ranger Handbook* briefing. Following a roll call, Hall pushes through brief statements of the situation as it relates to enemy forces and the commander's intent, the mission they've been given, and his concept of mission execution. He makes his assignment of team leaders—Byron O'Kane will have the A-team and Antonio Costa will lead the C-team. Then there are assigned equipment lists. Each man carries between five hundred and eight hundred rounds of ammunition, depending on his weapon and assigned team equipment. Team equipment assignments include shoulder-fired rockets, radios, first-aid kits, demolitions, time fuse, claymore mines, 40mm grenades, and an enemy-prisoner-of-war kit with handcuffs and blindfolds. The list goes on. Hall also assigns duties within his ODA—radioman, point man, designated compass man, designated pace man, EPW handlers, and so on. He also makes assignments regarding who is to handle various portions of the operations order. Then the team goes to work. Each man has personal and team gear to prepare and pack, and information to prepare for the operations order—the permission briefing, sometimes called the patrol leader's order. The patrol order is set for 0800 the following morning. Eight-one-one will be up most of the night making preparations. I ask Jan why he had put Sergeant Hall in charge and not one of the newer men.

"Sergeant Hall is a good briefer—a very thorough briefer. I wanted the younger men to see it done right. There is a lot of training value for them to see it done well."

At 0800, their rucks, about ninety pounds per man, are lined up along the wall of the equipment bay, and the men are in cammies and wearing fully loaded combat vests. Hall again calls the roll and checks with each man to ensure his personal and team equipment is ready and good to go. After a time hack, he begins the formal operations order.

"All right guys, listen up. This will be your briefing for Target 001, the ambush of a foot patrol at grid 5211, 8693." He turns to a map on the wall. "It's a bend in a stretch of unimproved road between these two intersections right here. Everyone got that?"

There's a rustle of activity as each man finds the target on his map. They've rehearsed this, and all of them have that section of the map neatly folded in their map cases with an acetate overlay of the target area. They're all on the same sheet of music. For the next two hours, Sergeant Hall directs the detailed operational briefing that is the patrol leader's order. He directs the team members to synchronize their watches, then calls on Tim Baker to brief them on the weather conditions. Roberto Pantella gives an overview of the terrain features and vegetation; Antonio Costa gives a breakdown of the enemy forces in the objective area.

"OK, everyone, stand up," Hall calls out to his team. "Roll heads left, now to the right, now everybody run in place." There is pounding of boots on the worn linoleum floor for about thirty seconds. "That's enough, guys. So, we're all awake. Now let's talk about the mission and how we plan to execute it. Everyone gather around the terrain models and pay close attention."

The two sand tables have been sculpted into scale models, one of the objective area and the other, a larger scale, of the target area. With a pointer, Sergeant Hall takes them over the key points and danger areas of the operation. "We'll insert by helo here. If we take fire on the way in, the pilot will clear off the insertion point away from the direction of the enemy fire, and if we're airworthy, we'll abort the mission. If we crash, we set up standard security and call in the backup helo for extraction. If we take fire after we're on the ground and the helo clears off, we'll abort the mission and move to coordinates 5360, 8602 and call for extraction. These coordinates will also serve as a rally point if we are separated on the ground and have to abandon the insertion point."

Following his briefing format, Hall covers the key points on the way to the objective, at the objective, and on the way to the extraction point. He details actions at danger points, actions at road crossings, actions at rally points, actions at a patrol base, actions on the objective, actions on clearing the objective area, and actions at the exfiltration site. He walks the team through the mission from the time they have boots on the ground until they are recovered.

"Questions?" Sergeant Hall asks. There are none. Eight-one-one stares back at him through bleary eyes. They're all going into the field with very little sleep. "OK, Ranger Altman will give the command-and-signal portion of the briefing." Altman brightens at being addressed as a Ranger, which he is not. He steps to the front of the room and reviews the standard hand and arm signals that 811 has used over the past several weeks. He then goes over each radio, the call signs they will use, and their assigned frequencies. Hall again takes over, checking his watch.

"OK, it's now 1037. I want everyone freshly cammied up, rucked up, and mustered outside for inspection at 1100."

The team members blacken their faces and help each other ruck up. Tim Baker, who's the assistant 240 gunner with the machine-gun tripod, carries a ruck of just over a hundred pounds. In accordance with operational security doctrine, the men sanitize the briefing bay, scrubbing the whiteboards and destroying the sand-table terrain models. Outside the hut, Sergeant O'Kane inspects his A-team, Specialist Costa the C-team, and Sergeant Hall inspects them all. The student ODA then files over to a designated training area near their barracks, where the men rehearse actions at danger crossings and actions at the objective. Eight-one-one then test-fires its weapons and returns to the main compound where its helo, a four-by-four truck, is waiting. The men board this notional helo in the reverse order they will exit the truck. Then they rehearse the helo insertion, leaving the back of the truck in orderly fashion and moving quickly into a security perimeter. The men of 811 can now do these things in their sleep, and they're not far from just that. These are very tired soldiers. Early afternoon, they make their helo/truck insertion and begin their patrol to the objective area. Jan halts them a short distance from the insertion point.

"OK, men, bring it in." Eight-one-one gathers around their cadre sergeant. "Sergeant Hall, that was an excellent briefing. I liked the conduct of your inspection and the rehearsals. For you newer men, take note of this. Inspections and rehearsals are important. I know you're tired and there's a tendency to take shortcuts, but don't. That's part of being a professional—doing the routine and mundane tasks again and again. When you do this for real, on deployment, you'll often have had less sleep than you had last night and the last few weeks. We train like we fight, and that means doing it when our butts are dragging." Turning back to Hall, he says, "You're done, Sergeant." Then he says to Captain Santos, "Sir, you're the patrol leader for the first mission. Take a few minutes with your team and let's drive on."

The first mission is still a roadside ambush of a foot patrol—something they've done many times. Santos leads them to a secure position above the road and moves forward with O'Kane and two others for a closer look at the ambush site. A short time later he returns, briefs the team, and they move up to a rally point, a small clearing a hundred meters from the ambush site, where they dump their rucks. Normally, two men would remain behind to provide security for the team's equipment, but there's nothing to be learned by watching the rucks. With Jan's approval, Santos takes the entire team to the ambush site. First he sets his left- and right-side security elements—two men each to guard the flanks and notify Santos if or when there is movement on the road. The security elements each have an AT4 rocket launcher so they can engage enemy armor should it appear. Santos then sets in the gun. He sites the M240 with a good field of fire in the direction of an approaching enemy squad. Tom Kendall sets up on the gun with Tim Baker laying out ammo. Then the two of them begin to gather brush and foliage to camouflage their positions. It's now midafternoon with plenty of daylight, so they take special care to remain hidden. A short distance away, Santos places Byron O'Kane and his A-team in a position where they are well concealed, but can quickly assault the kill zone of the ambush. It's a classic L-shaped setup, with the A- and C-teams forming the L. Santos places himself between his gun team and his assault team and then they wait, as do Jan and I down on the road, but well outside the kill zone.

Twenty minutes later, five role players in black uniforms, khaki field coats, and AK-47 rifles come wandering along the road. When they enter the kill zone, they're cut down by a withering volley of blank automatic-weapons fire. On Santos's order, the A-team sweeps through the kill zone and quickly searches the dead enemy bodies. Amid all the shouting and shooting, David Altman calls out the elapsed time at thirty-second intervals. It's a hit-and-run mission and speed on target is essential. The weapons and equipment taken from the dead enemy soldiers are dumped in a pile; Captain Santos calls in his security elements from either flank. The squad melts into the roadside foliage in a security perimeter. Sergeant Aaron Dunn places a dummy block of C-4 explosive on the collected guns and gear. Santos nods at him.

"Fire in the hole!" Dunn calls out and pulls the fuse igniter. "Fire in the hole!" the team echoes.

"Burning!" Dunn yells as he checks his firing assembly to ensure the time fuse is burning properly.

"OK, Sergeant O'Kane," Santos orders, "take us out of here." O'Kane sends Dan Barstow, the A-team point man, off on a pre-arranged direction from the ambush site. The rest of the team follow in squad order, with Costa counting everyone off the target to ensure that no one is left behind.

"OK, men," Jan calls after them, "hold it up, and let's bring it in again." Sergeant Janss holds a critique session that includes input from the risen-from-the-dead role players. He asks Santos, O'Kane, and Costa what they think they could have done better—what their teams could have done better. From my perspective, it was a textbook setup and execution. "There was one point where the volume of fire died off," Jan tells them. "You can't slack off and give them time to recover—you stick it to them and you keep sticking it to them. But overall, it was a good ambush. Your time on target by my watch was four and a half minutes. That's excellent." He consults his notepad, tears off a sheet, and hands it to Matt Anderson. "Captain Anderson, you're now the patrol leader. Kendall, you take the A-team and Altman, you have the C-team leader. These are your next coordinates. You need to be there no later than 2000. At that location, you will be met by a friendly agent who will give you further direction. How's your commo with the cadre base station?"

"We have good commo, Sergeant," Anderson replies.

"Good. Take a few minutes to sort yourself out and shift around your equipment, then head out to the linkup point with your contact."

"Roger that, Sergeant."

"And good luck. Make me proud."

"Roger that, Sergeant."

The role players walk back to a Humvee they had parked in the woods a few hundred meters away. They'll return to the cadre base camp set up on the edge of Fort Bragg's Nijmegen Drop Zone to await their next stroll through the kill zone of this ambush site. Sergeant Janss makes his way back across the piece of terrain that 811 just covered. A few hundred meters off one of the main roads, Gary Courtland has pitched a tent and set up a small camp. He and Jan will alternately work the ambush scenario. Later that evening, shortly after Jan links up with Courtland, another student ODA finds them. That team is given its mission and the ambush site coordinates, and the ODA sets off with Courtland following it. He and Sergeant Janss will make the trek to and from that same ambush-site scenario many times over the next three days, watching student ODAs kill the same role players and conducting after-action critiques.

Eight-one-one continues its operational odyssey. It takes the men about two hours to reach the grid coordinates Jan gave them. There, in the fading light, they find a tent and a man sipping coffee by a fire. It's cold but clear, with the temperature scheduled to dip well into the mid-thirties. The student ODA quietly sets up security with the man and the area around the tent well covered by team gunners. Captain Anderson and Specialist Kendall then approach the man by the fire. He's in the role of a Pinelander, someone sympathetic to the Americans but very wary. They exchange greetings, and the man tells them about an enemy installation he has seen that serves as an ammunition resupply depot. He shows Anderson and Kendall where it is on the map. Anderson questions him carefully about the terrain, the type of installation, and guard-force activity. Once back with the team, Anderson checks in by radio with his command element at the Nijmegen base camp. He's ordered by the base commander to attack the supply depot, 811's second target, at first light.

Matt Anderson leads 811 away from the Pinelander's camp a few hundred meters, where they go on another security halt. There he makes his way around the perimeter, briefing his men in twos and threes. "Here's the deal," he whispers to them. "We have a raid target that's about five klicks [five kilometers, or five thousand meters] east of here. I plan to cover as much ground as we can while we have some light. When we get to the target area, we'll set up a patrol base this side of the target and do the recon. Our scheduled hit time is at first light. The same standard procedures and signals remain in effect. Let's get ready to move out."

Eight-one-one moves into its patrol base shortly after midnight. The men set out security and begin to rotate the personnel on watch, while the others get a few hours of sleep. Anderson, Kendall, Dolemont, and Baker get no sleep. They go forward to conduct the recon of the target. They move around the target, making observations and taking notes. The sentry role players at the ammo depot don't get much sleep, either, as they man a guard post and perform roving security duties for the benefit of the student raiders moving silently out in the bush. Anderson leaves Baker and Dolemont with a squad radio to keep eyes-on the target while he and Kendall return to the patrol base to brief 811 on their target. Well before dawn, they return to the target site and dump their rucks. Then Anderson goes about the business of placing his C-team in a good fire-support position and his A-team in a good assault position. They move carefully and quietly in the predawn darkness. Before the sun is up, the bark of the 240 shatters the dawn. Moments later, the 811 A-team swarms over the enemy ammo depot like a medieval plague. When the site is secure, it becomes a cataloging-and-destruction exercise. There are boxes of ammunition and shipping crates of rifles, rockets, and claymore mines. Anderson directs the inventory of the cache, and then 811 rigs ordnance for demolition.

After Sergeant First Class Warner, the cadre sergeant at the ammo depot target, gives them an after-action critique, 811 gets a new set of coordinates. Then Sergeant Warner, based on written instructions from Sergeant Janss, makes leadership changes and releases 811 to continue its journey. None of the men in 811 know how many targets they have before them or even how many days they will be in the field. They do know this is the twenty-ninth day of their thirty-five-day Phase II training. All they can do is patrol to their next set of coordinates and radio in for instructions. With Hall and 811's two officers finished with their leadership duties, the X-Rays begin to take their turns as patrol leader. Specialist Kendall assumes duties as the patrol leader for the third target, a raid on an enemy radio-relay site. At this target, there is a designated time for the attack, and the team is given intelligence that a courier with sensitive information is to visit the site around noon. Kendall has to get his men in place and be prepared to initiate his attack when the courier arrives. Eight-one-one works the target area in a steady downpour. At 1155, a cadre sergeant arrives in a pickup truck, only to be shot to pieces as 811 makes its assault.

At this target, 811 has some problems. The communication between Kendall and the C-team is not what it should be, and the base of fire from the C-team is poorly coordinated with the A-team's assault. As a result, two of the enemy at the site escape and run off into the woods. Kendall sends Hall and Santos to track them down. The senior cadre sergeant at the radio-relay target covers all this in the after-action critique.

"I don't have to tell you that you had poor coordination with your fire-support element," the cadre sergeant tells them as we stand around a large fire at the target site. "That's why you have to have an alternate method of communication if, as it happened here, your squad radio fails. Now, two of the bad guys ran off when you made your assault. This can happen. So what do you do? Let them go? Chase them down? Chasing after them can be very dangerous—they know the lay of the land and you don't. Shoot them? Very soon, you're going to be operating in a reality-based world, not a school-solution world. Every shoot/no-shoot decision is driven by tactical imperatives and the area situation. Is the guy who runs just a scared dude? Does he represent a future tactical threat? Is he an al-Qaeda leader? Will killing this guy serve the mission or simply make insurgents of his extended family? These are life-and-death decisions, and you guys are going to be making them for real. Are you with me here?"

Eight-one-one's patrol to the target area, the target recon, the setup, the attack, the chasing down of enemy soldiers, and the after-action critique are all made in a December downpour. The ODA, the cadre sergeants, the role players, and the writer are all soaked to the skin. "OK, guys," the cadre sergeant tells 811, "you're on your own time. When you're sufficiently dry and warm, let's get back at it." Then the exercise continues.

Specialist Costa is the patrol leader for the fourth target, the recovery of an injured NGO (nongovernmental organization) worker. The worker, an International Red Cross employee, is in the hands of mountain tribesmen who are camped near the edge of a pine forest. They're bandits, so the environment is semipermissive, which means not totally hostile. Costa sets out two sniper elements to cover the camp while he and PFC Baker approach the tribesmen to negotiate for the release of the NGO worker. It takes a show of force and a promise of future payment to gain the release of the worker.

The fifth target finds them. Private First Class Pantella is leading 811 to the next set of coordinates when his point man spots a vehicle and a file of enemy soldiers heading their way. The team quickly sets a hasty ambush and engages them. After the firefight, the exercise becomes a drill in searching the EPWs and the vehicle for sensitive information. As on all the other missions on this final field exercise, the target cadre sergeant holds an after-action critique. Eight-one-one is doing a lot of things right, but there's always some aspect of the mission or the engagement that could have been better. The learning never stops.

From my perspective, I'm very impressed with the time and attention given to these training scenarios. Some role players are soldiers from Fort Bragg awaiting the start of their SF training, or former SF candidates recovering from injuries acquired in a previous class who will return to training when they are healed. Others are volunteers from various SOF and non-SOF units based at Bragg. They work hard; it's not easy being a target, nor is it all that pleasant getting roughed up in an EPW personnel search. I'm able to get out to see a few other student ODAs working in this training area. I try to be objective, but they don't seem quite as proficient or as professional as 811. But then, 811 is my team. It could be I'm just a little biased.

The sixth target is another raid, but with a twist. The target tasking is again radioed to them. It is a small enemy base camp that is reported to hold an American POW. Sergeant Dunn, the former radar technician, is the patrol leader. Dunn puts his team in security perimeter and sends out two recon teams to observe the target. In the remaining daylight, they observe the camp and the security patterns, and identify the small cage where the captured POW, a downed pilot, is being held. Back at the security position, Dunn briefs his team; the plan is to set a sniper overwatch and move the gun to a support position where their field of fire can bear on the small guard force but away from the caged American. A sniper overwatch calls for a good shooter to be in a position where he can protect his teammates who have to assault the target. The fire support and assault have to be choreographed to cut the prisoner away from his captors. Eight-one-one does its job, and after the chaos of the raid, a dazed former POW in a tattered flight suit, supported between Sergeant Barstow and Captain Anderson, is bustled away from the camp. A few hundred meters from the target, the cadre sergeant gives them their after-action critique and a new set of coordinates.

Target seven, another radio tasking, is yet another cache. Private First Class Tim Baker is the patrol leader, and they reach the site well after dark. The role players are two civilians who have a large store of equipment, all from U.S. military stocks. They are black marketeers. Baker and his A-team leader, Sergeant Daniel Barstow, are able to get close—it's a dark night with drizzle on and off, and the camp is well lit by a large fire. After his fire support and sniper overwatch are set, Baker and Barstow hail the camp and walk in, weapons slung. They pretend to be hunters, and Barstow plays the role of a drunk. They want to buy supplies, but the black marketeers want too much money. An argument breaks out, and Baker signals his team; the two pretend hunters drop to the ground, and 811 quickly assaults the camp. Sergeant Stan Hall leads the search team as they take inventory and prepare the cached materials for demolition. He finds a booby trap, a wire tied to a hidden smoke-grenade spoon. Hall is the only candidate to find and disarm it; all the other student ODAs find it the hard way. Meanwhile, Dolemont finds a cadre pickup truck stashed in a nearby ravine. He pulls into the camp to extract the team. The senior site cadre applauds Dolemont's initiative, but makes him surrender the pickup. Eight-one-one gets a very positive after-action critique and moves on to target eight. Unbeknownst to them, it's their last target.

Specialist David Altman is the leader for target eight. It is a long patrol to the final objective. This is their fourth day in the field. They've walked about twenty-two miles, not including all the reconnaissance movement in and around the targets. It's rained most of the time, and the one night that it was clear, the temperature dropped close to freezing. While they've not been told as much, 811 senses this is its last target. Just before midnight, 811 is met by a good old boy with a shotgun and a bluetick hound. Playing the role of a Pinelander who is out hunting, he tells Altman about a group of bad guys who are camped at the site of a plane crash. He says they are holding an American captive. Altman radios this information into their commander and is told to recover the pilot and retrieve a black box aboard the aircraft. Eight-one-one finds the crash site and spends most of the night preparing for a dawn assault. This is a difficult target. The crash site is the fuselage of an old Navy S-2 Tracker—a carrier-based antisubmarine aircraft. It's anyone's guess how this aircraft got to this training site on Fort Bragg. Near the aircraft, there's a campfire and a man in a flight suit tied to a chair. Men with AK-47s roam about the site on an irregular basis. The preassault reconnaissance also identifies a spider hole in which one of the security guards is hiding. Altman briefs 811, breaking his ODA into fire support, assault, search, and POW-handling teams. At dawn of their fifth day in the field, they make their move on the crash site. The POW handlers manage to creep close to the pilot before the shooting begins, which is a diversion away from the captive's location. They toss out smoke grenades and make a dash to secure the pilot and spirit him away. The assault team deals with the guard force, including the man in the spider hole. All goes well until the search team, led by PFC Pantella, finds the black box inside the aircraft. It's booby-trapped, and they set it off—a smoke grenade that quickly drives them from the interior of the hulk. Still, 811 was one of the few teams to successfully recover the pilot. After the critique, the team moves to its last set of coordinates. It's a familiar location; it's where they were inserted. They are bone tired, but they move in good tactical order. And their spirits are good; they're headed for the extraction site with the prospect of hot chow and a hot shower in the not-too-distant future.

Eight-one-one is one of the better student ODAs in Class 1-05. This is not just my observation; the cadre working the eight final targets agree. Like most of the other student ODA cadre sergeants, Jan made the patrol-leader assignments but let the senior leadership run the squad. He has a lot of confidence in Sergeant Hall, Specialist Dolemont, and the two officers. While this final field exercise is a chance for the student ODAs to lock down their Special Forces tactical skill set, it's also a report card of sorts for the cadre sergeants. Their pride is on the line. Whose guys are good, and whose are not so good? Whose student ODAs can be innovative in a tactical environment and whose are capable of little more than a rote execution of the basic skills? By late Saturday afternoon, day thirty-two of the training, all the student ODAs are back at the Rowe Training Facility.

For 811, the final days of Phase II are taken with gear overhaul, weapons cleaning, and a full inventory of sensitive items—specifically, the radios and night-observation devices. One morning before breakfast, there's a final round of training in unarmed combat. In a frosty corner of the Rowe Training Facility, the ODAs circle up and take turns with one man in the middle. The soldier in the arena has to fend off attack after attack, using the techniques the men have learned during the phase— breaking choke holds and slipping out of headlocks. They pull their punches and kicks, but there are still a few bruises and bloody noses. Back in the team hut, 811 completes a final round of peer evaluations. On day thirty-four, Jan spends fifteen minutes to a half hour with each man, reviewing his performance—his strong and weak points, and his ranking within the ODA. For the twelve men in 811, training is over. They will move on to Phase III. For Captains Anderson and Santos, they'll begin the 18 Alpha officer course, which will prepare them to be unconventional-warfare planners and foreign-internal-defense specialists. The enlisted men will start the specialty training that will qualify them for their individual Special Forces military occupational specialty, or MOS.

PFC Tim Baker, Specialist Antonio Costa, Specialist Tom Kendall, and PFC Roberto Pantella will all begin 18 Bravo training to become Special Forces weapons sergeants. Sergeants Aaron Dunn and Daniel Barstow are off to train as 18 Charlies, Special Forces engineering sergeants. Sergeant Stan Hall, Sergeant Byron O'Kane, and Specialist Frank Dolemont will all attend the 18 Delta course to become Special Forces medics. Specialist David Altman alone will train to become an 18 Echo, a Special Forces communications sergeant. The MOS training assignments are made at the end of Phase II based on the needs of the Special Forces groups, the aptitude of the soldier, and his stated preference. All of the MOS training, except for the 18 Deltas, will last some twelve weeks. Combat-medic training is a twelve-month course. Most of the billets for 18 Delta training are reserved for the regular soldiers, men who have invested enough time in the Army to be considered career soldiers. A few of the X-Rays from Class 1-05 will attend the Special Forces medic training, but most are those who have had prior medical training.

Day thirty-five is when the commander's review board convenes. Appearing before the board are the men who underwent retraining and reassessment while the rest of Class 1-05 conducted the final field problems. There are also a few men who did so poorly during the final exercise that their performance will be addressed by the board. As with the previous boards, the candidate's training packets are closely reviewed, and the cadre sergeants speak to the performance of each man. At this stage of the game, there are no psychologists present, and there is little discussion about a man's potential; they talk mainly about his performance and his character. Then the candidate is brought before the board, questioned, and allowed to speak to his performance. His fate may be determined at that time, or the board may ask him to step outside while they deliberate. The board, identical to the midcourse board, is chaired by the battalion commander, Lieutenant Colonel Jim Jackson. His battalion command sergeant major, Frank Zorn, and his phase company commander, Captain John Block, are seated to his right and left. Close by are the phase first sergeant, Stew Donnally, and Sergeant Major Rick Martin, from Phase IV. Since most of the board's work addresses candidates in the reassessment detail, those cadre sergeants who ran the retraining ODA are on their feet a great deal, speaking to the performance or nonperformance of those soldiers.

This board takes their work *very* seriously, perhaps more seriously than the Phase I board that selected or deselected marginal candidates. After Phase II, the attrition in Special Forces drops off dramatically. Most of the enlisted men finishing Phase II will become Special Forces soldiers. For the officers heading to Phase III, there is more attrition ahead. So the Phase II board process—the midcourse and final review boards—is an important cut. This is especially true for those men who have just been given one more chance in the reassessment ODA. The discussion among the board and the cadre sergeants is spirited, to say the least. Special Forces cadre sergeants have no problem speaking their minds to battalion commanders and command sergeant majors. At one point, the debate over a candidate became so heated, I had to excuse myself and leave the room. I felt this was strictly in-house business. As an outsider, I can't comment on the merit of their findings, but one thing was clear: These professionals are passionate in their commitment to select the right men, and only the right men, for this very important job.

Of the eighteen men granted a reprieve in the reassessment ODA, only one man was sent forward to Phase III. PFC Jamie Wagner, Specialist Scott, and the single captain were relieved from the course. But Specialist Scott and his marvelous knack for languages were not lost to Army special operations. Sergeant Major Zorn took him to Fort

Bragg, and introduced him to the 3rd Battalion command sergeant major, the senior NCO in charge of psyops and civil-affairs training.

Of the 341 officers and enlisted men who began with Class 1-05, 280 will begin Phase III—a success rate of 82 percent. This is up from the historical average of three in four who make it through Phase II.

On the evening of day thirty-four, Class 1-05's last night at the Rowe Training Facility, my wife and I join 811 in the team hut for a quiet celebration. Alcohol is not allowed at the Rowe Training Facility, but I asked Jan if it would be permissible for me to bring in some eggnog with a little snap to it. He allowed that it would be all right. So Julia and I carry in some spiked and nonspiked nog to the team hut along with a portable CD player. That evening, with Bing Crosby singing "White Christmas," we are honored to share some Christmas cheer with 811.

"Thanks for this little celebration," Captain Miguel Santos says, speaking for his teammates as he raises his cup, "and thanks for hanging with us during the phase."

"Thank you for letting Julia and me share this evening with you," I reply. "And for me, it was an honor to be a guest member of student ODA 811." Then, raising my paper cup with the spiked nog, I add, "Gentlemen, to success in Phase III."

"To success in Phase III!"

Author's Note: Soldiers selected for Phase II who are coming from combat support and combat service support units, like 811's Sergeant Aaron Dunn, are now being sent to the Special Forces Preparation Course prior to Phase II. They will join the X-Ray soldiers for this pre–Phase II, small-unit-tactics training. Soon after completion of Class 1-05's Phase II, SERE (survival, evasion, resistance, and escape) training was made a part of the Phase II curriculum. Those 280 soldiers from Class 1-05 who complete Phase III and IV will take their SERE training after they complete Phase IV. Special Forces SERE training will be addressed later in this book.

CHAPTER SIX

THE 18 SERIES

With the exception of those who will train to become 18 Delta Special Forces medics, the new Phase II graduates crowd into the large auditorium of Aaron Bank Hall, the sprawling special operations academic facility at Fort Bragg.

"On your feet!" a cadre sergeant barks, and the class rises as one.

A crisp, wiry sergeant in a freshly starched uniform strides quickly to the front of the large room. "Good morning, men. Take your seats. Welcome to Phase III. My name is Gary Baxter, and I'm the 4th Battalion command sergeant major. The colonel will be with us soon, but I wanted a moment with you before he arrives. First of all, congratulations on successfully completing Phase II. We know you're tough, and we know you can function in a tactical environment. Now you have to get down to the serious business of learning your trade. A few things to keep in mind. Fort Bragg is not Camp Mackall. This is a military post, and we live with a number of regular Army commands on this base. Stay straight, neat, and have a military haircut at all times. We're all soldiers.

EARTH TO SPACE. An 18 Echo candidate sets up his PSC-5 satellite radio for a commo shot during Max Gain, the 18 Echo final field problem in Phase III.

209

Be in a correct uniform at all times." The command sergeant major pauses to measure his audience. "This is an academic environment, and you have liberties during this phase that you don't have in the other phases of this course. Don't abuse them. You've all come too far to let an off-post incident or a DUI get you kicked out of here. I don't want to see you in my office. And you don't want to see me, so don't get sent for. Think about your goals, men, and why you came here. Don't blow it." Baxter glances to his right to a figure who seemed to have materialized along the wall. He is a short man with dark hair and a quiet manner. "Gentlemen, the battalion commander. Ten-HUT!"

Lieutenant Colonel Robert Sandoz makes his way to the center-front of the auditorium. He surveys the men in his audience—the men he is charged with training. Sandoz commands the 4th Battalion, 1st Special Warfare Training Group. After a moment of introspective silence, he speaks to them in a measured, clear voice.

"Gentlemen, let me echo the command sergeant major's welcome. Phases I, II, and IV are all essential in your journey to become a Special Forces soldier. But Phase III makes you a Green Beret. Over the course of the next three months, you'll receive the skill-based training to qualify you for your MOS. For you enlisted men, as weapons, engineering, and communications sergeants, and for you officers, as detachment leaders. My cadre are very passionate about their job as trainers. I'm going to ask each one of you to match their passion and dedication with your very best effort. Make no mistake about this, men, you are training for war. What you learn here will mean the difference between mission success and mission failure. It can also mean life or death for you and your teammates. This is a deadly serious business.

"My cadre are all experienced, proven Green Beret instructors. They can train any soldier in any army. But their efforts can only do so much. You have to bring the right attitude to this training. You have to want this training and information more than anything else in the world. Your desire to learn has to match that of my cadre to teach. This is a teaching environment. We will not talk down to you, disrespect you, or screw with you. But we will teach you." The battalion commander paces a moment, then turns to the class.

"You officers will have a tremendous responsibility when you go to your groups. But before you leave here I have to be satisfied—completely satisfied—that I can trust you with the responsibility and welfare of ten Special Forces NCOs. You enlisted men also have a responsibility. I have to be convinced that you can do your job—that you can lead and follow as a member of a Special Forces ODA team. It's very simple. Everyone in this room is going to war. Think about it, gentlemen, and good luck."

"FEET!" someone calls from the rear of the auditorium, and there is a scramble as the class rises. Lieutenant Colonel Sandoz steps to the side of the room to be replaced by Command Sergeant Major Baxter.

"That's it, men. We do our job; you do yours. No more, and certainly no less." Baxter consults his notes. "You each know the location of your respective company areas and where you are supposed to report after you leave here. Some of the finest first sergeants and trainers in Special Forces are waiting for you. Don't disappoint them. You're dismissed."

The officer candidates and the prospective weapons, engineering, and communications sergeants head off for their respective training companies. The next time they'll be in the same room will be in one of the two big classrooms at Camp Mackall when they begin Phase IV. That is close to three months in the future. Most of them will be there, but not all. None of them are thinking about that right now. What lies ahead for each man is months of hard work and the mastery of a dizzying array of technical information. The 18 Delta candidates from Phase II Class 1-05 will never rejoin the others, except by chance as teammates on an ODA at an active Special Forces group. The Special Forces medical sergeant curriculum is an intensive, twelve-month course that is both demanding and technical. This scattering of Class 1-05 into the various 18-series military occupational specialty (MOS) training curriculums presents a special challenge for me.

Up to this time, I've had the luxury of tagging along after a class, a student ODA, or an individual candidate as they went about their business. In most cases, the journey of one man mirrored the journey of the class. Now there are five training venues that are going on at the same time. Most of this training is conducted at Fort Bragg, so now I'll have an hour commute from my quarters at Camp Mackall to whichever training site or classroom that I wish to attend. It'll be a busy three months. And while I'll spend time at all venues, most of my time will be with the officers. If, in the words of Captain Walt Carson, the selection phase company commander, "Special Forces is an officer-led, enlisted-run organization," then why so much time with the officers? Every soldier on an ODA team, officer and enlisted, is a leader. Yet the enlisted soldiers, be they medics or communications sergeants, will usually join an ODA as the junior medic or the junior communications sergeant. To call them simply technicians would undervalue the versatility of these men, but the new 18 Bravos, Charlies, Deltas, and Echos will have the luxury of playing a role on the team. In most cases, they will be supervised and mentored by veteran team members. The enlisted leadership on an ODA will come from senior sergeants, specifically the 18 Zulu team sergeant and the 18 Foxtrot intelligence sergeant. Many of these men will have been on the job for close to two decades. In Carson's words, they have the experience to "run" the team as well as to lead in selected operational roles. During Phase III of Special Forces training, the enlisted soldiers will focus on the technical material within their specialties. Their leadership role in an ODA, certainly in the key leadership positions, may be years in the future.

This is not the case with the officers. They're being trained and groomed to become detachment leaders—ODA team leaders. Captain Matt Anderson or Captain Miguel Santos might well find themselves leading an detachment in Afghanistan, Colombia, the Sudan, or Iraq eight months from the completion of their Phase III. They'll be responsible for the operational planning and tactical thinking of their detachment's operations. Chances are their first deployment as a team leader will be a combat deployment. Other SOF units, notably SEALs and Rangers, bring their officers along more slowly. They deploy these officers in assistant-team-leader or deputy-unit-leader roles. The officer in charge of a SEAL platoon—the Navy SOF equivalent of an ODA—may be on his third combat deployment as a SEAL before he is the team leader. Special Forces officers have only their previous branch experience, their maturity, and their Q-Course training to rely on. They'll have no apprenticeship. These officers, when assigned to an ODA, are team leaders; they will sink or swim. In this wartime reality, they will perform or be relieved of command. The training of officers to qualify as 18 Alpha Special Forces detachment leaders will be taken up in chapter 7.

In Phase III, the enlisted soldiers will learn the mechanics of their specialties. They'll learn to perform these duties in support of their ODAs and teach these skills to others. During this MOS training, they'll continually be reminded that they are teachers as well as warriors.

THE 18 BRAVOS—THE SPECIAL
FORCES WEAPONS SERGEANTS

Most Special Forces phase training begins with some form of a come-to-Jesus meeting with the senior enlisted member of the training cadre, usually a master sergeant serving in capacity of the first sergeant. Eighteen Bravo training is no different, except that playing the role of the first sergeant for my Bravo phase is Sergeant First Class Rick Blaylock. Blaylock runs the weapons MOS training for Bravo Company, 4th Battalion. This class of 18 Bravo candidates is designated as Class 1-05.

"All right, guys, listen up. This will be your orientation briefing for the training that will qualify you as an 18 Bravo Special Forces weapons sergeant. From my point of view, you are the most important man on the team. This is not the Peace Corps. The work of a deployed Special Forces detachment will almost always involve weapons systems. Since 9/11, that has meant getting rounds on the bad guys before he can get rounds on you. Or training others, your teammates or local forces, to put rounds on the bad guys. The Bravo curriculum calls for sixty-five days of training. Given holiday periods and weekends, you will be with us for three months. But out of that sixty-five days of classroom and range time, you'll have to put in a lot of off-duty study time. There's a lot to learn. Maybe some of you guys think being a Bravo is just being a gunslinger. Well, there's that, but there's a whole lot more."

Blaylock quickly PowerPoints his way through the curriculum and weapons systems. Weapons systems include antiarmor rockets, antiaircraft rockets, a wide range of pistols, rifles, machine guns, submachine guns, sniper rifles, and grenade launchers, and indirect-fire weapons such as mortars and artillery. Within each of these types there are U.S.-made and foreign-made weapons. A Special Forces soldier has to be able to fight with his weapon, his ally's weapon, or the enemy's weapon. The first sergeant pushes on, slide after slide, weapons system after weapons system. Every pistol, rifle, machine gun, rocket, rifle, or mortar is considered a weapons system. Each one has to be mastered.

"As a detachment weapons sergeant, it will be your job to train your teammates," Blaylock tells them. "You will be the primary weapons system trainer of foreign and allied troops, and you'll have to be able to train them in *their* language. You'll have to know how to set up and manage firing ranges—here and overseas. The maintenance and inventory of all team weapons are your responsibility. The maintenance and inventory of all night-observation devices and night-vision goggles are your responsibility. It will be your responsibility to project, source, and order all ammo for your deployments. Along with the detachment engineering sergeant, you'll be responsible for the storage and security of all weapons and demolitions.

"You have operational responsibilities as well. The team leader will look to you as his primary adviser for weapons and tactics, offensive and defensive. You'll assist the team sergeant with operational fire-support plans. You'll be responsible for building terrain models and associated briefing graphics. You'll help with the operational planning to include infil, exfil, and route planning to and from the target. As an 18 Bravo, you'll have to be thoroughly familiar with the computer-based Special Operations Debriefing and Retrieval System. And there are a slew of administrative issues and reports that are your responsibility as an 18 Bravo."

I can see the look of dismay begin to grow on the faces of the new Bravo candidates. They really had no idea that there were so many weapons and so much to learn.

"I'll be honest with you," Sergeant Blaylock told me later, "the Bravo MOS is considered the least challenging and least technical of the specialties. That's why we get a lot of the X-Rays and the younger soldiers here. Some guys come in with the attitude that 'It's an Army school; how hard can it be?' We have to get past that in a hurry. They have to learn and master the capability, tactical use, and maintenance of each of these systems, and they have to demonstrate proficiency with them on the range."

Rick Blaylock is a square-shouldered, well-built soldier who looks as if he spends a fair amount of time in the weight room. He resonates authority, power, and competence. Blaylock grew up in Gettysburg, Pennsylvania, and has been in the Army for fifteen years. He has only been in Special Forces for eight years, but he has made three deployments to Afghanistan and one to Iraq—all combat deployments. He has just been selected for promotion to master sergeant and is awaiting orders back to 3rd Group for duty as an ODA team sergeant. It was my sense that while he has a passion for teaching, he wants to get back to the fight.

The new Bravo candidates begin in the classroom, a very old classroom, with lots of very modern weapons—day after day, weapons system after weapons system. There are fifty-some systems in all. Basically, they must know how to load, clear, disassemble, reassemble, bore-sight, zero in, and fire all commonly used military personal and light-infantry weapons in the world. They also have to be able to overhaul and repair weapons that are not functioning properly.

"They hand me an M4 that will not cycle on semiautomatic or automatic fire," Specialist Antonio Costa tells me of his training. "I have to look at the weapon and figure out what's wrong. It could be a bent firing pin, an improperly assembled weapon, or a missing part. Then I have to get out the spares kit and fix it. We spend a lot of evenings in the weapons rooms taking apart guns and putting them back together. We're getting so we can almost do it in our sleep."

The weapons systems taught at this Phase III include the following:

PISTOLS

Smith & Wesson M10	.38	United States
Colt Govt. M1911	.45	United States/others
Browning Hi-Power	9mm	Belgium/others
Beretta M-9	9mm	Italy/United States
Makarov	9mm	Russia
Heckler & Koch USP	.45	Germany
Glock 17	9mm	Austria
Heckler & Koch P-7	9mm	Germany

SUBMACHINE GUNS/MACHINE PISTOLS

M/45-Swedish K	9mm	Sweden
Madsen M/50	9mm	Denmark
Beretta M12	9mm	Italy
Sterling L2A3	9mm	Great Britain
Uzi	9mm	Israel
Heckler & Koch MP-5A3	9mm	Germany
Scorpion VZ61	9mm	Czech Republic

RIFLES/CARBINES

M14	7.62×51mm	United States (Colt and others)
Colt M16A2	5.55×45mm	United States
Colt M4A1	5.56×45mm	United States

Famas G2	5.56mm NATO	France
Simonov SKS	7.62 × 39mm	Russia
Heckler & Koch G3	7.62mm NATO	Germany
FN FAL	7.62 × 51mm	Belgium
AK-47/AKM	7.62 × 39mm	Russia
AK-74	5.45 × 39mm	Russia
Steyre AUG	5.56 × 45mm	Austria

SHOTGUN

Winchester M1300	12-gauge	United States

MACHINE GUNS

Kalashnikov PKM	7.62 × 54mm	Russia
M240B (FN MAG)	7.62 × 51mm	United States (Belgium)
M249 (FN Minimi)	5.56 × 45mm	United States (Belgium)
M60	7.62 × 51mm	United States
MG-3	7.62 × 51mm	Germany
Browning M2HB	12.7 × 99mm (.50 cal)	United States
DShK M38/46	12.7 × 109mm	Russia
Mk44 (mini-gun)	7.62 × 51mm	United States

GRENADE/ROCKET LAUNCHERS

M79	40mm (40 × 45)	United States
M203	40mm (40 × 46)	United States
Mk19	40mm × 53mm HV	United States
Mk47	40mm × 53mm HV	United States
AGS-17	30mm × 28mm	Russia
AT4	84mm	Sweden
Carl Gustaf M2	84mm	Sweden
RPG-7	40mm launcher	Russia

MORTARS

M29A1	81mm	United States
M224	60mm	United States
Podnos 2B14	82mm	Russia

A portion of the classroom time is devoted to simulators, including the call-for-fire simulator. The modern call-for-fire simulator is a room-sized video game. One whole wall of the simulator is a visual presentation of terrain. The candidates are arrayed in raised tiers before the huge projection screen with maps, protractor, an observed-fire reference card, and a call-for-fire guide. Their reference is that of a ground observer on a mountain looking into a valley. Each student makes a call for fire using proper radio call signs, procedures, and target descriptions, and with reference to the position of nearby friendly forces. The simulator projects the targets and the fall of shot onscreen—in this case, the splashes of 105mm artillery. It even has sound effects with the whistling of incoming shells and the KRUMP of explosions. Calls for fire are made using grid coordinates or polar plot coordinates, adjusting from a known reference point. The lessons learned in adjusting artillery fire are helpful when the class begins working on the range with mortars.

"I love mortars," Private First Class Tim Baker tells me after he came off the mortar range. "You can do a lot with a mortar, and you can teach the use of mortars to others. It's a simple weapons system and a basic defensive weapon, but there's a lot to know about it. We qualify in three qualification positions. First you have to crew the mortar. You have to set up and lay in the tube, shoot a few rounds to set in the baseplate, and get your aiming stakes calibrated. Then you elevate and traverse the tube as the spotter walks the rounds onto the target. You can't see the target, you just make the adjustments and drop the rounds in the tube.

"The second position is the spotter and probably the most fun job.

You spot the fall of shot and adjust it onto the target. In the spotter's position, you are in contact with the plotter; you give him the corrections, and he passes them on to the mortar crew. The plotter probably has the hardest job. He has to take the corrections from the observer and convert those heights and distances to issue the proper orders for the mortar crew. The plotter has to know where the mortar tube is and where the observer is. There's procedures for all this, but you have to understand the relationship between the guys on the tube, the observer, and the target. The next time I do this, there could be a gang of bad guys moving on a friendly position, and I'll have to be able to get those mortar rounds on target quickly."

Back at the Bravo training area, the candidates spend a day with the gun trucks—Humvees that are modified for Special Forces application. They're sometimes called general military vehicles.

"You guys need to listen up," Sergeant First Class Don Adams tells the prospective Bravos as he stands atop one of the two gun trucks, "because you're going to spend a great deal of your time in these vehicles on deployment." The gun trucks have only a passing resemblance to the standard Humvee; both have undergone extensive modification. "And when you're in one of these, never forget that you *are* a target."

Sergeant Adams joined the Army after he graduated from Parkway South High in St. Louis in 1990. He's been a Green Beret since 1993, and is qualified as a sniper and in military free-fall parachuting. Like First Sergeant Blaylock, he's from 3rd Group. Adams has made deployments to Ghana, Haiti, Ivory Coast, Senegal, Mauritania, Djibouti, Qatar, Yemen, Bosnia, Afghanistan, and Iraq.

Sergeant Adams explains how the deployed Special Forces detachments have come up with a whole protocol for the storage of equipment and ammo, including where to keep personal weapons if a soldier is driving or manning one of the vehicle weapons systems. The modifications are the evolution of trial and error—what works and what doesn't. This knowledge is handed down from team to team.

Given the speed and tactical requirements of Special Forces work, and that they are moving at night whenever possible, they use unarmored Humvees.

"All of you should learn how to weld if you don't already know how. There's always a welder handy when you're deployed. Make the modifications as necessary for your team and mission requirements. And don't forget that as a weapons sergeant on your detachment, you have to see that all guns on the truck are working and serviceable and that the ammo is in good order. You also have to see that every man on your team knows how to load, man, and use every weapon. This means you have to schedule live-fire drills for your team; don't assume that your junior engineer—or the senior one, for that matter—knows how to use a mounted 240 or an Mk19 grenade launcher."

Throughout the course, the Bravo candidates alternate between the classroom and the firing ranges. The classroom work is more heavily weighted during the early part of the course to allow for more range time during the latter portion of the instruction. They're routinely tested on all material and weapons systems. On the ranges, they get to shoot, and that's why many of these Special Forces candidates wanted to become weapons sergeants.

At the sniper ranges, they spend time with the Remington M700 SOPMOD (special operations modification), the standard sniper rifle in the Special Forces inventory, as well as the heavy-caliber and special-purpose sniper systems. In the classroom, they receive a thorough orientation on foreign sniper rifles. On the rocket ranges, they fire the two rockets in the U.S. inventory, the AT4 and the Carl Gustaf. The AT4 is a light weapon that gives a squad-sized unit in the field an antiarmor capability. The Carl Gustaf is larger and more accurate. Still a squad weapon, it is usually carried when the squad's primary mission is launching rockets. They also fire foreign-made RPGs, or rocket-propelled grenades.

"After firing the Russian-made RPG-7, I see why it's causing us such headaches in the hands of the insurgents," PFC Roberto Pantella tells me. "It's a very user-friendly and accurate weapon."

The prospective Bravos receive training on surface-to-air rockets, the U.S.-made Stinger and the Russian-made SA-7 Strella. All training I observe is with simulators. These are very expensive weapons systems, and so are the targets, so there's no live-fire training with the SAMs.

Standoff weapons systems include grenade launchers and recoilless rifles. Some of these systems are quite dated, while others feature the latest in technology. The 106mm recoilless rifle, married up with a .50-caliber spotting rifle, is identical to the ones we used in Vietnam—very accurate and very lethal. Forty-millimeter grenade launchers have been around for a while as well. The M79 and M203, the latter now adapted to the standard M4 rifle, have been in inventory for forty years. Automatic, high-velocity grenade launchers are relatively new. The newest is the Mk47 grenade launcher.

"You won't believe what the Mk47 can do," Specialist Tom Kendall tells me. "It has a laser range finder with a CRT screen. You just put the laser on the target, match the sighting mechanism to the laser, and fire. It's a Nintendo game. Your first round is on target—one shot, one kill. The Mk19 is a fine weapon, but the 47 is unbelievable. It's great for static defense, or it can be mounted on the ring turret of a Humvee."

During the last few weeks of training, there are two field exercises. These are mini outings designed to keep the Bravo students in the field so they can begin at dawn and work straight through into the night. One of these is a three-day exercise at Camp Mackall. At a training site that for all practical purposes could be a Special Forces base in Afghanistan, Iraq, or anywhere else in the world, the prospective weapons and engineering sergeants work on the construction of a base camp and its defenses. The Bravo candidates fill sandbags, build mortar pits, construct rifle and machine-gun emplacements, string concertina wire, and develop security-patrol procedures. In ODA-sized teams, they build sand-table terrain models of the camp defenses and position toy weapons to best advantage and with interlocking fields of fire. After a cadre sergeant approves their plan, then they go out and position real weapons to defend the camp in keeping with their terrain-model plan. This exercise will be repeated many times in foreign lands during their Special Forces careers.

The second field exercise amounts to camping out on the firing ranges at Fort Bragg. The cadre and support staff truck in weapons and ammunition, and the Bravo candidates are treated to a final round of shooting, firing as many of the weapons systems as possible. The most popular event during this field evolution is the combat range. Each candidate is armed with his personal M4 rifle and standard Beretta 9mm pistol. The targets are silhouettes at ranges from ten to twenty-five yards—close-in killing range. The drill is transition—rifle to pistol, pistol to rifle. Rounds on target with the rifle, then quickly drawing the pistol—primary weapon to secondary weapon when speed counts.

"You guys got to be aggressive—this is the business of killing," Rick Blaylock tells them. "If you're going to your secondary weapon in a tactical situation, you're in trouble. If that rifle jams or you're out of ammo, you have to get to that pistol—fast. It's kill or be killed—you or him. Most of your range time has been static firing—shooting for nice groups or double-tapping a silhouette target. In a gunfight, you're going to shoot that son of a bitch until he goes down, and you're going to keep shooting him. Get aggressive; get mean; get pissed. You kill him, or he kills you."

Blaylock and Don Adams walk along the firing line—instructing, exhorting, encouraging, and chastising. They also watch their student shooters closely for safety procedures during this fast-moving shooting training.

"You're in a fight, get angry!"

"Be quick, but be smooth."

"Don't take your eye off the target as you transition from one weapon to the other."

"If you're going for that pistol in a fight, you're in a world of shit. That bastard wants you dead; you get some rounds on him, or he'll get rounds on you."

During a break in the shooting drills, Blaylock gathers the class around him. "Guys, this is no-shit, lifesaving, downrange stuff. The skill and emotion you bring to a gunfight will win the day. You have to develop the mechanics and the muscle memory, but you have to be aggressive. Controlled emotion will help you win the fight. Your total focus is to kill that dude before he can kill you. When you get to your groups, you'll have to drill yourselves and your teammates just like we're doing here today. Then you'll be the guys behind the firing line helping your teammates to shoot better. Remember, you're training for a fight to the death; let the rage and the bullets fly."

For the better part of a full day, the class stands toe-to-toe with cardboard silhouette targets and blazes away—rifle to pistol and back to rifle. At times, you can hardly see the ground for the spent shell casings.

The Bravo candidates come off the ranges, clean weapons for a final time, and prepare for their comprehensive final exam. I ask Sergeant Blaylock about attrition in the phase.

"We don't have all that much attrition in this MOS phase. We had three from this class. One guy hurt himself during physical training and will be recycled to the next class. The other two were men who shouldn't be around guns at all; they simply haven't the awareness you must have when handling weapons. It seems like every class we have a few men—not many, but a few—who have no weapons sense. Another reason for the low attrition is the work of my cadre. If a guy's having trouble with a weapons system or does poorly on one of the exams, we work with him at night and drill him until he gets it right. If a man comes in here focused and determined to learn, we'll get him through."

I found PFC Tim Baker at the weapons-cleaning table on one of the final days. "Looks like you're about through here. What did you think of the weapons phase?"

"It was awesome, sir. There was so much to learn—there is still a lot to learn." He grins. "It was a challenge, but I've never had so much fun in my life. What an experience."

"What was the most important thing you learned?" I ask.

After a thoughtful pause, he says, "It's the emotion and measured fury that you have to bring to a gunfight. I came here to learn about weapons, but I had never thought about fighting—I mean, what it takes to fight and win. On the combat ranges, that changed. When it comes to a fight, you need all your skill and professionalism, but if you want to win that fight, you have to bring a controlled rage as well. We're training to be warriors."

"Good luck on the final exam," I reply. "And see you in Phase IV."

"That sounds awfully good, sir. See you in Phase IV."

The 18 Charlies—the Special Forces Engineering Sergeants

I catch up with the 18 Charlies as they are training at Camp Mackall. When I arrive at the base camp training site, it looks a lot different from when I was here only few days ago with the 18 Bravos. The skeletons of three buildings, in various stages of construction, have risen from the floor of the camp. The training facility rings with the sounds of a residential construction site—pounding hammers, the shriek of skill saws, and the steady din of generators. It is late afternoon, but there are portable floodlights in place so the work can continue after dark. Swarming over the three structures like an army of ants are eighty-some members of Engineering Sergeant Class 01-05. The training site looks like a crash project of Habitat for Humanity. All that is missing is Jimmy Carter hammering nails on the roof.

It's a sunny, cloudless January day with the temperature creeping into the high fifties. Most of the students have shed their blouses and work in T-shirts. All of them wear leather carpenter's belts, looking like extras on the set of the TV series *Home Improvement*. Two cadre sergeants and a civilian contractor sit on a stack of plywood watching the students work. I join them, and we watch the progress of the work. After a while, it becomes apparent that the three construction crews are in a race. One group is pulling up plywood sheets for the subroof and nailing them in place. They're clearly in the lead. The other two crews are still setting their roof joists.

"What do the winners get?" I ask.

"Nothing," Master Sergeant Ron Wyman replies. "And it's not really a race. Whichever crew is in the lead gets the first crack at the materials as they're delivered to the site. The guys who finish first just get to brag while they help the other crews finish."

The buildings are post-and-pier, single-story plywood huts built three feet off the ground, with stairs to a single door, and a window framed into each of the other three sides. These structures are exactly like those that housed my SEAL platoon in Vietnam and the ones that Special Forces ODAs now occupy in Afghanistan today. The camp itself, the same one the 18 Bravos sandbagged and fortified, is a triangular compound bordered by rolls of concertina wire. This, too, is familiar. It seems the triangular-shaped Special Forces compounds that once dotted the highlands of Vietnam are now springing up in Afghanistan.

"I spent a lot of my youth in camps like this," the civilian instructor tells me. He's a grizzled man of indeterminate age.

"Camp construction and defense was almost a lost art," Master Sergeant Wyman says with an easy smile and a touch of respect in his voice. "Fortunately, we still have a few old dogs like Howard here to show us how it's done."

The civilian instructor grins. "It's always nice when something you knew and did way back when is of some use to the new generation."

Every so often, one of the candidates would come over to where we're sitting to ask a question. Usually, it was directed to the retired Green Beret. I had to suppress a smile. Nothing pleases an old warrior more than being sought out by a young warrior. I'm speaking from experience here.

The 18 Charlie class had spent a total of seven days in the classroom and the shops at Fort Bragg before coming to Camp Mackall for three days of hands-on construction. In those seven days, they received instruction in all aspects of construction—from pouring foundations to installing corrugated metal roofing. Classes include construction design, reading blueprints, masonry, electrical wiring, concrete, structural calculations, and material management.

"We hand the student construction teams a set of blueprints," Wyman says, "and they have to take it from there. They have to develop a list of materials to include type and grade of lumber; the quantities of nails, bolts, and fasteners; how many bags of concrete; the amount and gauge of wiring; and so on. We begin at Fort Bragg, staging the materials and building the trusses. Then we come out here and put it together."

Master Sergeant Wyman came from 7th Group. As a Special Forces engineering sergeant, he's built houses, drilled wells, and constructed bridges all over Central and South America as well as in Afghanistan. Wyman is a lead instructor with Bravo Company, 4th Battalion, and he's in charge of teaching building and construction techniques to the 18 Charlie candidates.

"I can identify with these kids who are just coming into the Army and Special Forces in the X-Ray Program. I was one of them." In the early 1990s, there was an X-Ray-like program that took soldiers from basic training and assigned them to the groups in kind of an apprenticeship. Then they were sent to the Q-Course. "Every once in a while one of my cadre sergeants will get down on the X-Rays for not understanding the Army way of doing things, or that they're too green to train for Special Forces duty. I remind them I'm an X-Ray, sort of, and ask them if they have a problem with me wearing a Green Beret. That quiets them down in a hurry.

"When they get out here to Camp Mackall," Wyman continues, "they do it all, and they do it strictly to federal building code—pour foundations, set joists, frame in windows, set trusses, hang doors, and pull wires. Some of these kids have never handled a saw or used a level. I'm not sure they even teach high school shop any more."

The buildings literally go up before our eyes. "They seem to be working well and without a lot of direction," I observe.

"We have a few ringers in this class to go along with the guys who have never driven a nail. About fifteen of the X-Rays were journeyman carpenters before they signed up, so we have some talent and experience on this job site."

Two candidates who are new to the construction business are Sergeant Aaron Dunn and Sergeant Daniel Barstow. "The last thing that I built was a birdhouse for a Cub Scout project," Dunn says.

"This is terrific," Barstow declares as he takes his tool belt off for the last time. "We learned how to build things; now we get to learn how to blow them up."

After the buildings are finished, the class secures their building tools and turns their attention to the camp defenses. For another two days, they build wire obstacles, bunkers, sandbag shelters, and fighting positions. The Charlies work closely with the Bravos on base defense projects. They then return to Fort Bragg to begin their demolition and explosives training.

Many of the regular soldiers have handled explosives, and all of them have made up dummy charges with time fuse and inert blasting caps during Phase II. Now they get down to the serious business of tactical demolitions: charge calculation, charge placement, mine warfare, and target analysis. Classes begin with basic nonelectric and electric firing assemblies. The nonelectric assemblies are straightforward time-fuse, fuse-igniter, blasting-cap configurations with emphasis on the precise calculation of time-fuse burn times. The nonelectric firing assemblies have tactical and nontactical applications. The electric firing assemblies are used for administrative and construction demolitions in which the charges are command-detonated electrically through wire firing lead. Later on, they will learn about radio-control devices to initiate explosives and the use of standard military radio-detonation sets. One of the more difficult and math-intensive portions of the engineering sergeant curriculum is charge calculation and placement. There are formulas for just how much explosive will shatter, crack, cut, or penetrate an obstacle or material, and the exact placement of the charge to achieve the desired result. A small amount of explosive, placed just right, can surgically cut a steel I beam or a heavy wooden timber. The candidates learn to use detonation cord, or det cord, to initiate explosive charges, as well as a primary explosive. During the classroom and range work with demolitions and firing assemblies, the emphasis is always on safety. The handling and use of military demolitions is highly procedure driven. It's safe work if procedures are scrupulously observed.

On the Fort Bragg demolition ranges, the 18 Charlie candidates use a whole range of military explosives, including satchel charges, cutting charges, cratering charges, and shaped charges. They rig and detonate these explosives for tactical and construction—or destruction—applications. The load limit on the Fort Bragg ranges is four hundred pounds, which allows for some very big bangs. From military demolitions, they move on to the murky world of improvised munitions. These range from construction applications, such the mixture of fertilizer and diesel oil for earthmoving applications, to the making of IEDs—improvised explosive devices—for when military explosives are unavailable. Special Forces engineering sergeants have to be able to handle a wide range of modern, state-of-the-art military explosive devices and commercial explosives. Because they often work in primitive Third World situations, they have to know how to handle foreign explosives and what may have been state of the art thirty or forty years ago. Or they must improvise.

Throughout the engineering sergeant training, there's an emphasis on tactical demolitions—the use of demolitions in combat operations and the ability to teach those skills to others. Often the best way through a locked door in a tactical situation is by using explosives. The

18 Charlie candidates learn to use breaching charges and the various uses of the Special Operations Forces Demolition Kit. They are also introduced to the special-purpose munitions, which are well beyond the scope of this book.

"I particularly liked improvising with explosives," Daniel Barstow tells me. "You can get very creative. We first learned how you do it if you have the right military explosives or your demolition kit is with you. Then we'd do it if you had to improvise. We learned you could breach a wooden door by snaking det cord back and forth on the door and securing it with duct tape. But that doesn't work for metal doors. *But* if you snake det cord across a couple of IV bags [bags of saline used for medical purposes], the hydrostatic shock'll take down a metal door. These are good things to know."

A very important part of the course is the section on mines. Land mines have useful defensive applications in many places where Special Forces detachments go, but they are also indiscriminate weapons. During the Cold War and in areas of ethnic conflict, tens of thousands of land mines were sown throughout Southwest and Southeast Asia and the Middle East. They are a favorite tool of the insurgents. Therefore, Special Forces engineering sergeants have to have a good working knowledge of U.S. and foreign mines.

Most U.S. mines—there are seventeen in inventory—have a direct tactical application, and some of them can almost think for themselves. Some can lie in wait for a period of time for a vehicle to come by. Others can cut a path in concertina wire or a path in a minefield. All U.S. mines currently have a "life," which means they will explode or become inert after a period of time. The same is not true of foreign mines. The prospective 18 Charlies pay special attention to the twenty-five kinds of mines that can be found in Iraq and the fifty-nine kinds found in Afghanistan. Most found in Iraq and all but one found in Afghanistan are of foreign manufacture.

Eighteen Charlies learn basic render-safe procedures for mines and unexploded ordnance, but they are not military explosive ordnance disposal technicians. Most of what they do is to identify the mine or ordnance and explode it in place with a countercharge.

"We've been accumulating an impressive array of manuals and handbooks on mines," Aaron Dunn explains. "There's a lot we can do to help the locals deal with unexploded ordnance and to clear the area around their towns and villages of mines. Not only do we have the reference materials, but there are secure Web links we can access to learn more or to identify something we've not seen before. There's a lot to being a good engineering sergeant, and you're always learning."

"It's not all just putting up buildings and blowing things up," Sergeant First Class Carl Pennington, one of the demolition instructors, tells me. Pennington is a veteran 18 Charlie engineer from 10th Group. "Engineering sergeants have other duties. On deployment, they usually have primary responsibility for maintaining the vehicles. They also serve as the team supply sergeants and accountants; they help the team leader with the money and dealing with receipts. When the detachment deploys and redeploys, they supervise the loading and packing. On the operational side, they work with the team leader and the Bravos on route planning, infiltration, and target analysis. They serve as the specialists on terrain features. The 18 Charlies handle issues relating to tactical resupply, including the air-dropping of bundles. If the mission calls for infiltration by air, the ODA's Charlie is the primary jumper for demolitions. And along with the Bravo, they're responsible for the storage and accountability for munitions and demolitions. He's a very busy guy. If he's the senior engineering sergeant, he also has to supervise the junior Charlie. If he's the junior Charlie, he can get stuck with just about any job. Oh, and one more thing: He's responsible for cross-training the other members of his team in engineering and demolitions."

The final nine days of the 18 Charlie training are spent in the field. The class moves into the training base camp at Camp Mackall, but not into the buildings they constructed a few weeks earlier. They sleep in tent barracks and conduct their mission planning and briefings in tents erected within the camp. Over the course of the nine-day FTX, they will plan and conduct twenty-five to thirty missions in student ODAs.

"It's like the final field exercise in Phase II," Daniel Barstow tells me. I find him as he is gearing up in preparation for a training mission. "We usually conduct one daytime mission and two at night. The rest of the time we're planning, rehearsing, or trying to grab a few hours of sleep. The big difference from the Phase II fieldwork is that we patrol back to the base camp after every mission to get ready for the next one."

"Another difference," Aaron Dunn says, "is that every mission is a demolition raid or a target that requires the application of explosives. We plant charges on bridges, buildings, tanks, towers, trucks, trains, artillery pieces, old helicopters, and disused cruise rockets. Usually, we make an assault, secure the target area, plant the demo, and try to get off target as quickly as possible."

I was assigned to the student ODA of Sergeant First Class Nguyen Pham. When I arrive at the base camp, Pham's ODA is preparing to attack a petroleum storage site. The designated team leader had just given his warning order, and the team is busy preparing for the mission, which amounted to preparing charges to destroy an oil storage tank at the target location. The team leader calls them into the briefing tent for a quick thirty-minute patrol leader's briefing, straight out of the *Ranger Handbook*. The student leader races through the briefing, but slows as he goes through the actions on target. The team moves outside the tent, where there is a crude sand table of sorts—two-by-fours nailed together on the ground with loose dirt for sand. The petroleum site is represented by a tin tuna can. After a short rehearsal, the student ODA rucks up and leaves the camp to patrol to the target site. Sergeant Pham and I drive there and await the arrival and attack by his student team.

Sergeant Pham speaks with a halting accent that says English is his second language. He is five-ten, slender, angular, and with a very precise manner. I perceive both strength and a sense of purpose in Sergeant Pham.

"First Group?" I ask, thinking he would be assigned to the group with responsibility in Southeast Asia.

"That is correct."

"Vietnamese?"

He smiles. "Correct again. My father was an ARVN [Army of the Republic of Vietnam (South Vietnam)] officer. We came to this country when I was a little boy." The smile broadens a little. "Perhaps, Captain Couch, you and my father fought together."

"Perhaps," I reply, "I had that honor."

"We allow the students to go through the briefings quickly," Pham tells me while we wait for the student ODA to appear, "but without omitting any steps in the mission-planning format. This gets them thinking about tactical application of explosives they will use in Phase IV. On these training missions, we grade them on their actions on target and specifically on the construction and placement of the charges. We also spend time with them in setting up the briefing tent and establishing security. This briefing tent becomes a secure isolation facility in a tactical situation. The isolation and briefing areas are also the responsibility of the engineering sergeants."

We are about fifty meters from the target, an old, disused oil tank. The tank is part of a mock-up air-base complex just off the Luzon Drop Zone at Camp Mackall. Nearby there's an old plywood control tower and several aircraft with welded oil drum fuselages and sheet-metal wings. At a small campfire near the oil tank are two role players in black uniforms and AK-47s with blank firing adapters.

"What about the explosives?" I ask, knowing they can't use real charges at Camp Mackall. And I happen to live just a half mile down the gravel road from the drop zone.

"Everything is real except for the explosive charges. They use real time fuse, real blasting caps, and real det cord. It will make a bang, but it will not damage the tank."

Our attention is captured by the bark of an M240 machine gun from a fire-support position in the nearby woods. The two guards return fire, but they are quickly overwhelmed by the skirmish line that sweeps toward their position. Then there follows the normal shouting and shooting that accompanies the A-team as it makes its assault. After firing dies off, the team leader takes charge.

"Set security! Prisoner handlers, search the EPWs! Demo team, set your charges!"

The soldier kneeling next to one of the team leaders calls out the time. "Ninety seconds . . . Two minutes!" He carries one of the team's two radios and is in contact with the B-team leader, who has moved his men from the fire-support position to secure the perimeter. When the demo team leader has charges in place, and the patrol leader has inspected them, he calls, "Fire in the hole!" Then things stop.

Sergeant Pham comes forward and the prospective engineering sergeants gather around him. Pham conducts a critique of the explosive-charge placement. In this case, the canvas-covered wooden-block charges are braced against the metal skin of the tank by cut wooden branches. The charges are linked by det cord and dual primed with nonelectric firing assemblies. It's a crude, field-expedient, and very professional-looking job. Sergeant Pham points out a few ways it could have been done better and several ways it could have been done differently.

"Specialist Smith."

"Right here, Sergeant."

"What is your time delay."

"Two minutes, Sergeant."

"You may proceed."

Specialist Smith nods to his demo team leader, and again the cry "Fire in the hole!" rings out. This time it's for real. "Burning!" the demo team leader calls out as he inspects the time fuse. Sergeant Pham, myself, and most of the student ODA retreat to a safe distance. A few of the student 18 Charlies are set out on the nearby roads to make sure no one inadvertently approaches the target. At two minutes, three seconds, there's a sharp crack as the caps and det cord explode.

"Very good, Specialist," Pham tells his team leader, "and better a little late than a little early. Go police up the demo blocks and make your way back to the base camp. And remember, you are still tactical."

"Roger that, Sergeant."

Before the team can get off target, a Humvee roars across the open area from behind the dummy airplanes. A man is leaning from the window of the passenger's door, firing an AK-47.

"QRF [quick-reaction force]! QRF!" the team leader yells, and the candidates begin to return fire. The Humvee slews to a stop under a hail of blank fire. The team leader regroups his men, and they leapfrog back into the tree line near the target tank.

This field training exercise is the last evolution for the 18 Charlie Class 1-05. Before coming out to Camp Mackall, they'd taken their last written test, the target-analysis examination. They are all but finished with Phase III. I find my guys, Barstow and Dunn, packing their gear for the trip back to Fort Bragg.

"Now that you're about finished," I ask Aaron Dunn, "how does this compare with repairing aircraft radars?"

"It's a lot different, but I like it. I've been to a few Army technical schools, and they were hard. This one was just as hard, but here we had to bring it from the classroom to a tactical environment. We learned the technical aspects of construction and demolitions, and then we came out here to apply them in the field. And since it's Special Forces training, we had to do this when we're tired and haven't had much sleep."

"Sergeant Barstow, how does this stack up with Army military police work?"

Daniel Barstow grins. "It's a lot more challenging than what I was doing with the MPs. You have to respect demolitions, but blowing things up is a helluva lot of fun."

"So it's on to Phase IV?"

"Gear maintenance, and a good solid night's sleep," Barstow replies, "then on to Phase IV."

THE 18 DELTAS—THE SPECIAL
FORCES MEDICAL SERGEANTS

The 18 Delta medical sergeant curriculum is one of the most challenging and unique military training courses in this or any other army. This medical training is worthy of a book, let alone the few pages I'm able to devote to it here. In addition to the 18 Delta candidates, combat medics from the Army Special Operations Aviation Regiment, the Navy SEALS, the 75th Ranger Regiment, and the Air Force Special Tactics Teams all train at the $40 million Joint Special Operations Medical Training Center at Fort Bragg. The Joint Special Operations Medical Training Center operates under the JFK Special Warfare Center and School as its own training group and is the only MOS training that does not fall under the 1st Special Warfare Training Group. This facility is usually referred to by its acronym, the JSOMTC, but here we'll just call it the Medical Training Center.

The first thing the 18D candidates see when they enter the student entrance of the Medical Training Center is the Special Operations Medic Combat Pledge:

> As a Special Operations Combat Medic, I pledge my honor and conscience to my country and the Art of Medicine.
>
> I recognize the responsibility that may be placed upon me for the health and the lives of others.
>
> I confess the limitations of my skill and knowledge in caring for the sick and injured.
>
> I promise to follow the maxim *Primum mon non nocere*—first do no harm, and to seek the assistance of more qualified medical authority whenever available.
>
> Those confidences that come to me in my attendance of the sick, I will treat as secret.

I resolve to continue to sustain and improve my medical capabilities throughout my career as a Special Operations Combat Medic.

As a soldier/sailor/airman I will place all considerations of self below those of my team, my mission, and the cause of my country.

The Medical Training Center is a special and unique medical training facility—complete with state-of-the-art trauma simulators, operating rooms, a cadaver laboratory, and, like all medical schools, facilities for live-patient training. For the 18 Delta candidates, it's twelve months or more of classroom study, medical field drill, and internships that will make them qualified paramedics, emergency medical technicians (EMTs), and the finest combat medics in the world.

The first part of the 18 Delta training, or Special Forces Medical Sergeant Course, is the twenty-six-week Special Operations Combat Medic Course. Here they get classroom work in anatomy, physiology, pathology, patient assessment, and pharmacy training, as well as the basic classroom work that goes with EMT and paramedic qualification. The 18 Delta candidates perform clinical rotations in civilian hospitals and in civilian emergency and trauma centers. They also ride in civilian ambulances to work with emergency medical service paramedics on 911 calls. These clinical rotations and paramedic excursions have taken place at medical facilities in St. Petersburg, Tampa, Jacksonville, Richmond, and other civilian clinics. Before they graduate from the combat medic course, the 18 Delta candidates will have worked to save lives in actual trauma conditions and assisted in at least one birthing. But these soldiers are training to be more than EMTs and paramedics. They must be warriors and healers, sometimes both at the same time. One unique exercise during the course is the trauma-lanes training at the Medical Training Center. I've experienced some realistic military training, but nothing as intense or as well choreographed as the trauma-lanes training of the 18 Delta course.

"This introduces the student medics to working in a tactical environment," Chief Tony Balestra tells me. Balestra is a Navy SEAL chief petty officer and the senior Navy medical corpsman assigned to the school. He's a graduate of the 18 Delta medical training and rated as a Navy independent-duty corpsman. Chief Balestra escorts me to a wooded area behind the school but still within the perimeter of the facility grounds. The Medical Training Center is considered a secure facility, and visitors like myself have to be with an escort. Along a strip of grass near the woods is a series of army tents that are equipped as field infirmaries. These treatment facilities mirror what a Special Forces medic may have at a guerrilla base or a firebase in Afghanistan. There's a treatment table inside each along with the associated trauma equipment found in a mobile field hospital. It's like we're on the set of the *M*A*S*H* TV series.

"The students work in training units of five students and one instructor under simulated combat conditions," Balestra explains. "One is the primary student medic, one the patient, and the other three are squad members who can observe the treatment. The medic will have his aid bag, which he has packed and prepared for this exercise. With the exception of the wounded man, they're all in combat gear with load-bearing vests, extra magazines, weapons, and helmets." At the edge of the woods, Chief Balestra turns me over to a staff instructor and his student training unit. They're about to begin a trauma exercise.

"We grade each student in three areas," Instructor Mike Burke tells me as his students gear up. Burke is a retired Special Forces medic and a licensed physician's assistant. Like most 18 Delta instructors, he's a wealth of battlefield casualty knowledge and experience. "The first is their initial assessment of the patient, and it is an under-fire assessment. The student medic must conduct immediate lifesaving measures to control bleeding and restore breathing. Once those measures are addressed, he has to move his victim to cover and relative safety for more in-depth assessment. When out of immediate danger, the medic conducts what we call a rapid assessment. This is also a graded evolution. It's a head-to-foot inspection followed by field treatment to stabilize the patient. Treatment might include tourniquets, splints, braces, IVs, morphine, and the like. Then he has to rig the patient for casualty evacuation. Before transportation, the student medic has to fill out a form 1380. The 1380 tells the field hospital of the care given to date, the field diagnosis, meds—that kind of information." One of the students appears at Burke's elbow.

"We're all ready, Mister Burke."

"Well, then, let's go to work." Burke turns to a student with the aid bag. All of them are in battle dress. "OK, medic. We're under ineffective fire, and there's an enemy force probing our position that could make an assault at any time. You've got a wounded teammate up there. Let's get him."

Burke clicks his stopwatch and motions for me to follow. We trail the student squad up a shallow rise and some thirty meters into the woods. There, a wounded soldier lies moaning. And he *looks* wounded. His face is blue, and he's having trouble breathing. There is a large gash in his thigh that is literally squirting blood. And there is a bullet wound in his chest.

"Hey, buddy, how you doing?" The student medic shouts to him as he drops his rifle to the ground and slings his aid bag from his shoulder. "Talk to me, man, tell me where it hurts." The medic tends to the wounded man while the other three students take firing positions where they can provide security for the medic but still observe the treatment. The student checks his patient's airway and applies a tourniquet to the spurting wound, all the while talking to his patient, asking him about his condition.

The wounded student has just come from the moulage tent where his face was tinted blue-white, the bullet holes were applied with a Magic Marker, and a rubber leg gash was glued to his thigh. A bottle of fake blood is taped under his armpit and connected to the wound by a thin tube, allowing him to pulse with arterial bleeding. Instructor Burke also has a squirt bottle of stage blood to keep the wound blood-soaked. This guy's in bad shape.

WELCOME TO FORT BRAGG. A Pre-SFAS cadre sergeant makes a careful appraisal of a newly arrived Special Forces candidate.

THE CATERPILLAR. Pre-SFAS students link up, boots on shoulders, for collective push-ups during physical training on day one of the preparation course.

NAVIGATION PRACTICAL. A Special Forces soldier must be able to navigate with a map, a compass, and a protractor anywhere, anytime. Student Number 78 plots his course.

HOME FREE. Just in from navigation practical, Pre-SFAS student Number 70 catches a few winks in the base-camp area.

STAND AND DELIVER. Student Number 8 reports to the Pre-SFAS phase review board to determine if he will be allowed to move on to SFAS and Special Forces selection.

LOG TEAMWORK. Special Forces candidates in SFAS work together to manage their section of a telephone pole. Proper handling of the logs requires teamwork.

CHECKING IN. An SFAS candidate checks in with a point sitter on the land navigation course. When logged in, he will get a new set of coordinates and be off to his next point.

CONGRATULATIONS. First Sergeant Billy Sarno congratulates Private First Class Roberto Pantella on reaching the last point of the Star, the navigation final exam.

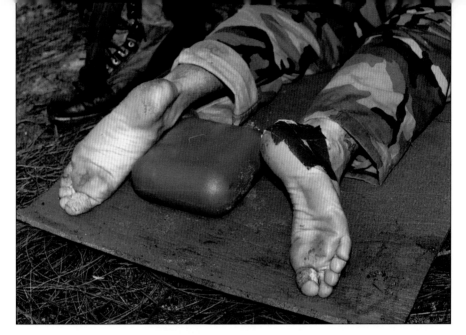

DUCT TAPE. SFAS candidates can move as far as eighteen miles a day under their rucksacks. Sometimes a little duct tape is needed.

SARE EVENT. An SFAS officer candidate is confronted with a war-crime scenario that involves partisan-force role players.

TEAMWORK. Moving a dead jeep through soft sand is a team effort. Everyone has to carry his load or the team fails.

MAKEUP! A Special Forces student gets cammied up for a field problem. Throughout the Q-Course, students apply and reapply face and hand camouflage.

OUTDOOR CLASSROOM. Sergeant First Class Sid Warner, ODA 812 cadre sergeant, holds class in the rain for student ODAs 811 and 812.

CLAYMORE CLASS. Sergeant First Class Paul Janss, student ODA 811's cadre sergeant, demonstrates the proper use of a claymore mine.

VERY CAREFULLY! Two Phase II cadre sergeants demonstrate the proper technique for searching an EPW—an enemy prisoner of war.

THE GUN. An M240 medium machine gun set up for an ambush. The two camouflaged lumps in the foreground are Private First Class Tim Baker and Specialist Tom Kendall.

LIKE THIS. Sergeant First Class Paul Janss demonstrates the right angle for covering fire to Captain Miguel Santos.

FIELD INSTRUCTION. Sergeant First Class Paul Janss, upper right, briefs five members of student ODA 811 before they continue with their tactical field problem.

TAKE FIVE. Private First Class Tim Baker takes a break during Phase III, 18 Bravo training at Camp Mackall.

TRANSITION. Private First Class Roberto Pantella holsters his M9 pistol, getting ready to go to his M4 rifle. In time, he'll do this without taking his eyes from his target.

LONG GUN. Specialist Tom Kendall settles in behind the scope of an M24 sniper rifle.

GUNFIGHT FORM. Private First Class Tim Baker engages a target under the watchful eye of 18 Bravo cadre sergeant Don Adams.

CONSTRUCTION AT CAMP MACKALL. Sergeants Aaron Dunn and Daniel Barstow and their 18 Charlie classmates on the roof of a student project during Phase III.

CARE UNDER FIRE. A student combat medic applies a tourniquet during the trauma portion of the 18 Delta course. He then readies the patient for casualty evacuation.

18 ECHO FIELD OFFICE. Tools of the Special Forces communicator—rucksack, rifle, radio, and a toughbook computer.

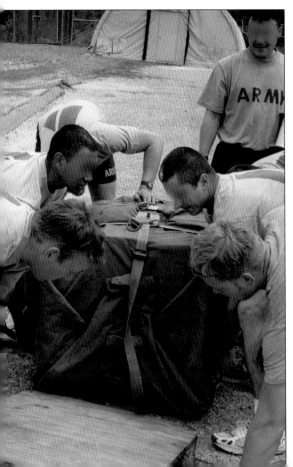

AERIAL RESUPPLY. Student ODA 915 prepares a bundle for airborne delivery in Phase IV. Clockwise from top, standing: Specialist David Altman, cadre sergeant, Sergeant Andrew Kohl, Sergeant Brian Short, and Sergeant Aaron Dunn.

DEMO INSTRUCTION. Sergeant Aaron Dunn, one of ODA 915's engineers, gives his team a class on demolitions during the pre–Robin Sage mission-readiness exercise.

IT'S A GIRL. Captain Santos and his daughter Anna—two hours old—with the author. Santos was granted a six-hour pass from Phase IV to see his firstborn, then returned to his team to parachute into Pineland and the Robin Sage scenario.

CHECK EQUIPMENT! ODA 915's cadre team sergeant, Troy Blackman, checks Staff Sergeant Tom Olin's reserve parachute. Note: This is a practice, nonequipment jump.

MARCH OF THE PENGUINS. Student ODA 915 under full combat load waddles to waiting Casa transports that will drop them into Pineland.

AIRBORNE! ODA 915, six of them in two Casa aircraft, insert into Pineland and the Robin Sage exercise. Each man jumps with a hundred pounds or more of equipment.

WE DO IT THIS WAY. Captain Miguel Santos briefs a contingent of Pineland guerrillas on the Rules of Land Warfare and the humane handling of enemy combatants.

DRESSING OUT THE PIG. Sergeant Andrew Kohl, back to camera, and Staff Sergeant Tom Olin do the honors. The pig provided a non-MRE dinner for thirty men.

ALLEGIANCE TO PINELAND. Captain Miguel Santos and members of student ODA 915 administer the oath of allegiance to two new guerrilla recruits during Robin Sage.

CONVOY BRIEFING. Iraqi Army scouts are briefed by a Special Forces sergeant prior to a Humvee convoy run from Al Asad to Hit. Author in center of photo. *Photograph courtesy of Staff Seargeant Chris Stanis.*

EIGHTEEN X-RAY AND THE AUTHOR. A year after their time together at Camp Mackall, Tom Kendall and Dick Couch spend a few moments together in Iraq.

"That enemy fire is getting closer," Burke tells his student. "What are you going to do?"

"His breathing is more regular now," the student medic says as he checks the tourniquet. "I'm ready to move him."

"Do so," Burke replies.

The medic calls in his security, and they become litter bearers. They move the patient across a shallow ravine, where Burke allows they're at a safe location—for a while. There the student medic begins his rapid assessment. He checks the patient's torso and each limb for additional injury. Further inspection of the fallen soldier yields a broken leg. As the student medic works, he says what he's doing and thinking. "Breathing rapid and shallow," the medic reports. "As you find it," Burke replies. On taking his patient's blood pressure and pulse, the medic says, "One hundred twenty over 80, pulse 90 and strong"—the actual condition of the patient. Burke replies, "Ninety over 60, pulse weak and rapid," and the medic treats his patient accordingly. The medic splints the leg and gets an IV started. The patient seems to have a neck injury that interferes with his breathing, so a neck collar is put in place. The patient's now ready to be evacuated.

After a critique by Instructor Burke, the patient is carried out of the woods to the field hospital tent and hoisted upon a treatment table. There he will be tended by another student training team. The new team of caregivers will have the advantages of the field hospital equipment, but must work from the information given them on the 1380 form provided by the student medic in the field. The field hospital care and treatment is the third area of evaluation. A new student medic takes charge and continues to assess the patient's injuries and conduct treatment.

Perhaps the hardest job is playing the victim. He's a stage prop—all marked up, moulaged, and dressed to look like a battlefield casualty. He has to lie there and exhibit the assigned symptoms and stay in character as much as he can. It takes thirty minutes or more in the moulage tent to get made up, and nearly that much time to get cleaned

up. And being a patient is also a learning experience; the student caregivers learn to handle others as they would like to be handled.

The trauma lanes are a good preparation for the field paramedic
and EMT internship duty. After the twenty-six-week combat medic
curriculum, the 18 Delta students have a short break before continuing
with the second half of their Special Forces Medical Sergeant Course.
The second half is the independent practice portion of the training. It
begins in the lab with blood work, urinalysis, pharmacology, and par-
asitology, with follow-up work in disease assessment and management. The trauma training continues with advanced work in treating
multiple battlefield patients. The prospective Special Forces medics
also receive training in surgery, anesthesia, nursing, and postoperative
care. And since combat medics may be the only medical option in a
primitive area, they receive training in dental anesthesia and extractions. They also train in veterinary medicine, herd management, and
food inspection.

Far more than the other MOS trainees, the 18 Delta candidates
work in an academic and clinical environment. The Medical Training
Center has a modern medical library, and the students have a wireless
network for access to classroom materials and the instructor staff.

"I thought the combat medic course was a grind, but the independent
practice training is even harder," Byron O'Kane, now Staff Sergeant
O'Kane, tells me when he is two-thirds of the way through his 18
Delta training. "There's a lot to learn in the surgery and anesthesia
training. You have to learn it, demonstrate proficiency in the operating
room, and you have to stand for your oral boards. After that, we'll
have another internship out in a civilian hospital, where we spend time
in the operating room and clinical settings. It's been a long slog, but
I'm beginning to see the light at the end of the tunnel. I'm looking forward to getting finished and back out into the field."

"On to Phase IV."

"On to Phase IV."

Of the three soldiers in my student ODA from Phase II who chose

18 Delta, Sergeant Byron O'Kane proved to be the superstar. He was the honors graduate in his 18 Delta class. Sergeant First Class Stan Hall graduated in the middle of the class, but without any recycle time. Only about half of those who start the 18 Delta training are able to go straight through without having to retake one or more portions of the course. One in five finds this MOS is not for them or is too difficult for them, and they are usually assigned to another Special Forces MOS training venue. Specialist (now Sergeant) Frank Dolemont, the combat veteran and tactically the most proficient of my guys in Phase II, had trouble with the academics and was recycled to a following class. He's still working to become a Special Forces medic.

It is interesting to note that the 18 Delta Phase III MOS training is nearly three times as long as Phases I, II, and IV combined.

"We've trained you to save lives on and off the battlefield," First Sergeant Gavin Haines tells them when they leave the Medical Training Center as Special Forces qualified medics. Haines is a twenty-two-year veteran who grew up in central Oregon. He is a Thai speaker who has spent most of his career with the 1st Special Forces Group. "You are a healer. Your job is to take care of your teammates and to cross-train them in combat casualty care. But never forget that you are a Special Forces soldier. When you put that Green Beret on, you are a warrior first and a medic second."

THE 18 ECHOS—THE SPECIAL
FORCES COMMUNICATIONS SERGEANTS

Perhaps next to the 18 Deltas, the 18 Echo communications sergeant MOS training is the most difficult. Technically, it might be the most challenging. Prior to 18 Echo Class 1-05, the communications sergeants, like the medical sergeants, had a longer Phase III than the other MOS curriculums. Through January 2005, the 18 Echo course was a month longer than the 18 Bravos, Charlies, and Alphas. The extra time was needed for the Echos to learn and drill in international Morse code. Morse code is no longer a requirement for Special Forces communications sergeants.

"Even without the code requirement," First Sergeant Larry Blowers tells me, "we have a lot of information to get across in a very short period of time. Weapons, engineering, and even the medical requirements of MOS training change slowly. In the communications world, the technology changes every year, every class. Even if the radios don't change, there may be a modification to an existing radio or antenna system or a software application that changes. Since we're a part of an evolving military communications system, there are changes within that system as well. On the positive side, the systems keep getting smaller, more reliable, and more user-friendly. Still, the 18 Echo communications sergeant has to learn each new system, incorporate this into his communications planning, and teach it to the other members of his detachment. So while the newer radios are easier to use, they do change, so the learning never stops. And this means we have to give our Echo candidates a thorough grounding in communication basics and computer technology. More and more, if you can't use a computer or maintain a computer in the field, you can't communicate."

First Sergeant Blowers is a solidly built master sergeant who grew up on the Gulf Coast. He has just over twenty years in the Army and will return to the 3rd Group when he finishes training new 18 Echos. His current job description is first sergeant, Charlie Company, 1st Special Warfare Training Group. Blowers knows communications and has something of a facility for languages; he speaks French, Spanish, Haitian-Creole, and Korean, and can make himself understood in Serbo-Croatian.

"Our training here is a three-pronged approach," the first sergeant continues. "Our students have to understand communication theory, computers, and, above all, be able to communicate in the field. A good commo sergeant is one who is out there at two a.m. with his radios, trying to establish or improve his commo link. A communications sergeant has to make comms anywhere, anytime, and under any conditions."

The 18 Echo candidates are trained at two locations. The classroom work that relates to computers is done at Aaron Bank Hall at Fort Bragg. The fieldwork and the classroom work on radios take place at the communication training facility on the eastern side of Fort Bragg, a portion of the base known as Eureka Springs.

"The first thing we learned were computers," Specialist Justin Keller tells me. The big man from Denver, the former college wrestler and bouncer, had been tapped for communications training. I note that a great many other X-Rays with college degrees, like Specialist David Altman, are in Echo training. "When most people think of Army communications, they think of a radioman in the field with a handset to his ear. There's that, but the portal to most of our radios is through the computer. Everyone has some knowledge of computers. Some like me could just do e-mail and word processing. A few in the class were computer techs before they came into the Army. And you'd be surprised how many guys worked at RadioShack or Circuit City. We spent almost three weeks on computers, and working with the one we use in the field. It's a ruggedized PC designated as the CF-18. We call it a toughbook. We learned field maintenance and how to take them apart and reassemble them, so they can replace components on deployment and make upgrades to components. We also learned how to set up work groups and local area networks, or LANs. The basic program is a version of Windows 2000 Professional. We all became very proficient at using a computer."

The 18 Echo curriculum includes antenna theory and radio wave propagation. The candidates are introduced to a host of military radios, but focus on the care, maintenance, and operation of the radios that are currently in use in the Special Forces groups. Then there are the peculiarities of military communications that include message format, authentication procedures, operational procedures, common abbreviations, acronyms, and prowords. The 18 Echos must also master secure communications, which involves cryptographic coding and decoding—or, more simply, using crypto.

"We really learn and use four basic radios," Specialist Altman explains. "The first, heaviest, and probably the most important is the AN/PSC-5D. We call it the PSC-5. It's our primary satellite communications, or SATCOM, radio, and weighs about twelve pounds—eighteen with batteries in it."

The PSC-5 can do a lot of things. It is a multiband, multimission backpack radio that can operate in the UHF and VHF frequency ranges and can be used for line-of-sight or satellite communications. One cadre referred to the PSC-5 as the king of radios. The 18 Echo candidates train on this radio and use it primarily to transmit text and imagery by satellite from remote locations back to the forward operating base.

"There are three other radios that we have to know," Altman said. "Our primary HF or high-frequency radio is the AN/PRC-137F. The 137 is used for HF voice traffic and for ALE transmissions—automatic link establishment messages. The automatic link is kind of amazing. When you type up a long message and send it on ALE, the radio chooses the frequency, at the lowest power setting, and sends the message when it finds those parameters. It makes for a very secure transmission. Then we have the AN/PRC-148. We call it the 'embitter,' for MBITR, or multiband inter-/intra-team radio. It's a handheld FM Motorola-type radio that's very light, less than two pounds, and durable. This a great radio and can do a lot of things, including satellite communications, but we use it as a secure, line-of-sight radio for squad communications. And finally, we have the AN/PRC-119F. The 119 is a heavy radio like the PSC-5, and we use it for FM voice transmissions, often as a patrol base radio. We not only have to know how to use the radios, but we have to carry them, along with extra batteries. On a good day, I weigh a hundred forty-five pounds. Sometimes I think my combat load, with the radios, weighs more than I do."

The Echo candidates not only have to know the radios, they're also responsible for developing communication plans to support tactical missions and base camp operations. A deployed ODA may have several teams out in the field and must maintain secure communications with those teams as well as the higher command at a forward operating base. A communications sergeant also has to train the other members of his team in the use and care of the radios and in the execution of the current commo plan. And like his brother weapons, engineering, and medical sergeants, he will have to teach these disciplines to allied soldiers in their language.

Communicators and operational planners have long been indoctrinated in the PACE protocol when developing communications plans. PACE stands for primary, alternate, contingency, and emergency methods of communications. "That's still a part of our planning and thinking," one of the cadre sergeants told me, "and the students need to learn this. It'll be part of their communications plan they'll have to develop and brief their plan for every operation. But with today's modern, secure communications, you really only need a primary and an alternate. And we often have secure satellite phones. I've been to some pretty remote places on the Afghan-Pakistani border, and my Iridium sat phone was clear as a bell. But then sometimes there's no coverage or your phone just goes down. Or the guy you want to talk to has a bad phone. Then you better find another way to make commo."

The initial part of the 18 Echo curriculum is focused on learning the theory, learning the equipment, operating the equipment in the classroom setting, and operating the equipment under field conditions. Toward the end of the course, the Echo candidates are spending a lot of time outdoors communicating. There are two outdoor exercises. The first is a mini field exercise in which the class bivouacs outside the Eureka Springs communications facility, and the candidates erect antennas and run commo drills with all four radios. The instructor staff is right there with them, to help and answer questions. It's an opportunity to set up and use all the radios, and to lock down the procedures and operation of each one. The second is a field performance exercise and the final exam for the 18 Echos. The twelve-day exercise is called Max Gain.

During Max Gain, the candidates will have to communicate with each radio under tactical field conditions for an extended period of time. The exercise begins with full ruck, weapons, ammunition, rations, and a load of radios. They operate in five-man teams. Each team has two PSC-5s, two PRC-119s, two MBITRs, and one PRC-137—and a lot of extra batteries. They also carry two CZY-10s, or "Crazy Tens," pocket-size crypto devices that are used to load crypto into all radios. The Crazy Tens are a very highly controlled item. The teams leave the commo facility with each man carrying between 90 and 110 pounds of gear. A few of them are even heavier. This burden is shared equally by weight, if not by the man packing the weight. At 150 pounds, David Altman carries the same load as Justin Keller does at 250; both shoulder a ruck weighing a hundred pounds. They patrol under full tactical discipline for only a few miles, then set up in patrol base camps with eight commo teams per camp. While at the base camp and the outlying commo sites, the Echo candidates have to keep up tactical disciplines, just like they did in a patrol base back in Phase II. This means they live out of their rucks, observe the two-man rule, and never get beyond an arm's length of their weapon. At night, the candidates take their rifles into the sleeping bag with them. At least two men are on security duty at all times.

One team will occupy the base camp while the other teams patrol out at least two hundred meters to set up team commo sites. There they string up field antennas for HF communications and erect the portable, ray-gun-looking antennas for satellite communications. Two men take up security positions while another two rig antennas and begin to set up their radios. The fifth man is an observer. I follow Justin Keller and his team to their comm site.

"We do a quick tactical setup and get ready to make commo. From here we will do SATCOM with the PSC-5 and high-frequency voice with the 137. With the SATCOM, the timing has to be precise. We each have designated fifteen-minute windows in which to get our message off and to receive a receipt for it. Then we rotate positions. Then the next guy has fifteen minutes to sanitize the radio and set it up for his transmission window. We call them block times—fifteen minutes to set up and fifteen minutes to make commo. Each of us will send two messages, which will keep us here at the team site for five hours or so. Then we pack up and head back to the patrol base. Back at the base, we will send an ALE message on the 137. We also have hourly FM commo checks with our forward operating base on the PRC-119 and intra-squad comm checks with the MBITRs. Tonight, we'll be back out again for more SATCOM on the PSC-5."

In the tactical configuration of the team commo sites, I note that they are always ready to move and fight. When they are talking, the radios are still in the rucks so they can shut down and leave quickly if required. I also watch as they set up two of everything, including two toughbook computers, so if a computer or a radio fails, the operator on the block time can quickly change out a faulty component.

Each candidate's SATCOM message, text or imagery, is beamed to a satellite twenty-three thousand miles in space and back to the commo facility just a few miles away. There, a team of staff communicators receives and acknowledges each transmission. The facility is manned 24/7, and these are graded transmissions. Inside the commo facility is a large board that identifies each individual message, the Echo candidate who sent it, and any irregularities of format and procedure. During the course of the Max Gain exercise, each candidate will make a total of fifteen graded SATCOM transmissions.

"Block time is evaluation time," Keller says. "For the most part, I didn't have any trouble, but on a few of them I was sweating it. Fifteen minutes isn't much time if something's not working. But we've been trained for that; it's called the ABCD protocol—antenna, batteries, connections, data. Ninety-nine percent of all problems come to this. When the gear doesn't work, you begin a formatted series of trou-bleshooting procedures. A loose connection almost caused me to miss my comm window, but I got it fixed in time to make commo."

"High-frequency communication is all about the antenna," David

Altman explains to me. "We use either an elevated dipole or an in-verted 'V' configuration. For Max Gain, we were communicating with a commo station in Florida, some four hundred miles away. The signal has to skip between the earth and the ionosphere to travel that far, so we have to adjust the antenna to get a good signal—to achieve the right bounce. But the PRC-137 is a good radio. We had ten graded HF voice and HF ALE transmissions on the 137."

In 18 Echo Class 1-05, there are seventy-some students out working in two patrol bases for Max Gain. The cadre pretty much leave them alone, but stop by periodically to see if there are any problems and to ensure they are maintaining a tactical posture. The patrol base loca-tions are each scheduled for one move to drill the candidates in break-ing camp, along with the radios and the aerials, and setting up in a new location. One of the patrol bases gets a little sloppy in their fieldcraft discipline and are forced to move a second time to refocus their atten-tion to tactical detail. The cadre, based on feedback from the commo facility at Eureka Springs and in Florida, know if an individual candi-date is having trouble. Usually, it's a technical issue or a piece of gear that needs to be swapped out. Then the staff is right there to work with the student communicator. As one cadre member puts it, "The groups need these guys, and we want to give them every chance to succeed."

"When they finish with Max Gain," First Sergeant Blowers tells me, "we feel they can communicate to standard—anytime, anywhere. Dur-ing the course of twelve days in the field, they'll be hot, cold, attacked by bugs, and get rained on. That's what we want; they still have to communicate. Commo is very important in the operations of a de-ployed Special Forces detachment. This is why we put them out there and have them do it again and again and again. It's our responsibility and their mission to see that they can make commo anytime and under any conditions. We also want them moving around in the woods under a load. It gets them thinking about Phase IV, where they'll move un-der this much gear or more, and they will be walking a lot farther."

"How about class attrition?" I ask him.

"Our job is to get these guys through this, and by and large we do. If they're having problems, we come in and work with them at night or on the weekends. We lost two from this class. One was for a family problem, and he'll probably be back. The other was a guy who for some reason just couldn't handle the technical material. Hard as we tried, we just couldn't get through to him. It's like that sometimes, but we try to get them all through here and on to Phase IV."

"Never been in the field that long," David Altman says of Max Gain. "But I learned a lot, and I'm ready to communicate in Phase IV. I also learned that I'm going to have to build a better ruck to see if I can shed a few pounds. We carry a lot of gear."

"This was a challenging course," Justin Keller reflects. "I was a little beat up from Phase II, so the classroom time at the beginning allowed me to heal up. I know we have a ways to go, but I'm starting to think about duty with an ODA team. The 18 Echo is in the middle of everything, and I can't wait to do my job on deployment as a communications sergeant."

"But first there's Phase IV."

"Oh, right, Phase IV. I'm looking forward to that as well."

At the end of Phase III, the 18 Bravos, Charlies, and Echos join their officers, the 18 Alphas, for a return to Camp Mackall and Phase IV. By now, most of them, to one degree or another, know each other. They are joined by a contingency of 18 Deltas who began their combat medic training over a year ago. Ahead for these soldiers is a crash course in unconventional warfare and the storied Robin Sage exercise.

CHAPTER SEVEN

THE DETACHMENT COMMANDER

Following the battalion commander's and battalion command sergeant major's briefing to the Phase III gathering, the class officers make their way to the Alpha Company area at Aaron Bank Hall. There they meet in a classroom with Major Jim Brooks, who commands Alpha Company, 4th Battalion, 1st Special Warfare Training Group. Brooks came to the training group from Iraq, where he served with the Free Iraqi Forces in Nasariyah. Brooks is a quiet, understated man whose soft demeanor belies his reputation as a top Special Forces professional. He lays out the administrative, academic, and professional requirements of the course.

"I don't have to tell you gentlemen just how important the next three months in your Special Forces career are. What you learn here will determine your success as a detachment commander. We'll throw a lot of information at you—so much you might feel smothered at times. Work through it. This is information you will take with you to war."

Major Brooks then introduces his company operations warrant

TEAM LEADER.   Captain Miguel Santos confers with his team in the field during one of the Phase III tactical drills.

officer, Chief Warrant Officer Frank Bonner. In contrast to his company commander, Bonner is animated and direct.

"Good morning and welcome to the 18 Alpha curriculum. Let me echo what the major said; the next three months are going to be challenging and important. From here, you will break up into your small groups, where most of your work in this phase will take place. Before you do, I'm going to brief you on your duties and responsibilities of your team warrant officer—your 180 Alpha. As team leader and detachment commander, you'll have a lot of talent and experience to help you get the job done. Your 180 Alpha is an important part of that talent pool. He's your assistant detachment commander and he can do a lot of things, but his primary job description is to assist and advise. Remember that, gentlemen—assist and advise. He will also command in your absence."

Bonner quickly goes over the history of warrant officers in Special Forces. Warrant officers have been serving as assistant detachment commanders since 1993. Warrant officers are drawn from the ranks. Typically, a capable Special Forces soldier will move along a career path that leads to becoming an ODA team sergeant—a sergeant major and the senior enlisted man on the team. A few of these superior-performing Green Berets will elect not to take the team sergeant route and take the path that will lead to their becoming commissioned as a warrant officer.

"Your warrant officer can do a lot of things for you," Chief Bonner tells the new 18 Alpha candidates. "He's a wealth of experience— experience that ranges from your budget to your training. And above all, remember where this guy is coming from. He has enlisted history and possibly enlisted history with the team and the team sergeant. Like you and the team sergeant, he is a type A personality and wants what's best for the team. You, the team sergeant, and the warrant are the top three on the ODA. What the team does, how it trains, and any problems on the team are going to be handled by the three of you. There may be times when you disagree and have to go behind closed doors to work it out. That's OK. As team leaders, you are the final authority and will make the final decisions, but don't overlook the fact that you may have as much as forty years experience between that warrant and that team sergeant. Get to know these guys; break bread with them. Listen to them and treat them with respect."

Chief Bonner goes on in detail about the duties and responsibilities of the assistant detachment leader. "And one more thought before I let you go. As a detachment leader, you're the boss—the final authority on that ODA. But keep in mind that when dealing with your warrant and your team sergeant, it's their team. You will come and go, but in most cases, they will remain with the team. Good luck to all of you."

Chief Warrant Officer Bonner releases them, and the officers head for their team rooms. There they will meet the key instructors for their Phase III training—perhaps the most important individuals in their entire Special Forces Q-Course training: their two small-group instructors.

"One of the most important things I do here as the battalion commander," Lieutenant Colonel Robert Sandoz told me, "is to find and select the right officers and noncommissioned officers to serve as small instructors for officer training. My command sergeant major and I personally interview each of them, and not all that I interview are right for the job. There was a time in Special Forces when we got less than the best here for instructor duty. That was true for all phases of training. But that's no longer the case. To build the force properly, you have to bring your best back here to train the new men, especially the new officers. The good ones naturally want to stay in operational rotation. We're at war, and they want to keep their guns in the fight. My job is to convince our best officers and NCOs that they can contribute to the fight by coming back here and passing their experience along to the new detachment leaders."

The officers are broken down into ODA-sized groups for their phase training. In my group, along with Captain Miguel Santos and Captain Matt Anderson, there are two other infantry officers, one of them coming from the 75th Ranger Regiment. There is a field artillery officer, an engineer, an air defense officer, and a chemical warfare officer. There are also two foreign officers, one Czech and one Pole. All are captains. Among the Americans, five are married, two have never been married, and one is divorced. Both of the foreign officers are married. Matt Anderson is divorced with two daughters, and Miguel Santos and his wife are expecting their first child in four months. All of the American officers, with the exception of the chemical warfare officer, have been to Ranger School. As in other phases of training, the group will train and function as a student ODA. My group is designated as ODA 912. The ten officer candidates file into the 912 team room and take their seats. The walls of the small classroom are plastered with maps, organizational charts, briefing formats, combat photographs, and technical information. This will be 912's home for the next three months when it's not traveling or in the field. Their homeroom teacher and senior small-group instructor is Major Eric James.

"Good afternoon, men, and welcome to 912 and Phase III. My name's Eric James, and this is Master Sergeant John Rameres. We'll be working with you for the next three months. The master sergeant is a former marine and a combat veteran. He came to Special Forces from Southern Methodist University by way of the post–Gulf War X-Ray Program. Get to know him; there's a lot you can learn from him to help you be successful in this phase. All of you want to lead an ODA—to become detachment commanders. After this phase, Master Sergeant Rameres will be returning to 7th Group as a team sergeant. We're a small community; he may be your team sergeant. I especially want to welcome the allied officers. We look on the allied officers as training aides, as well as brothers in the international special operations community.

"There's a lot of information in this phase that you're going to have to get your arms around. Master Sergeant Rameres and I are here to educate, train, and mentor you. We're also here to push you—to see that you understand the mechanics of planning and executing special operations as well as understand the big-picture special operations environment. There's a lot to learn, and you'll put in a lot of long, hard hours to get through this. All of you were outstanding in your branches before you selected for Special Forces; you will work hard to be average here. You'll leave here with the tools to solve difficult, complex, and ambiguous problems. You'll learn to plan operations on a level you never thought possible. A lot of this will be death by PowerPoint, but we'll spend some time in the field as well. We'll counsel and evaluate you. This phase of training is designed to identify and improve on your strengths. It's also designed to point out your weaknesses so you can work on them.

"I'm very passionate about this training and the skills you must have if you're going to be an effective detachment commander. If I yell at you, don't take it personally. I'm a fire-and-forget kind of guy. If there are problems, call me anytime, and that includes at home. If you have an issue, let's get it resolved. I've been married quite a while, and my wife understands my commitment to this business and this training. If there's someone in your life, then this job will affect them and will undoubtedly create hardships for them. Your wives, girlfriends, and/or fiancées are welcome to call or e-mail my wife if they want to talk about it. No problem."

James hurriedly writes his home phone, cell phone, and e-mail on the board. Eric James is a straightforward, square-jawed officer from 10th Group. He's been in the Army for eleven years and in Special Forces for six. He's from Colorado and has a degree in mechanical engineering, as well as a master's degree in unconventional warfare. He has made deployments to Kosovo and was with the Kurds in northern Iraq for Operation Iraqi Freedom. James comes across as an open and affable officer with a passion for getting the job done right. He also projects a very crisp, no-nonsense approach to his work.

"Time is very short, gentlemen," James continues, "and you have a great deal to learn. The next time you see some of this material it will be downrange and it'll be for real—with lives and the mission on the line. Master Sergeant Rameres and I will be watching to see that you're engaged and putting forth your best effort. I'll always ask, 'Is this guy doing the best he can with the knowledge he has?' For staying in shape you are on your own; big-boy rules apply. You'll take the phase six-event physical fitness test, the one with the bench presses and pull-ups, now and when you leave the phase. You should be stronger at the end." He pauses a moment to survey his student officers. "This business is like no other. There are very broad left and right boundaries. Work hard and use your time well. When we're here in the team room, bring your lunch if you like. We'll eat together and talk about Special Forces."

Major James then pushes through the phase administrative details and evaluation criteria. On a break from the classroom, I speak to a few of the officers about their senior group instructor.

"Don't let that Boy Scout image fool you," one of them tells me with a note of resignation in his voice. It seems Major James's reputation was a pass-down item from previous classes. "The guy's a workaholic," another student officer says, "and a perfectionist. We'll bust our ass every day and every weekend to get through this phase."

The 18 Alpha curriculum for this class, Class 1-05, is broken down very precisely into blocks of instruction: five days of MOS orientation, ten days of adaptive thinking and leadership (ATL), and five days of strategic reconnaissance and direct-action analysis and planning, followed by a ten-day field training exercise, a fourteen-day foreign-internal-defense training module, thirteen days of unconventional-warfare training, and four days of advanced special operations training. The final four days of training is a full-immersion unconventional-warfare planning drill that will prepare the student captains for the extended unconventional-warfare exercise and field problem of Phase IV—the Robin Sage exercise.

The MOS orientation is a crash course in the duties and responsibilities of detachment specialties—one day for each. Assigned to Alpha Company are a cadre of experienced senior Special Forces sergeants who serve as instructors and support staff. On successive days, these veteran sergeants lecture the future detachment leaders on what their brother technical specialists can do for them and their teams. They also bring to the class an impressive array of weapons, radios, night-observation devices, cameras, laser designators, and (inert) explosive firing assemblies for hands-on training. A cadre medical sergeant accompanies the officers to the Joint Special Operations Medical Training Center for briefings and a facility orientation. By the end of the week, these captains more clearly understand the capabilities and responsibilities of the weapons, engineering, medical, and communications specialists who will be their teammates. Again and again I heard these veteran Green Beret trainers caution the officers: "These men are the subject-matter experts in their MOS, but you have to manage and supervise them, and take an interest in what they do. And remember, they know the gear and the weapons systems. The company supply sergeant will have you sign for this equipment—all of it. Ultimately, you're the one who'll be held accountable if something goes missing."

The adaptive thinking and leadership (ATL) training module is a unique experience for the 18 Alpha candidates. This is a relatively new block of training and, in some ways, as difficult to put into words as it is to put into practice. The purpose of this training is to equip Special Forces officer candidates with the ability to change or modify the way they approach problems and unfamiliar situations. The ATL training also helps them to understand how *others* perceive them. Much of Special Forces work is about relationships—relationships with superiors, subordinates, indigenous counterparts, hostile parties, insurgent actors, and nongovernmental organization types, to name a few. Put simply, often the success of a detachment commander is his ability balance the goals, needs, and cultural norms of others with his mission requirements.

"Special Forces personnel routinely deal with the unfamiliar," Major Ed Deagle tells me. Major Deagle is a trained psychologist who administered the three-and-a-half-day classroom portion of the ATL training. Deagle is a scholarly man, very approachable, and has none of the rough edges of the men he is training. He has an easy sense of humor, and he's very perceptive.

"Many of these officers bring with them a set of decision-making skills that've proven successful in traditional or more structured situations. The adaptive process is just that. We first want to develop their sensitivity to changes in their environment—changes that may affect their approach to a situation. Quite often, they do what they have always done in a new situation, even when their approach does not apply to the existing conditions. Second, we want them to change or modify their approach in a manner that will be successful—one that will move them to a resolution of the problem or desired outcome. And finally, we want this change in behavior or approach to be driven by some shift in the environment. When things change, so do they."

"At first, this concept was hard for me to get my arms around," Matt Anderson says of his ATL training. "I understood what not to do, as I have my own way in which I approach problems or people. I guess we all do. For me, the ATL training forced me to step back a moment and see the problem—to take an additional moment to evaluate the situation and not rely on old techniques. I was one of those guys who would question the problem if my solution didn't work or was marginally effective. You can't do that; ATL teaches you to focus on how *I* can change to better handle the problem. The classroom drills helped a lot."

One of the scenarios is a negotiation. On one side of the negotiation is the student team leader, who has to arrange transportation for his team across a piece of arid and unfamiliar terrain in North Africa to their base camp location. He has limited funds to make these arrangements, feed his men, and support his mission. He also knows the locals to be crafty, sometimes unreliable, and out to make a quick buck. The trek to the base camp is long and dangerous. The team leader has to make a good bargain and a safe bargain. On the other side of this negotiation is an ATL student playing the part of a local merchant. The merchant has invested his family's money in trucks and knows the Americans can be profitable customers. He also knows that he has the only trucks available, but the journey will be dangerous, and it would be catastrophic to lose the trucks. Yet he needs to make this deal to stay in business, and it has to be a good deal. Like his countrymen, the merchant enjoys the art of negotiating, and holds those who don't negotiate in low esteem. The team leader and the merchant enter negotiations. Each has a best deal, an acceptable deal, and a bottom-line deal position. Each knows what, for him, is a bad deal. Under the precepts of adaptive thinking, both have to read the human terrain—the other person—as they work for the best possible outcome.

"This kind of negotiation is very typical," Ed Deagle says of this scenario. "Special Forces detachment leaders do this all the time. But the thinking behind the negotiation exercise has a much broader application. These ATL techniques will work for solving problems in a range of strategic, tactical, diplomatic, and leadership situations. They are particularly helpful in cross-cultural situations and when stress and emotion are factors in decision making. We try to give these future team leaders the tools to make better decisions. Some of them come to this quickly, and some are very hard to pry out of their old ways of problem solving in a structured environment. A few of them will see this as hocus-pocus and change very little. Others will readily adapt to it, and it will become a valuable asset in their leadership toolkit."

Following the classroom work, the 18 Alpha candidates begin a six-day field problem designed to challenge their decision-making ability in an unfamiliar environment and with ambiguous instructions. The students begin with a historical, political, military, cultural, religious, and geographical overview of the Pineland scenario. Pineland is a mythical nation around which much of the Phase IV training is built. They are briefed at a simulated forward operating base, where the commander tasks them with gathering certain physical and human intelligence. Their mission is to determine the feasibility of American support for a resistance movement in the country of Pineland. The resistance group they are to contact is known to oppose the Pineland government, which is unfriendly to the United States. They are infiltrated in two-man teams by helicopter to the outskirts of a metropolitan area—usually the outskirts of Richmond or Raleigh-Durham. Once on the ground, they must cache their equipment, change into civilian clothes, and "infiltrate" into the city. They are armed only with contact instructions for their first partisan linkup. This exercise has gone by a number of different names, but it's currently called the Volkmann Exercise.

"This is a full-on role-playing scenario," Eric James says of the exercise, "and the students have to stay in role and play the game if they're to learn from it. They have information about their first contact and where to meet them. Each member of the team will take the lead in three or more meetings where they'll have incomplete information about the parameters of the meeting and about the individuals whom they must contact and extract information. Information is parceled out to the officer candidates depending on how well they handle the meeting and their elicitation skills."

Following the meetings, the teams exfil to a safe area and are returned to base, where they're debriefed by a Special Forces officer playing the role of a joint special operations task force intelligence officer. During this debriefing, each student captain presents the information he collected and any corresponding conclusions. Then he's evaluated on how he did or did not meet the commander's objectives and intent.

"This is a rude awaking for many of these guys," Eric James says. "Very little in their military experience has prepared them for this. They are used to dealing with subordinate soldiers and superior officers with clear-cut lines of authority and communication. Now they must deal with a resistance fighter or sympathizer who has his own frame of reference. For the student, the turf is unfamiliar, their marching orders are vague, and they have varying degrees of control over their environment. It challenges the limits of their interpersonal skills. After each meeting, the resistance member role player fills out an in-depth critique of the meeting. What the student takes away from the meeting and how the role player perceived the exchange are often very different. It's a huge learning experience, but only if the students stay in character. This is the first of many such meetings during this phase. They will conduct dozens of them during Phase IV and the Robin Sage exercise."

There are fifteen days devoted to strategic reconnaissance and direct action. Five days are devoted to mission planning in the classroom at Aaron Bank Hall, then the all-officer student ODAs travel to Fort A. P. Hill, an Army base in central Virginia, for field training. Each ODA is given a target package with the mission of conducting a strategic recon- naissance of the two targets in the package. The student officers know that they'll probably be tasked with a follow-on direct-action strike immediately following their reconnaissance. In my student ODA, ODA 912, the assigned team leader is Captain Larry Shaw. Shaw is chosen to lead because he is a chemical warfare officer and the only American officer in 912 not to have been to Ranger School. Major James wants him to get as much time as possible in planning and leading small-unit operations. The foreign officers are excused from this particular class exercise for a special briefing in Washington. The other captains in 912 are assigned duties within the ODA, those of team sergeant, intelligence sergeant, communications sergeant, and the like. The planning process is not unlike that in Phase II, but far more detailed and analytical. This formatted approach to planning is called the military decision-making process, usually referred to as MDMP. It is both methodical and com- prehensive, and—if used properly—allows for creativity in the plan- ning process, but forces the planners to examine every aspect of the mission. MDMP is the common format of special operations and joint- service operations. It allows SOF components such as Special Forces, Rangers, and SEALs to share planning doctrine with conventional forces.

"This is the only time in Phase III you will plan as a student ODA and take that planning into the field," Eric James tells 912. "The foreign- internal-defense and unconventional-planning exercises will be far more detailed and rigorous. So we let you cut your teeth on the reconnaissance and direct-action problem. It'll give you a chance to work and plan as a team. It's also a chance to get creative and apply your adaptive-learning training to a tactical problem. This is an opportunity to have some fun and take chances. In your planning, think about novel ways to execute your mission. Don't get too clever, but forget the book. Think about ways to accomplish your mission with minimum exposure and least chance of compromise."

Nine-one-two attacks the problem, and begins to build alternate courses of action to accomplish its mission of observing its assigned targets. The team considers various courses of action and works up plans for infiltration, exfiltration, time on target, actions on target, and the host of logistical, contingency, and mission-essential tasks associated with the operation. There are medical, communications, and weather annexes to prepare. As a team, they're all nimble with computers and the mission-planning software. Each of these captains has his personal version or versions of standard MDMP format—modified, tailored, and annotated from previous tours and planning previous operations. This planning software is carried on their personal laptops and on one or more thumb drives. A thumb drive is a small, removable computer storage drive a bit smaller than your thumb. When the drive is not plugged into the back of a computer, it's often carried around the candidate's neck on a lanyard.

"A thumb drive on a lanyard is the staff officer's ID badge," Captain Miguel Santos says with a grin. His role on the team for this exercise is the intelligence sergeant. Santos is one of the better mission planners in the student ODA. "I've been planning missions and small-unit tactics since I was at West Point. Every time I do this, I learn something, and that leads to a shortcut or a way to do it better the next time." He fingers the small cylinder around his neck. "Every lesson learned goes here, and it's available when I need it."

Nine-one-two plans for two days and formally presents several operational courses of action to its forward operating base commander, who is played by Major Brooks. Brooks agrees with the single course of action it recommends, and the team begins the more detailed work that will turn the chosen course of action into an operable mission plan. This planning begins at Fort Bragg and continues when they arrive at Fort A. P. Hill.

The facilities at A. P. Hill are excellent, and there are no distractions.

As a young junior-grade lieutenant back in 1969, I trained at A. P. Hill with SEAL Team Two. The current facilities are Spartan and similar to those at the Special Forces training areas on Fort Bragg—dated wooden buildings with barracks space at one end and a planning bay at the other. The planning bays are cluttered with easels, whiteboards, tables, folding chairs, laptop computers, equipment boxes, MREs, field gear, and weapons storage lockers. For three days, 912 plans for its recon mission with the expectation of a follow-on direct-action tasking. The goal of much of this planning effort is the operational briefing for the forward operating base commander. This briefing is called a briefback. In this case, the commander is played by the Fort A. P. Hill base commander, who, by chance, happens to be a Special Forces officer.

Captain Shaw's plan is simple and straightforward. The eight-man ODA will insert some four miles from the target area. The men will then patrol to the area and establish a base camp to support their mission. Shaw and his communicator will man the base camp while two three-man reconnaissance and surveillance teams will move closer to the targets and establish patrol bases. The plan is for the two recon teams to lay up during the day and move about at night to survey the targets—a mobile radar site and a communications relay station. The briefback reflects the general political and military situation in the nation of Pineland. Shaw's presentation is very smooth and professional, with various members of the team sharing the briefing duties. The real learning comes from the feedback from the commander's comments.

"Good job," he says to Captain Shaw, but he's really speaking to all of them. "You touched on all the mission critical issues and peripheral information. A couple of things. Since this is, for now, a reconnaissance mission, stress the importance of remaining undetected. Your guys have to know just how important this is, and remaining undetected has to drive your planning and your movement near the target.

"As soon as you get on the ground and into the target area, get off a situation report to me as soon as you can. There'll always be a very anxious forward operating base commander waiting to hear from you.

He wants to know if you are all right, and he wants some ground truth. You are ground truth. Other commanders will likely key in on your information, right up to the area task force and regional commanders. You are now the best and most current information source." He pauses to consult his notes. "You have a good plan, but keep it flexible as your recon teams will need to see things firsthand. If and when you are tasked with a direct-action follow-on mission, you'll want to plan with their recent observations. You've probably already gamed a direct-action operation, but be open to the best and safest way to accomplish the mission. Right now, you may think the best option is to engage the target with a sniper weapon. Change the plan if your ground analysis shows this is not the best way to do this. Don't underestimate the value of a simple standoff weapon like your M203 grenade launchers. They can be very effective against a soft target like a radar site."

The battalion commander leaves, and Eric James begins his critique. "I agree with the colonel; it was a good briefback." Then he begins a long list of "do better" and "consider this" items.

"When talking weather, terrain, enemy movements, and quick-reaction forces, talk about how these factors affect *your* mission. And always focus on the simplest way to accomplish your mission. On the positive side, Captain Shaw, I like the way you positioned yourself in base camp and in a position to support both of your reconnaissance teams. It's a strong command-and-control position. Some commanders would like to see you in the primary recon team, but I think you have better overall control in the base camp. It means that you're in for a few days of sitting on your butt in a hide site, but it's best for the mission.

"Again, you did a lot of things well, but as team leader you have to sell yourself, your plan, and your team to your commander. During the planning, intelligence drives the operational plan; during the briefing, your command of the intel will help you sell your operational plan. Be confident. Don't look at your briefing slides; look at him. Speak in a clear, command voice—look him in the eye. Say things like 'Your intent is' and show him how your plan addresses his intentions. He may have other tactical options. Give him every reason to have confidence in your ability to carry out this mission.

"There's another reason you want your immediate commander and everyone else up the chain of command to have confidence in you," James tells his captains. "A lot of commanders want to micromanage you in the field. The last thing you want is some guy back in a rear area calling you every few hours to ask you how it's going. It's in your interest to give the higher-ups every reason to trust you and to let you do your job. This is especially true for routine tactical missions or missions that are administrative in nature. A detachment commander recently back from Afghanistan told me he had an emergency request to send his medic to a forward position to tend to some friendlies who had been wounded by an IED. He sent his junior medical sergeant and his senior weapons sergeant to take care of it. The area commander, a conventional-force guy, ordered him to go—he wanted the detachment commander on the end of the radio so he could call every fifteen minutes and see what was going on. It was nothing his two sergeants couldn't handle. The detachment commander had his team sergeant in the field with a platoon of local militia and wanted to be near his ODA base camp. He finally had to tell his commander to let him do his job or to relieve him. You have to know your team and your stuff, and you have to be respectful, but you also have to stand your ground."

Nine-one-two conducts its rehearsals, sanitizes its briefing spaces, and boards its insertion helo—in this case an old six-by-six Army truck. The men are dropped off late afternoon for a four-mile night patrol to the target area. The temperature is in the mid-thirties, it's raining, and their rucks top out at about ninety-five pounds. They'll be in the field for five days with no resupply. Just before dawn the following day, the three elements of 912 go to ground in their hide sites. In most reconnaissance and surveillance missions, the recon teams move at night and hide out during the day. Choosing and preparing a good hide site is an art form. They'll usually look for a small depression or a narrow ravine to start with. Then they move about the area to find fallen branches to bridge the depression. A woodland-pattern tarp is placed over the branches and covered with sticks, vegetation, and leaves. Most teams carry a can of spray adhesive so the leaves will cling to the tarp and look natural. You can walk within a few feet of a good hide site in the daytime and not see it. Before the elements go to ground for the day, they rig jungle antennas, using a slingshot to carry a weighted line over a tree branch to hoist the wire antenna into the air. When the sun is full up, 912's two hidden recon teams are in communications with Shaw in the base camp on their handheld MBITR radios. In the base camp, Captain Shaw raises the forward operating base on his PRC-137. By midday, the cadre are out looking for the student teams to see how well they're hidden.

The drill is to put eyes on the targets for two days, noting the security arrangements, guard-force activity, and operational activity. All this is relayed back to the forward operating base—in this exercise, a cadre sergeant manning a base-station radio. These are long days and uncomfortable days, but this is the essence of strategic reconnaissance—observe without being seen. On the third day, Captain Shaw receives a radio message that calls for the targets be taken out at exactly 2345 the following day—fifteen minutes before midnight. The tasking calls for the radar site and the communications facility to be inoperative for four hours. Per the Pineland scenario, Navy fighter jets flying from carriers offshore are scheduled to conduct strikes at strategic targets inland, and a gap in the radar coverage must be opened to give them access to their targets. That evening, Captain Shaw calls each of his recon teams in and tasks them with their respective direct-action missions. Based on their observations of the targets, each team plans and executes their assigned strike. One team finds the power supply unit for the mobile radar site and places a dummy block of C-4 explosive on the unit at 2340, with a five-minute delay. The other team creeps to within forty yards of the communications facility and simulates a strike with an AT4 rocket. Nine-one-two reconstitutes itself at a prearranged rally point and patrols from the area.

The men are holding a loose security perimeter at a roadside clearing in a sleeting rain when the six-by-six helo comes to collect them.

The mission after-action review at the A. P. Hill barracks facility is quick, as snow is beginning to stick and the forecast calls for more. The tired, wet captains quickly pack out their personal gear and the exercise support equipment, and climb into the bus for the ride back to Fort Bragg.

"It was good to do a mission like that start to finish," Matt Anderson says of the experience. "Major James made us move through the planning process in excruciating detail. Just when you think you have it right, he comes along and wants it done better. Once we were in the field, we got a real feel for a true reconnaissance mission. It's been a while since I set up housekeeping in a hide site. Once in position, we were able to move about at night to get eyes-on the targets from various angles. The actual hit on the target was pretty anticlimactic, which is as it should be. The preparation is everything."

With the exception of the fieldwork that was part of the adaptive thinking and leadership training and the A. P. Hill exercise, most of the 18 Alpha training is focused on operational analysis and mission planning. In addition to the pure planning drills or command post exercises, there are scheduled classes on the political and interservice aspects of Special Forces operations. These blocks of training are sandwiched around the planning exercises. On occasion, training and instructional opportunities present themselves that may trump scheduled training, or are conducted after hours or on a free weekend.

Among the scheduled training is a half day of tracking. More specifically, it's a class on countertracking, or what a team in the field might do if they suspect they have a tracker after them. The men learn how a tracker works, what he looks for, and what they as a tactical unit or an individual on the run behind the lines can do to delay a tracker. The cadre instructor is a crusty master sergeant who has built his own spore pit out behind Aaron Bank Hall. Most Americans, he tells the captains, can be tracked by the trash they leave behind and their tobacco products. There is also a half day at the close-air-support simulator, a facility not unlike the call-for-fire simulator on which the weapons sergeants trained. Calling in close air support and calling in artillery are similar. Among the unscheduled briefings is that of an AC-130 gunship pilot. The AC-130 Spectre is a modified version of the venerable C-130 turbo-prop medium transport. The AC-130 Spectre has been armed with 40mm and 105mm guns. It is a very stable platform that can deliver an accurate and sustained rate of fire. An AC-130 can take out a building and leave the one next to it undamaged. It is particularly lethal against lightly armored vehicles and troops caught in the open. The AC-130U model also has an impressive suite of IR, thermal, and low-light-level sensors, as well as a substantial communications capability. The pilot, an Air Force captain, is the wife of one of the 18 Alpha candidate captains.

One of the more interesting unscheduled training opportunities comes with a visit by CBS News correspondent Lara Logan. She is no stranger to speaking to the military, and her presentation draws equal numbers of 18 Alpha candidates and Special Forces cadre. She outlines the duties of the press in general and her job as an investigative reporter in some detail. "I saw her more than I saw some of the guys on my ODA during my last trip to Kandahar," one of the cadre sergeants observes quietly. While it is a cordial exchange and Ms. Logan takes all questions from the floor, I can tell that the veteran cadre who had recent tours in the combat zone are very skeptical of the press. "They have a job to do, and so do we," another of the cadre says to me. "She's pretty competent and she's a hard worker, but we have to be *very* careful in dealing with the press. As a rule, unless I'm directed by higher, I simply just avoid talking to them."

"It's good for these guys to see and hear a reporter," Major Brooks says of Logan's visit, "and someone they've seen on TV. It's one less variable for them going on deployment."

Whenever there's a free minute of training time, Major James gives 912 some insight on life as a detachment leader and some of the things they need to be aware of. One of these is his personal equipment briefing.

"You're going to be very busy when you get to your detachment, so you'll want to have all your personal operational gear set up and ready to go. You'll get a standard issue, but if you're like me, you're going to want to customize some of your own gear. And that comes out of your pocket, something my wife still wonders about. But if you're going to be a professional warrior, you may want gear that's tailored for you." In the front of the room, an array of operational gear is laid out. "I bought a custom rucksack that suits my needs and some of the loads we carry in cold-weather operations with 10th Group. It holds my chow, sleeping bag, mission-specific equipment, ammo, clothing, that kind of thing. This is my load-bearing equipment vest; you can see that it is nonstandard. If you want one thing custom made, it's your LBE vest. This is what you will fight with when you dump your ruck or if you're out on quick-strike, direct-action mission. Your LBE should hold your ready ammo, a radio, compass, GPS, a trauma pouch, maybe some PowerBars, and whatever you might need to keep you alive for a day and keep you in the fight. As far as your standard BDUs, get some additional pockets sewed into them so you can stash a ready magazine, your survival maps, a day/night signaling device, a secure Iridium phone, an extra tourniquet, or whatever else you might need if you're away from your LBE and an emergency arises.

"You'll be issued body armor, but I recommend that you look to a custom vest—a body-armor plate carrier that'll allow you to operate with a full set of armor or perhaps with only the front and back plates. Sometimes you may want to remove the side plates for mobility. You'll wear this body armor under your LBE and under any number of standard and nonstandard uniforms and hadji dress, so you want it to be comfortable. Your group will issue you the plates, but I highly recommend you buy your own vest.

"On a standard deployment, you have to be prepared to move around in civilian clothes and in different settings. So you need to be able to dress casual, semicasual, and business casual. We call it rough, smooth, and slick. Rough is a T-shirt, jacket, and jeans; smooth is slacks and an open-collared shirt; and slick is coat and tie. As an ODA team leader, you have to be able to walk into an embassy, a tribal leader's home, or a downtown bazaar. You're probably never going to pass for anything but an American, but try to avoid the cowboy boots, ball caps, and big belt buckles. If you're lucky, you can pass for a Canadian or a German in an airport. The objective is to blend in and keep a low profile. Try to find a jacket that is reversible with good pockets and with one side a dark green or brown. You want it to be loose in case you have to wear body armor under it or carry a weapon. In this business, you have to be prepared to be operational or go operational at a moment's notice. We're not spies, but a team leader's work may require him to go about in civilian clothes."

Also scheduled for the 18 Alphas are four days of advanced special operations training, a classified block of instruction that trains the officer candidates in special intelligence collection techniques.

Midway through the phase, the officers of 912 are scheduled for their midcourse review. Major James and Master Sergeant Rameres spend an hour or more with each of them discussing their performance—where they are strong, and where they are weak. I sit in on a few of these sessions, and they are candid, honest assessments of each individual. The individual evaluation covers professional disciplines such as mission planning, briefing, and fieldcraft, but the focus is on demonstrated interpersonal skills and the candidate's decision-making abilities. At the beginning of Phase III, all of the officers took The Attentional and Interpersonal Style (TAIS) inventory. Most of the midcourse review focuses on the individual performance during the Volkmann Exercise and how that performance correlates to the TAIS results. Typically, Major James begins these interviews with open-ended questions.

"How would you rate your performance so far?"

"Tell me, because you've never stated it in so many words and I didn't pick it up in your autobiography: Why do you want to be in Special Forces?"

"Where do you think you're weak?"

"During the Volkmann encounters, you came across a little harsh and strident. Even during your debriefings, you were a little defensive. Do you think this is accurate?"

After challenging the candidate in areas where his performance may have been lacking and weak, Major James and Master Sergeant Rameres move on to positive areas and what the individual candidate might do to work on his deficiencies.

"From what I've seen, your performance in the Volkmann Exercise and field exercises is consistent with the comments from your TAIS. You are quiet, and that's OK, but that often makes you seem arrogant and above others. You need to be aware of how you come across to others."

"Your TAIS suggests that you have a high opinion of yourself and that you hold yourself to a very high standard. This tendency to be the best and to achieve excellence often prevents you from taking advantage of the opinions of others or of changes in the environment."

"You're doing well, but you need to work to improve your situational awareness and your negotiating skills—your interpersonal skills. Intellectually, you like the challenge and have a do-it-myself attitude. This can limit you. Learn to ask questions and take advice from others—to weigh others' opinions."

"You seem to attach your identity to your achievement. People like you are prone to put the job ahead of their families—way ahead—and that's a trap all of us have to work on and try to avoid."

"Your TAIS rated you as overanalytical and perhaps slow to come to a decision because you thought too much about it—made it too complicated. I saw that a little bit during the field training at A. P. Hill. Then when you make a decision, you defend it, even if new data questions that decision."

Most of these counseling sessions end with some recommendations to work on weaknesses.

"Since you seem to overanalyze, try to be brief and concise and go quickly to the bottom line. Find a peer buddy in the class, someone you trust. Tell your peer buddy this is an area you're trying to work on, and seek his feedback."

"In every situation that calls for a decision, ask the opinion of someone else on the team. If you don't understand how they came up with that decision or position, ask them to explain it. This will allow you to make a change or to validate your original position."

After the midcourse review, and prior to the next block of instruction, 912 and the other 18 Alpha candidates take two days off for sustainment training. They have an equipment jump one day, and spend another on the firing ranges with combat shooting. A day of airborne operations and a day of shooting are scheduled for the Charlies, Deltas, and Echos during their Phase III as well. The Bravos, the weapons sergeants, need only to make the jump.

Nine-one-two moves on to the foreign-internal-defense planning exercise. FID is an important tasking of Special Forces, both historically and as it relates in the current operations in Afghanistan and Iraq. Foreign internal defense and counterinsurgency, or COIN, are closely related. It is the business of working with other nations and other cultures to defeat insurgency. In my opinion, it is the single most important skill set of Army Special Forces. This unique ability to work "by, with, and through" another culture in the conduct of counterinsurgency operations is what makes the Green Beret the most essential warrior in our military today. The U.S. Army is the service component tasked with counterinsurgency, but that capability is a function of big Army's ability to find and kill insurgents—a near-impossible task if the insurgents find refuge in the local population. Patrolling neighborhoods in Humvees and cordon-and-search tactics are not effective in defeating an insurgency. Perhaps this sells our conventional military presence a little short, but one thing is clear: The difficult business of rooting out a well-organized and well-financed insurgency *cannot* be done without the help of the local population. Orchestrating this help is the stock in trade of Special Forces.

The foreign-internal-defense module begins with lectures on the mechanics and infrastructure of an insurgency, and the role of the adviser in working with the local military and police forces in a foreign country. As with most Phase III officer training, the scenario is built around a planning exercise. In FID training, the exercise is to plan a Special Forces ODA deployment called JCET—joint/combined exchange training. In this scenario, the country is Ecuador and the insurgents are the FARC, or Revolutionary Armed Forces of Colombia. The same principles apply for a similar FID deployment to Afghanistan, Iraq, the Philippines, Indonesia, or just about anywhere else when a friendly government is threatened by insurgents.

The first several days of the FID exercise are classroom intensive and focus on the specifics of planning and coordinating a JCET deployment. It begins with tasking and funding—who wants the training done and who pays for it. If the training is requested by the host nation, then the request for U.S. assistance is handled by the Department of State and the money comes through State from Title 22 funding. If the JCET was initiated by Special Forces with the objective of training a Special Forces ODA team, and was approved by the U.S. Special Operations Command, then the funds are taken from the military budget in the form of Title 10 funds. No matter where the money comes from, the ODA will deploy with the idea of training the host nation's military or constabulary in military skills they can use to defend themselves against the insurgents. In the school planning scenario, the opposition is the FARC, one of the few remaining insurgencies with a Communist ideology, which has a narco-terrorist history. They are still active, with tentacles reaching into several South American nations, including Hugo Chávez's Venezuela.

"I was the assist detachment commander for the FID problem," says Miguel Santos. "But we all work the problem as a team. The process is the same as for a strategic-reconnaissance or a direct-action mission.

We get the tasking and begin to game out various courses of action. Each of these alternatives is examined for how it'll work in practice and how it addresses the commander's intent—his vision of the mission and the desired end state. We get pretty far down in the weeds of each one, building a task organization, analyzing the host nation's requirements, planning logistics, building training plans, building timelines—that kind of thing. Once we work up several alternative plans, we decide as a team which course of action we think is best and run it by Major James, just like we would present it to our battalion commander."

"OK, I'll go with your course of action," James tells OD 912 and the designated team leader, Captain Jim Toohey. Toohey is a tall, intelligent officer who came to the Q-Course from the Army Corps of Engineers. He and the rest of 912 are assembled in their team room at Aaron Bank Hall.

"Now you have to get into the details. Think about every aspect of your mission: what you can do to make it succeed, and what might come up that'll interfere with your mission. You have to think very hard about the unit you are going to train—get into that unit commander's head. Remember that as advisers, you have to be able to conduct company- and battalion-size operations and assaults on a 'by, with, and through' basis, *and* you have to do this within *their* capability." James clicks on the PowerPoint, and a series of items begins to slide onto the screen in the team room. "A couple of things for you to consider as you return to your planning sessions."

- Match the training environment to the operational environment.
- Know as much as you can about the enemy *they* have to fight—in this case, the FARC.
- Be very careful how you train and offer to help. They may think they're doing a pretty good job.
- You will be dealing closely with embassy personnel. Understand the attitude of the ambassador to your being there and the dynamics within the country team.

- How does the host-nation commander view the training you are bringing to him?
- Have previous ODAs been there? What did they do? How were they received?
- Your communications and medical planning have to be spot on. Think about what may happen if one of your men or the men you are training gets hurt. Game it out.
- Make a friend of the embassy liaison officer. Your rapport with him, or her, is very important.
- We plan using our military decision-making process—MDMP—but how do they do it?
- How do they train? Get a feeling for a day in their life—do they sleep late? Do they take siestas? Do they live in garrison or will you be training men who live with their families?

"This is a short list," Major James tells them, "but you get the idea. You can't plan enough, and you can't think about these things enough. Look two or three moves ahead. An action on your part to solve the immediate problem may create multiple problems down the road."

Prior to the deployment of an ODA, a delegation from the team, usually two men, will visit the host nation to conduct a predeployment site survey. Within the context of the JCET training exercise for this FID problem, this becomes a series of role-playing events. Captain Toohey and Miguel Santos "arrive" in the host nation and go to the embassy. Their first meeting is with the embassy liaison officer, who is played by Major Brooks. Brooks's character is a lieutenant colonel who is a logistics specialist, new to the job, and knows little about the work of Special Forces. Brooks, seated behind the desk in his office, is dressed in a white shirt and tie as he would be in an embassy setting; the captains are dressed in slacks and open-collared shirts—they're smooth. The venue, as with most role-play training that has limited student participants, has Captains Toohey and Santos conducting the interview with the rest of the team standing behind them along the wall to listen and learn. "Lieutenant Colonel" Brooks tries to ensnare Toohey with a Special Forces demonstration at the airport and to assist him with some embassy staff work. Captain Toohey neatly sidesteps these requests. Following the interview and critique, the site-survey team and their observers climb into vans and head out to the host-nation training area—in this case, the 82nd Airborne pre-Ranger training camp.

A civilian role player in the guise of an Ecuadoran corporal takes them around the camp where the ODA will train the Ecuadoran unit—a counterinsurgency battalion. Toohey and Santos ask questions, make notes, and take pictures. Then they are led to a building where they conduct a meeting with the host-nation battalion commander. The two ODA advance men know from his bio that this commander is wealthy by birth, well educated, may have higher political aspirations, and has earned a reputation as a good commander in the field. The commander wants to talk about politics and America. Toohey and Santos have to work hard to keep him on the subject of their training mission. Following the interview, there's a critique. What did they learn? What could they have done better to establish rapport? How could they have better handled the meeting to keep the conversations on point?

On their way back to the notional embassy and before they conclude their site survey in the host nation, Toohey, Santos, and company negotiate several more role-play encounters that challenge their ability to think on their feet and their interpersonal skills. Those encounters are omitted here to preserve their training value for future 18 Alpha officer candidates. The site-survey team and the other members of 912 head back to their team room to begin working on the JCET backbrief for their battalion commander.

Nine-one-two works all afternoon and most of the night to prepare their JCET predeployment briefing, or briefback. A battalion commander from the 7th Special Forces Group is seated at the table in the briefing room at 0800 the following morning to receive their briefing. Captain Toohey and 912 push through their formatted briefing, with the battalion commander stopping them on occasion to ask a question.

And as with most briefings, much of the learning comes from the post-briefback critique. The commander compliments the team on their planning, then flips through his notes and ticks off a number of items the team should consider or consider in more detail when planning a training mission to another country:

"Don't forget that the host-nation commander has been fighting for a while. Listen to him. What does he say about his capability? What do battalion-size operations mean to him?"

"As you rehearse for the deployment, don't forget teaching rehearsals; they're very important. If you're going to train at altitude, rehearse at altitude."

"Verify ammo requirements on the ground—ensure you have what you need, who is providing it, and what are the arrangements for storing weapons and ammunition."

"Alcohol. Know customs and have a plan. Some cultures are hard drinkers, like eastern Europeans, and some cultures don't drink at all."

"Be prepared to deal with the press. War-game out the hardball questions. They're there to get the goods on you and to embarrass you. You have to protect yourself and the host-nation force."

"Security; this is big issue. There are people out there who want to kill you and kidnap you. Game out your security plan. Is there a history of vehicular kidnapping of Americans? Can you carry a gun while you're out in civilian clothes?"

"One of the main jobs of your predeployment site survey is to gauge embassy support and commitment for your mission. The same for the host nation."

"You as a team leader have to understand the range and depth of *their* problems. Gear and procedures are different in Macedonia than in Africa or Afghanistan."

"Every move you make has an effect on the local economy. Think about this as you contract for services."

"You have to war-game the training and decide if you are going to conduct the training for the host-nation force or if you're going to train the trainers—their senior training sergeants. The latter is usually better, as we can get them to do the job so we can go home. At all times, do what's best for the men you have to train."

"And always, always, always see to the safety of your men. Good luck to all of you."

Following the foreign-internal-defense planning exercise and brief-back, the men of 912 secure their FID training materials and prepare for a trip to Washington. Well before dawn the following day, the officers of Class 1-05 are on a bus bound for D.C. There they will receive classified briefings from the deputy director for special operations at the Pentagon, and representatives at the State Department, the Defense Intelligence Agency, and the Central Intelligence Agency.

For the most part, these programs are designed to give these future detachment leaders some feel for the organization of these agencies and departments, how they communicate with the Defense Department, and how their overseas representatives and programs may interact or support the work of Special Forces. At State, they spend time with a former ambassador who speaks about his relations with ODAs that worked within his country. At the CIA, they meet with senior officers of the Special Activities Division. Most of these briefings have a Middle East/Afghanistan/Iraq bias.

Nine-one-two musters in the team room at 0700 following their return from the nation's capital. "I know you guys didn't get back until late last night," Major Eric James tells his captains, "and you may find yourselves a little short on sack time from here on out. There's a lot of ground to cover and not much time left. Now we begin unconventional warfare. The UW planning exercise will be intense and take you deeply into the Pineland order of battle and the Robin Sage exercise scenario that is a big part of Phase IV.

"You all saw the detail that goes into planning a mission to help an allied force defend itself against insurgents. Now we're going to plan an insurgency. *We* are the ones who're now going to help the insurgents to oust the government in power. Although we don't call them insurgents anymore; they are now guerrillas or freedom fighters. Guys, let me tell you, this is hard stuff. Most of you have worked with battle staffs with a full complement of operational planners, logisticians, communications specialists, combat support elements—the whole enchilada. As a team leader taking an ODA into a UW environment, the whole thing falls to you. You are not planning a single mission; you are planning a whole campaign. You have the formatted MDMP to guide you, but it's only a guide. You'll have to ask a lot of questions and get very detailed in your planning. In a UW scenario, every move you make has to be gamed for its impact down the line—how it impacts your guerrilla force, how it affects the local population, and how it supports the commander's intent and your mission."

Major James passes out an exercise message that tasks student ODA 912 with preparing to enter the nation of Pineland ahead of conventional coalition forces. Their mission is to train and organize the irregular forces that now oppose the government of Pineland, and to conduct an unconventional-warfare campaign. They are also to provide intelligence and condition the battle space for an invasion by coalition forces. He gives them a few minutes to read the tasking.

"Your planning has to take into account the capability of the guerrilla force in place and the capability of the enemy. How can you target the enemy's command-and-control infrastructure with your force? Think of the reaction of the enemy; what do you want to show on the battlefield—what's your signature? You can think way out of the box; your only constraints are a reasonable measure of support and the moral and legal constraints that're always part of what we do. I want to see some good thinking on how to get the job done with minimum risk to you and the local assets you have available to you. In the Robin Sage exercise, there will be both physical and exercise constraints that are artificial. In this planning exercise, you can turn yourself loose—be creative within reason. This is downrange important. You *will* do this for real.

"As you build your potential courses of action, keep in mind that

you are preparing your sector for a follow-on conventional allied operation. What intelligence can you send back to help with that operation? What's the suitability for the primary and secondary roads to
support division-sized movement? How effective are the Pineland
internal security forces? How do you identify spies among the guerrillas you are going to train and take into battle? What are the potential
targets that you can begin to identify that will degrade or disrupt the
enemy's mobility? What are your plans for the demobilization of your
guerrilla force after D-day? See what I'm getting at? You've a lot of
planning to do and a lot of questions that need answers. And every
move you make has to be thoroughly war-gamed. What does that decision mean now and how does that decision affect events in the campaign that will take place tomorrow and the next day?

"You'll have only a single day to work up your courses of action
and present them to the commander tomorrow morning. Give these
options a lot of thought, and which one you will recommend and why.
Captain Santos, you will be the team leader for this one. The rest of the
assignments are posted on the board. Good luck, gentlemen."

Miguel Santos smiles slowly and shakes his head. He seems to have
known he would be tapped for the final problem. It'll be 912's most
difficult challenge in Phase III, but Captain Santos is perhaps the best
planner in the student ODA.

"OK," Santos says to his team after James leaves, "who's my intelligence sergeant?"

"Right here," answers the captain from the 75th Ranger Regiment.

"Get started on building an intel file and see that everyone is read
into the problem. Also start listing additional information requirements we'll ask for as we move into the problem. Who's my assistant
detachment commander?"

"Right here, Miguel."

"You and the team sergeant start building a timeline and milestones
leading to the courses of action briefing at 0800 tomorrow morning."
Santos checks his watch. "For the next few hours, it's a mission-

analysis drill. What you don't find in the scenario file and message traffic, get it on the information requirement list. OK, guys, let's get it done." ODA 912 breaks into a flurry of activity.

The officers work through lunch and send out for pizza for the evening meal. About 2100, Major James drops by to see how they're coming on their courses of action. He studies each one carefully. The one they have selected and directed much of their extended planning effort on is not what he had in mind.

"That's why you have to war-game each of these approaches; look weeks down the line at where each course of action will take you. Think about how long you'll be in the field under this scenario. What happens if there's no aerial resupply? What if the guerrillas fail to provide the mobility you need? If this is your initial target list, how're you going to move about to hit them all? And think about these targets. Your job is to do what a smart bomb cannot do, like snatching a Pineland leader from a moving vehicle or hitting an armory to get arms for your guerrillas."

After some discussion, a new "recommended" course of action is chosen, and 912 goes back to work. They work through the night, and at 0800, a weary group of captains briefs Major Brooks on the range of options considered for the mission and the course of action they think will best serve the mission and the commander's intent.

With a course of action chosen, the heavy lifting of planning an unconventional-warfare mission shifts into high gear. Information is fed to ODA 912 by the training cadre as they respond to intelligence data requested by the student ODA. There are briefings from the scenario command-staff intelligence officer on current events in Pineland and from the command-staff operations officer to refine the commander's intent, key tasks, and the desired end state of their mission. Other briefings, with cadre sergeants serving as support staff personnel, cover communications, medical support, and logistics. Nine-one-two also speaks to the pilot who will be supporting the mission and interviews a refugee from Pineland. There's also a briefing by a legal officer from the 7th Group. Part of what he tells 912 is exercise related and a great deal of it is real world.

"You're always going to have rules of engagement—ROEs will be a fact of your deployed life. And, you're always going to be concerned with the safety of your men. That said, the basis of ROEs is 'proportional response.' ROEs are rooted in political, military, and legal parameters. Civilians are protected persons, and you are accountable for any harm that comes to them through your actions. You have a right to self-defense, but if civilians get hurt or killed, you'll have to be able to articulate your position in the action. Know and understand the standard ROEs and how those ROEs apply to your area of operation. Rules of engagement have to be part of your planning, here in the Q-Course and down range. And the Robin Sage exercise in Phase IV is the last time you'll see an enemy in uniform. Remember, we have ROEs; they do not."

Captain Santos and one of his men conduct these interviews or receive the briefings with the rest of the ODA in close attendance. Master Sergeant Rameres sits in on all of them and conducts a short critique after each.

"Always remember that no matter whether it's a local civilian or the battalion communicator or a pilot, every one of these people can help you with your mission. Take a moment or more as necessary to build rapport and elicit every scrap of information you can. You need what these people know and can do for you, and if you're not sure of what they're telling you, ask the question a different way. And be careful what information you give. With the pilot, tell him only what he has to know to support your mission. He may become a POW, and you don't want him to have the details of your movements on the ground."

Three days after the course of action briefing, Captain Santos stands before Lieutenant Colonel Jim Jackson, the 1st Battalion commander, to deliver his briefback. He begins with an overview of the mission, a restatement of the commander's intent, and the desired end state. Then he plunges into the mechanics of the operation. All of the team members contribute, but Santos does most of the talking. The briefback details ODA 912's mission, the team leader's intent, task organization, threat analysis, concept of operations, logistics, command and signal, and personnel issues. Two hours and seventy-six PowerPoint slides later, Santos asks if there are any questions. There is close to an hour of critique and discussion of 912's planning effort. Lieutenant Colonel Jackson's comments are a balance of the exercise briefback critique and considerations for real-world operational planning.

"You have to plan carefully and you have to plan methodically," Jackson says in closing. "Don't forget the administrative issues. It's easy to go past the admin stuff and into the meat of the mission. Get into the details that protect your people. When you deploy for real, make sure your men have a will made out. Make sure it's in writing how and where they want to be buried and who gets the insurance money. Keep track of your funds; helos crash, and money gets burned up. These are real-world issues. Build these details into your training scenarios—you'll soon be doing this down range, where it counts. Looking ahead to Robin Sage in Phase IV, you'll have one more time to do this in training before it's real—real lives and real bullets. If you can manage an unconventional-warfare campaign within the political, military, and cultural boundaries of the Pineland scenario, you can handle any unconventional-warfare or foreign-internal-defense situation in the world. That's where we are going with this. We'll see you gentlemen out at Camp Mackall in a week or so."

The last item before the student captains from 912 leave Phase III is their final counseling sessions. These sessions are much like the mid-course counseling, but more in depth. The 18 Alpha candidates' Special Forces training folders are getting pretty fat by this stage of the Q-Course. Each one is a detailed chronology of the officer's performance, along with specific comments and evaluations since the beginning of Phase II. There are summations of counseling sessions, TAIS coaching points, Volkmann Exercise performance reports, role-playing contact reports, debriefing reports, self-assessment reports, leadership assessment reports, peer evaluations, spot reports—both positive and negative—and their physical training scores. This is not the first special operations training venue I've been around, and I can say I have never seen this much attention to so much detail—such focus on individual performance and analysis. Each man's jacket has eight to ten pages of typewritten assessment and critique information.

The End of Phase Counseling Evaluation usually begins with an overall recommendation for continuation in the Q-Course. As the senior small-group instructor, Major James rates every member of 912 regarding his technical, physical, and mental performance. This evaluation goes into specifics about the candidate's strengths and weaknesses, as well as the progress he has made during the phase. Where credit was due, he gave it.

"It was noted by the cadre and his peers that Captain Smith transitioned into the unconventional mind-set more quickly than almost anyone in the class."

When criticism was warranted, James did not pull his punches. "While I have seen some improvement, Captain Smith still has tendencies to be argumentative and abrupt in his dealings with others. If he can continue to improve his verbal and nonverbal communications and actions, he may be able to overcome this glaring weakness." For all of these officers, this is by far the most formal and detailed critique they've received in their military careers.

On Thursday of the final week, 912 and the other officer ODAs are turning in their materials and phase-related equipment, and completing *their* evaluations that rate the 18 Alpha curriculum and the cadre. Everyone gets a critique. The student officers will have a long weekend before they begin Phase IV. I stop by the team room that afternoon to thank Major James and Master Sergeant Rameres, and wish 912 well in Phase IV. I catch Miguel Santos just as he is finishing up.

"Three down and one to go," I remark. Captain Santos will get his Special Forces tab and Green Beret sooner than most because he is SERE qualified and a Spanish speaker, which means he could graduate from the Q-Course when he finishes Phase IV.

"Yes, sir," he replies. "And I'm glad to have this one behind me. Phase IV won't be easy, but I hope it won't be as hard as this. I haven't studied this much since finals week at West Point."

"But you passed Phase III, right?"

He pauses a moment before replying. "Yes, sir, I passed, but this was a bit of an awakening for me. I've always been a hard worker, and I've always done well—at West Point, in my year group from West Point, and at my previous commands. Here I was average—maybe below average. Major James had a few good things to say in my final counseling session, and more than a few areas where he feels I came up short—where I need to improve. I'm not questioning him, but it's been a while since I've been hammered on like that."

"So what now?"

Santos gives me a tired grin. "I guess I need to spend a quiet weekend with my wife and think about all this. Then attack Phase IV on Monday and try to do better. You're going to be with us out at Camp Mackall, aren't you, sir?"

"I wouldn't miss it for the world."

Author's Note: As mentioned in these notes following previous chapters, the Special Forces Qualification Course is a dynamic, changing process. Nowhere in this evolving process are these changes more dramatic or rapid than in the training of future detachment leaders. Without getting into specifics as to the then and now, let me just say that current changes to the 18 Alpha curriculum include the training and integration of the international student officers, physical training (cadre and student ODAs now conduct team physical training on a daily basis), an expanded Advanced Special Operations training block, and modifications to the adaptive leadership training and Volkmann Exercise. Training venues have also changed, with more of the training conducted away from Fort Bragg at remote sites.

CHAPTER EIGHT

ROBIN SAGE

At 0500 on a Monday morning in mid-April, 308 18 Series MOS-trained officers and enlisted men, along with their operational gear, muster in the parking lot of Aaron Bank Hall at Fort Bragg. Technically, they're still Green Beret candidates, but they are trained Special Forces soldiers. Because of the training before them, the Phase IV cadre refer to them as students. They are once more broken down into student ODAs and board an assortment of buses, trucks, and semitrailers that resemble cattle cars. After a stop at the armory to draw weapons, they head for Camp Mackall and the Rowe Training Facility. They are Class 2-05 for this phase of training. Once there, they pretty much know the drill. By 1000, the students have found their assigned team spaces—the all-too-familiar barracks/team-room facilities. For Phase IV, they're a combination of Quonset-hut-style buildings and temporary mobile-home-type condo bays set on post-and-pier foundations with common sidewalls. Only in Phase IV, these

---

HERE'S THE PLAN. Colonel Chissom and Sergeant Major Johnson, flanked by two guerrillas, listen as Specialist Antonio Costa briefs them on the ambush of a Pineland Army patrol.

287

team huts become isolation facilities. Within the training scenario, these are ODAs preparing for war. The student ODAs quickly settle into their quarters and draw additional equipment for the phase— radios, medical equipment, night-vision goggles, military GPSs, and a considerable amount of consumables like Chemlites, flares, MREs, and blank ammunition. After the equipment draws, each man lays out his personal and assigned team equipment on a poncho liner for inspection. By midafternoon, the candidates form up next to the battalion headquarters, the same area where many of them received their SFAS briefings. One of the phase cadre sergeants quickly covers the now-familiar rules for Special Forces training at Camp Mackall—no nonmilitary books, no cell phones, no personal computers, and no personal GPSs. Then the 1st Battalion commander steps in front of the formation.

"Gentlemen, welcome back to Camp Mackall," Lieutenant Colonel Jim Jackson says to Class 2-05. "This is it, Phase IV. This is where you take everything you've learned and put it all together in an operational environment. We expect you to work with indigenous forces in an unconventional-warfare scenario. That means dealing effectively with military, paramilitary, and civilian personnel. This phase is all about managing the human terrain. The indig forces you will work with will have different motivations and values than you. This is probably the last time many of you will train men for war that speak your language. You'll have to find common ground and to pursue common interests with these men; you'll have to win them over. It's all about people. Your job is to teach them, train them, and bond with them. It's a by, with, and through business, in this phase and on deployment in the Special Forces groups. Like all phases of training, we have performance review boards. There are three things that will get you to the board. The first is an inability to positively interact with others. The second's the inability to grasp the material we teach here. Before you head into the field on Robin Sage, we'll be teaching you some important skills. Show us a poor learning curve and you will find yourself recycled to the next class. And the last thing that'll get you to the review board is lack of focus or not taking this training seriously. The Robin Sage exercise is one long, continuous stage performance. Get your head in the game and keep it in the game. Treat the training scenario like the real thing—be an actor and stay in character.

"Finally, I want you to enjoy this training, and get all you can out of it. If you stay in role and work the scenario, it can be very rewarding. The guys coming back from combat deployments say Afghanistan is Robin Sage on steroids. Robin Sage and the Pineland scenario isn't just some war game. It's effectively trained several generations of Green Berets in unconventional warfare and foreign internal defense. This is real-time, downrange stuff. Take it seriously, gentlemen. A year from now, all of you will be deployed and in harm's way. Command Sergeant Major?"

Sergeant Major Frank Zorn steps before the class. "It won't get any better than this," he says with an easy grin. "Nobody's shooting at you, which, by the way, is the last time you will have it that way. If you are taking real fire, it's not part of the training. There are some locals out there that like to shoot guns. If the rounds are real, go admin. Otherwise, stay in the game—stay involved. There's always something that you can do, something that needs doing. If there's a problem, *be a part of the solution.* This training is for people who think—people who are aware of what's going on around them and can anticipate what's going to happen next. There'll be a lot of opportunity for you to do something stupid. Don't. Even when no one else is around, play the game for real. And you 18 Deltas, let me see a show of hands." There is a smattering of hands from the group. "OK, I want you to repeat after me, 'I am a warrior first and a medic second.' Go on, say it." They do. "Thanks, that's all I have. Have fun, work hard, train hard, and train like you fight, because you'll be taking these skills to the fight."

The next man to address the class is Major Mike Kennedy. Major Kennedy is a lanky North Carolinian with a quiet, serious manner.

He grew up in Chapel Hill, less than a hundred miles from Camp Mackall. He has a bachelor's degree in history from the Citadel and a master's in defense analysis from the Naval Postgraduate School. Kennedy has been in the Army for fifteen years, the Special Forces for ten. He's spent most of his time with the 3rd Group and is a French speaker. In addition to several tours in Africa and Bosnia, he has made three rotations to Afghanistan. Mike Kennedy is thc commander of Echo Company, 1st Battalion, and the man responsible for Phase IV and Robin Sage. Robin Sage, the most complex and diverse military training exercise in the United States, rests squarely on his shoulders.

"Welcome to Phase IV," Kennedy tells Class 2-05. "Congratulations for getting to this phase in training. How many combat veterans do we have here?" About 30 percent of 2-05 raise their hands. "If I asked this question eighteen months ago, it would be half that many. If I ask that question of this group eighteen months from now, it would be 80 percent. Those of you who haven't seen combat soon will. Phase IV is pre-mission training. This is the last chance to rehearse those skills you'll take to war. The skills you'll use in Robin Sage—small-unit tactics, your MOS training, air infiltrations and resupply, and working with indigenous forces—are the things you'll do when you get to the fight. What you fail to learn here can get you or one of your teammates killed. Here, we'll hold you to a proficiency standard, or you'll be recycled or relieved. You have to perform. You're not a rifle squad; you are an ODA, and we expect you to think, adapt, improvise, and overcome. In short, you have to make it happen.

"Your reputation is also at stake. These cadre sergeants will know if you are a slacker—trying to do just the minimum. Ninety percent of my cadre sergeants will go back to the groups as team sergeants; you'll see them again. They all have memories like elephants. Take ownership and leadership within your teams. You captains and team sergeants have to step in and show the way when things get hard, and they will get hard. You guys in ranks have to lead from within the team. Do what needs to be done. Good luck."

The class breaks from the formation and heads for their team huts. My student Operational Detachment Alpha is student ODA 915. Nine-one-five has some familiar faces and some new ones. Leading the team is Captain Miguel Santos, the student detachment leader. He'll be in charge of this twelve-man ODA during Phase IV and Robin Sage. Along with him will be many from his, and my, Phase II student ODA. The team's 18 Bravos, or weapons "sergeants," are Specialists Tom Kendall and Antonio Costa and Private First Class Tim Baker. The 18 Charlie engineering sergeants are Sergeants Daniel Barstow and Aaron Dunn. The communicators, or 18 Echos, are Specialists Justin Keller and David Altman—the big guy from Denver and the little guy from Tennessee. Lost from the Phase II team are Stan Hall, Byron O'Kane, and Frank Dolemont, who are all in combat medic training. Also missing is Captain Matt Anderson, who will command another student ODA in Phase IV, and the rugged PFC Roberto Pantella, who, due to the surplus of weapons sergeants on 915, is assigned to another Phase IV ODA.

Joining my Phase IV ODA is a single 18 Delta medic, Sergeant Andrew Kohl. Sergeant Brian Short, who, like Antonio Costa, is in the National Guard, is also an 18 Echo communicator. Nine-one-five will have a fourth communications sergeant in Staff Sergeant Tom Olin, who, as the senior enlisted soldier, will serve as the team sergeant. Nine-one-five will also have another officer, a foreign-exchange student from Botswana, First Lieutenant Patrick Kwele. Kwele will serve as the assistant student detachment leader. Let's take a closer look at the new guys.

Andrew Kohl is a veteran of Operation Iraqi Freedom and has been in the Army for four years. He was an all-state high school cross-country runner from Wisconsin. After a year of college, he decided to enlist in the Army. "I've an uncle who served in Special Forces, and he's been urging me to do this. After I saw what the SF were doing in

Iraq, I knew this was what I wanted to do." "Doc" Kohl has been
in combat medic training longer than his teammates have been in the
Q-Course and longer than the X-Ray candidates have been in the
Army. But his combat medical training was as brief as he could make
it. He was one of the minority from his 18 Delta class to go straight
through training with no recycles.

Brian Short grew up in Minneapolis and has a bachelor's degree and
a master's in communications. Captain Santos immediately tapped him
to serve as 915's intelligence specialist. Sergeant Short was working as
an assistant manager at Wal-Mart when he joined the National Guard
to help pay off his college loans. He knows that by volunteering for
Special Forces training, he's guaranteed himself a combat deployment.
He's assigned to the 20th Special Forces Group, and is the only one in
915 that knows the exact day when he will deploy with an operational
detachment to Iraq. And that deployment will be only days after he
graduates from the Q-Course. I asked him what he'll do when he
returns. "I'll have to wait and see. I may go back to my old job at Wal-
Mart, or I may elect to go into the active Army. Right now I have to
focus on Phase IV, the rest of the Q-Course, and my deployment."

Staff Sergeant Tom Olin, twenty-five, has been in the Army for six
years. He is from Montana, and began his military service with the 1st
Cavalry Division as a Bradley Fighting Vehicle driver. This is his second try at the Q-Course. He was dropped from training in 2003 during Phase IV and is now back for the second try, having served a tour
with the 10th Mountain Division in Afghanistan. He declined to talk
about his previous attempt at Special Forces training, saying only that
"I made some mistakes the last time I was here, and I won't make
those same mistakes again. I'm back here because this is what I want
to do; I want to be a professional Special Forces soldier."

First Lieutenant Kwele is part of the ongoing international military
student program in U.S. Army and Army Special Forces. There are foreign officers as well as enlisted soldiers in Class 2-05. They participate

in all aspects of the Q-Course except those classroom evolutions where classified material is discussed, which include some classroom training during Phase IV. Before they enter American military training, the international students are carefully screened and in some cases attend language training in America. They're also counseled in our customs and cultural norms—issues that range from the treatment of women to automobile insurance. This includes our military standards of conduct, which may differ from their home nation's service. One such standard is the position and esteem which our Army affords noncommissioned officers and which may or may not be the case in the guest soldier's army.

Patrick Kwele is a lean, handsome, ebony-skinned African, with a shy, engaging smile. He is polite, almost formal, and speaks English with the precision of an Oxford don. Every foreign student in the Q-Course has a military sponsor who mentors them and helps them during training and outside of training hours. Kwele's sponsor for the Q-Course is a former Ranger Regiment captain from Texas. "My girlfriend and I took Patrick home with us for Christmas," the former Ranger said. "We hit every cowboy bar between New Orleans and Austin. I think we probably corrupted him a little along the way, but boy, did we have fun. And I have a standing invitation for a home-cooked meal the next time I'm in Gaborone. He's a great ally, and he's become a good friend."

At the team hut, the men continue to settle into their quarters while they await the arrival of their cadre officer and cadre sergeant. The thirty-six-day Phase IV curriculum can be broken down into three parts: classroom training at the Rowe Training Facility, preparation for Robin Sage, and the Robin Sage exercise. A word about Robin Sage. It is one of the most intense and well-choreographed military training exercises I've ever witnessed, and I've seen my share of military training exercises.

Robin Sage is a storied field exercise that ranges over some fifteen counties and eighty-five hundred square miles of south-central North

Carolina, from Camp Mackall north to Greensboro, west to Charlotte, and south to close to the South Carolina border. This wide usage of public and private lands is made possible by a mosaic of land-use agreements. There are a great number of patriotic farmers and landowners, including race-car legend Richard Petty, who allow the use of their property for this exercise. A number of rural communities take part in this exercise and act out the part of the Pineland citizenry. To train these 300 Special Forces candidates, there will be over a thousand support personnel: over 350 contract role players, 400-some volunteer auxiliaries, and 250 or more military and civilian contractor personnel. In addition to the support personnel, there are the soldiers who play the role of the guerrillas—the freedom fighters in this unconventional-warfare mega-exercise. These soldiers also serve in the role of opposition forces—usually enemy soldiers. They come from all over the Army and include National Guard components, marines, and, on occasion, West Point cadets—wherever the Army can find men and women to come and serve in this capacity. These soldiers play the role of Pineland guerrillas that have to be trained and led into battle by the student ODAs. This ad hoc guerrilla army can range from 400 to 600, depending on the availability and the size of the Phase IV class. The optimum mix is two guerrillas—or "Gs," as they are called—for every Phase IV student. With our forces committed to the global war on terror, finding soldiers in this quantity with the time to support this training has been a challenge.

Robin Sage is the third name given to this comprehensive Phase IV Special Forces training exercise. The origin of the name is unclear and often disputed among Special Forces veterans. It's generally thought that it came from the North Carolina town of Robins and Special Forces colonel Jerry Sage. Sage, an OSS veteran, was a former 10th Special Forces Group commander.

The logistics, coordination, command, and control of this exercise, as you may imagine, are formidable. And the exercise play, while highly formatted and supervised, is free flowing. The direction and development of the exercise scenario is, within bounds, driven by the capability, performance, and decisions made by the student ODAs. Each ODA is tasked with a mission to infiltrate the fictitious nation of Pineland, link up with their assigned guerrilla band, and conduct an unconventional-warfare campaign. Their mission is to orchestrate guerrilla operations in advance of a planned invasion by conventional coalition forces. Robin Sage is a complex, freewheeling, wide-ranging military/paramilitary exercise on a scale that I've never before experienced. It's worthy of a book, not just the chapter I'm able to devote to it here.

In the 915 team room, the student ODA gathers to meet their assigned cadre team sergeant and cadre team officer.

"Captain Santos, you up?"

Santos looks around the team room and finds his student team sergeant. "Sergeant Olin?"

"We're up, sir," Staff Sergeant Olin replies.

"We're up, Sergeant," Santos tells the 915 cadre team sergeant.

"OK, bring it in. I've got some word to put out." Sergeant First Class Troy Blackman is from southern Ohio and joined up right after high school. He has been in the Army for twenty years and the Special Forces for fifteen. All of his time has been with the 5th Group. Blackman deployed as a young sergeant for the first Gulf War and most recently to Afghanistan for Operation Enduring Freedom. During the intervening decade, he has made more than a few deployments to the Middle East and Southwest Asia. He can converse with the locals in Arabic. Blackman hopes to be on the next promotion list for master sergeant and return to the 5th Group for an assignment as an ODA team sergeant. Sergeant Blackman flips through his notebook, then looks up to survey his student team.

"I have a few things for you before we get started. First of all, I want you to understand that this is serious training. I'm serious, the captain's serious, and I expect you to be serious. Stay focused, be a team, help each other, and work for the common good. You've all come too far to screw up now. At the top of my list is integrity. Don't lie, cheat, or steal. Violate our standards of integrity and you are gone. Violate UCMJ [the Uniform Code of Military Justice] and you may do time. UCMJ is an acronym for jail. In addition, you'll really piss me off. I care about this training and about Special Forces. You're all needed in the groups and in this war. Don't demean me or this training.

"A few no-nos. We use blank ammo, but even so, accidental discharges and negligent discharges will get you out of here. Lie about it, and you're gone forever. 'Fess up, and you're gone from this class, but we might be able to get you back for the next class. All training materials are classified DTNB—don't tell no body. Play the game. No interaction with anyone that's not in the course. Once you go into isolation for the final problem, you will not talk to anyone in another ODA."

Sergeant Blackman covers team room protocol; he wants 915 to keep their spaces clean and orderly. Inside, they can be informal; but outside, they have to be in a full and correct uniform, and observe the buddy system. Blackman then asks for each man to introduce himself and to state why he chose Special Forces. The reasons range from the patriotic to the boring civilian job to the inactivity of their conventional unit.

"I came into Special Forces because I was looking for a challenge," Blackman tells 915, "and I stayed in Special Forces because I get to serve with the greatest guys in the world. I have two families—my wife and two boys at home, and I have my brothers in SF."

A tall man standing off to one side speaks for the first time. "I joined Special Forces because I wanted to work with other cultures and to operate with the freedom and independence that you can only find in Special Forces," Captain Garrett Childers tells the student ODA. He's 915's cadre officer. "As many of you know, that kind of freedom is seldom given to a junior leader in a conventional unit." Captain Garrett Childers is six-two and lean, with something of an academic bearing and a perpetually mild expression. He's a West Point graduate with ten years in the Army, half of that in Special Forces. His father was with the World Health Organization, so Childers grew up in South America and Europe. He's fluent in Spanish and French. His operational time has been with the 7th Special Forces Group. Captain Childers has made several deployments to South America, a rotation in Afghanistan, and a rotation in Iraq.

"I want to see good leadership," Captain Childers continues, "from top to bottom. I'll look for strong leadership from the senior members of the team and from the junior members as appropriate. Use your time well to front-load your standard patrolling procedures and to get back into tactical form. It's been a while since you were out there working as a team. Planning will be important. You senior guys should be familiar with MDMP. I'll count on you to help the junior men to understand the military decision-making process and how to prepare and deliver briefing materials. You'll be challenged tactically and intellectually. The game here is to make good decisions with some thought to the second and third effects of that decision. You'll have to game out every situation and every decision. Work hard, pay attention to detail, and take care of each other."

The phase begins with the classroom work, learning about air operations and clandestine airborne infiltration into a denied area. During Robin Sage and often on deployment, ODA teams are resupplied from the air. The information comes to them by PowerPoint and a stack of Army and Air Force publications and field manuals. They learn about the rigging and preparation that go into preparing pallets and personnel for a tactical airdrop. There are protocols for marking a drop zone, signaling, authentication, surveillance, and bundle recovery. Communications with the aircraft are very important. The engineering sergeants are responsible for preparing and rigging bundles for aerial resupply and for parceling out the dropped supplies and packing these supplies off the drop zone. Class 2-05 learns about the management of airborne resupply using U.S. and allied aircraft. They also learn to deal with Third World situations in which pilots may not have GPS, nav aids, night-vision goggles, or reliable aircraft. Every airborne drop has to be planned, and there are the mathematical calculations that go with determining the release point and the impact point. Bottom line, a Special Forces soldier has to know how to set up and manage aerial resupply from any type of aircraft, under any weather conditions, in any terrain, anytime, anywhere. Considerations can range from the location of nearby power lines to the pilot's skill and ego.

After two days of classes, 915 builds two pallets with twelve cases of MREs each. That afternoon the team parachutes, with full equipment, into the Luzon Drop Zone at Camp Mackall. Later that evening, they prepare the DZ for aerial resupply and guide in the aircraft, a twin-engined Casa, that drops their bundle. Staff Sergeant Olin directs the preparation of the DZ for a daylight drop. Five other members of 915 form the recovery team. They break down the bundle and pack the boxes of MREs and the parachute off the drop zone. The chow, parachute, and pallet are loaded on a truck that will take the gear back to the Rowe Training Facility. That night, Sergeant Dan Barstow is in charge of the aerial resupply. He directs 915 as they rig the drop zone for a night drop.

After the air-operations block of training, 915 and the other Phase IV ODAs return to the compound to begin three days and evenings of classes on unconventional warfare. This classroom work is tailored to helping them to support and manage the Pineland resistance forces in the Robin Sage exercise. For the officers, much of this is familiar from Phase III. For the enlisted soldiers, it's a cram course in guerrilla warfare. These three days of Insurgency 101 in a crowded classroom could have been terribly dull and laborious had it not been for the talented delivery of the cadre sergeant instructors and civilian contractors who make these presentations. Most are well punctuated by historical and anecdotal examples. Much of the material focuses on the three key components of an insurgency. The first are the guerrillas, or freedom fighters, the action arm of the insurgency and the overt irregular/ paramilitary forces the student ODA will be most concerned with. Interestingly, when they are on *our* side, we usually refer to them as guerrillas or partisans or freedom fighters. When *they,* the men in the hills, oppose a government we support, we call them insurgents. The second is the underground. The underground is the clandestine, cellular organization that conducts subversion, sabotage, and intelligence collection activities. The future political leadership that arises from a successful insurgency comes from members of the underground. And then there's the auxiliary, the volunteers who support the insurgency with logistics, transportation, and security. The future Green Berets are told that in an unconventional-warfare scenario, it's critical that they understand these three components of an insurgency and that they establish good rapport with each of them. Again and again, the trainers hammer on the necessity of understanding their freedom fighters or guerrillas from the perspective of *their* wants, desires, goals, problems, values, and culture.

A lot is crammed into these three days of instruction; it exhausts the candidates and the writer—logistics, security, intelligence, caching equipment, linkup procedures, guerrilla bases, guerrilla training areas, mission support sites, emergency procedures, communications, demobilizations . . . the list goes on. There were two blocks of instruction I find particularly compelling. One is on negotiations and the other on cross-cultural communication. The material and the delivery are first rate. In the crowded, stuffy classroom, I can feel the weary candidates perk up during these presentations.

The class on negotiation is presented by a retired Special Forces sergeant major who had trained at the Harvard Law School's Program on Negotiation, the U.S. Army Peacekeeping Institute, and the State Department's National Foreign Affairs Training Center. "Understand that there's always a basis for negotiation," he tells Phase IV Class 2-05, "and each side has a range of options. You have the tactical-force option: small-arms fire, close air support, and smart bombs—that sort

of thing. And there's the nontactical option, or trying to influence someone else to see things your way. We negotiate all the time—when we
buy a new car, when we want to watch the ball game and our wives
want to watch a movie. The regular Army usually negotiates with
tanks, armored personnel carriers, and attack helicopters. In Special
Forces, we often have to be persuasive in our work—it's the nature of
working by, with, and through others. In Afghanistan, our first order of
business was to get the tribes of the Northern Alliance to quit fighting
each other and to fight the Taliban. It took a lot of negotiating to do
this. The guys who accomplished that had to understand where those
tribal leaders were coming from. I mean, *really* understand them—their
reservations, their history, their customs, and their ambitions. In your
negotiations during Robin Sage and deployed downrange with an operational ODA, you'll have your frame of reference—what you want to
accomplish, your best-outcome position, and your bottom-line position. But you better understand the issue from *their* perspective as well.
You may need help or information from some nongovernmental organization, and the local person heading that NGO may be some West
Coast, liberal-educated, no-leg-shaving, Birkenstock-wearing female
uniform-hater. And you gotta deal with her. The terrain can change
swiftly. You may be dealing with a tribal elder in the morning, with the
embassy security officer at noon, and that scratchy lady at the NGO
later in the afternoon. You need to use your maturity, professionalism,
and common sense. If you're a head butter and not a people person,
you may have some problems. Negotiation and mediation are tools,
just like small-unit tactics, weapons, and close air support."

The program is followed by a scenario-based persuasion exercise.
This four-hour presentation is a cooked-down version of a graduate-
level semester on negotiations. Following the negotiations block of
instruction, Class 2-05 plunges into cross-cultural communications.
This block is presented by a very capable, veteran cadre sergeant.

"The more you know about another culture and can communicate
with them, the better you can do your job. Understanding them, gain-

ing their trust, avoiding their taboos, and presenting yourself in a favorable light from *their* perspective is critical. Language is the essence of their culture. If you haven't the time to learn the language, study common phrases—hello, thank you, excuse me—that kind of thing. Also, be aware of important nonverbal communication. To Arabs and Africans, showing the sole of the foot is a great insult. The OK sign means screw you in Latin America. In some cultures, eye contact can be insulting.

"Religion is the overriding cultural value in some societies. Understand their beliefs and mythology and learn to avoid things that offend. Customs in many places have the force of law. In a Muslim country, T and A is toes and ankles. In Nigeria, I once had to eat the heart, eyes, and brains of a goat. It was their delicacy and presented to me as a point of honor. I not only ate it, I relished it." He gives the class a helpless shrug. "Tastes just like chicken. In northern Iraq, they dropped us a pallet of corn for our Kurdish fighters. Kurds don't eat corn—it's pig food. They used the corn as a helo landing-zone marker. In southern Turkey, there is no toilet paper in rural areas—just a bottle of water in what passes for a toilet. That's why in some cultures, they only eat with one hand. After an experience like that, you never go anywhere without a personal stash of TP.

"Don't overlook the interaction of culture in their family structure. Study their family customs. Know the role of women, children, and old people in their culture. Age is a virtue and measure of respect in some cultures. We value individualism and privacy. Not all cultures do; Asian cultures value the group over the individual. In some cultures, face is important—we Americans are direct, no matter what. And freedom underlies all our values. In some societies and families, freedom is way down on the list. But make no mistake about it, honoring their family traditions and cultural norms is one of the best ways to gain their goodwill and trust.

"Be very careful if the conversation is about religion, politics, personal questions, and geography. You can get into trouble really fast because it's often not what you say or mean, it's what they hear and understand. And be careful not to take offense when *they* mean no offense. For us, time is a biggie. We are punctual and value time; not so elsewhere. You leave the United States, and time takes on a whole new perspective. Most of the people you will work with will not own a wristwatch.

"We have to work extra hard, because we in America are very ethnocentric—we think our culture is superior. Why's that? It's because we've got moon rocks, and nobody else has moon rocks. This ethnocentricity breeds discrimination and disrespect; it can get in the way if your mission is by, with, and through another culture. And in SF, we have to work extra hard because our business usually involves guns. Are there any genuine U.S. Army squad leaders out there?" A few hands go up. "When you get a bunch of newly trained trivets from Fort Benning assigned to your squad, do you watch them pretty closely during their first time on the range? You bet you do. How about when you and another SF sergeant take one hundred of your non-English-speaking, new best friends out for a few hours of rifle training before you go trade real bullets with the enemy? Get your heart going? Maybe a little. Think it might help if you understand something of their culture and where they're coming from? You're going to see it all over there. Afghan militiamen often take their young sons with them on operations—six-year-olds with automatic weapons. I was four days in country on my first operation. A five-year-old gets off the truck with a bandoleer of ammo and a Makarov pistol—and he could handle it.

"Now, many of you are just wanting to know what you need to get by for Robin Sage. Never forget, Robin Sage is training wheels for the real thing. And for some of you guys from New York and California, Pineland really is a foreign culture. Robin Sage, and what you will see overseas, is all about rapport. It's about negotiation; it's about listening; it's about putting yourself in the other guy's position—seeing it from his side of the table. It's about balancing your priorities with his priorities. Rapport is very important in other cultures; it's important in Pineland. For you officers, much of what you'll be trying to do is understand your guerrilla chief. After you get close to him and you have some trust, you will want to know why he came to a position of power. Is it because he has money? Is it by force of will, religion, patriotism, or a place he held in the old order? And what does he want for the future? How does he see himself in the new order?

"For all of you, everyone in Robin Sage—the G chief, the auxiliary truck driver, the local guy from the underground, and especially the guerrillas—are there for you to work with, get to know, learn from, and understand. Today, it's role-play. A year from now, maybe less for some of you, it will be downrange and deadly serious. Good luck guys, here in training and in the real world."

Following the unconventional-warfare classes, 915 and the other student ODAs enter a four-day block of mission planning, mission-planning training, and preparing for their mission-readiness exercise. During this time, the team members spend time with their phone-book-sized background materials on the customs, history, politics, culture, economics, current events, and geography of the nation of Pineland. Regarding geography, the nation of Pineland is physically the south-central portion of the state of North Carolina. Pineland is bordered by the equally mythical nations of the Republic of Columbus to the south, the Republic of Appalachia to the west, and the United Province of Atlantica to the north. Each member of 915 has to know all about these nations as well as the country they are about to invade—Pineland.

Captain Santos and First Lieutenant Kwele hold classes in the team room to bring the others up to speed on MDMP—the military decision-making process—and, more specifically, their roles in helping to plan the mission. All of them have some familiarization with mission planning, but most of this is tactically orientated planning as outlined in the *Ranger Handbook*. This is in-depth planning that carries into the mechanics of linking up with and training a guerrilla army. On the third day of this reading and planning work, Major Kennedy, in the role of their forward operating base commander, holds a staff mission briefing for all the ODA detachment leaders and their assistants.

"Don't lose sight of my objective," he tells his team leaders. "Your primary task is to disrupt the Pineland army and the Pineland security forces, and to condition the battlefield in advance of conventional forces. Training your Gs is only part of what you have to do. Once you infil into your areas of responsibility, you are ground truth. You're to continue with your area assessment and report intelligence back up the chain of command. Secure, reliable, accurate communications are an important part of your job. I'm not too concerned about format, but I am concerned about your painting a clear picture of the battlefield. Real world, what you report can go straight up to the White House.

"Read carefully the motivations and problems of the locals you're training. Always be studying your guerrilla counterparts with an eye to how they can be most effective against our common enemy. And while you and your Gs are working toward a common goal, be thinking about what their future agenda might be after the hostilities are over. Think downstream. Understand the second- and third-order consequences of what you do. And while you'll be immersed in the details of training your Gs and conducting missions, think about demobilization and the role of Psyops and Civil Affairs in the aftermath of the fighting.

"You'll be challenged, and you'll be confronted with dilemmas. You will have to think your way and negotiate your way out of these dilemmas. And through all this, never forget that you are an American Special Forces ODA with the full backing of the U.S. government. Your skills and presence are needed. Invite, even demand, respect. Don't allow yourself to be marginalized; retain your weapon and your rights as a leader and an American. You will have to think and conduct yourself as a Special Forces soldier at all times."

Following Major Kennedy's remarks, the team leaders and their assistants receive a series of briefings from cadre serving as the forward operating base intelligence, supply, and communications officers. Then it's back to the team huts for more planning and preparation.

Late afternoon on day twelve of Phase IV, 915 and the other teams leave the Rowe Training Facility on a three-day mission-readiness exercise. This is a short field exercise designed to develop and rehearse their standard operating procedures and to brush up on their tactical movement as a team. They'll also conduct mission-specific rehearsals for Robin Sage. The exercise begins with an equipment jump. The heavily laden teams are trucked to the Camp Mackall Army Airfield, where they board C-130s and are dropped into nearby Luzon Drop Zone. Once on the DZ, 915 gathers at the rally point and patrols off the DZ to their assigned linkup point. There they're met by their cadre truck, one of the large four-by-four trucks that support the training. Nine-one-five piles into the back of the truck and the canvas flaps are pulled tight. They are then driven all over the back roads of Camp Mackall. The drill is for them to estimate their speed and direction of travel without visual reference. In the back of the big truck, the members of 915 huddle around their maps and try to track their movements with penlight and compass. Shortly after midnight, the men are dropped at their training area, surprisingly not too far from where their back-of-the-truck navigation said that they would be.

They are up well before dawn conducting preplanned cross-training, beginning with combat first aid. Most student ODAs in Class 2-05, like 915, have only one medic. Sergeant Andrew "Doc" Kohl drills his teammates in combat casualty care, including assessment of the victim, controlling bleeding with tourniquets and bandages, splinting, CPR, and giving IVs. The training is much like the trauma lanes in the combat medic training, but without the makeup and fake blood.

"Get a system of assessment and treatment in your mind and follow it each time you work with a casualty," Doc Kohl tells his teammates. "Do it the same way each time."

After medical training, the 18 Echos run the team through some comm drills. They train on the PRC-119, the PSC-5, and the PRC-148 MBITR radios, all radios they will take with them into Pineland, and on the KL-43, a small keypad used to send a text message when a toughbook computer is not available. Specialists David Altman and Justin Keller serve as primary trainers and drill their teammates on each radio—how to set in the frequency, adjust the power setting, and transmit. After the commo training, Sergeants Aaron Dunn and Daniel Barstow, the team engineers, hold a class on demolitions using dummy charges, det cord, and blasting caps, but with real time fuse and real time-fuse calculations. They cover circular and linear charges, charge placement, knot tying with det cord, the dual priming of charges, and the safety considerations associated with nonelectric firing assemblies. They set up demo training lanes, so each man can set up a charge and dual prime it. Then the weapons sergeants, Baker, Costa, and Kendall, hold a quick familiarization on the M240 and SAW machine guns, and the optimum placement of these weapons systems. They also inspect their teammates' personal M4 cleaning kits. Where they're deficient, they provide their teammates with spares.

Sergeant Blackman stops by late morning to see how they're doing. He gives them a short, informal class on linkup procedures for Robin Sage, along with some ideas to get them thinking about near and far recognition signals in a rural setting. He watches his team's training for a short while, then leaves without comment. These cross-training drills serve two purposes. The first is that they get the whole team up to speed on what they need to know in the way of first aid, communications, weapons, and demolitions for the Robin Sage exercise. The second is that it is practice teaching for the teachers. The new 18 Series specialists will be teaching these same skills to their guerrillas—the Pineland freedom fighters.

After the MOS cross-training, the team begins a long patrol to their new training area. Along the way, they conduct a mini Phase II course to review basic patrolling, raid, and ambush procedures, reaction to fire, countersniper procedures, hand and arm signals, danger crossings, security halts, and the whole range of small-unit tactical skills. Afternoon becomes night, and they continue to patrol and drill until they reach their second layup position and go to ground for the night. Ten of them bed down, while two remain awake on watch. Sergeant Blackman and Captain Childers had carefully reviewed their team's training schedule prior to the exercise, but pretty much leave 915 to train on their own. I move around to see a few other Phase IV ODAs conduct cross-training and small-unit-tactics drills, and their cadre sergeants were often right there with them. I ask Miguel Santos about this.

"It's on us," Captain Santos says after their first full day in the mission-readiness exercise. "We know what we have to do, and the guys are committed to getting it done and getting it right. Sergeant Blackman told us what he expects out here, and we don't want to disappoint him. We all think pretty highly of him—Captain Childers as well."

The second day of exercise is interview day. Nine-one-five patrols about a mile to the training site and dumps their rucks in a wooded area near one of the lakes on Camp Mackall. This is where the eight student ODAs assigned to their forward operating base gather for this day's training. There are eight training stations. Each station or venue is a tarp rigged among the trees with a table and four or more chairs. At each station, there are two contract role players who support this exercise and Robin Sage. Almost all are former Green Berets who now work for Northrop Grumman. The student ODA is briefed/read into each scenario by their cadre team sergeant. Then two members of the ODA are designated as the team leader and team sergeant. They approach and make contact with the two role players waiting at the station. The rest of the ODA members gather nearby so they can observe and listen.

For 915, the first scenario is a Belgian medical nongovernmental organization, Doctors Without Borders, working in Afghanistan. The

ODA is new to the area and wants to make contact with the NGO— get to know them, see what they can do for the NGO, and see what they can learn. Specifically, the ODA wants to know about insurgents in the area. The men know the doctors move freely about and treat both sides. The NGO reps distrust the military. It's not a personal thing, but they want to keep their distance and maintain their neutrality. They do want military help if things get out of hand, and perhaps some supplies that the NGOs find scarce. Staff Sergeant Olin and PFC Tim Baker are the team leader and team sergeant for this encounter. Olin asks how things are going and if there's anything they can do to help. The NGO rep allows that he has a broken sterilizer and needs a new one. Tom Olin tells him he'll see what he can do to find one, and asks about the insurgent activity in the area. After a semicordial back-and-forth conversation while the other members of the team observe, Olin and Baker say good-bye to the two NGO workers. Time is called in the exercise play, and 915 gathers for an immediate critique of the session.

The other venues pose different and challenging dilemmas, but issues commonly encountered by deployed ODAs. One is with a Pineland guerrilla chief. This is a first meeting between the G chief and the Americans who have just arrived in area. A guerrilla on security checks them out, and the chief welcomes them to his fire under a patch of canvas suspended between trees. The G chief has problems—wounded men, low supplies of food and ammo, lack of weapons. Sergeant Dan Barstow and Specialist Tom Kendall meet with him to work out the G chief's problems and the relationship/status of the newly arrived Special Forces team. The third scenario deals with a black marketeer. He has food, ammunition, grenades, weapons, medical supplies, and women—all for sale. Sergeant Aaron Dunn and Specialist Antonio Costa try to find out what he has, how much, and whom he's selling it to. ODAs prefer not to work with the black market, but sometimes there's no alternative. Dunn and Costa's job is also to find out where he's getting his wares. After a bit of bargaining, they buy a sack of potatoes as a show of faith and to maintain contact. In the critique, the cadre sergeant observing this venue puts black-market activity into perspective for 915.

"You're always going to have needs, and you'll always be buying and contracting with the locals for those needs. In Special Forces, you just can't run down to the battalion supply sergeant. You'll try not to deal with the black market, but you may have to. In some countries, and in regions of just about every country, you'll find the black market. A black marketeer knows you can probably put him out of business. You may use this leverage to get some useful intelligence. Regarding dealing with the locals in general, expect to pay a fair price and perhaps a premium, but no more. Be gracious, and even tip them. Local knowledge and setting limits can keep you in the best place to negotiate. Every team has a guy who's good at this—loves buying used cars, making deals, likes haggling. Let him deal with the locals when you need something."

The next venue or dilemma is a rogue U.S. contractor in Afghanistan. This is a fellow American who's in Afghanistan for the money, and Sergeant Brian Short and Specialist Justin Keller have to engage him. In the scenario, they need intelligence that the rogue contractor may have, but the contractor's clearly in Afghanistan for different reasons than the Special Forces team. "There are many legitimate contractors who'll be able to help you with your mission," the role players tell them during the critique, "and some will try to screw you. You have to look carefully at their motives and establish the basis for your relationship. If they're in it for themselves, to the detriment of you, your mission, and your nation, let them know that you and your posse may just come back and put them out of business. And immediately report this up the chain of command."

At the fifth encounter, Sergeant Andrew Kohl and Specialist David Altman link up with a Pinelander who is part of the auxiliary that is to transport the team through a dangerous area. Kohl, the team leader, has 1,000 don (the currency of Pineland is the don) for making arrangements. This member of the auxiliary's a good old boy and friendly, and asks them for money for a local orphanage he says he is running. The student Green Berets have to make their own assessment. They also have to refocus him on the job at hand—getting the team moved safely. They have to not only negotiate his fee, but talk about what to do if they get stopped by the Pineland security forces and what to do if there's any shooting—how they're going to keep him safe. They have to get a quick read on him—what are his real motivations and interests? How reliable is he?

The final three problems or dilemmas involve the whole team with each acting in their team assignment. All three relate to the Robin Sage scenario, but could be any unconventional-warfare or foreign-internal-defense assignment anywhere in the world. Captain Miguel Santos leads his team into the first of these, which is a meeting with a G chief and several of his guerrillas. The meeting runs along predictable lines as they talk about money, food, weapons, and medical needs. Then a Pinelander reporter wants to take a picture of the Americans with the guerrillas. Both Captain Santos and Sergeant Olin protest; they cannot allow this. The G chief insists, and there's a spirited debate about the photo. They reach a compromise and sit back down to drink a toast to Pineland. Two members of 915 have secretly been told by one of the cadre sergeants to refuse to drink for religious reasons, and an argument breaks out over this refusal.

"This is something you'll have to deal with," the cadre sergeant at the venue tells 915. "You may cite mutual respect for your customs or ask them to honor your religious belief, but you're going to have to resolve it on terms acceptable to them. That means you may have to drink some god-awful brew when you'd really rather not."

The second dilemma arises in a discussion with a G chief who's baiting caches with food and killing unarmed enemy soldiers when they come for the food. Captain Santos tries to dissuade the guerrillas from this, saying this isn't honorable and will cost them face with the local population. He also gently threatens the withdrawal of his support if they continue to shoot unarmed combatants. The third dilemma comes to them in the form of an armed intruder who approaches the group and tries to disrupt the meeting. There's a question of whether to talk to challenge the intruder or just shoot him.

"Two lessons here, guys," the cadre sergeant at this station tells them. "The first is that you can never forget that you're American fighting men, and you'll be bound by certain standards and your ROEs. You may not always be able to enforce those on the people you work with, but, consistent with your mission, you have to try. The second is that security is a twenty-four-hour a day job. When you're out there on the tip of the spear, things can change in a heartbeat. You may have to quickly reorient yourself and take action. It's on you, and you can never let your guard down. If the team leader and the team sergeant are locked up in negotiations, the rest of you have to set security and watch their backs."

Day three of the mission-readiness exercise is a tactical Olympics of a sort. Nine-one-five is matched against student ODA 912. The two teams begin with a five-mile, four-point land-navigation course over which they have to move in tactical order. The final point brings them to a sparsely wooded training area on the western edge of the Camp Mackall Army Airfield. There the student ODAs prepare for the head-to-head competition, but first they change into dry clothes. The nav course took them through some streams and draws. Nine-one-five was penalized for not finding one of its nav points, so it starts the remaining events with a time penalty.

The competition takes the two teams several hundred meters up the wooded area and back. It's a race against each other and the clock. Along the way are stations where the men must perform individually and as a team. The starting positions are about fifty meters apart, so each team can see how the other is faring in the competition. Sergeant Blackman walks with 912 and Sergeant First Class Bill Viafore, 912's cadre sergeant, walks with 915. Both cadre sergeants want their own team to win, but they're more concerned that the teams perform to standard and display the proper skills. This is their final tactical tune-up before Robin Sage.

The route laid out by the cadre teams for the student ODAs challenges them on a range of tactical disciplines. Initially, each man in turn must fire a magazine of blank ammo through their M4 rifles. Each magazine has a bad round, which means the shooter has to fire, clear the jammed weapon, and continue to fire. Another event has them set up and fire a short belt of ammo through the M240. Again, there's a bad round. Clearing a jammed round from a 240 often requires muscling the big gun, sometimes with a boot. Time is added for procedural mistakes. At another station, the team has to rig two demolition charges with dual-initiated, nonelectric firing assemblies. Both charges are to be timed with a two-minute delay. Time is added for nonoptimum charge placement and for fuse burn times inside or outside the two-minute window. In the weapons drills, the 18 Bravo weapons sergeants cannot participate, and in the demolition drill, the 18 Charlie engineers can't play; it's all on how well they cross-trained their teammates.

The final event is a medical-commo drill. A man on each team is "shot" and has to be stabilized, cared for, and evacuated. The care is in the form of treatment for bleeding and shock. He needs resuscitation, CPR, and an IV. The 18 Delta medical sergeants can only observe. Then the casualty has to be carried on a litter to the edge of the airfield clearing and readied for casualty evacuation. The teams have to put out marking panels and prepare the helicopter landing zone to move their casualty. Each team has to rig a field-expedient antenna and hoist it at least thirty feet into the air. Then each of the non–18 Echo communicators has to set up and transmit a message on the PRC-119. The last man on the radio drill calls in the helo, a four-by-four truck. The team puts out smoke on the LZ for the pilot/truck driver, and the casualty is loaded onto the evacuation helo. All the drills are executed in simulated tactical, under-fire conditions. That means the teams have to be thinking security and teamwork start to finish.

Nine-one-five manages to come from behind and win the competition, but I thought both teams did well. The cadre viewed the exercise with a more critical eye. Both teams sit in together during the after-action review.

"Command and control," Captain Childers begins, "that's a biggie for me. When that team leader's busy, someone has to jump up from the perimeter and take charge. Your team leaders and team sergeants seem to know their stuff, but they can't do it all. When the team leader is head down, ass up on a job, someone has to pick up the slack and watch the big picture—be ready to take charge and react. Another thing, whatever you do, do it properly. Too many of you out on security just found a twig or a small tree for cover. That's unacceptable. Set up your ruck for protection. Find the best and biggest tree to give you cover and support for your firing position. Do the little things to the best of your ability—never slack just because you are not in the center of the action or doing a visible task. This is a time for passion about all tasks, large and small."

"In some of the evolutions, you did well," Sergeant Viafore tells 915 and 912, "and in others, you disappointed me. That 240's very important. Everyone has to know how to quickly clear a jam on the big gun and get it back in the fight. If that jammed round won't come free, get mean and clear it. Men can die if you don't. When one of your teammates went down, you were way too slow. There were too many guys standing around, waiting for someone else to take charge; it took you too long to get to the guy who was hit." There is an edge to Sergeant Viafore's voice, and he speaks with feeling. "Hear me on this, guys. You have a sacred duty to go to the aid of a man who is down. If a medic isn't there, and he wasn't in this drill, you're the medic—do something. Nothing's more important than saving a brother's life. Too many times in this training, you waited for someone else to take charge. Like the captain said, if the team leader's busy or the team sergeant isn't there, jump in and make it happen. You're all leaders, every one of you. Now, this criticism may be negative, and maybe I'm not giving you credit for all the things you did right out there, but this is a harsh business. This is Special Forces, not some liberal-arts, feel-good program; we don't have time for your self-esteem. If it's not right, we have to get it right and fast—we're at war. The same'll be true when you get to an operational team. If a guy's doing something wrong, you jump in his shit until he gets it right. When I get done here at the training command, I'll be back on a team, and maybe some of you will be my teammates—my brothers. Maybe a year or two from now, I'll be doing something wrong and you'll have to jump in my shit and get me straight—hear what I'm saying. In Special Forces we train each other— that's true here, and it will be true when you get to your team at group."

The final evolution of the mission readiness exercise is a gunfight. Late that afternoon, 915 and 912 rechamber and rebarrel their M4s to adapt to Simunitions, or Sims. Sims are 9mm paintball rounds that are adapted to the standard M4 rifle. They have the same cyclic rate of fire and short-range trajectory as the real thing. The rounds make a splotch and a sting when they hit, but nothing more. A few of the older soldiers have trained with Simunitions, but for most, this is their first time—their first firefight. The contestants in a Sims fight wear protective goggles and face masks. A good Sims fight is the dream of every little boy who played war games when he was a kid. I was one of those little boys.

There's a deserted training compound nearby that 915 elects to defend. A squadron of National Guard H-60 helos are training at the airfield, and they agree to insert the attack element—912. It's the honor system; if you're hit, you go down. Soon it's game on, and the two teams are running and gunning. When it's over, 915 has more men standing, but then the advantage always goes to the defender. Sergeant Blackman calls the two student ODAs in for the after-action review.

"OK, this training was a bonus for you and a game—a paintball fight—but what did we learn? The basics work, right? You guys in 912 had a hard job, assaulting a fixed position with the enemy alert and ready for you. But you executed a fire-and-maneuver attack pretty well. Remember, a steady volume of covering fire is key to the success of the maneuvering element. Also keep in mind, plywood and twigs may stop a Sims round, but not a real one. Real bullets are for keeps, and concealment is not necessarily good cover. And basic infantry tactics work, even for us high-speed, Special Forces guys."

Nine-One-Five and 912 patrol back to the Rowe Training Facility. They overhaul their gear that evening and get a good night's sleep, perhaps for the last time in Phase IV. Ahead of them are four days of intensive planning and preparation before they infiltrate into Pineland for Robin Sage. The student ODAs are now under strict isolation protocol. They can interact with their higher command and those role players assigned to their forward operating base, but no one else. This is the final countdown to Robin Sage.

In the 915 team room, Captain Santos staffs out the planning assignments for his team. There's a lot to do, but they have been thinking about and working toward this since they arrived at Camp Mackall. There are six computers in the team room. All are on a local area network that supports Robin Sage. Weather data, mission-planning software, and the full Pineland scenario—history, economic data, politics, geography, demographics, and maps—are in the database. Seldom did I go into 915's team room, day or night, and not find a soldier at each of the computers.

The drill is not unlike what took place in the planning rooms during the mission-planning exercises of the 18 Alpha's Phase III. Only these are a group of soldiers, not officers with mission-planning experience, and five of Captain Santos's ten enlisted soldiers have been in the Army less than eight months. His assistant detachment leader is an excellent officer, but he's new to the mission-planning doctrine as practiced in the American military. The heavy burden for supervising and planning and the mission briefback will fall on Miguel Santos.

Everyone has a hand in the planning and in preparing equipment for the mission. A great deal of the initial planning effort falls on Sergeant Brian Short, the team's intel sergeant. He begins to work up the intelligence picture and format it for the briefback. The weapons sergeants have to plan ammunition requirements, both what they and the team will carry in and what has to be staged for the resupply bundles. They also have to identify weapons spare parts and build repair kits; there are no armories in Pineland. The engineering sergeants have their demolition requirements in the way of explosives, det cord, time fuse, and their demo kits. They're also tasked with building the resupply bundles—bundles that are to be staged for scheduled airdrops and for on-call air resupply. The lone combat medic has his medical bag to prepare, along with the medical equipment and meds he will be taking in for training and administering to the guerrillas. There are also real-world issues like poison ivy, cuts, and infections. He, too, has equipment for the resupply bundles. All of them have equipment to stage for team operations, training of the guerrillas, and aerial resupply. And all of them have input for the briefback.

Perhaps the busiest soldiers in 915 are the commo sergeants. They have to program and test the radios that they'll be jumping with into Pineland. Nine-one-five will take in a single PSC-5, which will be their primary SATCOM radio, and one PRC-137, which will serve as their FM-ALE link for their periodic situation reports. They'll have one PRC-119 to serve as a mission-support radio and handle intersquad traffic. The 119 is to function as a base station for the six PRC-148 MBITR tactical or squad radios. The team will also have a KL-43 and two toughbook computers. They'll train the guerrillas on the 119 and 148 radios. The commo sergeants also prepare backup radios for on-call resupply in case the radios they take in fail or are damaged during the insertion. All of them have to be loaded with crypto and tested.

Amid the planning and gear preparation, there are briefings by the forward operating base personnel on rules of engagement, current intelligence, logistics, public affairs, and tactical deployment issues. These briefings are exercise related and real world—especially regarding public affairs. Robin Sage is a big event, and there are reporters out in the field wanting to talk to soldiers, and the Phase IV students are instructed on how to deal with them. There are also scenario-related briefings. One is with a Pinelander who recently came out of the area of Pineland that they will be going into. Another is with a Special Forces sergeant who was in Pineland on a JCET deployment two years ago. These scenario briefings are conducted by the officers and the 915 team sergeant, Tom Olin. Nine-one-five works well into the nights, with the team members averaging about four hours of sleep.

"There's so much to do," Sergeant Olin says, "and so very little time to get it all done. There are so many details to attend to. We'll be out there fourteen days, and everything has to be front-loaded—what we take in and what we'll get through aerial resupply. Sometimes it overwhelms you. Then you have to get out your planning lists and start working the issues one at a time. The guys are starting to zone out, but they're still getting things done."

The briefback is scheduled for the third day of the four-day planning and preparation window. By late afternoon of the second day, Captain Santos and his team have their planning largely complete and are starting to rehearse for this final mission briefing. Santos and First Lieutenant Kwele will handle large portions of the briefing, and Sergeant Short will deliver the intelligence summaries. For the MOS-specific portions of the briefback, Tim Baker will address weapons-related topics, Daniel Barstow will speak to engineering, Andrew Kohl, of course, will discuss the medical portion, and David Altman will brief the communications. Tom Olin is on for weather and logistics. By early evening, the 915 briefing team is in full-on rehearsals, while the other members of the team continue to prepare equipment.

Just before midnight, I get a call at our cabin from a friend of Miguel Santos. It seems that his wife is in labor and Captain Santos is

about to become a father. Santos and his wife had planned for him to
be absent for the birth and had flown his wife's mother over from
Germany several weeks ago to be with her daughter. Nine-one-five *is*
in isolation and the briefback *is* scheduled for 0900—a little over nine
hours from the time I got the call. And yet Womack Army Medical
Center at Fort Bragg is only forty-five minutes away and it *is* their
first child. It takes me five minutes to dress and another five minutes
to get to the team hut. Nine-one-five is still working, but the briefback and their equipment are in good order. After a few phone calls—
duty NCO to cadre team officer to company commander and so
on—915's team leader receives permission to leave Camp Mackall.
Moments later, Miguel Santos and I are in my pickup truck and
headed for Fort Bragg. Anna Santos is born while we're en route, but
the new dad is soon with his family. I grab a few hours sleep in my
truck before we head back to Camp Mackall; the new father has had
none. By 0600, we are back at the team room. Captain Santos gets a
hearty round of congratulations from his teammates, and 915 begins
a final rehearsal for the briefback.

The briefbacks, or mission briefings, are taken seriously in Special
Forces—certainly so in Phase IV training and Robin Sage. The officer
acting as 915's battalion commander to take the briefback is Lieutenant Colonel Matt Stark, commander of the 2nd Battalion, 7th Special Forces Group. The team rises as he enters the team room, and
Captain Santos introduces himself and the members of his team. Lieutenant Colonel Stark takes his seat, and Santos begins with a concise
statement of his mission, then plunges into the Pineland situation and
threat evaluation. As in the rehearsals, other members of 915 follow
him with their portions of the briefback. The briefing is very detailed
and very technical, with a great deal of acronyms and military jargon.
Fortunately, I had been through Phase III, so I could follow most of it.
Ninety minutes and 115 PowerPoint slides later, Captain Santos concludes his briefback.

"The men have worked hard," he tells Lieutenant Colonel Stark, "and they're prepared to carry out this mission. We're good to go, sir."

The team is sitting in two rows to the side of the table where the colonel took the briefing. "That was a good job," Stark begins, "especially given the time you've had to devote to it. I'd like to say that you'll have more time for planning down range, but that may not be the case. I like your approach to training your G force, but don't try to jump right into it with the guerrillas. Settle in with your Gs and build some rapport first. And you, Captain, are going to have to sell this plan to the G chief before he allows you to train his men. Again, try to get a read on him before you begin training. He may be strong politically, but is he strong tactically? Is he strong organizationally? You have to make a quick assessment of him—help him where he is weak, yet stay in the background and not make him look bad to his men." He pauses to consult his notes. "Your infil plan is a good one, but more detail is needed. You have to plan for every imaginable contingency, from a man getting injured on the drop zone to being compromised on the drop zone. Until you make a safe linkup and are in the security of the guerrilla base, you're in Indian country, and you have to take all security precautions. And when you are in the G base, you'll still have to tend to your own security. In Robin Sage, and later on when you deploy for real, always be thinking about security. In Special Forces, you'll never really be free of that responsibility."

Lieutenant Colonel Stark again consults his legal pad, checking off notes as he makes each point to 915.

"Past training your guerrillas and taking them on operations, make a careful risk assessment on each and every mission—take the time to game it out from a risk perspective.

"Do what you can to stay away from air resupply, it puts you and the aircraft at risk. Work with your Gs and the auxiliary to get what you need, if you can.

"A word about the equipment you are going to jump in. The tendency is to go in heavy. Assume some risk on food and water. You can find water on the ground, and you can do without food for a while. Try to cut down on your weight so you can move better. This is a good time of year temperature-wise, so you can cut down on your snivel gear.

"Medical. Be ready for real-world issues—sprains, cuts, infections, that kind of thing. For the future, know your teammates and know their injuries. Guys get hurt. Don't put a man or a team at risk because a guy's hurt and wants to suck it up and go in on the mission.

"Communications. I want a situation report as soon as you're safely on the ground. It'll make me feel good. Until I hear from you, I'll have a quick-reaction evacuation force in full readiness until I know you are on the ground and moving safely. Situation reports. I want a situation report daily; I want to know what you need and the current intelligence. Intel reports and situation reports will drive decisions at the highest level—even to national command authority level, your lips to president's ears. You are the ground truth—all before this is dated information.

"Be aware of what Civil Affairs and Psyops can do for you, especially during demobilization and the political climate that will follow the cessation of hostilities."

He looks at the two rows of soldiers that make up 915. "One of the hardest things you may have to do in this exercise is to keep your focus. This is as real as it gets without real bullets. Flip the switch—get your head in the game and keep it there. This is a real operation. Life and death. Talk to each other; if one of you gets down, then another of you is going to have to kick him in the ass. Play it for real, to the max of your ability, and you'll leave here with skills that you'll need and be thankful for down range. Do well in Robin Sage, and you'll be ready for duty with a Special Forces operational detachment."

Lieutenant Colonel Stark rises, and 915 is on their feet a nanosecond behind him. He shakes each of their hands and takes his leave. I sat in on other briefbacks, and each commander handled it differently. Some interrupted to ask questions of the briefer. Others aggressively challenged the team leader, and still others would quiz the team—asking the ODA junior weapons sergeant about guerrilla weapons training or the senior communicator about far recognition signals. The afternoon following the briefback is the time for the Phase IV written examination, a comprehensive exam that tests military knowledge in all aspects of unconventional warfare. To prepare for it, each member of 915 pairs up with someone who has a different MOS—a Bravo with an Echo, the Delta with a Charlie—and they grill each other on their specialties and what they've learned to date in Phase IV.

While 915 and the other student ODAs plan, prepare, brief, and test, there's a curious gathering of soldiers in the parking lot just outside the Rowe Training Facility compound. A steady stream of trucks and buses brings soldiers from Fort Bragg to Camp Mackall. This contingent is a mix of 82nd Airborne veterans, a National Guard unit from Wisconsin, and a service support company from Fort Benning. These are the Gs—the guerrillas who will serve as Pineland irregulars for the Robin Sage exercise. They're organized into their guerrilla bands and then, along with their G chiefs, head out to their G bases. There the G chiefs, who are mostly veteran role players of Robin Sage, will read them into their roles as irregular soldiers and get them in character, as well as the uniform of a Pineland guerrilla. For some of the combat veterans from the 82nd, they'll have to dumb-down their military skills. For the service support soldiers, they will learn some new skills. All of this is part of a realistic unconventional-warfare training scenario and the capstone of Green Beret training.

I asked Lieutenant Colonel Jim Jackson why, in the light of the global war on terrorism, Robin Sage did not morph into a foreign internal defense or counterinsurgency scenario with a Middle East/ Southwest Asia flavor. "It's been talked about," Jackson told me, "but Robin Sage has met the test of time. If these Special Forces students can handle what we throw at them here in Pineland, they can handle unconventional warfare, foreign internal defense, and counterinsurgency warfare anywhere in the world."

Late on the afternoon of day twenty, 915 is on the tarmac at the Camp Mackall Army Airfield, awaiting its turn with several other student ODAs for airborne insertion into Pineland. Parachute is not the only way into Pineland. Teams have gone in by truck and by mule. The classroom work, the planning, the gear preparation, and the briefings are all behind them. Now they're going to war, inasmuch as war can be arranged in an unconventional-warfare training scenario. Captain Santos has checked each of his men, and a cadre jumpmaster has checked them all. Sergeant Blackman and Captain Childers, like two mothers getting their children ready for the bus for the first day of school, are checking everybody. The men are heavy—each of them has a hundred pounds of gear, more or less, plus the weight of the main parachute and the reserve. The only man who is light, equipment-wise, is Specialist Justin Keller. The parachutes have a training-load limit of 350 pounds, and he personally makes up 250 pounds of that weight. Some of his gear will be jumped in by his teammates, and he will recover it once they are on the ground.

The weather is drizzly and the wind's gusting up to fifteen miles per hour—marginal for Army airborne training operations. Bands of dark clouds march across Camp Mackall Army Airfield. It's approaching dusk. "If the wind's under thirteen and we have the ceiling, we go," says Sergeant Blackman. "The rain won't matter." Aircraft land, take aboard student ODAs, and leave. Finally, it's 915's turn. Two Casas, small twin-engine transports, belonging to the Army Special Operations Command Flight Detachment, land to collect 915. The heavily laden soldiers waddle to the aircraft like a file of penguins, six on one aircraft and six on the other. As they board the aircraft, I race across Camp Mackall from the airfield to the Luzon Drop Zone in time to see two planes pass over the DZ in close formation. It's raining, and all but dark. All twelve come out clean, and 915 is under canopy. One by one, the men drop their rucksacks, which fall to the end of a nylon tether. First the ruck, then the soldiers, slam into the DZ. Once on the ground, the men gather up their gear and parachutes, then make their way to the rally point on the northeast corner of the drop zone. They pile the chutes by the side of a road and mark them with a Chemlite for retrieval by exercise support staff. Then, after a head count and an equipment check, the ODA moves off in patrol formation to link up with the Pineland auxiliary.

In the real world, as in Robin Sage, linking up with partisan forces on contested ground is chancy business, one that must be done with care and caution. This will be the first test for 915. Following 915 that evening are myself and two civilian Northrop Grumman OCE (observer, controller, evaluator) personnel—simply referred to as OCEs. Either these two civilian controllers or Captain Childers and/or Sergeant Blackman will be on-site or with 915 at all times. Both OCEs are retired career Green Beret sergeants. The primary linkup site for 915 is a small bridge that spans one of Camp Mackall's lake-overflow gates. It's a two-mile patrol from the DZ rally point to the linkup. Once we are close, Captain Santos puts the team in a security perimeter and sends Sergeant Tom Olin and PFC Tim Baker ahead to exchange recognition signals with the Pinelanders. Signals are given, but not returned. Olin and Baker move closer and signal again. Then the shooting starts. Santos can only recall his scouts and make for the alternate linkup point. But the alternate is only a half mile away, and is sure to be compromised by the shooting. So it's on to the contingent linkup site.

"I learned a lesson on that one," Captain Santos later reflected. "You cannot have your secondary linkup within earshot of your primary. So I walked my team all night because I didn't plan well enough."

And walk they did. The contingent linkup site is close to an eight-mile hike from the primary. So 915, carrying close to a hundred pounds per man, walks ten miles that first night, all of it in the rain. Nine-one-five, the OCEs, and the writer are pretty beat up when we arrive at our destination, an abandoned rural church just off Camp

Mackall proper. It's 0300, and 915 has been on the ground for seven hours. The team goes to ground for a few hours' rest and the 18 Echos rig their PSC-5, find their satellite, and transmit their first situation. There's a dedicated satellite that supports Robin Sage and the nineteen ODAs scattered across Pineland.

Nine-one-five's contingent linkup is scheduled for 0600 that morning. First Lieutenant Patrick Kwele and Specialist Antonio Costa change into civilian clothes for the meeting. Well covered by their teammates hiding in the woods, the two soldiers wait by the road in front of the church. Soon a pickup truck slowly approaches. Kwele and Costa exchange bona fides with two members of the Pineland auxiliary, then call in Captain Santos. After some negotiations and the exchange of 1,000 don, an agreement is struck for them to be picked up by truck later that morning. The auxiliary returns at the appointed time, this time in two old pickup trucks, and 915 clambers aboard. The truck beds are wet and dirty, but then so is 915. The soldiers are covered with heavy tarps, and the little convoy sets out to meet with the head of their assigned partisan group—their G chief.

While 915 is making their final preparations for insertion into Pineland, I go out to visit its guerrilla base. It's located a sloping piece of acreage populated by scrub oak trees, low vegetation, and an occasional pine, all surrounded by freshly planted soybean fields—private land made available to the Army by a local farmer. The ground is located several miles north of the town of Raeford. It's rural North Carolina farm country. The cadre have set up their camp about a quarter-mile from the G base to support the 915's exercise scenario, or "lane." Here, well away from the G base, the cadre, OCEs, and additional role players will await events in the exercise play to unfold. I park my truck at the cadre camp and make my way down a dirt road that bordered a bean field, then take an overgrown path into the woods that meander down a shallow slope and into the G base. There, in a small clearing, I find a large tarp covering a fire pit with six to eight boxes and stools around the fire. A large store of wood is stacked nearby. Next to this gathering place there's a small tent with a table that holds a modest supply of canned goods and MRE rations. A fifty-five-gallon drum is blocked up on a crude wooden cradle with a filler cap on the top. Scattered down the gentle slope are small tents and low shelter tarps tied in among the trees. These are the guerrilla "hooches." It has the look of Andersonville. As I approach, a large man with a goatee, tan ball cap, and dark fatigues is addressing some two dozen men dressed like himself. All wear the same black field uniforms, but there's a smattering of camouflage jackets and hunting vests.

"OK, men. Thanks for all your hard work in getting the camp set up. For the next two weeks, you are no longer American soldiers in the United States Army. You are Pineland freedom fighters—living on the edge and suffering here in this guerrilla camp for the freedom of our beloved Pineland. In this camp, you'll always address me as Colonel or Colonel Chissom, and Sergeant First Class Johnson here is now Sergeant Major Johnson. Our uniform is the black guerrilla fatigues of the Pineland freedom fighter and your civilian baseball caps.

"Forget all you learned in the Army; you've had no formal military training. I don't want to hear any Army slang. If you were a city boy before you came into the Army, be a city boy here. If you were a farm boy, you're a farm boy again. You may know how to shoot a rifle, but you're not a marksman, and you've maybe put a dozen or so rounds through your weapon. You may have seen a hand grenade, but you've never thrown one. This afternoon, I want you to study your Pineland packets and get in character. Do not get buddy-buddy with the SF students when they arrive; they're here to learn, and they learn by interacting with you and by teaching you how to become soldiers."

Then Colonel Chissom lays down camp rules—trash in bags for daily pickup, only toilet paper in the latrine trench, keep the water barrel full, stay in small groups, take care of your gear, stay in character, and so on. "After today, I don't want to hear any chatter about NASCAR, Jennifer Lopez, or current events. We live in Pineland, and we don't have radios out here. I don't want to see any Game Boys or earphone wires coming out of your ears."

Then Captain Garrett Childers seems to materialize out of the woods, as he and Sergeant Blackman would often do over the next two weeks. Colonel Chissom nods to him as Childers steps before the group to address them. "I'd also like to thank you for being here," Captain Childers tells the guerrillas. "I know some of you may not want to be here, but well, that's tough. It's not the first or last time you'll draw a detail you don't like. Play the game while you're here, and perhaps you can have some fun and learn something. Two things. First, be safe. If you're not sure that a local you meet or who happens to come by is really part of the scenario, err on the side of caution. Identify yourself as a serviceman who's participating in a military exercise. Show your military ID, if necessary. There are some good old boys out here who live in a very small world, and may not know who we are or why we're here. Second, for the next two weeks you're actors. This may surface a whole new career for some of you after you leave the Army. Again, I appreciate your help and count on you to stay in character in order for us to properly evaluate our candidates. Myself and my cadre's time will be taken with the students, so take your direction from Colonel Chissom. Oh, and this is Mister Couch. He's a writer and not part of the scenario, but will be observing you and the Special Forces candidates during this exercise."

After the meeting breaks up, I approach the G chief and introduce myself. "I guess, Colonel, that I'll be taking my direction from you as well. Please let me know if I'm in the way at any time."

He laughs and offers me a firm hand. "Oh, I doubt that you'll be in the way, sir, but I'll let you know. Make yourself at home. Things are pretty informal here in camp, and as you probably know, some evolutions are preplanned and some of them will flow from the actions of the student ODA."

Bill Chissom is a retired Special Forces master sergeant from Clarksville, Tennessee. His dad was a career soldier, as was he; he's been retired less than a year. This is his third Robin Sage as a G chief. Five of Chissom's twenty-six years in Special Forces were as an instructor at the Special Forces Q-Course, so he knows Robin Sage well. The rest of his time was with the 3rd and 5th Special Forces Groups, where he made over *twenty-five* overseas deployment rotations. Chissom is a veteran intelligence sergeant and team sergeant. Now he's a colonel in the guerrilla movement struggling to topple the current government in Pineland. "We need quality Special Forces soldiers in this war on terror," he told me. "Nine-eleven should never be forgotten nor ever be forgiven—ever."

The two pickup trucks deliver 915 to a safe-house location on Camp Mackall near the main entrance, some seven miles from their contingency linkup point. The men are beat, and they look it as they file from the trucks into the clearing, where there's a small cabin and a fire pit with log sections for seats around the fire. There, Colonel Chissom is waiting for them, along with Sergeant Major Johnson and three other armed guerrillas who stand on the periphery. Sergeant First Class (now Sergeant Major) Johnson is the senior enlisted soldier in Chissom's guerrilla band.

"Welcome to Pineland, Captain," Chissom says, rising to greet Santos. "We're glad to have you here to help us with our struggle." They exchange greetings, and the colonel bids them to sit with him around the fire. "I'm not very happy about last night," he says in a measured voice. "That cost me a lot of money. I had to pay drivers and bribe guards at the checkpoints. One of my men was killed, and now I have to take care of his family." After a brief negotiation, Captain Santos gives him 30,000 don, almost a third of the money he brought with him. "What else did you bring for me? Food? Ammo?"

"We brought both," Santos replies diplomatically, "but we only have what we could carry. And that we'll share with you. What we really brought are ourselves. I have with me a team of professional soldiers. We're here to help you with your struggle. Your fight is our fight."

"Oh, that's good, Captain, real good," Chissom concedes, "but you have to understand, you're outsiders; you're gonna have to work your way in here. You see, my men have been fighting for a long time, and they've lost a lot—their homes, their families, their friends. They gave it all up for the struggle. We're fighting for our land; we want our life back—we want to build a new nation and start new families. You say our fight is your fight? Tell me, Captain, why're you here? Why did you come to Pineland?"

"Those who have taken power in Pineland seized the government without a fair vote—without the permission of the citizens," Santos replies. "They're robbing you and your people; they've taken what is rightfully yours. We're here to help you regain your land and your nation."

Colonel Chissom thinks about this and nods thoughtfully. "OK, I'll buy that. How about you," he says, pointing to Specialist David Altman.

"I believe in freedom," Altman replies. "And I believe in helping others fight for it."

"And you?"

"Our great-great grandfathers fought for our liberation from England," says Sergeant Daniel Barstow. "We're here to help you fight for your liberty."

"I've learned that freedom and liberty are precious," replies Specialist Justin Keller. "We Americans can't enjoy our freedom if yours has been taken away."

"I'm a professional soldier," says Sergeant Andrew Kohl. "I believe in what you fight for, and it's my duty to fight alongside you."

Chissom appears satisfied with this. "All right, I'll accept that. We'll fight together, side by side. So, before we leave here and go to our camp, we'll honor you with a small freedom-fighter's ceremony. Since we are brothers in the same cause, we must share a toast to our fallen warriors. This is a sacred undertaking."

The particulars of this ceremony and the contents of the toast are omitted from this text in the spirit of preserving one of the mysteries of this Robin Sage training lane. I can say that what was served was not a gourmet offering—far from it. Yet the men in 915 soldier through this ritual because they *really* want to wear that Green Beret. After the meeting, while the team waits for the auxiliary and their pickups, Captain Childers takes Captain Santos aside.

"OK, last night was a ballbuster, but that can happen, here and later on—down range. When things turn to shit, you have to focus on command-and-control issues, and the guys have to get past their misery and drive on. You have to refocus them—get their heads back in the game and on the mission. It's combat leadership. Last night, they started thinking about their pain and forgot about the team and their job. Don't let them do that. As a detachment leader, you'll always have the tough choices: let them rest now when they really need a rest, or push them so you can get them more quickly to a safe place. They have to suck it up and follow you. A lot of Robin Sage is managing chaos and not losing your cool when things turn to crap. During the initial days of the Afghan campaign, it was chaos. But we got through it and accomplished our mission there. Only patience and persistence prevailed. It's the same here. Robin Sage is designed to prepare you for this. Now, step it up. Take charge of these guys and make it happen, OK?"

"Roger that, sir," Santos replies, "and thanks. I guess I needed to hear that—again."

Nine-one-five arrives at the G base early in the afternoon. The rain has finally stopped, and there are a few sun breaks amid the passing clouds. Colonel Chissom points to an area of the camp where they can dump their rucks, then disappears into his tent. Sergeant Olin looks for Sergeant Major Johnson to talk about the camp duties and security, but he's nowhere to be found. And there are no other guerrillas about. Santos and Olin walk the perimeter of the camp, talk about security, and wonder where everyone is. The other members of 915 set about stringing up some poncho shelters and lay out their gear to dry. By midafternoon, there is a rustling of activity about the camp as Colonel Chissom, Sergeant Major Johnson, and a few of the other Gs begin to gather at the fire pit under the large tarp near Chissom's tent. Chissom invites Captain Santos to join him by the fire.

"Things seemed a little quiet around here this afternoon," Santos offers in the course of the conversation.

"It's our custom here in Pineland," replies Chissom, "to observe Ra-haa between eleven a.m. and three p.m. During that time, the men are free to sleep, tend to their own needs, or meditate. It is a private time for us."

Later, Tom Olin will ask his team leader, "How the hell are we going to train these guys if they all take four-hour naps in the middle of the day?"

"I don't know," Santos tells his team sergeant, "we'll just have to figure out a way."

During the course of that first afternoon and evening, Captain Santos works to engage Colonel Chissom, and Staff Sergeant Olin tries to go one-on-one with Sergeant Major Johnson. Sergeant Olin and Sergeant Major Johnson are able to work out some shared camp-duty and camp-security issues between the Gs and 915. Things seem to be moving forward as more of the Americans are invited to join the fire. Then there is a dustup between Olin and Johnson. One of the Americans began asking about how the guerrillas train. That prompted Johnson to ask Santos, Olin, and the others in 915 to leave the fire. It seems they had begun talking about training without first observing the Pineland custom of engaging in small talk before turning to business. This is considered bad form in Pineland.

"If you and your men are so anxious to work and train," Colonel

Chissom tells Santos, "then your men can take the camp security duty tonight and my men will sleep."

It's another tough night for 915. Half of them sleep while the other half man the three security outposts that guard the camp. Captain Santos and Sergeant Olin are constantly on the move, checking on sleepy soldiers in their security positions. As they go about their duties, they talk about the importance of building rapport and understanding these foreign fighters they are there to train.

The following morning, things are better as 915 and Gs take up camp chores. The guerrillas have been briefed to be a little standoffish and make the Special Forces candidates draw them out. Captain Santos does a quick inventory of the limited food stocks in the G base and proposes to Colonel Chissom that the Americans and his Gs pool their chow resources, and share-and-share alike. Colonel Chissom warms to this. On the advice of the ODA weapons sergeants, the camp security positions are repositioned to better protect the camp. Doc Kohl moves about, checking on the health of each of the guerrillas. He asks Sergeant Major Johnson if he can hold sick call for the Gs and, if there are any of his men who serve as medics, he would like to meet them. Andrew Kohl is proving to be a quick study in the by, with, and through art. Soon he has two Gs assigned to him. He doesn't talk medicine, but asks them a lot of questions about Pineland and themselves. Later that morning, two Pineland fighters arrive at the G base and ask to see Colonel Chissom. Colonel Chissom greets them warmly, but later expresses his displeasure with Captain Santos. "Your security should have told me they were here before I had to meet with them."

The two visitors, who will turn up periodically throughout the Robin Sage exercise, are a Colonel Merced and one of his lieutenants. They are, for want of a better term, a roving band of patriots—kind of a special operations force working for the liberation of Pineland. Merced has some intelligence on the movement of the Pineland security forces and the dreaded Pineland Condor Squadron, a particularly capable counterinsurgency element of the Pineland Army. He also has information for a potential target for that evening—the regular movement of a squad of Pineland soldiers between two Pineland security installations. Merced and Chissom are clearly on the same side, but Santos notes a change in his colonel's comportment in Merced's presence. He senses almost equal measures of trust and distrust between the two, and that they may be political rivals. Later that day, he will report this in his daily radio situation report.

That afternoon, during what should have been the Ra-haa period, Sergeant Brian Short, coming off security duty, finds Captain Santos.

"Hey, sir, something's up. I went to get one of the Gs for security relief at 1500 and he wasn't in his tent. I checked around, and they are all gone. Their gear and their hooches are still here, but the Gs have all bugged out."

Santos and Olin begin to look around and quickly find that Short is right. They can find neither Colonel Chissom nor Sergeant Major Johnson. Santos considers this, then turns to Olin.

"OK, I want half the guys on security while the other half pack their gear and get ready to move out quickly. Then trade out; I want the team ready to move on a moment's notice. This may be some kind of test, or it may be that there's some kind of a threat in the area. At any rate, we have to be ready to fight or get the hell out of Dodge."

Nine-one-five quickly gets ready to move. Then late that afternoon, the Gs begin to straggle back into camp in twos and threes. Finally, Colonel Chissom and Sergeant Major Johnson return to the G base. It seems that Colonel Merced told Chissom in private that the location of the camp may have been compromised and that there was the threat of a raid by a Condor strike element. The fact that the Gs quietly left without telling the Americans clearly says that they still don't fully trust them. Santos tells Chissom of his disappointment, but the colonel passes it off as an internal security issue.

That evening, Chissom tells Santos that they are going to act on

Merced's intelligence and ambush a Pineland security squad that will be in the area. He asks Santos and two of his men to go along as observers. Santos accepts and offers the assistance of one of his SAW machine gunners to help with the ambush. They leave the G base on foot a few hours after dark—three Americans, Colonel Chissom, and five of his Gs with the two OCEs and myself trailing along behind. Halfway to the target area, Chissom stops to brief his men on how they're going to arrange the ambush. The intelligence has the enemy moving along a disused railroad track. Chissom wants his men arranged on either side of the track to take the enemy soldiers in a crossfire.

"Uh, if I may, Colonel, may I offer a suggestion?"

"What is it, Captain?" Chissom says irritably.

"You may want to stagger your men on either side of the track, or better yet, put them in an 'L' formation so you won't be shooting at each other."

"This is the way we do it—the way we've always done it. Why do you want us to change our tactics now?" The colonel is clearly upset.

After a heated discussion, Santos is able to show them the potential for fratricide in an opposing cross fire. Chissom grudgingly concedes the issue, but he's clearly resentful. The small force continues the mission. They patrol for another hour to the target location. Shortly after midnight, a five-man squad of the Pineland Army comes up the tracks and is cut down by the guerrilla band. On Santos's recommendation, Chissom put the SAW at the foot of the L with an excellent field of fire. It's a textbook ambush and the enemy solders have no chance, and go down in a hail of blank automatic-weapons fire. In spite of the tactical success, things go sideways. As the Gs strip the dead enemy of their weapons and ammunition, Chissom offers Santos the honor of firing into the body of one of the fallen soldiers. Santos refuses, and another argument breaks out. Chissom accuses him of cowardice, and Santos tries to explain that this is against his rules of engagement. The

Gs form up behind Chissom in a show of support. Then Santos suggests they talk later; guerrilla strikes are suppose to be hit-and-run operations.

They're no more than a half hour into their trek back to the G base, retracing their steps, when Santos politely suggests that it might be dangerous to return the exact same way they came. Chissom explodes.

"How dare you *again* question my authority! This is my turf, my country, my fight, and this is my band of freedom fighters. You Americans are foreigners. You are arrogant! You are rude! And you know nothing of our struggle here! Maybe it would be better if you go back to where you came from and let us fight on alone."

We are on a back road along the edge of a cotton field. I can see the dim lights of a farmhouse a few hundred yards away and hear a dog barking in the distance. A half moon peeks from behind a cloud to illuminate this confrontation that's taking place, literally, in the middle of nowhere. You can cut the tension between Santos and Chissom with a knife. It's my sense that Colonel Chissom is *really* upset and that Captain Santos is *really* struggling to hold his temper and work within the scenario. The others—the Gs, the other two 915 soldiers, and the writer—watch in apprehension as the two men square off. Only the two OCEs, standing well off to the side along with me, seem to take it in stride.

"You dress me down in front of my men," Chissom continues, "you tell me how to do what we've done many times, and then you rush me away from the ambush site and we have no ears to show for it!"

"Ears?" Santos questions.

"The ears of the Pineland Army swine," Chissom says with a show of great exasperation. "How do we celebrate the death of our enemies if we do not take their ears?" Then he stalks off in the direction of the G base. The guerrillas follow him, and the Americans follow them.

"Is it always like this?" I ask one of the OCEs as we drop back from earshot of the others.

"In one form or another," he says. The OCE I spoke with retired after twenty years in the Army with close to sixteen years in 5th Group. While on active duty, he deployed to Kuwait, Somalia, Iraq, Bosnia, and Saudi Arabia. He was an 18 Echo communications sergeant, and for two years he served as an 18 Fox intelligence sergeant. "Bill [Chissom] is a good one. He seems to know when to challenge the students and when to back away from them. But make no mistake about it; this is real. When you work with other cultures, being right or tactically sound doesn't always make them like or trust you. This captain's pretty sharp, but he's letting his tactical competence become an obstacle to doing his job. It's easy for us to see it, standing back and watching." The former Special Forces sergeant chuckles. "Now, Captain Santos, there, he's sweating bullets and wondering what the hell he did wrong."

When we get back to the G base, Colonel Chissom goes straight to his tent. Santos huddles with Sergeant Olin to compare notes. Olin has something of a victory to report. He and Sergeant Major Johnson talked for a few hours around the fire, and Johnson will allow the 18 Bravo sergeants to begin holding classes on weapons maintenance and the use of the M240 machine gun tomorrow. Santos retrieves his toughbook computer from his ruck and types up a brief report on their first mission with his G force. These situation reports are sent by PSC-5 via satellite or PRC-137 high-frequency transmission and retrieved at the 18 Echo/Eureka Springs communications center at Fort Bragg. These transmissions are then forwarded to the Rowe Training Facility at Camp Mackall. The cadre serving as the forward operating base communicators receive these messages, reply as necessary within the exercise scenario, and file a copy of the message traffic in Captain Childers's in-box, where he or Sergeant Blackman retrieve them on a daily basis.

The next morning, Captain Santos, after three restless hours sleep, finds Colonel Chissom by the fire pit.

"Mind if I join you, sir?" Chissom says nothing, but motions for him to take a seat. Santos desperately wants to have it out with

Chissom—confront him, air it out, and move on. This direct approach is how most American military officers—and American business executives, for that matter—handle these issues. But last night, Santos, Patrick Kwele, and Tom Olin talked about it, and now Santos is prepared to deal with it differently.

"I need to apologize for last night, Colonel," Santos says. "Our customs and military traditions are very different from yours. There are some things my country forbids me to do and will hold me strictly accountable for. Yet I failed to appreciate just how hard it is for you and your men in your struggle for freedom. Perhaps I need to work harder to understand your ways and the gallant efforts of your freedom fighters. I hope we can still work together for the liberation of Pineland."

Chissom nods slowly. "I think I understand, Captain, and we do need to work together if we are to free our country. Let us try to be allies."

That morning, Doc Kohl holds sick call for the Gs—there are real-world issues with poison oak, a few cuts, and a brown recluse spider bite. The latter is a serious matter; Kohl dresses the bite and starts the soldier on antibiotics. Later that morning, a cadre medic, in the guise of a Red Cross worker, stops by to check Kohl's diagnosis and treatment. The ODA weapons sergeants begin to hold classes in weapons and tactics, and the communicators work with the Gs on the PRC-119 and PRC-148 MBITR radios. The training is supervised by First Lieutenant Kwele and is going so well that the Gs are an hour into Ra-haa before they realize it and head for their hooches to rest. Captain Santos stays close to Colonel Chissom, engaging him on issues that range from future joint operations to his vision for Pineland after the peace is won. That afternoon, Sergeant Olin and Sergeant Johnson agree that the three security positions that guard the camp will be jointly manned by one American and one Pinelander.

The relationship between Captain Miguel Santos and Colonel Bill Chissom will continue to blossom and then become strained, as relationships will between the Gs and 915. Some of this is scenario driven to generate teaching points, and sometimes it's the reaction or response to the conduct of 915. I find it surprising how the soldiers in the role of Pineland guerrillas take so well to their persona of insurgents. On occasion, I find them being overly cooperative, as I know they're secretly rooting for the 915 Special Forces students, but for the most part they live and act the part of Gs. The time and attention that go into this one scenario, or lane, to train twelve Special Forces candidates is simply phenomenal. Twenty-eight soldiers work in shifts around the clock to train the twelve, plus the part-timers in the form of Colonel Merced, the auxiliary personnel, and other role players. And this is *one* lane. There are *twenty-four* other scenarios being played out across the state of North Carolina. A total of twenty-five student ODAs working under three forward operating bases are embedded with their guerrilla contingents, all working to liberate this small nation called Pineland.

I was able to get out to see some team leader/G-chief interaction at other G bases during the previous Robin Sage class, Class 1-05, and they struggled, just like Captain Miguel Santos is with Colonel Chissom. Each student ODA scenario or lane is a scripted, well-tested, well-thought-out series of events designed to challenge and teach these Green Beret students. These scenarios are also flexible and can be advanced, or delayed, or modified, within limits, depending on the decisions and actions of the student ODAs. In some lanes, certain businesses and sometimes whole communities are in on the game. There are stores that will sell goods and food for don, with the store owners later exchanging the don for greenbacks. There are meetings at night with members of the underground in basements under bowling alleys. Intelligence on critical targets is passed over the counter by coffee shop owners to SF candidates dressed in civilian clothes. To the credit of these patriotic citizens, I'm not sure this civilian-supported military training could take place anywhere but central North Carolina.

By the third day, the operational tempo picks up. The Gs are short on weapons, so First Lieutenant Kwele, Sergeant Dunn, and Specialist Costa are sent to make a weapons buy on the black market. The auxiliary who is to take them to the rendezvous with the arms dealer manages to drive off (on instructions from Sergeant Blackman) without Patrick Kwele, leaving Dunn and Costa to negotiate the buy.

"That taught me a lesson," Costa said of the evolution. "I was the junior guy and thought I'd just be along for security. Then the lieutenant gets left and suddenly I have to inspect, test, and make the buy. From now on, I'm going to pay better attention to the mission brief. You never know when you'll have to step up and take charge."

The first major target is a railroad bridge. This is one of the preplanned targets that 915 worked on before they inserted into Pineland. They knew they would have to blow the bridge, but didn't know exactly when. Their forward operating base commander radios them with instructions to take out the bridge close to midnight the following night. Sergeant Dan Barstow is to be in charge of this operation. He elects to send in Specialist David Altman and PFC Tim Baker, along with two Gs, the night before for the mission reconnaissance. For this mission, Baker is to be in charge and Altman the recon-team communicator.

"David and I work well together," Baker tells me. "We were in the same boot camp company and the same jump-school stick. With the exception of Phase III, we've been together since we joined the Army. We're battle buddies, and we'll handle this recon."

They are to put "eyes-on" the target for twenty-four hours, then bring Barstow and his men in, link up with them, and do the job. The bridge is eight klicks (eight thousand meters—about five miles) from the G base. Barstow wants commo with his recon element, but there is some question of using an MBITR radio since it is at the limit of the small radio's range. Altman is made to take along the more powerful, and bigger, PRC-137 to talk to the PRC-119 serving as the G-base radio.

"I didn't spend all that time in Phase III learning about radios," Altman says with some irritation, "not to make that commo shot with an MBITR. I know I can do it."

The recon team goes in and finds a good perch above the railroad trestle. They observe the guard force, which turns out to be a maritime unit that has regular foot patrols on the bridge and a Boston whaler that patrols the river. Altman, who brought along both radios, finds a shallow rise above their position and rigs a ladder-line, J-pole antenna to the small, handheld MBITR. "I had great commo with the G base, and I was transmitting with only a tenth of a watt of power." He passes along the recon team's observations. Armed with this new intelligence, Daniel Barstow, Sergeant Brian Short, and the four Gs who will be with them plan their mission throughout the day. That evening, under Dan Barstow's direction, the team delivers a briefback to Colonel Chissom. Chissom is happy to see his Gs delivering portions of the mission brief. Shortly before midnight, PFC Baker and his recon element link up with Barstow and the assault team. Together, they attack and eliminate the enemy force guarding the bridge. There are five of them sitting around a fire by the river, and the attackers are able to get quite close before they open fire in a one-sided assault. With the guard force neutralized, they place their charges on the rails, pull their time fuses, and move off for their extraction point. After they've cleared off the target, I remain with the OCE who will retrieve the dummy charges. He's a former 18 Charlie engineering sergeant. He times the time-fuse burn from the "fire in the hole" to the puffs of smoke at the base of the inert caps. Both burn times of the dual-primed charges are very close to the allotted five minutes. The OCE also grades the quality of the det-cord tie-in and the placement of the charges.

Sergeant Barstow's team and the recon element are not the only teams in the field. Soon after Barstow and company leave camp for the attack on the bridge, Specialist Justin Keller, along with Sergeant Aaron Dunn and two Gs, set out to recon the drop zone for the pre-planned aerial resupply the following evening. They're collected by the auxiliary in yet another old pickup truck and taken to a location several miles from the G base. Keller has a military GPS called a plugger and verifies that they are at the right location. Then they settle in to put eyes-on the vacant field for the next twenty-four hours.

Back at the G base, Sergeant Olin is manning the base-station PRC-119 and receives Dan Barstow's report that his mission was a success. Captain Santos and Olin immediately send out a satellite transmission on the PSC-5 that the railroad trestle is now unusable and will be for several weeks—mission accomplished. After the recon and action elements return, Sergeant Barstow conducts a quick after-action review. It is now 0300, and his recon element has been up for well over thirty-six hours—the others for more than twenty. The OCE allows that charges, as placed and rigged, would have done the job and offers a few tips on how they could have done it differently or better. Then Captain Childers steps before the group.

"I'll be brief, and then you guys can get some rest. It's very important that on a reconnaissance you don't get detected. The mission will still go if you get no information, but don't get seen. Have your priority intelligence requirements down pat. What is the information you need from the recon? How safely and far away from the target site can you get this information? Do the job in the safest and most secure way possible. Nice job overall, Sergeant Barstow, but a word about your briefing. In putting together your task organization, you have to address a whole spectrum of 'what ifs.' What if there's no commo? What if the auxiliary doesn't show? What if the auxiliary's compromised? What's your absolute go-to-hell fallback plan at each stage of the operation? Think about and talk about what might be your most dangerous courses of action. See what I'm getting at? Think security, security, security, OK? Again, good job. Now get some rest. It's already tomorrow, and there's a lot more coming at you."

After the after-action review breaks up, Childers takes Captain Santos and First Lieutenant Kwele aside. "I know it's hard waiting it out in the base camp while your guys are out on a mission. Real world, you'll have your contingency procedures and your quick-reaction-force procedures in place if needed. But mentally, you almost have to write those men off—think about not seeing them, because you'll have too much to do to worry about them. You have to trust them to do the job, but make sure you and they have a clear understanding of what you and they will do if things turn to shit. That usually means a total loss of commo, like if they're in a Humvee and get hit by an IED that blows out all their radios."

Captain Santos is still worried about the confrontation between himself and Colonel Chissom on their first operation. He wants some resolution on the issue of how to treat enemy dead and wounded. Their discussions around the fire lead Santos to ask permission to brief the Gs on *his* rules of engagement. Chissom agrees, and the next morning he calls in his guerrillas so Santos can speak with them. Chissom sets him up for success.

"This is a change for us, and I know it'll be hard for some of you. I believe that maybe we Pinelanders need to rethink how we've been doing this. Let's hear what Captain Santos has to say."

"First of all," Santos tells the assembled guerrillas, "let me say how proud I am to be serving with you. We are all honored to be a part of your struggle to liberate Pineland. As you and Pineland emerge and join the family of free and democratic nations, you will be expected to treat your enemies in a more humane way—in a way that is consistent with international standards."

Santos goes on to tell them what they can and cannot do—basically, that they cannot shoot to kill if an enemy poses no threat, and that they cannot shoot an enemy soldier who surrenders. There are challenges from the ranks of Pineland freedom fighters. Specifically, they point out that prisoners have to be fed and wounded prisoners have to be cared for. As guerrillas, they have limited stocks of food and medicine. Don't those serving the current regime deserve to die? And how are they to be given their bonuses if they have no ears for proof? Santos smoothly handles these objections, saying that the whole world will soon know of the conduct of the Pineland freedom fighters and judge them accordingly. Captain Childers and I watch this presentation from behind the group.

"He handled that pretty well," Childers says. "We like for these future team leaders to be put on the spot and have to articulate the Rules of Land Warfare and rules of engagement. Captain Santos did a good job."

At least a few hours each day are taken with MOS training. The Bravos take their G trainees through individual movement and move on to coordinated squad tactics. The Charlies teach nonelectric fire assemblies and charge placement. The guerrillas who are out on the security positions now make all the radio checks back to the base-station radio. And Doc Kohl now has five Gs that he's teaching about trauma care. They work on the basics of combat medicine, and he has them giving IVs to each other. At first, he was not permitted to set up a central dispensary, but now he's allowed to do this in the supply tent.

The daily G-base life has finally fallen into a pattern. There are teams out at night, sometimes day and night, and during the day there's training, camp chores, and security duty. Meals are MREs, although the Gs have smuggled in a supply of treats they share with the Americans on occasion. Among the most odorous duty is the filling in of the latrine, and extending the trench for the next day's business. Upstream from the latrine, literally, is a meandering stream that the Americans and the Gs use for water. The water is packed up the hill to the camp in buckets, and poured into the community water drum. Doc Kohl keeps close watch on the filling and the purification of the water. The treatment tablets don't make it taste or smell all that great, but it's potable and safe.

That afternoon, the aerial-resupply recovery team briefs Colonel Chissom on their mission. They're in radio contact with Specialist

Justin Keller and his recon element at the drop zone. Keller reports in every three hours, and it is all quiet on the resupply DZ—a cow pasture made available by yet another patriotic North Carolinian. Sergeant Brian Short will lead the recovery element, with Andrew Kohl and three Gs on his team. Based on information provided by Justin Keller and his maps, he has a sand-table, on-the-ground, in-the-dirt mock-up of the drop zone. Sergeant Short briefs the situation and makes assignments for the signaling of the aircraft and humping the equipment off the drop zone and to the auxiliary pickup. ODA 915's intel sergeant is an excellent planner and briefer. He quickly covers their recovery plan, including the most probable courses of action and the most dangerous courses of action. The Gs, who are becoming familiar faces, as are their noms de guerre—Gator, Red Dog, and Pigpen—brief the command and signal, weather, and coordinating instructions.

When they are finished, Chissom looks to Captain Santos. "This looks like a good resupply operation, and we really are getting low in chow and ammo, but I have a question. How come your guys always lead and my freedom fighters always follow? Do you Americans always have to be in charge?"

Santos pauses, but only for a second. "No, Colonel, they don't. Why don't we look into having one of your men lead the next operation?"

Chissom grunts his approval, but Santos knows he's missed an opportunity. An aerial resupply, while a technical evolution, is relatively straightforward—unless they get compromised. He knows he could have allowed a G to lead the operation while his men attended to the communications and technical issues relating to the airdrop.

Captain Childers and I drive out to the pasture drop zone to watch the evolution. This is a blind drop, which means that if the signals are in place at the right time, the resupply aircraft makes the drop with no communications. Brian Short has made a linkup with Justin Keller, and they're in position and waiting. The drop is made, but there are problems with getting the recovery team quickly to the pallet and getting the stores safely off the drop zone. Then the auxiliary driver with the pickup truck is late coming back for them. When he finally arrives, the driver wants a portion of the supplies, and a heated debate takes place on the edge of the drop zone. "Look, pal," Brian Short tells him firmly, holding his weapon at the ready, "we work for Colonel Chissom. You take us back to the camp, and if the colonel says you can have some of these rations, then we'll give them to you then."

At the G base following the resupply mission, Captain Childers gives them a critique of the operation. "Keep your briefings simple and gear the briefing to the Gs. They have to understand what's going on. And so does the colonel. Stop using grid this and grid that; grid coordinates don't mean anything to these people. Did you notice Colonel Chissom always taking off and putting on his glasses? He doesn't see too well. Point to the map and use the terrain models. Also, you did this with two briefings, one for the recon element and one for the recovery element. It should have been a single briefing. The recovery team is there to mark the drop zone and hump the gear off the DZ, but the recon element has to be prepared to mark the DZ and handle the drop if the recovery element is late or gets compromised. An aerial resupply mission may look easy, but it's not, and it has to be done right. This is not some huge DZ at Mackall or Bragg—it's some barley field or a pasture you've never seen before. You have to check it out for security, and verify that all the data you had going in is still valid. Then you have to make your calculations and set up the markers in a tactical environment. And when the bundle hits the ground, you have to quickly deal with it. This is a very important skill set. If you can handle a blind drop with no commo here, then you will have no problem in Afghanistan, Colombia, or wherever. Within a year, most of you will do this for real, and I mean with real bad guys in the hills watching you."

After the others disperse, Childers calls over Miguel Santos and Tom Olin. "Your guys are doing a pretty good job, but their briefings need more polish. I know you're busy and you're tired, but make your team leaders come to you for a practice session before they make their mission briefback. They'll do better with a practice, and you can help them with any problems. And you should know what they are going to say before they say it in front of Chissom. Oh, and another thing. Cross-loading. Your guys are pretty good about cross-loading equipment on a mission, but have them cross-loaded here in camp and when they're out on security. They have to be ready to move and support each other in a fight at any time, OK?"

"Roger that, Captain," Olin replies.

"Only delegate the cross-loading assignments to your weapons sergeants," Childers says. "They should be on this. As team sergeant and team leader, you are both too busy to be dealing with that." Captain Childers leaves them, and Santos and Olin are joined by Patrick Kwele to review the security rotation and the morning's training.

"It's always something," Olin says, "something we forgot or something we could do better."

"Always," Santos replies as they bend to the task of planning the day, "but that's why we're here."

The next day, there's more confrontation. The resupply brought in ammo, MREs, and more money—more don. The ammo and the MREs were stored in the supply tent. This morning, two cases of the MREs are gone. Olin reports this to Santos, who takes it up with Colonel Chissom.

"Are you accusing my men of stealing?" he says with a show of anger.

"I'm saying that *we* are missing some food," Santos replies, trying to keep the emotion from his voice, "rations for *our* men. I have inspected the Americans, and they do not have the missing rations. What do you think we should do now?"

"I do not have to inspect my men. They would not steal, as the penalty for stealing is death." The missing MREs go unresolved and Santos chooses not to pursue the matter.

Pay for the Gs had been an ongoing topic between Santos and

Chissom since their arrival—how much and when. They agreed that
the funds the Americans brought with them would go for operational
needs, but when the resupply came, the men would get paid—payment
in arrears for their service and a week in advance. It was also agreed
that the Gs would sign a pledge of loyalty to the new government of
Pineland. The signing and the pay would take place at the same time.
But the Gs refused to sign the pledge, and only a few of them can read.
A compromise was struck—they would take an oral oath—but not
until some words were exchanged between Sergeant Major Johnson
and Staff Sergeant Olin.

That evening, the team and the Gs stand down. First Lieutenant
Kwele is put in charge of the G base while Colonel Chissom, Captain
Santos, and Sergeant Olin attend a meeting called by the Pineland guerrilla force area commander. The meeting is ostensibly to talk about
operations and the course of the campaign for the liberation of
Pineland—what needs to take place before the U.S.-led coalition forces
arrive. The assembly is held in an old barn and attended by what seems
to be a host of locals, mostly retired Green Berets in the role of
Pinelanders—a colorful gathering, to say the least. This gallery of area
residents, underground and auxiliary, numbers about fifteen. Chissom
sits with the area commander, along with Colonel Merced, at a table.
Miguel Santos and Tom Olin are seated in low chairs before the table
and are bathed in floodlights. The setting has all the makings of an
inquisition.

"I was led to believe that you American Special Forces would join
our freedom fighters and work together against the enemy," the area
commander begins. "But I'm told this is not happening. I hear there
are problems, and I want to know what's going on. Why aren't the
Americans and our fighters working more smoothly? How come the
Americans always lead? What's this about working through Ra-haa
and the men having to sign a pledge before getting paid for service?
Why are you not killing more Pineland security forces? And I just

learned that three of our freedom fighters have deserted from your base. What about this, Colonel Chissom?"

Chissom, like Santos, is on the spot with the area commander. The colonel pushes through a list of excuses, most of which lay the issues at the feet of the Americans. Now it's all on Captain Santos. He's in the docket and on the defensive. And this is the first that he's heard of the desertions. The meeting lasts two hours. Shortly afterward, Santos tells me, "This was longest two hours of my life." For Captain Santos, it was a verbal gauntlet, with hard questions coming from several quarters. He was squirming, and so was I. I like this young officer, and my heart went out to him during this ordeal. In the end, both Santos and Colonel Chissom pledge that they will work together for the greater good of the cause.

"You have to game out a meeting like you game out a mission," Garrett Childers later tells his detachment leader. "Think in terms of most probable courses of action, most dangerous courses of action, and everything in between. This time, they put you on the defensive and kept you there. But you had no fallback courses of action, no alternative plan. You and your team sergeant need to talk it out and develop backup plans if things go sideways on you, like they did here. You have the skills and training to work your way out of situations like this. Use them. And you have to learn to control your emotions—show them nothing. In most cultures, emotion is a sign of weakness. Now, did you learn something from the meeting?"

"Yes, sir."

"Fair enough; let's drive on."

This was an emotional experience for me personally. I came from the meeting shaken. I thought they ganged up on Miguel Santos—it was a verbal mugging. It was a degrading experience, and I felt for him. Why, I asked myself, should an officer in the United States Army have to submit himself to this kind of an ordeal? It took me a while to sort through this evolution—to understand the teaching points and the necessity of this kind of training. And the kind of war we're training these men for.

In conventional warfare today, we have the upper hand. We have the money, the firepower, the logistics, the technology, and the battlefield capability. All of these mean little in an insurgency. Captain Santos is being trained for insurgency and counterinsurgency, where he has limited tools, where he has to negotiate for mission success, where he is often well out of his comfort zone and has to use his training, smarts, savvy, and cunning to get the job done. Bottom line, if *they*—the Colonel Chissoms of the world who represent our allies in the local population—are critical to the solution, and they certainly are in working the human terrain of an insurgency, then *we* have to work with them. Our American conventional, fire-superiority, might-is-right, why-don't-the-locals-get-off-their-ass approach will not win the peace in the face of a dedicated insurgency. As much as my heart went out to Captain Santos during his ordeal, it's but another step in preparing him to fight *our* war.

The following morning, Captain Santos and Colonel Chissom begin the morning under a strained cordiality. "He dimed me out," Santos says later in the day of his G chief, "but I have to get past that. We have a war to fight."

For the next several days, the Americans and the Pineland freedom fighters conduct a series of missions. There are always one or two teams in the field. There's a mission to neutralize a water purification plant, to ambush a Pineland Army supply truck, to disable a microwave relay station, to cut a rail line, and to conduct a strike on a Pineland Army armory. There's another aerial resupply drop. Most of these targets require a recon team to put eyes-on for a full twenty-four hours before the mission is carried out. Each of these targets requires a full-on mission-analysis, mission-planning work-up. And there are always the constants that keep 915 from getting more than just a few hours sleep here and there—security duty and camp chores. There are issues of personal hygiene that are essential when men are in the field this long. Twice a day they strip and search each other for ticks. About every third or fourth day they shave. Bathing involves a hand cloth and a canteen, followed by a wipedown with a Handi Wipe. By contrast, I have it easy. I'm able to slip back to my cabin for a few hours each day. There I strip and toss my clothes in the washer, and my wife inspects *me* for ticks before I hop in the shower. After a change of clothes and a hot meal, I'm back on the job. The soldiers in 915 are out there for the duration. (Think about it as you sit back and read this text. I can't remember the last time I went two weeks without a shower, can you?) The men in 915 are getting weary, they're short on sleep, and they still have a campaign to fight. They have a lot to learn, and the learning is not easy.

"Often the students do what they think the cadre wants them to do," Sergeant Blackman tells me. "They are still playing cops and robbers, trying to get through the problem with the school solution. One of our challenges is to get a young soldier to see a problem and figure out how to best solve it, calling on his training, his intuition, and his imagination. If he gets outside the guidelines, the instructors can always step in, but we want to see them solve problems, not check the boxes. The ones that get it, that've made the leap from conventional to unconventional thinking, will really surprise you.

"During one class, I quietly parked my truck on a back road and walked through the woods to watch the students attack a target. I moved carefully and quietly so they wouldn't see me. They made the hit and did a pretty good job. I was headed back to my truck, but when I got twenty meters from it, the engine roared to life, and it drove off with the whole squad in the back. Well, I knew I'd locked it, and I knew I had the keys. It seems their security element had spotted me and sent one of their street-smart kids after the truck. He shimmed the door and hot-wired the ignition, and they were gone. I chased after them, cussing a blue streak. About five minutes later they came driving back slowly, all of them with a big grin—asked if I needed a ride."

"What'd you do?" I ask.

"What could I do? I told them that for future exercise play, cadre trucks were off-limits, but that they'd earned a ride back to the G base."

On day seven, the G base is moved to a location on state game lands a few miles southwest of the town of Pine Bluff. The Gs move in the morning and the auxiliary trucks bring the Americans in that afternoon. The new location is more secure in that it's protected on one side by a swampy marsh, and that means lots of mosquitoes. But this base camp can be guarded with two security positions. Later that afternoon, a dilemma surfaces when Colonel Merced brings in three new recruits. Colonel Chissom says he doesn't trust the new men; he thinks they might be Pineland Army spies. The new men are quickly blindfolded and made to kneel with their hands tied behind their backs. There's talk of executing them to be on the safe side. Chissom turns to Captain Santos.

"I'll let them live, but you have to take charge of them and vouch for their conduct."

Santos sidesteps this one. "Colonel, these are Pinelanders and they're your people—your responsibility. Perhaps we should question them further to assess their loyalty."

Chissom says he will take responsibility, but whatever happens, happens—indicating he may just shoot them. On further questioning, the new recruits are found to be loyal partisans and allowed to remain in the G base. The ODA gives them the Pineland oath, pays them, and gives them a quick class on the Rules of Land Warfare—what is and is not acceptable in their combat operations.

"What if the colonel decided to execute them?" I ask Miguel Santos later.

"We were ready for that, but there is only so much we can do in that situation. Intervention would threaten our mission, and the actions of the new recruits could only erode my position if I'd taken responsibility for them. We have some leverage with Chissom, and I was prepared to use it if he threatened to shoot them."

"Captain Santos did the right thing," Bill Chissom says of the dilemma. "Sometimes we take it further and prepare the new men for execution to see how the team handles it. But make no mistake, this kind of thing's happening in Special Forces compounds today in Afghanistan and Iraq. Who can you trust? Who do you let come into your base camp, and what do you let them see of your physical setup and your security measures? And how do you handle a situation where one of your indigenous leaders wants to mete out justice to someone on the spot? This is real world."

The day after the G-base relocation, as it turns out, is a national holiday in Pineland. For the Americans, by chance, it's Mother's Day. The occasion is marked—for the Pinelanders, not for Mom—by a pig roast. Part of the duties of the men on security duty the previous night was to keep a roaring fire going to make a bed of coals. Sunday morning, a freshly killed whole pig is delivered to the camp. The Americans and the Gs gather for a class in pig preparation. As the team medic, Doc Kohl is in charge of dressing out of the pig. A cadre medic is on hand to supervise, to talk about the cuts of meat, and how to inspect the entrails to avoid eating a contaminated animal. As it turns out, Tom Olin is the most experienced with a boning knife and cleaver. He'd worked in a butcher shop in Montana between college and the Army. For many soldiers, this is the first time they've seen a recent kill hung and dressed out. The whole gut-clean-dress evolution, thanks to Sergeant Olin's skill, takes only an hour. The cooking takes the whole day. Sergeant Blackman brings in a bag of rice, some carrots and onions, and some seasonings. It's a real feast, and the only non-MRE food 915 will get in Pineland—almost.

Midday, one of the Gs on water detail comes back from the stream that drains into the marsh near the camp. "There's a big snake down there," he reports, "right where we get our water. I tried to scare him off, but he won't budge."

Tom Olin goes back with him to investigate and returns with a four-and-a-half-foot cottonmouth—a really fat one. Short then proceeds to skin and dress the snake, and it joins the pig in the holiday celebration. Tastes just like chicken, but rather tough chicken.

Camp activity and operational activity begins to mesh with ODAs and Gs working together—almost blurring their differences. On Captain Santos's recommendation, 915 and the Gs settle into groups of three—one American and two Pinelanders. They become battle buddies. They keep their rucks together so if they have to bolt, they stay together and fight together. Their hooches are side by side.

During the evening on day nine of Robin Sage, Captain Childers takes 915's officers and team sergeant aside. "There'll be a lot going on and as we approach the final days of Robin Sage, things will accelerate and become more chaotic. Your job is to bring some order to these events. That means you have to focus on the big picture, so you'll have to delegate things like security, commo, and base chores. One thing that can help is to have your team supply sergeant keep a running tally on your consumables—chow, ammo, demo, and water. Brief the colonel on these twice a day. It lets him know you're on top of things, and it's a chance for a positive interaction."

The cadre camp is located on the edge of a field near an abandoned tobacco drying shed. Quite often when I visit the camp, I find Sergeant Blackman on a stool in the woods near the shed, hunched over his computer. There is a DC power cord running from his pickup to the computer. Evaluations have to be made and training records kept up to date. For each exercise or block of training, each candidate is rated on tactical performance and/or leadership—good, bad, excellent—and recommendations are made as necessary on how to improve that performance or leadership.

On day ten, 915 and its guerrillas are joined by two more cadre—or perhaps semicadre would be a better term. They are two staff sergeants from the 7th Special Forces Group at Fort Bragg. They'll help with the training for the balance of the Robin Sage exercise and serve in opposition-force roles for the final problem. Both were in Robin Sage about this time last year, and both just returned from a combat rotation in Afghanistan. They are helpful, critical, and very supportive. There's an instant bond between these two new Green Beret veterans and the candidates. It's a good dynamic. They are not cadre in the same way as are Sergeant Blackman, Captain Childers, and the OCEs. As Brian Short puts it, "They are us a year from now."

Also on day ten, the communicators receive a priority message from their forward operating base. There is to be a document drop that evening. Nine-one-five is tasked with finding a secure location and setting up the drop. At 2130, Sergeant Olin and his recovery team are crouched on the edge of a farmer's field, prepared to receive the package. Due to the short notice and the urgency, there is no time for a twenty-four-hour eyes-on, so Captain Santos sent along First Lieutenant Kwele with a ten-man security element to protect the recovery team. At the appointed time, Short sends Aaron Dunn out into the field. He breaks out a lime-green Chemlite and begins to swing it on a three-foot cord. From the air, or anywhere in the area, it looks like a spinning lime-green disk. David Altman comes up on the PRC-119 air-to-ground frequency.

"Dustbin Two-Seven, this is Oscar Delta Alpha Nine-One-Five, do you copy, over?"

"Uh, roger Nine-One-Five, hear you five by, over, over."

"OK, Two-Seven. We are in place. Authenticate my signal, over."

"We hold a light-green circular strobe, over."

"Roger the green circular strobe. Standing by for your package, over."

"OK, Nine-One-Five, starting our run now. Two-Seven, out."

A few moments later, a dark form flashes over the field. It's a low, quick pass with the long snout of a Pilatus Porter STOL aircraft briefly visible. A drogue chute blossoms from under the wing with a packet attached. Olin's recovery team has the package in a matter of moments. They call in the security element and begin to patrol to the extraction point, where two auxiliary pickups are waiting for them. A few hours later, Santos, Kwele, Olin, and Short are gathered around a makeshift table going over documents and photographs. All wear camping-type headband lights. The documents contain their mission tasker and the intelligence information for their final target.

"OK, guys, this is it. I'm going to spend some time with this material. It'll be with me at all times if you need it. Patrick, you make security rounds." To Olin and Short, Santos says, "You two grab some sleep. At first light, I want the team mustered and ready to begin a full-on mission-planning effort."

The next morning, Captain Santos briefs Colonel Chissom on their mission. "I'd like to get right to the mission analysis and mission planning. Why don't I bring in six of my mission planners, and you and Sergeant Major Johnson get a half dozen or so of your men, and we'll lay this out for them together?" Chissom agrees with this approach, and soon they're all gathered around the fire pit. Santos does most of the talking. Already, Sergeant Aaron Dunn, 915's best terrain-model man, is poring over the intel photos and starting to build a scale likeness of what appears to be a prison complex. A senior member of the resistance, the man who's destined to become the president of a liberated Pineland, has been taken prisoner by the Pineland Army forces, and being held at a local correctional facility. Nine-one-five's mission, and that of their irregulars, is to set him free.

Captain Santos makes team assignments and 915 starts to work. Each American has one and sometimes two Gs working with him. That night, Miguel Santos and Brian Short leave the camp in civilian clothes with a member of the auxiliary. Their destination is the Pine Court Motel to meet with a partisan with intelligence on the prison. The Pine Court is not a four-star hostelry. Their contact is an informant and a member of the underground. He's also a North Carolina state trooper and a retired Green Beret. When Miguel Santos knocks on the door, it's opened by a woman. "C'mon in, guys," she says with a generous smile. "You're right on time." She's attired in loungewear. Santos and Short, thinking they have the wrong room, start backpedaling.

Then the trooper appears, in uniform. "It's OK, guys," he tells them. "With the Condor teams out, we can't be too careful." The woman is his wife. She watches TV, while the captain, his intel sergeant, and their informant go over a sketch of the prison and some aerial photos Santos brought along. They talk about the layout, guards, patrol routines, and access to the interior of the prison. Their informant knows a janitor at the prison. He says he'll have him unlock one of the back gates—if he can.

The next morning, Captain Santos is back with his team planning for the mission. While they're occupied with their maps and terrain models, Sergeant Troy Blackman quietly grabs two of the Gs and says, "Get your rucks and follow me." He takes them out of G base, slipping carefully between the two security posts. When they're well outside the camp perimeter, he asks to borrow one of the Gs' rifles. He checks to ensure the weapon is loaded with blank ammo and shoots them both.

"OK, guys, you're shot. Start calling for help."

"Medic! Medic, I'm hit—help me! Help!" Doc Kohl and four others respond on the run, two Americans and two Gs. They patrol on skirmish line to the two wounded men. Then Sergeant Blackman shoots Kohl. "OK, your medic just got shot," Blackman tells the others. "Now what are you going to do?"

Several others arrive from the G base to provide security and to help with the casualties. Sergeant Blackman dictates wounds: head wound bleeding badly, leg wound bleeding badly, abdominal wound, pulse weak and rapid, blood pressure dropping. It's a full-on medical drill for 915 and its Gs. They get a pressure bandage on the abdominal wound, a tourniquet on the leg, and some IVs started. An auxiliary truck arrives to take the two Gs to a regional medical station for treatment; Doc Kohl is pronounced fit for duty.

"We needed to take a few of the Gs out of the G bases, so we have a more robust opposition force during the final problem," Sergeant

Blackman tells me off to the side, "so we created this training scenario. This way we get some medical training and collect some men to serve with the opposing forces."

"I'd just come off security duty and was sound asleep," Sergeant Kohl says of the drill. "I came out of a total fog—didn't know where I was, what day it was. I was running up the trail with my aid bag and my rifle before I really came awake. Guess that's the way it'll be downrange."

Captain Santos and his planners work straight through the day. This is to be a two-ODA, two-G-force operation, with some twenty-four Americans and forty-five Pineland freedom fighters making the attack. It'll be a complex and challenging undertaking. Nine-one-five will be teamed with 912 for the operation. That evening, after an exhaustive day of planning, Captain Santos, Sergeant Olin, and two of their Gs are taken to a safe house well out in the countryside. There they meet the team leader, the team sergeant, and two Gs from student ODA 912. Inside the safe house, the resistance sector commander, a contract role player in the character of a Pineland resistance-force general, is conducting the proceedings. Attending the general are Colonel Chissom, 912's G chief, and Major Mike Kennedy, the American forward base commander, who has just "parachuted in" that afternoon for the meeting. All of them are drinking beer—nonalcoholic O'Doul's. The Pineland liberation battle plan is reaching a critical phase. The invasion forces are ready, but this senior resistance political leader has to be made free to lead the new order. The two student ODA delegations, each in turn, present their plan to free this key Pineland leader. For both 915 and 912, their guerrilla counterparts do most of the talking. The game now, as I'm taken aside and told, is *not* how well the ODAs can do the job, but how well they've schooled their Gs to do the job. The empaneled cadre, G chiefs, and sector commander will select one ODA to lead the mission and one to support the mission. Their criteria? Which ODA has done the best job in training their guerrilla force. Up front, whose Gs are the best mission briefers.

While the cadre and guerrilla leaders talk and evaluate the two presentations, the two team leaders and their contingents mill about in front of the safe house. It's a soft North Carolina spring night. While I wait it out with them, I spend a few minutes with Sergeant Major Rick Martin, the Echo Company sergeant major and Major Kennedy's senior enlisted adviser.

"At this point in the training," Martin tells me, "the 'by, with, and through' concept of conducting a campaign should be taking hold. Sometimes the light goes on and sometimes it doesn't. Our job is to turn that light on. It can happen early on and, hopefully, sometime before Robin Sage is over. For a few, it doesn't go on until they are standing in front of the review board with that deer-in-the-headlights look. It'd be easy for me to say the reason we don't reach more of these soldiers is that they are spoiled, or immature, or soft, or spent too much time with video games, or whatever. The bottom line is that we're getting bright kids and motivated, patriotic kids. If we don't reach them, then the problem is on us. We are always looking for new ways to teach and reach these guys. What motivated my generation, or even the candidates here five years ago, is different today. We're always asking, how do you turn the light on? For a few, a very few, we yell at them—try to goad them into the proper mind-set. Others, we use reason. Some respond to the intellectual challenge, and for some it's the enjoyment of teaching military skills to others—this can be fun stuff. And for many it's simply the prospect of inclusion into this brotherhood. But it's a moving target, and we have to move with it. We have to turn that light on."

The two ODA contingents are called back into the house, where they're told that 912 will take the lead and 915 will assume the role of the support element. As the candidates and their guerrillas file out, I can see that Miguel Santos is deeply disappointed.

"This is going to be a great operation," he says to no one in particular. "I really wanted to lead it." Sergeant Major Martin is within earshot and comes over to him.

"Sir, from what I've seen and heard, you're a good officer, and when you get to your group, you're going to be a good team leader. But take this on board as a lesson. It's not how good *you* are; it's how good *they* are. Now, for whatever reason—training, personality, experience, whatever—912's Gs were a little sharper than yours tonight. So they got the job. Understand this and drive on. OK?"

"Roger that, Sergeant Major."

For most of the night, the senior members of the two student ODAs and selected members of their guerrilla bands plan and prepare for the prisoner rescue operation. The following morning, the team leader for 912 gives his briefback to the two G chiefs and their general. Captain Santos, Sergeant Brian Short, PFC Tim Baker, and five of 915's Gs are part of this briefback. They hastily mount out and are inserted by auxiliary truck just after midnight to survey the target. Santos and his men are the recon element for the operation. Well before dawn, they patrol across a cow pasture, hop a barbed-wire fence, and make their way through a dense thicket to the perimeter of the prison.

Captain Santos and his senior guerrilla pull back into the woods and set up a patrol base, well hidden in the woods. Then two recon and surveillance teams are set out on opposite sides of the target. They are in place with eyes-on when the sun comes up. Both teams have MBITR radios and are in contact with Santos in the patrol base. The resourceful Brian Short has put up his antenna high in a tree. He has his PSC-5 set at full power, and is able to reach 912's G base some thirty klicks away. That's an HF, line-of-sight transmission of some eighteen miles—quite a communications feat. Every four hours, Santos and his recon element send back reports of guard-force activity and suggested attack routes for the assault on the prison. They'll also serve as a reception element for the main force when they arrive and guide them to their jump-off locations for the attack. But it's a miserable night and day for the recon element. It's turned warm and muggy, and the mosquitoes are a dense swarm in the moist air. I surrender my remaining stock of bug repellent to the recon element before heading off to the disused prison to await the final event.

The evening brings no relief from a hot sultry day, with thunderheads building in the fading light. Soon there's lightning on the horizon and the rumble of thunder. The abandoned prison is a brick-and-stone structure with three-story guard towers on opposite corners of the square-shaped, cinder-block walls. The buildings are a cluster of single-story brick structures with iron lattice-work windows. A twelve-foot chain-link fence topped with concertina surrounds everything. The facility is deserted but for roving sentries and a single guard in each tower. Another guard stands by the main gate, which is closed but not bolted. In a white-brick holding area with a stout metal door, a handcuffed Northrop Grumman employee, a former Green Beret in the role of a Pineland resistance leader, awaits his redemption. It's an Alcatraz-like movie set.

"The prison was closed down about ten years ago," Captain Childers tells me as we wait for events to unfold. "This is the first time we've used this facility in this lane. We'll have to see how it works out." We're in the tower closest to the woods. There's about 150 yards of open area between the woods and the prison. Midway from the walls to the woods in one quadrant there is a large equipment shed, and in an adjacent quadrant there is the warden's cottage. Both are suitable as cover to marshal an assault force. A few minutes after dark, I watch as a string of dark forms peel out from behind the shed and drop on line to take up a fire-support position. That would be 915 and a complement of their Gs. Then two files of similar dark forms spill from the other side of the shed and make for the main gate of the prison. Suddenly, there's a commotion from the far side of the complex, and shots are fired. After a brief silence, a lively firefight breaks out as one of the assault elements pours through the unlocked back gate. From then on, all is yelling, running, and gunfire. There's the pop-pop-pop fire from the lighter-caliber weapons punctuated by the deeper automatic bark from the M240s.

The assaulters pour into the prison, some of them engaging the guard force while others race for the holding area that houses their objective. Meanwhile, there's the whoosh of rising pop flares and the whistle and bang of artillery simulators. And smoke—lots and lots of smoke. The prison compound is soon awash in the harsh yellow light of parachute flares. And to add to the surreal drama below me, the skies have opened up to a solid, steady downpour. Then I hear the assault force yelling, "Turnkey! Turnkey!" which I assume to mean that they have their Pineland resistance leader in tow. The attackers fall back under the cover of their fire-support element. A few of them have wounded comrades in fireman's carries, and I see four men running with a fallen soldier in a soft litter. There's another round of smoke grenades as the assault force and their support element retreats to the cover of the shed and into the woods. The last of the parachute flares winks out, leaving a darkened prison complex, the stench of sulfur and cordite, and a steady rain.

"That was amazing," I tell Garrett Childers, "simply amazing."

He grins. "It was a show, all right. And I guess it'll have to do until they get to the real thing, which, for some of them, is not all that far off."

The OCEs follow the candidates back through the woods to their exfil points. The cadre gather in the parking area near a gaggle of government pickup trucks to talk about the assault and to exchange notes on who did what, and what should be covered and emphasized in the after-action review. Nine-one-five returns to its G base tired, wet, and excited. Two of the Gs and one American were left behind to guard the camp, and they have a roaring fire going for the returnees. Soon they're joined by Garrett Childers and Troy Blackman. Sergeant Blackman gives them a quick after-action review, but there's little he can address specifically, given the confusion of that many soldiers moving about in the rain and the smoke.

"You guys did a good job on the recon. The guard force thought they heard you moving in the woods last night, but they weren't sure. As for the assault, it went as well as could be expected, given the numbers involved and the command-and-control issues that go with a force of that size. What I want you to take from this is that when the shooting starts, you can only rely on how well you planned the action, how grounded you are on your unit tactics, and how much you can count on that guy beside you. If he's a brother Green Beret, all well and good. If he's one of your Afghan or Iraqi militiamen, then you'd better have trained him well and know what he can and cannot do."

The next morning, it's camp chores, cleanup, and demobilization of the guerrilla force. The former guerrillas are given a bonus of 3,000 don for their service and an honorable discharge from the Pineland resistance force. Captain Santos thanks and praises them in a short ceremony. Each former G is also given a commendation for his patriotic contribution to the future of Pineland. Real world, Captain Childers will write an official letter of commendation for Sergeant Major Johnson, now once again a sergeant first class. Doc Kohl gives them a quick mustering-out physical, and that afternoon, two big four-by-four trucks collect them for the trip back to Fort Bragg. It's like the last day of scout camp, and there are some bittersweet farewells between the Americans and their Gs. Several of the former Pineland guerrillas told me that when they get back to their units, they'll start the process that will get them to SFAS. For the Americans left at the G base, there are civil-affairs projects that amount to trucking around to the various target locations and safe houses to clean up any debris or trash left from the training. Phase IV and Robin Sage are essentially over, and while they get a full night's sleep, two men on rotation are awake at all times and on watch. Colonel Chissom turns in early. The following day, he is up early, supervising the final cleanup and breakdown of the base.

"Good luck and God Bless," he says to 915 as he shakes each man's hand. "When you get to the fight, remember what you learned here and make us proud."

Nine-one-five rucks up for the final time. The men are loaded, but not quite as heavy as they were when they parachuted into Pineland two weeks ago. Captain Santos leads them up to a clearing above their

G base, where a truck will soon collect them and take them back to Camp Mackall. They're a tired bunch of soldiers, but there is a look of achievement in their eyes. "By God, it's over, and we did it," I hear more than once. They dump their rucks and wait for the truck. I find Miguel Santos, who is speaking quietly with First Lieutenant Patrick Kwele.

"So what's next?" I ask them.

"I will attend an advanced school here at Fort Bragg," Kwele says with his precise diction, "and then I will return to Botswana and take up my duties. When I return, I will become commander of one of our scout companies."

"I'll go directly to 7th Group," Miguel Santos says. "I attended SERE school before my last deployment, and I think that'll allow me to validate the Special Forces SERE requirement." As a Spanish speaker, he has already validated his Special Forces language requirement. "But first, I've a couple weeks of leave on the books. That'll give me a chance to get to know my new daughter."

"From Robin Sage to two a.m. feedings and changing diapers?"

"You got that right, sir," he says with a big grin, "and I can't wait."

Phase IV Class 2-05 is all but done. Back at the Rowe Training Facility, there's the now-familiar equipment inventory, equipment overhaul, and equipment turn-in. The radios, night-vision goggles, GPSs, and other sensitive items have to be accounted for and made ready for Class 3-05. Throughout the phase and after every major evolution, these items were inventoried. Now, 915 makes this accounting for the last time. There are course critiques and a final round of peer evaluations. There are general counseling sessions and lengthy individual counseling sessions. Captain Childers and Sergeant Blackman sit with each man for a candid assessment of his strengths and weaknesses; those areas in which he performed well and those areas in which he can improve.

"How'd it go?" I ask Miguel Santos after his meeting with his cadre mentors.

"All right," he says with a tired smile. "They were more generous then than I thought they might be, but they certainly didn't hesitate to talk about my shortcomings. And to be honest, their criticisms were totally in line and fair. There are some things I still need to work on—probably will always need to work on. But y'know something, sir. I think that if God himself were to come through the Q-Course, in every phase there would be a cadre team sergeant to point out his deficiencies and tell him what he needed to do to correct them."

There is also the Phase IV Commander's Review Board. The board composition is much the same as those in Phases I and II: company and battalion commanders, company and battalion sergeant majors, and selected cadre sergeants. Before a candidate appears before the board, his performance is addressed by his cadre team officer and cadre team sergeant. Nine-one-five had no candidates for board consideration.

"This is a tough business," Sergeant Major Rick Martin says of the Phase IV review board's work, but it was my sense that he was talking about the Q-Course and Special Forces work in general. We talk during a break in the board deliberations, and are joined by Group Command Sergeant Major Van Atkins. He didn't sit on the board, but was there to observe.

"To get to our level—the Special Forces detachment level—you have to get to the Robin Sage level," Atkins says. "If our students don't get in character and play *this* game, it's hard to play the game for real on deployment. If these students can't drop into character with their G chiefs and the other role players, or even with the G soldiers, what're they going to do with their platoon of Afghan militia? We can't leave Afghanistan or Iraq until the Afghans and the Iraqis can do the job, and they can't do the job until we train them to a point where they can take over. A lot of people think the tip of the spear for Special Forces is the business end of an M4 or kicking in a door. That's the easy part. For us, the tip of the spear is squatting by a fire with your Afghan company commander, sharing a little tobacco, and planning the next day's training. Or out there on the range with a group of Iraqi policemen who just drove down IED alley to get to the range to train with you. Some guys like to kick doors; hell, I like to kick doors—who doesn't? But for us, breaking bread around the fire with the locals is more important. And it serves two purposes. One, you may learn which door to kick—where the *really* bad guys are. And two, maybe in time we can train them to kick the door so we don't have to even do that. Being a good Special Forces soldier is all about training them to do our job. *And,* as soon as we train them to do the job, we can get the conventional guys off the checkpoints and Humvee patrols, and out of harm's way so they can go home as well.

"Most of us in the senior cadre, like the sergeant major here, have been doing this for a long time," the group command sergeant major adds. As I stand and talk with these two veterans, I remind myself that between them there's almost sixty years of experience. "We worked in the shadows before 9/11 and now, perhaps, not so much in the shadows. We've fought more than a few wars, and been immersed in foreign civilian and military cultures around the world. Now our job is to prepare the next generation to carry on. Their fight will probably be more difficult than ours and certainly more important. But as we assess and train these young soldiers, we must never forget how young and stupid we once were. That light Sergeant Major Martin speaks about so often didn't go on for some of us until we reached our Special Forces groups."

"We have to go back to work," Sergeant Major Martin says. "Good luck with your book, Mister Couch." He and Atkins return to the classroom where the phase review board is being held. As I watch them go, I'm reminded of Fredric March's line in *The Bridges at Toko-Ri.* March's character, a Navy admiral, in referring to the heroic performance of his carrier pilots, wondered admiringly, "Where *do* we find such men?" Indeed, where.

Phase IV Class 2-05 began with 308 candidates. Two hundred and eighty-four graduated from the phase. Fourteen were recycled to a future class, and ten were relieved and released to the Army for future assignment.

Author's Note: Like all phases of Special Forces training, Phase IV and Robin Sage are continuously being evaluated, refined, and upgraded. There was a recent pilot Phase IV in which Phase III graduates were first sent to language school, then to Phase IV. The language was Arabic, and the Robin Sage–like exercise was shifted to the Army's National Training Center in California. There, the students worked with Arabic-speaking role players during their unconventional-warfare field exercise. The results of this pilot program will be the basis for language-centric Robin Sage training.

EPILOGUE:

AFTER-ACTION REVIEW

With the completion of Phase IV Class 2-05, most of the successful candidates will begin their final journey toward the Green Beret. A very few, like Captain Miguel Santos, will take a few days off and head for their assigned Special Forces group. In the case of Captain Santos, it's the 7th Group based at Fort Bragg. Because he's met the requirements of the Q-Course for survival and language training, he'll don his beret ahead of his former Phase IV classmates. For the others, there's Survival, Evasion, Resistance, and Escape (SERE) School and Special Operations Language Training. Before my time at Fort Bragg and Camp Mackall, there were two graduation ceremonies for Special Forces students, one that awarded the Green Beret and another that awarded the "tab." Most of us are familiar with the beret, but what's perhaps most coveted by these chosen soldiers is the tab—a small arc of cloth that rides just under, and conforms to, the left shoulder seam of the soldier's uniform. It simply says, "Special Forces."

COMBAT REHEARSAL.   Iraqi soldiers from the Albu Nimr tribe, working with an SF ODA in western Iraq, practice room-clearing drills in preparation for a combat mission.

That tab will snuggle concentrically above their airborne tab, or, for soldiers like Miguel Santos, above their Ranger and airborne tabs.

Prior to the beginning of 2005, Phase IV graduates were awarded their Green Beret at a formal dinner ceremony and their tab at a more modest celebration when they completed SERE and language training. That's all changed. As mentioned in my note at the end of chapter 5, SERE training is now a part of Phase II and the Special Forces tactics portion of the Q-Course. More recently, language training is now being taught throughout all phases of the course, with special emphasis in Phase IV. There are some distinct advantages to these changes in that both survival skills and language skills are now part of the new Phase V and Robin Sage. The Pinelanders and the guerrilla chiefs can now, when practical, interact with the students in a foreign language. Language becomes a learn-it, use-it skill, just like communications for the 18 Echos and trauma care for the 18 Deltas. Moreover, it allows for a soldier to formally complete the Special Forces Qualification Course with the completion of Robin Sage. He can then be recognized in an appropriate combined ceremony that awards his beret and tab before sending him on to his group for duty. Those like Captain Santos, because they completed the Q-Course at odd times and in small numbers, often missed proper recognition of this milestone in their career.

"It'd have been nice," he told me, "but I have no complaints. I got to spend a little extra time with my family, and I got to a group sooner than most of the others. I have two new roles now; I'm a father and a Special Forces detachment leader. Life can't get much better."

I have elected not to deal at length with SERE or language training. SERE training is a nineteen-day Level C Code of Conduct course followed by a five-day Peacetime Governmental Detention/Hostage Detention course. Level C is a course for warriors "whose military role entails a relatively high risk of capture or makes them vulnerable to greater-than-average exploitation by a captor." In addition to survival and evasion training by some of the finest live-off-the-land experts in the world, the students are subjected to a detention phase that involves resistance to tactical interrogation in a realistic POW setting. Few courses in the military are as physically and emotionally challenging as the captive phase of SERE training at Camp Mackall. And few military training venues are as well monitored and supervised; the medical and psychological oversight is both comprehensive and redundant. This five-day detention training is all about how to resist all forms of exploitation and about the conduct expected when a soldier becomes a captive warrior.

One of the reasons I chose not to expand on SERE training is that much of the training is classified, as well it should be. It is how we train our warriors to deal with capture, to return with honor if they can and to die with honor if they must. It's serious business. In past wars, including my war, to be taken by the enemy was an ordeal—one that was painful and life-threatening, but one that you had a better-than-even chance of surviving. Your being taken captive was a collateral consequence of the conflict. Those were the good old days. In the current fight, quite often the objective of the enemy *is* the taking of captives—not for information or political advantage, but for ritual execution. To be taken captive can be a death sentence. And for that reason, content associated with the SERE portion of the Q-Course will not be addressed in detail.

I did speak with two recent graduates of SERE training—and by recent, I mean they had just finished the course when I interviewed them. Earlier that morning, they had been POWs. One was a staff sergeant with eight years in the Army, and the other was an 18 X-Ray specialist with just over a year in uniform. Both had that calm, satisfied, far-off look in their eyes that said they'd just put a very difficult and moving experience behind them. They had, after all, spent five days in a POW compound.

"We learned a great deal about fieldcraft and living off the land during the survival and evasion training," the sergeant said. "The cadre sergeants were a wealth of knowledge. Real world—or at least real-world North Carolina—I could survive out there and evade capture."

"And the training in the compound?"

"That was a learning experience as well, in a different sort of way." The staff sergeant looked from me to the SERE phase company commander, who was also present, and then back to me. "Well, sir, let's just say I have some idea of what it's like if, God forbid, I'm taken prisoner, and how to conduct myself when that happens. It's another component of the skill set—another tool in the toolbox."

"It's the hardest thing I've ever done in my life," the young specialist said. "The regular phase training of the Q-Course is hard, but not hard like this. I lost twenty pounds, and I didn't exactly go into this training chubby."

Assuming the weight loss was from the field-survival training, I asked, "But didn't they feed you in the camp—the POW compound?"

"Yes, sir. We got a bowl of rice."

"Daily, right?"

"No, sir. The whole time."

I sensed they were still digesting this experience and didn't yet want to talk about it. I also figured they probably wanted to get to the nearest Burger King. "One last question. Did you cry?"

For the first time, they smiled and both nodded. "Oh yes, sir, we cried," the sergeant replied.

I've yet to speak with a SERE student who didn't cry when they hoisted up the Stars and Stripes, which signaled the end of the POW-compound phase of SERE training. I did, but of course, that was a very long time ago.

Special Operations Language Training addresses the conversational, tactical, and cultural aspects of a foreign language. The instructors are native speakers, and one often sees them roaming the corridors of Aaron Bank Hall in native dress. In addition to native-speaking instructors and state-of-the-art language laboratories, there are computer-driven personal programs available, like the highly regarded Rosetta Stone series. The instructor-student ratio averages about eight to one.

Special Operations Language Training at Fort Bragg is taught in eight-week or fourteen-week iterations. Spanish, French, German, and Indonesian are eight-week curriculums; Russian, Farsi, Korean, Arabic, Tagalog, and Chinese are fourteen. Special Forces soldiers are sent to civilian language facilities for specialty languages, like Pashto, Thai, and Vietnamese. Once a soldier demonstrates a tested proficiency in a language, he becomes eligible for professional pay.

"In some ways, this is harder than being out in the swamps at Camp Mackall," Captain Matt Anderson told me. He was studying Arabic. "You get to go home every night, but you have to discipline yourself to turn off the TV, put on the headphones, and listen to your language."

The new Green Berets, with their tab, head out for their groups and duty in a Special Forces Operational Detachment Alpha—a real go-overseas, go-in-harm's-way ODA. For a few, there will be time for stateside training with their detachments prior to deployment. For others, when they check into their group headquarters, they will learn that their detachments are on deployment.

"We've had young X-Ray soldiers get on a plane for Afghanistan within days of leaving the Q-Course," a battalion command sergeant major from 3rd Group told me. "When he gets to the forward operating base, we send them right out to a team in the field."

"The new kids do just fine," said a team sergeant with 3rd Group. "We have a lot of confidence in the current training at the Q-Course and the new guys they're sending us. We get them right in the operational flow. They're green, but as long as they listen, they can help the team. Some are better than others, but we use them to the limits of their experience. We have a lot of work to do."

Training for the new men depends on the time available when they reach their detachment and the detachment's next deployment rotation. The twelve-man detachments specialize in various military disciplines: scuba, high-altitude low-opening (HALO) parachuting, mountain operations, maritime operations, and urban combat. If there's time, they will attend schools or courses that train them in these specialties. Given the current operations in Iraq and Afghanistan, the new guys almost always need time behind the gun. During whatever time is available to them in the form of predeployment, mission-readiness training, they do a lot of shooting. Time and school quotas permitting, the groups try to get their new men to formal tactical and shooting schools. There are two schools that top the list. First is the Special Operations Target Inderdiction Course, which is an advanced sniper course. The second is the Special Forces Advanced Reconnaissance, Target Analysis, and Exploitation Course. This course is all about tactical battle-space management for small units in urban terrain. Both are high-speed courses that prepare the new SF soldiers for the realities of modern combat. But when the detachment is due for rotation overseas, the new Q-Course grads will deploy with their teams. There is no leaving a man back to attend a school.

I found the notion of new Special Forces soldiers making a combat rotation within weeks of their Q-Course graduation intriguing. Newly minted Navy SEALS will have up to *eighteen months* of individual, team-centric, and predeployment training before they go into harm's way. I really wanted to see these new Green Berets in action. So I started back up *my* chain of command—JFK Special Warfare Center and School to the U.S. Army Special Operations Command to the U.S. Special Operations Command—and asked, "Any chance I can go over and visit some of my guys?" Long ago, I began to think of these new men collectively as "my guys."

"You want to go downrange?" I said I did. "Sure," they told me, "we'll get you there," and they were true to their word.

In May 2006, for the first time in close to thirty-five years, I found myself en route to an active theater. The last time I went to war—my war—it was on a C-54 transport plane, a version of the old DC-4. It was the same unpressurized, piston-engine museum piece that ferried soldiers to Korea. It took us forty-six air hours to lumber from San Diego to Saigon. On this trip, I began my journey on Delta Air Lines, connecting through Amsterdam on KLM into Qatar. I left Qatar on a C-130 transport from Al Udeid Air Base to Balad Air Base in Iraq. From there we attempted to reach Al Asad Air Base by UH-60 helo, but were forced to turn back due to a sandstorm. I finally arrived at Al Asad by way of a C-17 transport—a long way from my home in Idaho.

Al Asad is a hundred miles west of Baghdad. It was once used as an Iraqi air base during Saddam's regime, and there are several carcasses of Russian-built fighter jets scattered around the base. One of the protective revetments at Al Asad was given over to an Army Special Forces company of the 3rd Battalion, 1st Special Forces Group. The company's headquarters constituted a Special Forces advanced operating base, or AOB. The function of this AOB is to provide logistics, intelligence, and operational support for their five operational ODAs.

My first team visit was to an ODA located at a U.S. Army outpost well northwest of Baghdad. They share the facility with a battalion of mechanized infantry from the 1st Armored Division. The bases at Balad and Al Asad are large, secure installations with lots of creature comforts—chow halls, modern toilets, modular living quarters, and clean office spaces. The operational ODAs, however, live quite differently. The team house is an abandoned concrete Iraqi army barracks served by outdoor Porta-Pottis and a single crude shower. They cook in a makeshift kitchen, which means a lot of stove-top and microwave eating. They have their own generator, which affords them air-conditioning for their communal berthing and team spaces, but the generator noise is a constant companion. The single-room tactical center where the team does their operational planning is a crude concrete cubicle and has the look of a team planning bay at Camp Mackall—work tables, wall maps, and lots of laptop computers. Temporary wiring is strung everywhere. Those in the detachment live a lot like Phase II and IV students in the Q-Course. It was much hotter in western Iraq than in central North Carolina, but a dry heat with little humidity.

Getting to their location was a forty-five-minute high-speed run from Al Asad by armored Humvee. "It's game on when you leave the gate," the Special Forces major who commanded the company told me. There were five vehicles in our little convoy—two AOB Humvees and the three Humvees belonging to the Iraqi army. The latter were manned by Special Forces–trained Iraqi army scouts. The movement was briefed by our convoy NCO, a former 18 X-Ray and staff sergeant assigned to the AOB. He reviewed convoy standard procedures, including vehicle intervals, hand and arm signals, and various courses of action—actions on enemy contact, actions if we were hit by an IED, actions if one of the Humvees were to become disabled, and so on. On the roads in western Iraq, speed is life, and we drove at the top speed of the slowest vehicle. Most American casualties in Iraq today are from IEDs. Improvised explosive devices in the form of buried explosives or vehicular suicide bombers are on everyone's mind. They were certainly on mine as we left the gate at Al Asad. Our convoy NCO, riding in front of me in the passenger's seat, passed over the radio, "We're now in Indian country—everyone go hot!" The .50-cal gunners in the turrets cycled their weapons to chamber a round and everyone inside my Humvee with an M4 rifle did the same. That is, everyone but me. Eighteen months ago, this staff sergeant was an 18 X-Ray in Phase IV; now he was in charge of twenty-five Americans and Iraqis going into harm's way. On most of my Humvee runs, a junior team sergeant took charge of the convoy. Driving our Humvee in the lead vehicle on his run was the company command sergeant major. It's the way of Special Forces; when possible, senior sergeants put the junior sergeants in positions to learn and lead. We drove fast and occasionally swerved to miss a crater in the road from a previously detonated IED. Game on.

When we arrived at the ODA's outpost, the team was gearing up for a mission. The mission was a multiunit operation into a nearby village that was a hub of insurgent activity, for both local insurgents and transients coming in from the Syrian border. IED activity in the area was on the rise, and this operation was designed to do a bit of housecleaning. There were two other forces involved in addition to the elements with my ODA. There would be two platoons of mechanized infantry from the 1st Armored Division in Bradley Fighting Vehicles and two platoons of Marine Force Recon from a regional combat team with the 7th Marines. The Special Forces and mech infantry would drive to their objectives, while the Marines would be landed by helo some four miles from the town and patrol in on foot. An AC-130 gunship would be on call and orbiting overhead, and a section of Marine F/A-18 fighters would be circling as well. Each force had specific targeting in their assigned section of the village. It was to be a predawn coordinated attack.

My ODA was a "heavy" detachment with fifteen Green Berets. There were also two Marine Corps intelligence analysts, a four-man Civil Affairs team, and a single Navy corpsman assigned to the team. The detachment members looked very similar to my SEAL platoon decades ago: Their hair was longish, but not too long, and about a third of them had beards. They went about the team compound in shorts, T-shirts, and sneakers. The detachment commander was a short, lean Korean-American with a degree in literature from UCLA. He had the look of an undergraduate student. His quiet, capable leadership was well complemented by the veteran sergeant who ran the team. The team sergeant was a slim, outgoing master sergeant from San Antonio with full, neatly combed hair and a push-broom mustache. He was on his fourth rotation to Iraq. I asked him how many deployments he had made in his SF career. "I keep track of countries, not rotations, and I've been to sixty-three countries in my twenty-four years with Special Forces—so far." This team was a relatively young detachment with several team members on only their second and third rotation. Only one was on his first, and he was a former 18 X-Ray. And, of course, there was a story there. He was from Petaluma, California, and has a degree in engineering from Princeton. He worked as an analyst for a venture capital firm in San Francisco for five years before leaving it for the X-Ray Program. My favorite X-Ray question had become "How do you like this duty?"

"It's good work—something of what I expected and much of it is

what you could never expect, or could even imagine. And it's challenging, always a challenge."

"And your MOS?"

"I'm an engineer—an 18 Charlie. As a trained civil engineer, it was a
chance to do some hands-on construction work and, I admit, a chance
to work with military demolitions. I do like to blow things up. Of
course, as the junior detachment Charlie, I get more than my share of
the paperwork, but that goes with the territory."

"Any chance of reenlisting when your contract service is up?" This
had become my second-favorite X-Ray question.

"I'm not sure, and I'll have two years to think about it. Right now
I'm leaning toward getting out and getting a graduate business degree.
We'll see. Right now, I'm having fun; I like what I'm doing."

At 1300 on the day of our arrival, the team sergeant briefed his
ODA and the AOB support team on the following morning's mission.
This was more of a patrol order than a full-on mission briefback for a
senior commander, but the key elements were the same. It had the feel
and format of a briefing by Sergeant Stan Hall with student ODA 811
during Phase II, or Captain Miguel Santos with 915 in Phase IV. The
briefing was for the ODA and addressed its role in the operation, one
that would focus on security, movement, and intelligence collection.
The assaulters for this mission, the actual door kickers, would be
Iraqis.

The assault phase of the operation would be carried out by members
of the Albu Nimr tribe. The team had been working closely with the
Albu Nimr for some time. The Albu Nimr are a Sunni tribe spread
across the border regions of western Iraq and into Syria. They number
about three hundred thousand and are known for their extensive
cross-border enterprise: They're smugglers. The head of the tribe is a
thirty-year-old university-educated Iraqi who recently assumed leadership of the tribe on the death of his father. The young sheik and his
family had their issues with Saddam, and they have their issues with
the new government and the Americans as well.

"The sheik is always polite and mannerly during our meetings," the team sergeant told me. "He speaks English, but we converse through interpreters. He wants us out of Iraq, but he knows he's not yet strong enough to resist the insurgents. Our insurgents in this area are locals, but there are many Saudis, Egyptians, and Syrians—mostly Syrians. He understands that we're here to train his soldiers, and that as soon as we've trained his guys to handle the insurgents and the security issues, then we can leave. That's what he wants; that's what we want. The Albu Nimr we train are a part of the Iraqi army in name only. They're in uniform, and they're paid as Iraqi soldiers, but their loyalty is to their tribe. They allow us to train them because their sheik has told them to cooperate with us. They learn quickly, and they're pretty damn good in the field. We like working with them."

The Special Forces portion of the operation would have four assault groups. Each assault group would have five Albu Nimr tribesmen— they would be the tip of the spear, the assault element. Backing them up would be a security element of four to five Iraqi army scouts. "We're there to back up both of them," one of the SF gunners told me. "We'll drive the lead vehicles and man the heavy machine guns in the Humvees. We'll also supervise the handling of detainees and searching the target houses for intelligence. Otherwise, it's their show."

Following the team sergeant's briefing of the Americans in the operation, each assault and security element was then briefed by the two detachment sergeants assigned to that assault group. There was a daylight rehearsal that amounted to room-clearing drills at an abandoned two-room house at the nearby firing range. The assault-group vehicles, two Humvees and an up-armored Chevy Luv pickup truck, rolled up to the practice structure and positioned themselves as they would on the real target. The Albu Nimr assaulters quickly ran to the building and set up in a stack at the main entrance. On the signal of their team leader, they kicked the door and cleared the rooms—by the numbers, just like a Phase II squad during Special Forces tactics training. The Iraqi army scouts set up security, and the Special Forces sergeants observed their team's action on the target. After a quick critique, they moved on to an adjacent range to test-fire weapons. The same drill was repeated at the night rehearsal, but for the test firing of weapons. After the night rehearsal, the assistant detachment leader, the team warrant officer, came up to me.

"Hey, sir, I'll be with the second assault group, and we have an empty seat in the lead vehicle. You want to go along?"

I considered this—and the assurances I'd given my wife about not going on combat operations—for about a nanosecond. "You bet I would."

In the early morning hours, we rolled into the outskirts of the town, multiple assault groups, several vehicles to each group. Close to the center of town, my assault group broke from the main body and headed for our assigned targets. A few high-speed turns, a short sprint down some very narrow streets, and we skidded to a halt. Our Albu Nimr assault element was quick and professional. The Iraqi army scouts, Shia recruits from Baghdad, also performed well. And the Special Forces sergeants whose men were making the assault were like proud soccer parents watching their kids take the field. The SF gunners in the Humvee ring turrets and the other ODA members on security were like birds of prey, watching the walls, rooftops, and alleyways for any sign of counterforce activity. There was no shooting in or around my assault group, but I could hear explosions from the marines operating a few blocks away. They were using explosive breaching charges, and we could hear muffled booms as they took down doors. There were follow-on assaults from information learned on the initial targets, but we were clear of the town before dawn.

We rolled back into the Special Forces compound shortly after daylight with twelve detainees. The little task group was after four targeted individuals—insurgents known by name with an active history of violence, intimidation, insurgent support, and IED activity. We got three of them. The others were brought out because they had multiple weapons, explosives, or documents in their houses that tied them with insurgent activity. Bringing out detainees, even documented insurgents, is not a grab-and-go business. Each detainee and his house has to be searched, and the results of that search documented. Each detainee's personal documents are taken from him and put in a ziplock-type bag and hung around his neck. He is then cuffed and blindfolded, and placed in one of the vehicles.

The marines were tasked with finding and capturing the head insurgent hiding in this village. Their job proved to be easier, or harder, depending on your perspective. Their target eluded them initially, but the insurgent leader and five of his bodyguards ran into one of the Marine security elements. They made the mistake of trying to fight it out with them. The marines killed all six, and cut off the head of the insurgent snake in this area. One marine was slightly wounded. When the ODA got this report later in the morning, the men were happy for the marines, and maybe even a little bit jealous.

The marshaling and management of the detainees was an operation unto itself. It took time and attention to detail, and had to be done properly in order to document the conditions of their detention so these insurgents could be dealt with appropriately. Their capture, detention, documentation, interviews, and transport had the makings of a crime-scene investigation as much as a combat operation. Each was given a quick medical examination by the team medics to ensure he was fit for transport. Most of the communication with the detainees was through interpreters. Two of these interpreters were permanently assigned to this ODA, and two others were brought along from the AOB for this operation. Two were U.S. citizens, one a local Iraqi national, and one an Iraqi national living in the United States awaiting citizenship. All were civilians, and all were under contract with the Department of Defense.

"I grew up in Basra and I came to the United States about six years ago," one of them told me. "I live in East Lansing [Michigan] and I'm a crane operator, but soon I will be an American citizen." Before I could ask how it was to be back, he told me. "I love Iraq and I love

Iraqis. They are a good people, and they deserve justice. These insurgents, they deserve justice as well—swift justice. I hate them for what they are doing to my country—my country, Iraq, and my country, America." He went on to tell me how we should be handling detainees, and it was quite a bit different than the criminal-apprehension, chain-of-custody, civil-liberty-awareness treatment that I observed. I had watched him during the operation and during the field interrogations. He was conscientious and passionate—a great asset to the team. On my way out of Iraq, I met him in Balad. He was heading for the U.S. consulate in Germany to finalize his citizenship.

While the team bent to the tedious task of processing the detainees, I was able to spend a few minutes with the Civil Affairs team and their team leader, a Civil Affairs major. "We're here to assist ODA and to do what we can for the locals, both to build confidence in the new government in Baghdad and to make the people a little more trusting of us." He showed me a list of their civil-affairs goals within their area of operations.

Water filtration project
Electrical system refurbishment
Village cleanup and sanitation
Road repairs
Improvements to the local clinics
Water main/pipe repairs
Humanitarian assistance—books, soccer balls and nets, classroom
    supplies and support

The ODA tried to spend as much time out on humanitarian missions as it did on combat/combat support missions. "One way or the other," the detachment leader told me, "there's a lot to do, and we stay busy." The afternoon following the operation, we made the run back to Al Asad. Our Iraqi army scouts element and their Humvees stayed behind, and we made the journey with three Humvees, one of them in tow. There was a mechanical problem with one of the ODA's vehicles and we had to tow it back to Al Asad for maintenance. Also part of the convoy was an armored LMTV Army truck that carried our twelve detainees. Like the Humvees, there was a ring turret atop the truck cab with a Special Forces sergeant camped behind a .50-caliber heavy machine gun.

I was able to spend time with two other ODAs during my time in Iraq. One of them was also located at the AOB. This team had, in the words of one of the detachment members, "drawn the short straw," and had to stay with the AOB. They occasionally ran their own operations, but for the most part they supported and augmented the other AOB ODAs. The other ODA I visited in western Iraq also lived in a deserted Iraqi army barracks with minimal services and the steady din of a generator in their little compound. They were colocated with a battalion of marines and a battalion of the Iraqi army, both charged with keeping critical infrastructures safe from insurgent activity.

Again, I sortied from Al Asad with a small Humvee convoy of Green Berets from the advanced operating base. We made this dash and came back in a single day. The trip focused on current intelligence requirements and medical issues. The team we visited was briefed by AOB personnel on updated procedures for operational intelligence collection, and we brought along a dentist to do some extractions for Iraqi army soldiers working with the ODA. For some of the Iraqis, it was their first visit to a real dentist. They came into the treatment room, which was the ODA medic's small makeshift dispensary, eyes wide with apprehension. The dentist, on loan from the 10th Special Forces Group, lay his first patient down on a wooden bench and went to work, a novocaine hypodermic in one hand and a flashlight in the other. That's when I left. I don't do well at the dentist's office at home, let alone a stone-floored, plywood-sided storage closet in western Iraq.

There were two former X-Rays on this team, both solid performers according to their team sergeant, who went out of his way to praise the new men. Both had interesting backgrounds, but one of them I would have to file in the unique category, or perhaps the uniquely suited category. He was a Brigham Young University graduate, and his two-year Mormon mission to South America had served to refine an ability he seemed to have with languages. Prior to this rotation, he could speak Spanish, Portuguese, Italian, Korean, and Tagalog—the latter from Special Forces Language Training. Now, with three and a half months in Iraq, he was getting pretty good at Arabic.

"I do well when I can control the conversation, like when I interview a detainee and can ask the questions—I know, to some degree, how he might answer. When someone questions me, or it's a fast-moving conversation, I have to ask them to slow down. But I'm getting better every day."

"It must be nice," I observed, having been a poor student of languages, "to have a knack for languages."

"It's not a knack," he informed me evenly. "It's commitment. Anyone can learn a foreign language if they want to. It takes a genuine desire to learn and the discipline to practice. And you have to go out of your way to find and practice with native speakers. The second language is easier than the first, and they get easier each time, but you have to make a personal commitment to learn the language." So much for my two years of Spanish and my inability to do little more than order a *cerveza por favor.*

The run back to Al Asad was hot, dusty, and uneventful. The following day, I was scheduled to visit another ODA near the Syrian border. This particular ODA was having a great deal of operational success and was considered one of the premier Special Forces detachments in Iraq. But the helo was delayed until late in the day and would not return until the following evening, too late for me to make the return connection back to Balad. That night, after the AOB contingent had left, I got to talking with one of the warrant officers at the AOB and learned that his sport was judo.

"There was a guy I met in the Q-Course," I told him, "who was a black belt and professional martial artist. You might know him; his name is Tom Kendall."

"Tom Kendall!" the warrant blurted. "He's here at Al Asad." Moments later we were in one of the AOB's battered Land Rovers and headed across the base for the compound. As the reader may recall, I met then Specialist (now Staff Sergeant) Kendall in Phase I during selection and was able to track him pretty much through Phase IV. He was now assigned to a special SF unit, one normally reserved for experienced soldiers, but Kendall had been an exceptional performer throughout the Q-Course. He was, as I was to learn, the only first-rotation 18 X-Ray to be assigned to this special team. We found him working out at the base gym. I hadn't seen him in over a year. It was like visiting one of your sons on the job a year out of college. The open, easygoing face was the same, but I'd never seen him with hair—no beard, but lots of hair.

"So, tell me, what's been happening to you since I last saw you?"

"Spanish language school, SERE training, and then to my group. Because of my team's mission, I got a priority slot for the Special Forces Advanced Reconnaissance, Target Analysis, and Exploitation Course. Our team has only been here a short while, and we've spent a lot of time in Baghdad, training the Iraqi counterterror units. We've been up here at Al Asad for some direct-action work, but most of the targets that would fit our force seem to be going to other units. So we're headed back to Baghdad in a few days, back to training the Iraqis."

"Do you like it?"

"For the most part." Kendall had always struck me as someone who wanted to take whatever he was doing to the next level and then some. I could see he was a little frustrated. "If things don't pick up this rotation," he said with an easy grin, "then maybe they will on the next one." I'd heard this from others in Special Forces. They were obligated to operate in battle spaces controlled by conventional-force commanders, which meant they often felt underutilized. But that's the nature of this kind of warrior, as much as it is the nature of any conventional-force restrictions.

"Think this is something you might want to do for a career?"

"I don't know," he said seriously. "I'm taking a wait-and-see attitude. My daughter starts kindergarten about the time I have to make that decision. For me, that's a big factor. We'll see when the time comes—maybe yes, maybe no." I wished him a safe tour, and we headed back across the base to the AOB compound.

The only other familiar face I saw on my journey was a senior commo sergeant on of the teams who was a cadre sergeant at Camp Mackall during my Phase IV. Time permitting, I'd have liked to have visited other teams. As it was, the next day I was on a C-130 back to Balad. I had a full day and night at Balad—time enough for me to bang out most of this epilogue and undergo two mortar attacks, one of them landing a round just outside the Balad special operations compound. Cheap at twice the price: I got to go on an operation with a Special Forces ODA, and I got to visit with Tom Kendall. Then it was a C-17 from Balad to Al Udeid Air Base in Qatar and the long trip back to Idaho. I arrived home tired, thankful, and feeling very, very blessed. Few special operators of my generation are afforded a chance to revisit their trade and to be with young warriors in the current fight. Thank you, Special Forces, for allowing me this opportunity.

This is the time in a book when I get to remove my careful-observer cap and take a few minutes to make a personal observation—on this war and the current business of special operations. And this strictly as I see it. The U.S. Army and the U.S. Army Special Operations Command have monitored me pretty closely during this effort. There was never a hint of censorship regarding my work, but they were engaged and read the text carefully. When they made a suggestion, it was just that, and usually in the interest of accuracy or specific information they would like to see omitted in the interest of training future Green

Berets. For the most part, I honored those suggestions. So let me now say, for the record, that the following is my take on the current fight, the role of special operations in this fight, and, by extension, our current force structure. These are strictly my opinions.

Semantics and words seem to play a big role in this conflict. First, the global war on terror, and the acronym GWOT that we see everywhere. It's very misleading. Terror, or terrorism, is a tactic, and just one of the tactics used by al-Qaeda and their allies in this war. Given that we're the good guys, the bad guys in this fight are the insurgents. So perhaps the global war on insurgency (or insurgents) would be a better phrase. And yet, while insurgency is a better word, it's still a tactic. We may not be fighting terror per se, but we're certainly up to our armpits in an insurgency. And is it really global? Sure, they attacked us in Washington and New York, and continue these attacks in western Europe, but *their* homeland is the Islamic world. Due to the nature of our open society, the insurgents can move about and even operate in our world, but because they've skillfully packaged their cause in an Islamic wrapper, the Islamic world is their base. If we can find a way to beat them there, then we'll win. And just who are "they"—these insurgents who use terrorism and promote insurgency? I've used the term "Islamists" and even "fundamentalists." Extremists, in the context of Islam, is a far better word. I wouldn't like to think that all of Islam is our enemy, but I do believe we are fighting Islamic extremists, and the prize in this conflict is the leadership of the Islamic world—oh, yes, and control of all those oil and natural gas reserves that happen to be in the Islamic world. *We* think it should come to a vote—some form of political/economic/universal consent of the people. This means a secular approach to governance, and some form of government with the consent of the governed. *They*, the extremists, think it should be their version of God's law, with themselves and their extreme clerics in charge. Unfortunately, because their tactics are terror *and* information, they've made this fight come across as a Crusaders-and-Arabs issue, painting coalition forces in a role of the invader/occupier. And that's why we have a whole lot of soldiers, sailors, airmen, and marines on combat deployment.

There are various layers of reality in this struggle. There is the reality of what is taking place on the ground in Afghanistan and Iraq—the "ground truth," as the Army likes to call it; there is the war as portrayed by the Western media; and there is the war as an element or chess piece in our political process. Regarding the American media, it is through their eyes that most of us perceive this war. I wish they would be as helpful to us in our fight as Al Jazeera is to the other side, but that's not how a free press operates, nor should it be. Does the media have a liberal bias? Possibly—even probably. But the driving force of our media coverage, which is dominated by television, is viewership—the ratings. We are a nation that has a fascination with violence, graphic video footage, and what might broadly be called, I'm sorry to say, dysfunction. We consume the stuff, and much of our media coverage is consumer driven. The war is no exception. Therefore, a suicide bombing in Baghdad, especially if there is some graphic video to go with it, is far more newsworthy than the civil-affairs projects of a Special Forces ODA in western Iraq.

Politically, well, this conflict has become a they-said, he-lied, we-should-have exercise in partisan politics. Bottom line, through executive leadership and congressional approval, this nation went to war. We invaded Iraq. That war, which we initiated, has become a nasty, protracted insurgency. Americans tend not to like lengthy military engagements; the insurgents know this, and even count on it. Few of the chosen soldiers I spoke with in Iraq saw this fight in political terms. They were too focused on training Iraqis, and trying to find and target insurgents. They did, however, wonder if their nation had the stomach to see this one through. They get CNN on satellite, even at the remote ODA locations.

"You watch news of the war on TV," a detachment sergeant told

me, "and it's unlike anything we see here on a day-to-day basis. You also see the approval polls for the war, and it makes you wonder. I don't care how we got here—we're here. And we have to stay here and help these people until they can do it on their own. For the nation, it's pulling out. For us, it's leaving behind friends you've promised to stand alongside until the job's done."

So much for the media and the political dimension. What's really happening over there? Are we winning? Can we win? This war, like all wars, will take time, treasury, lives, and national will. Do we have enough of these elements to see this one through to a successful or an acceptable resolution? I get asked these questions a lot, especially after I returned from Iraq.

Ten days in Iraq is not enough to see it all, but it was enough to dramatically raise my concerns. Quite frankly, I'm worried. We have lives at risk, and that may not change for a while; I flew with two flag-draped coffins on a leg of my trip back home. The casualties are a trickle compared to what they were or could be, but a single death in Afghanistan or Iraq is still an item on the nightly news. And more than a news item if that death is in your community or your family. The fact that this death is matched daily by the more than forty Americans killed on our highways by drunk drivers does not lessen *my* concern for this single fallen warrior. It does, however, speak to this war in terms of the current media consciousness. This war is costing a lot of money, but as compared to our gross national product and what we spent in the Cold War, including Vietnam, it's not all that much. Time and national will may well be the deciding factors. We are an impatient culture and an impatient electorate. Dedicated, skillful insurgents think in terms of decades. To use a sports analogy, we think in terms of athletic seasons, and politically, in election cycles. Militarily, we have problems. I recall a comment of Secretary Rumsfeld's a few years back: "You have to go to war with the Army you have." He's right, and we did. That said, the composition of our armed forces is wholly unsuited

to fight this war. What's really sad, for me, is that this is not unlike our experience in the Vietnam War—or the Vietnam Insurgency. To quote that great American, Yogi Berra, "It's déjà vu all over again."

We have a superb and highly professional military that has no peer when it comes to expeditionary and maneuver warfare. But today's enemies don't fight that way. They may posture in a conventional military manner, with parades and smart marching columns—as Saddam's army did and Kim Jong Il's army still does—but they cannot match us on the battlefield. In 1968, the North Vietnamese tried to mass their forces against ours during the Tet Offensive and at Khe Sanh. They took a terrible beating. Our media ceded these victories, but the enemy was crushed on the battlefield. So they stepped up their insurgency efforts, and five years later they sent us home. Saddam was a slow learner; it took a thrashing in the Gulf War and another trip to the woodshed a decade later for him to get it. But Saddam was a thug, and the people of Iraq were glad to see him go. So were others in the region, especially the Iranians. Like Tet and Khe Sanh, our invasion of Iraq was a tactical victory, and like post-1968 Vietnam, we face an entrenched insurgency with a very superior conventional force.

I speak often and at length with special operators returning from rotations in Afghanistan and Iraq. I spoke with as many as I could while I was in Iraq. They're proud of their service, and they feel they're gradually making a difference in their areas—their little sectors of the war. They believe the insurgents are, for the most part, a ruthless and foreign-driven influence, and that most Afghans and Iraqis don't want them in their country. They don't want us there, either, but they generally understand why we're there and the conditions under which we will leave. More than most in our deployed force structure, our special operators often deal with the locals on a daily basis, out in the villages and towns or helping to train the Iraqi and Afghan army and police units. On balance, they are not encouraged about our efforts to counter these insurgents. In traveling about Iraq, I was not encouraged by what I saw. Specifically, I was not encouraged by the nature of our

presence, our management of the war, and the restrictions imposed on our forces.

First, the nature of our presence. Our visible military presence in Iraq, frankly, borders on the obscene. We have taken Saddam's army and air force bases and made them into gigantic logistic, personnel, and convenience centers. There are post exchanges, Subway sandwich shops, latte bars, gyms, swimming pools, miniature golf, and massive messing facilities. The contract chow halls are overwhelming. Along with a lot of overboiled and fried food, there are ethnic dishes—Chinese and Hispanic mostly—sandwich bars, salad bars, fresh fruit, and an impressive selection of pastries—not desserts, but pastries displayed in pastry cases. Two of the chow halls where, I must admit, I ate like a pig had Baskin-Robbins counters. The personal quarters for the soldiers, airmen, marines, and an occasional sailor ranged from barracks living to two-to-a-container billeting modules, all air-conditioned—Spartan, but very comfortable. The showers and toilet facilities are modern, communal, and often spotlessly maintained by contractors. Most Iraqis don't live this well, and neither do soldiers in the Iraqi army. The bases I visited had extensive defensive perimeters that protected runways, aircraft, flight lines, motor pools, maintenance facilities, warehouses, command centers, and just about anything else you would see on a large military base in the United States. Except for the checkpoints, concertina wire, and the ten-foot-tall slabs of eighteen-inch-thick concrete used to create on-base minicompounds and contain indirect-fire attacks, these *are* U.S. bases. I found it troubling that these bases in Iraq have a permanent feel to them, much like the ones we have here at home.

Don't get me wrong, some very brave soldiers and marines go out on patrol, conduct operations, stand duty on checkpoints, and put themselves at risk to provide some measure of security and stability to Iraq. Convoy duty is often combat duty. It's hot, dangerous, dirty work, and they do it courageously and professionally. But then they retire to these huge, fortified American installations with replicated American amenities and count the days until the end of their rotation. This is a generalization, but a lot of our forces live like this. Those whose duties don't take them off base, and there are a lot of them, simply live out their rotations in this military twilight of a reconstituted America. Those scattered forces I saw in the outlying, smaller installations live a different life. So do those who do the heavy lifting of training the Afghans and Iraqis—like the Special Forces ODAs. They live much like the men they train.

The management of this war goes back to fighting the current war with the Army you have. In spite of the recent powering-up of SOF budgets, we still have a conventional force in the field and battle management by the regular Army or Marine Corps ground-force commanders. They own the battle space in Iraq and Afghanistan. There's an SOF command structure in these theaters, with joint special operations task forces and task units and forward operating bases and advanced operating bases—like the one I visited at Al Asad. But none of these "own" battle space; they provide only administrative, logistical, or intelligence support. If a detachment of Special Forces and their Iraqi army scouts or local tribesmen want to mount an operation against insurgent elements in the neighboring town or neighboring mountains, they have to get permission from the conventional commander responsible for that area or sector. Training of the Iraqi army or the Iraqi police is a conventional U.S. Army responsibility. They may ask for Special Forces help with this, and the smart military-training teams do, but they don't have to. A lot of field-grade and senior SOF commanders in Afghanistan and Iraq are in the position of "selling" SOF capability to an Army (or Marine) battalion or regimental commander. I'd like to see battle space or territory given to SOF commanders and subordinate conventional forces assigned to support them. I realize that this runs against the current military culture, but I think it's time to rethink our approach to fighting this enemy—even though less than one soldier in twenty in the active theaters is an SOF operator. We need a more robust SOF command-and-control structure. Maybe in the next war—or when the light goes on and we build and tailor a force to meet the threat and tactics of this insurgent enemy. Or the next one.

Finally, there is the issue of restrictions in the use of force. The rules of engagement and the Rules of Land Warfare, as you have seen, are drilled into future Special Forces soldiers in the Q-Course and are a fact of life for all our deployed forces in the operational theaters. The SOF operators in the field live with these rules, and many a battle-space commander lives in fear that they will be violated—that there will be an incident that will get him relieved of command and end his military career. The bad guys know these force restrictions and how to get around them. IEDs and suicide bombers kill our soldiers and marines, and they kill even more Iraqi soldiers, policemen, and civilians. Yet placing an IED is a crime, not so much an act of war. If an insurgent is caught with a shovel in his hand digging alongside the road, he can put his hands up and not be shot. He will, in all probability, be processed, sent to an interrogation center, and released. He knows it, the average Iraqi knows it, and so does that Army specialist out patrolling those mean streets in his armored Humvee. They see some of these guys more than once. However, if the act of placing an IED were to earn a bomber an on-the-spot bullet, then there would be fewer of them out there—a lot fewer. Some of the detainees I observed appeared to have smirks on their faces. They were known insurgents, foot soldiers, and they knew they would be back on the streets in a few weeks. The issue of security and the ability of a government to protect its citizens is paramount. IEDs and suicide bombers visibly threaten this—and from what I saw, they threaten it effectively. Again, most of our combat casualties on the nightly news are from IEDs.

I don't have an answer for this one; it's very dicey business. The special operators I speak with feel the level of insurgent violence could be dramatically reduced if they and the locals they train could take stronger action—specifically, against the bomb makers and the bomb placers. But the on-the-spot-bullet call is a difficult one. Any decision to shoot preemptively is a serious one—for those you make eligible for the bullet, certainly, and for those who have to make the on-the-ground decision to shoot preemptively. I say this with no regard for an insurgent who probably deserves this form of summary justice. I'm far more concerned about the American soldier, special operator or otherwise, who pulls the trigger. I care deeply for our soldiers and marines, and I want them to leave their field with honor; I want them mentally and morally intact when they return home. This, more than any other reason, is why we need to get this matter into the hands of the Iraqis and Afghans. Let them decide the fate of some Syrian or Saudi dirtbag insurgent who has come to *their* country to kill their citizens, or a member of their community or family.

There is a final issue, and it has nothing to do with rules of engagement or conventional-force application versus special operations—it's an in-house SOF issue. This is the emphasis *within* the special operations community regarding unilateral, direct-action operations as opposed to a commitment to train the locals. In a broad sense, both can be seen as counterinsurgency measures. The SOF proponents of direct action feel that if you find and kill enough senior-level insurgents, then the insurgent gears will grind to a halt and buy us the time to win local hearts and minds. They're trying to cut the head off the snake, and they did with the targeting and elimination of Abu Musab al-Zarqawi. Those who practice foreign internal defense advocate a by, with, and through approach—that the training of local soldiers and policemen should be a priority. The locals, once trained and fielded, are a whole lot better at the job than we are. Having done the former, albeit a long time ago, and seen the latter, I'm inclined to believe that training the locals to do the job is better—way better. It's a matter of preventive medicine or surgery. And while developing the language and cross-cultural skills is more difficult and more time consuming than purely tactical, behind-the-gun skills, it's what really sets the special operator apart from his conventional counterpart. What I'm saying here is that within special operations, we need more focus on foreign internal defense and counterinsurgency—these are the essential skills.

This applies not just to Special Forces, but to our Rangers and SEALs as well. This in-house attention and concentration is important now, as we deal with this insurgency, and as we prepare for the next one. It's the way our enemies will fight.

There's an old military adage that we usually fight the current war with the tactics of the last war. This is because wars supposedly change, and the military force that once proved effective is out of date—obsolete. We came into this war woefully unprepared to deal with an insurgent enemy; we simply lacked counterinsurgency capability in our force structure. In that regard, we learned little from Vietnam. I predict that the *next* war, or, better said, the next campaign in this one—the Regional War Against Islamic Extremists—will look a whole lot like this one. To be as unprepared as we were, especially with the decision to go into Iraq, was unfortunate. To be unprepared the next time, in the context of those we send into harm's way, will be criminal.

GLOSSARY OF

ACRONYMS AND MILITARY

NOMENCLATURE

1st SWTG	1st Special Warfare Training Group

18 Series military occupational specialties (MOS):

18 Alpha (18A)	Detachment commander
180 Alpha (180A)	Assistant detachment commander
18 Bravo (18B)	Weapons sergeant
18 Charlie (18C)	Engineering sergeant
18 Delta (18D)	Medical sergeant/combat medic
18 Echo (18E)	Communications sergeant
18 Foxtrot (18F)	Intelligence sergeant/18 Fox
18 Zulu (18Z)	Team sergeant/operations sergeant

APFT	Army Physical Fitness Test
ATL	Adaptive Thinking and Leadership
BDU	Battle dress utility (camouflage uniform)
BNCOC	Basic Non-Commissioned Officers Course
COIN	Counterinsurgency
DA	Direct action
DZ	Drop zone
EPW	Enemy prisoner of war
FID	Foreign internal defense

FOB	Forward operating base
Gs	Guerrillas
GPS	Global Positioning System
HALO	High-altitude low-opening
Humvee	For HMMVW—high-mobility multipurpose wheeled vehicle
IVW	Involuntary withdrawal
LBE	Load-bearing equipment (vest)
LMTV	Light medium tactical vehicle (an Army 4 × 4 truck)
LZ	Landing zone
MDMP	Military decision-making process
MOS	Military occupational specialty
NCO	Noncommissioned officer
NVGs	Night-vision goggles
Psyops	Psychological operations
ODA	Operational Detachment Alpha
ODB	Operational Detachment Bravo
OSUT	One Station Unit Training
Q-Course	Special Forces Qualification Course
QRF	Quick-reaction force
Radios	Radios used by Special Forces:
AN/PSC-5D	Also PSC-5; primary satellite communication/SATCOM radio
AN/PRC-137F	Also PRC-137 or 137; primary high-frequency (HF) radio
AN/PRC-148	Also MBITR, or "embitter"; multiband inter-/intra-team radio, a handheld FM radio
AN/PRC-119F	Also PRC-119; FM base-station voice radio
ALE	automatic link establishment (text message format used with PRC-137)

Rank Enlisted Army rank structure, junior to senior:

Private first class (PFC)

Specialist

Sergeant, or buck sergeant

Staff sergeant

Sergeant first class

Master sergeant—command senior master sergeant, often designated as first sergeant

Sergeant major—command senior sergeant major, often designated as the command sergeant major, or CSM

ROEs	Rules of engagement
SARE	Situational Awareness Reaction Exercise
SAW	Squad assault weapon
SF	Special Forces (refers to Army Special Forces)
SFAS	Special Forces Assessment and Selection
SFPC	Special Forces Preparation Course
SOF	Special operations forces (refers to Army, Navy, Air Force, and Marine Corps special operations)
SR	Special reconnaissance
SWCS	Special Warfare Center and School (John F. Kennedy Special Warfare Center and School)
TAC	Teach, advise, and counsel
UW	Unconventional warfare
VW	Voluntary withdrawal

ABOUT THE AUTHOR

Dick Couch is a 1967 graduate of the U.S. Naval Academy. He graduated from BUD/S Class 45 in 1969, and was the class Honorman. He was also first in his class at the Navy Underwater Swimmers School and the Army Military Free-Fall (HALO) School. As Whiskey Platoon Commander with SEAL Team One in Vietnam, he led one of the few successful POW rescue operations of that conflict. Following his release from active duty in the Navy, he served as a maritime and paramilitary case officer in the Central Intelligence Agency. In 1997, he retired from the Naval Reserve with the rank of captain. Dick and his wife, Julia, live in central Idaho.